ESSENTIALS
OF IRISH
BUSINESS
LAW

Fifth Edition

Áine Keenan

GILL & MACMILLAN

Gill & Macmillan Ltd
Hume Avenue
Park West
Dublin 12
with associated companies throughout the world
www.gillmacmillan.ie

© Áine Keenan 2008
978 07171 4380 1
Index compiled by Cover to Cover
Print origination by Type IT, Dublin

The paper used in this book is made from the wood pulp of managed forests.
For every tree felled, at least one tree is planted, thereby renewing natural resources.

A CIP catalogue record is available for
this book from the British Library.

'Table A, Companies Act, 1963' is reproduced
with permission of the Controller, Stationery Office.

The sinner and the saint are merely exchanging notes:
the saint has sinned, the sinner can be sanctified.
It is time that divides them; it is time that will bring them together.

Nisargadatta Maharaj, *I Am That: Talks with Sri Nisargadatta Maharaj*

CONTENTS

PREFACE TO THE FIFTH EDITION

The fifth edition has been written to respond to those significant changes in Irish law since 2004. Its main aim is to provide students with a broad knowledge of the principles of Irish law as it affects commercial transactions, and to increase their awareness of the need to consider the legal implications in the decision-making process. Like its predecessors, this book is designed primarily for students sitting examinations in third-level colleges and professional institutes, but it is also relevant to students taking any introductory law course.

I have continued to follow the style and layout of the previous editions, which proved so popular with students and lecturers alike, with each chapter containing:

(a) a list of the important topics covered by the chapter;

(b) a summary of the purpose of the chapter;

(c) a presentation of the related rules of law in a manner which will help students to assimilate the necessary facts;

(d) a list of the important cases and/or statutes referred to in the chapter, where applicable;

(e) a progress test based on, and cross-referenced with, the contents of the chapter; and

(f) useful Internet resources for further research.

In order to derive maximum benefit from this book, the text should be used in conjunction with the past examination questions at the end of each section, permission for use of which has been kindly granted by the Institute of Accounting Technicians in Ireland, the Institute of Certified Public Accountants in Ireland, the Chartered Institute of Management Accountants, the Association of Chartered Certified Accountants, the Institute of Chartered Secretaries and Administrators, and The Marketing Institute.

As with previous editions, I wish to acknowledge my deep appreciation and gratitude for the comprehensive assistance I have received from Louise Tierney BL. Her research has made this task so much easier.

There are many wonderful friends who have also supplied practical support, emotional encouragement and boundless generosity. I am especially indebted to Anjali, Joan Bree, Orla Carew, Michael Dineen, Francis Fay, Pat Hickey, Declan Keane, Anne Mathews, Margie Murphy, Barry O'Callaghan, Jude O'Neill, Nuala Perry and Margaret Riordan. Finally, my sincere thanks to Mrs Chhaya Arya of Chetana Ltd, 34 K. Dubach Marg, Kala Ghoda, Mumbai 400 023. for permission to reproduce the quotation on p. iii.

The law is stated on the basis of the material available to me as at 1 July 2008.

Áine Keenan
Mumbai

PROFESSIONAL EXAMINING INSTITUTES

Institute of Accounting Technicians in Ireland
Chartered Accountants House,
83 Pembroke Road, Ballsbridge, Dublin 4
(01) 637 7363
www.iati.ie

Institute of Certified Public Accountants in Ireland
9 Ely Place, Dublin 2
(01) 676 7353
www.cpaireland.ie

Association of Chartered Certified Accountants
9 Leeson Park, Dublin 6
(01) 498 8900
www.ireland.accaglobal.com

Chartered Institute of Management Accountants
45–47 Pembroke Road, Ballsbridge, Dublin 4
(01) 643 0400
www.cimaglobal.com

Institute of Chartered Secretaries and Administrators
PO Box 7568, Foxrock, Dublin 18
(01) 283 2451
www.icsa.org.uk

The Marketing Institute
South County Business Park, Leopardstown, Dublin 18
(01) 295 2355
www.mii.ie

Institute of International Trade of Ireland
28 Merrion Square, Dublin 2
(01) 661 2182
www.iiti.ie

Irish Institute of Purchasing and Materials Management
5 Belvedere Place, Dublin 1
(01) 855 9257
www.iipmm.ie

TABLE OF CASES

INTERNET RESOURCES

British and Irish Legal Information Institute
   www.bailii.org
Irish Courts Service
   www.courts.ie
Irish Legal Information Initiative
   www.ucc.ie/law/irlii

Part 1

INTRODUCTION TO THE
———— STUDY OF LAW ————

THE FUNCTIONS AND SOURCES OF LAW

Topics covered

- Functions of law
- Sources of Irish law

- Historical sources of law
- Legal sources of law

Summary
This chapter examines the purpose and effect of Irish law and how that law has come into being.

• Functions of law

1. The law is the body of rules imposed by a State upon its members which is designed to regulate human conduct within that State. The courts interpret these rules of conduct, decide whether they have been broken and pass sentence or make an award of compensation. A certain standard of behaviour is thereby maintained amongst the members of the State in the interest of the common good.

2. The law is not static. It changes and develops, reflecting the values and institutions of each era. Not alone does it define and safeguard rights of property and uphold public order, but it is also used to develop the national economy and to deal with social problems.

• Sources of Irish law

3. The term 'sources of law' is used in several different senses:

(a) historical sources – generally regarded as common law and equity;
(b) legal sources – the means by which the law is currently brought into existence.

There are five legal sources:

(a) legislation (statute law);
(b) subordinate legislation;
(c) the Irish Constitution 1937 (Bunreacht na hÉireann);
(d) European Union law;
(e) judicial precedent (interpretation of statutes).

• Historical sources of law

4. Irish law is a common law system derived from English law. It was implemented after a conquest which replaced the highly developed native Brehon laws. Since the foundation of the Irish Free State in 1922, however, Irish law has developed a character of its own with the coming into effect of a written Irish Constitution (Bunreacht na hÉireann) in 1937 and the enactment of different statutes.

5. Because of the similarities between the legal systems of Ireland and England, having in most areas of the law a common base, it is necessary to refer initially to the historical development of English law.

Common law

6. At the time of the Norman Conquest in 1066 there existed a primitive legal system based on local custom. Afterwards, these local customs were unified into one system of law with the King at its head. A judicial system was gradually established through the justices who travelled to different parts of the realm to settle criminal and civil disputes. Although these justices at first applied the customary law of the neighbourhood, often hearing their cases with the assistance of a local jury, they developed rules of law, selected from the differing local customs which they had encountered and applied uniformly in all trials throughout. This ancient unwritten law was made common to the whole of England and Wales, and for this reason was known as 'common law' (*ius commune*). The Irish generally became entitled to the benefits of the common law by 1331.

7. To commence an action before any of these courts a <u>writ</u> had to be obtained. This specified the ground of complaint and gave a brief summary of the facts on which the plaintiff required judgment. After a period of time it was decided that writs could only be issued in one of the established forms in order to bring a grievance before the royal courts. The fact that no new type of writ could be issued unless it was approved or developed by Parliament made the common law system very rigid and hence an inadequate way of providing justice.

8. Over the years, the common law grew into a rigid and harsh system. Rules of procedure were complex, and any minor breach of these could leave a plaintiff, who had a good case, without a remedy. Plaintiffs could be frustrated in civil actions, where the only remedy which the common law courts could grant was an award of damages. They could even find themselves unable to enforce a judgment given in their favour because there was no suitable common law remedy. The practice grew in such cases of dissatisfied litigants petitioning the King to exercise his prerogative power in their favour. The King, through his Chancellor, set up the Court of Chancery to deal with these petitions.

Equity

9. The body of law developed by the King's Court and administered by the Court of Chancery was called 'equity'. Initially, in dealing with each petition the Chancellor's concern was to establish the truth of the situation and to impose a just solution without undue regard for technicalities or procedural points. Gradually, the court began to be guided by its previous decisions and formulated a number of general principles, known as the 'maxims of equity', upon which it would proceed. These are still applied today when equitable relief is claimed.

10. The following are some examples of the many maxims:

(a) *Those who seek equity must do equity.* Persons who seek equitable relief must be prepared to act fairly towards their opponents as a condition of obtaining relief.

(b) *Equity looks to the intent rather than the form.* Although a person may pretend that they are doing something in the correct form, equity will look to see what they are really trying to achieve.

(c) *Those who come to equity must come with clean hands.* To be fairly treated, the plaintiff must have acted properly in past dealings with the defendant.

(d) *Equality is equity.* What is available to one person must be available to another. This reflects the effort made by the law to play fair and redress the balance.

11. Equity was not a complete alternative to the common law. Instead, it provided a gloss on the law by adding to and improving the common law. The major changes produced by the interaction of equity and common law included the:

(a) recognition and protection of rights by equity for which the common law gave no safeguard;

(b) more effective procedure of equity in bringing a disputed matter to a decision;

(c) development under equity of discretionary remedies.

12. By its nature, the Court of Chancery was bound to come into conflict with the common law courts. This rivalry was resolved in 1615 by a decision of the King that where common law and equity conflict, equity should prevail.

13. By the nineteenth century it became the rule for judges in the Court of Chancery and the common law courts to respect and follow previous decisions and precedents. Because the separate existence of the Court of Chancery and the common law courts was not satisfactory, it was decided to merge the administration of equity and common law. Reforms were introduced in Ireland by the Judicature (Ireland) Act 1877, which established a logical court structure, simplified procedures and fused the administration of common law and equity.

The Act decided that in cases of conflict, equity should still prevail over common law.

• Legal sources of law

Legislation or statute law

14. Legislation is the laying down of legal rules by an institution which is recognised as having the right to make law for the community. Such laws are known as statutes.

15. Our oldest statutes were ordinances made by English kings before parliaments existed, and which were applied to Ireland. The Parliament of Ireland made statutes for this country until the Act of Union 1800 joined Ireland and Great Britain in the United Kingdom of Great Britain and Ireland. Between 1800 and 1922, statutes applying to Ireland were made in the Parliament at Westminster. Upon the establishment of the Irish Free State in 1922, legislative independence was restored. From 1922 to 1937, the legislative source was the Oireachtas of Saorstát Éireann and, from 1937, under the Constitution, the Oireachtas. Legislation prior to 1922 continues in force, by virtue of Article 50 of the Constitution, to the extent that it is not inconsistent with the provisions of the 1937 Constitution.

16. Our current legislative body, therefore, is the Oireachtas which is empowered by our Constitution to legislate for the country. Article 15.2.1 states: 'The sole and exclusive power of making laws for the State is hereby vested in the Oireachtas: no other legislative authority has power to make laws for the State.' The Oireachtas consists of two houses, being Dáil Éireann and Seanad Éireann, and the President.

17. Superior legislation, i.e. laws enacted by the legislature, before they become law are known as Bills. A Bill must go through five stages in the Oireachtas. The first stage, which may take place in either the Dáil or the Seanad, consists of placing the title of the Bill before the House. After this, the Bill is printed but if it does not pass this stage then the Bill is defeated. Otherwise, the printed Bill is circulated and given a second reading. The minister responsible for guiding the Bill through the Oireachtas normally explains the nature of the intended legislation and often goes through the Bill section by section. The third stage is the committee stage. The 'committee' is normally the entire House, except where the Bill is of a highly technical nature, in which case it is examined by a standing committee representing the main parties and including some members at least who specialise in the relevant subject. The Bill is examined section by section and may be amended. The fourth stage is the report stage, at which further amendments may be made. If the government has undertaken in committee to reconsider certain points, it often puts forward its final amendments at this stage.

The Bill is then referred to the other House where a similar process may be followed. The fifth stage is the final reading. The Taoiseach presents to the President, for signature, the Bill as passed by both Houses of the Oireachtas. It is then promulgated by the President who publishes a notice in *Iris Oifigiúil* (the *Official Gazette*) stating that the Bill has become law.

18. If a statute or part of a statute is, at a later date, found to be repugnant to the Constitution, it can be declared invalid by the High Court and, on appeal, by the Supreme Court.

19. Judges have established certain guidelines – which are not rules of law – to assist themselves in interpreting statutes. The three recognised judicial approaches to statutory interpretation are:

(a) *The literal rule.* This is the basic rule of interpretation. A judge must give to words their literal or usual meaning unless the Act defines or restricts the meaning to be taken.

Case: Burke v. Aer Lingus (1997)

The plaintiff was injured whilst travelling on a shuttle bus between the aircraft and the passenger terminal, after having travelled on an Aer Lingus flight to Dublin. Article 17 of the Warsaw Convention provides that 'the carrier is liable for damage sustained in the event of the death or wounding of a passenger or any other bodily injury suffered by a passenger, if the accident which caused the damage so sustained took place on board the aircraft or in the course of any of the operations of embarking or disembarking'.

Held: The meanings of 'embarking' and 'disembarking' have a wider connotation which includes some activity by the passenger prior to entering or after leaving the aircraft. The shuttle-bus ride is an air related risk having regard to the nature and purpose of that part of the airport where it takes place, and hence 'disembarking' does not have to be strictly interpreted in accordance with its ordinary meaning and popular usage. The plaintiff's journey by shuttle-bus was therefore within the ambit of the Warsaw Convention.

Case: Dillon v. Minister for Posts and Telegraphs (1981)

The plaintiff, a candidate in a general election, submitted a sample of election literature to the Department of Posts and Telegraphs in order to qualify for free distribution of election material. The application was rejected on the basis that the literature contained a passage describing politicians as 'dishonest because they are being political and must please the largest number of people'. The defendant argued that this was in contravention of the requirement that material not be 'indecent, obscene or grossly offensive'.

Held: The passage, while possibly displeasing, could not be described as indecent, obscene or grossly offensive on a literal reading of the rules.

(b) *The golden rule.* Where a literal interpretation of the statute would lead to an absurd or inconsistent result, the courts will usually attempt to modify the strict grammatical meaning of words in order to avoid such a result. Where a statute permits two or more possible meanings that can be derived, application of the golden rule is not inconsistent with the literal rule, since the literal rule cannot be applied in such cases.

(c) *The mischief rule.* Where an Act is passed to remedy a mischief, the court must adopt the interpretation which will have the effect of remedying the mischief in question. The judge must look at the law which existed prior to the statute and then the defect in the law which the statute purported to remedy. The statute should then be construed in such a way to suppress the defect and advance the remedy.

Case: Nestor v. Murphy (1979)

The defendants, husband and wife, had executed a contract whereby they agreed to sell the joint tenancy in their family home to the plaintiff. They failed to complete the sale and the plaintiff claimed an order directing the specific performance by the defendants of the contract of sale. The defendants contended that the contract for sale was rendered void by the provisions of the Family Home Protection Act 1976 whereby the written consent of the defendant wife was required prior to the execution of the contract of sale.

Held: The purpose of the legislation was to protect the non-owning spouse by preventing the other spouse from disposing of the family home without his or her prior written consent. Since the defendants in this case were joint tenants of the property, the legislation was held not to apply.

20. Under the European Convention on Human Rights Act 2003, Irish courts are required to interpret law in a manner compatible with the provisions of the Convention. When someone is faced with a particular legal provision that they believe violates their rights under the Convention, they must ask the court to interpret it in line with the Convention rather than asking the court to invalidate the legal provision. In addition, the Act requires that due notice be taken of any decisions, opinions or judgments of the European Court of Human Rights on any matter in which the Irish court has jurisdiction.

Case: Foy v. An t-Ard Chlaraitheoir, Attorney General and Others (2007)

The plaintiff, who had undergone gender reassignment in 1992, took an action to secure a new birth certificate reflecting her female gender. She claimed that her right to respect for private life (Article 8) and her right to marry (Article 12) under the European Convention on Human Rights had been violated by the State's refusal to do so.

Held: Irish law was incompatible with the European Convention on Human Rights. The State's failure to provide for 'meaningful recognition' of the plaintiff's new identity violated her human rights and she was entitled to court costs and compensation for her lengthy court battle. Furthermore, the State was remiss in not recognising the rights of transgendered people five years earlier when most other European countries were doing so.

Subordinate legislation

21. Subordinate, or 'delegated', legislation arises from laws laid down by a body or a person to whom the Oireachtas, i.e. the superior legislature, has delegated power to make such laws. The Oireachtas has delegated power to government ministers, local authorities and other bodies to legislate for specified purposes only.

22. Delegated legislation saves the Oireachtas from debating local matters. It allows the government, or minister, to act quickly in emergency situations. It gives greater flexibility, because it can be changed easily and quickly when it becomes outdated or impractical. A statute, on the other hand, can only be repealed or amended by a subsequent statute.

23. Delegated legislation is implemented by statutory instruments, orders, regulations and bye-laws which have the same force of law as statutes passed by the Oireachtas.

24. Delegated legislation must be reasonable, must apply basic fairness of procedures and must be *intra vires*, i.e. within the confines of powers delegated under statute. If delegated legislation is beyond the powers of those exercising it, it may be challenged in the courts on the grounds that it is *ultra vires* and may be declared by the court as void.

25. Subordinate legislation is also scrutinised by the Seanad Select Committee on Statutory Instruments.

The Irish Constitution 1937 (Bunreacht na hÉireann)

26. The Constitution, which came into effect on 29 December 1937, is the basis of our law. The law of the Constitution:

(a) regulates the structure and function of the principal organs of government;
(b) regulates the relationship of these organs to each other and to the citizen.

It deals with such topics as the nation, the State, the President, the Oireachtas, the government and the courts. It also concerns itself with the Attorney General, the Council of State and the Comptroller and Auditor General. It contains a section which guarantees certain fundamental rights to every citizen. These include personal rights (Article 40) and rights relating to the family (Article 41), education (Article 42), private property (Article 43) and religion (Article 44).

27. The Constitution has a higher status than any other domestic law in that it may only be changed by a majority of voters in a referendum and in that any legislation which is held to be repugnant to the Constitution is invalid.

28. The President has the power under Article 26, after consulting the Council of State, to refer a Bill, before it becomes law, to the Supreme Court for a decision as to its constitutionality. Legislation enacted by the government may be referred under the Constitution to the High Court, and on appeal to the Supreme Court, by the President or by any party with an actionable interest.

Case: McKenna v. An Taoiseach, An Tánaiste and Others (1996)

The plaintiff had instituted proceedings in the High Court in which she claimed that the government had acted *ultra vires* and in breach of the Constitution by the expenditure of public funds in a campaign to advocate a particular outcome of a referendum. The plaintiff's claim was dismissed on the grounds that the purposes for which public monies were spent are matters for the government and the Dáil and it was not the function of the courts to resolve such disputes. The plaintiff appealed to the Supreme Court.

Held: Having regard to the importance of the Constitution as the fundamental law of the State and the crucial role of the people in the enactment of the Constitution, the use of public funds in a referendum campaign, which was designed to influence voters in favour of proposal, was an interference with the democratic process and the concept of equality.

Case: Murphy v. Attorney General (1980)

Article 41 of the Constitution declares that the State pledges to guard with special care the institution of marriage, on which the family is founded, and to protect it against attack. The plaintiff challenged parts of the income tax code which taxed a married couple living together more heavily than two single persons living together with similar incomes.

Held: The nature and potentially progressive extent of the burden was a breach of the pledge by the State to guard with special care the institution of marriage. The provisions in the Income Tax Act 1967 were therefore held to be unconstitutional.

Case: Educational Company of Ireland v. Fitzpatrick (1961)

Article 40 of the Constitution guarantees the right of freedom of association. Employees of the company, who were members of a union, in order to force their employer to employ only trade union labour, picketed the premises in an attempt to force all the employees to join the union.

Held: Employees who when being employed were not required to belong to a union had the constitutional right to disassociate. Thus, picketing for the purpose of forcing persons to join a union against their wishes was inconsistent with the right to freedom of association and, hence, unconstitutional.

European Union law

29. Since accession of Ireland to the European Economic Community in January 1973, the Constitution has no longer been supreme in all respects. A constitutional amendment was necessary to allow laws of the Community made externally, and not by organs established under the Constitution, to be part of our domestic law. Such a modification was accepted by the people in a referendum on the third amendment to the Constitution on 10 May 1972 and was enforced by special statutes, namely, the European Communities Act 1972 and the European Communities (Amendment) Act 1973.

30. The primary law of the European Union, which is contained in the principal treaties – the Treaty of Paris (1951) establishing the European Coal and Steel Community (ECSC), the Treaties of Rome (1957) establishing the European Economic Community (EEC) and the European Atomic Energy Community (Euratom), the Single European Act (1986), the Maastricht Treaty on European Union (1992), the Treaty of Amsterdam (1997) and the Treaty of Nice (2001) – takes precedence over domestic law. This is self-executing. Ratification of the treaties by a State means that the provisions become automatically embraced in the law of that State.

31. The secondary law of the European Union, made by the Council of Ministers or the European Commission, consists of regulations which apply to Ireland immediately without further legislation, and of directives which are made obligatory by special Irish statutes, statutory instruments or other political action. Recommendations and opinions expressing the Council of Ministers' and Commission's views may also be issued. These, however, are not binding, merely persuasive.

32. While it is true that membership of the European Union does restrict the supremacy of the Constitution, the directives to which Ireland must ultimately conform are issued as a result of negotiation and often agreement between the Irish government and the other governments of the European Union. The Irish government is dependent on the support of a majority of members of the Dáil to retain office. Therefore, the Oireachtas has indirect influence on the European Union law-making process.

Judicial precedent

33. Common law and equity have been developed through the centuries by judges in giving their decisions in the courts. Judge-made law involved the application of customary law to new situations, thereby maintaining consistency. As the law became more sophisticated, the decisions of the judges were recorded and reports were made of law cases. It became possible to follow previous decisions of judges and this brought about a level of certainty and progressive development in judge-made law. The reform introduced by the Judiciature Acts

1873–75 led to the modern doctrine of precedent which depends for its operation on the fact that all courts stand in a definite relationship to one another.

34. Judicial precedent is the application of a principle of law, as laid down by a higher court on a previous occasion in a similar case to the case before the court. This is known as the doctrine of *stare decisis*. A precedent or previous decision may be persuasive or binding.

35. A persuasive precedent is one which does not have to be followed by a court. The judge, however, may be influenced by it because it is worthy of the court's respect.

36. A binding precedent is a decision which the court must follow. This is based on the view that it is not the function of a judge to make law, but to decide cases in accordance with existing rules. Not all of the decision is binding on a later court, but only its authoritative element which is called the *ratio decidendi* (reason for the decision). This is the principle of the law upon which the judgment was based. The remainder, known as *obiter dictum* (by the way), are comments not directly related to the case and do not constitute binding precedent.

37. Not every decision made in a court is binding as a judicial precedent. The court's status has a significant effect on whether its decisions are persuasive, binding or disregarded. The higher the court, the more universally followed will be the decision. A superior court may overrule or replace a precedent set in a lower court. The old principle is then void of authority and is replaced by the new principle. Courts of equal seniority have no power to overrule each other, and decisions of such courts act as persuasive authority only. Finally, the court may decide that the *ratio decidendi* of the previous cases is not relevant to the current action because of factual differences which justify it in not following the earlier cases. This is known as 'distinguishing' the case, and allows a different legal principle to be formulated.

38. The highest court of authority in Ireland, the Supreme Court, binds all the courts. Because it is the highest court it is not bound by decisions of any other court. Since 1965, however, it has broken with its tradition of always following its own previous decisions, and also the decisions of those courts which had preceded it as the court of ultimate jurisdiction.

39. In *The State (Quinn) v. Ryan* (1965), the Supreme Court declared unconstitutional a statutory provision which it had previously declared constitutional in the earlier case of *The State (Duggan) v. Tapley* (1952). This more liberal approach was extended beyond the confines of constitutional issues in the *Attorney General v. Ryan's Car Hire Ltd* (1965). In this case, Justice Kingsmill Moore, while accepting the need to follow precedents in order to avoid uncertainty in the law, was of the opinion that 'the rigid rule of *stare decisis* must in a court of ultimate resort give place to a more elastic formula. Where such a court is clearly of the opinion that an earlier decision was erroneous, it should be at liberty to refuse to allow it, at all events, in exceptional cases'.

40. The Supreme Court will only overrule a previous decision where there is substantial agreement among the members of the court that there are compelling reasons for doing so. Hence, though not recognised in the Constitution, the doctrine of precedent is strongly adhered to in the courts.

Case: Kenny v. Trinity College and Dublin City Council (2007)

The plaintiff had objected to the building of a development consisting of new student residences at Trinity Hall, Dartry, Dublin 6. In 2003, the Supreme Court granted an application by the defendant to have the proceedings struck out, with the court's judgment having been given by Mr Justice Murray. In 2007, the plaintiff applied to the court to vacate the earlier order, stating in an affidavit that he had recently become aware that Chief Justice Murray's brother was a partner in Murray O'Laoire, Ireland's largest architectural practice and the firm which designed the Trinity Hall development.

Held: The Supreme Court set aside its earlier judgment on grounds of 'objective bias', or the possibility that an observer might perceive bias, even though the Chief Justice's brother was not in any way directly involved in the subject matter of the litigation.

IMPORTANT CASES

Numbers in brackets refer to paragraphs of this chapter

IMPORTANT STATUTES

European Convention on Human Rights Act (2003)

PROGRESS TEST

Numbers in brackets refer to paragraphs of this chapter

1. What are the functions of law? (2)
2. List (a) the historical, and (b) the legal sources of law. (3)
3. Explain how common law and equity developed as part of Irish law. (4–13)
4. Describe the stages through which a Bill must pass before becoming law. (17)
5. What is statutory interpretation? (19)
6. State the main advantages of delegated legislation. (22)
7. Describe how the Constitution has a higher status than any other domestic law. (27–8)
8. How are the principles of European Union law incorporated into Irish law? (30–31)
9. Explain the doctrine of *stare decisis.* (34–6)
10. On what grounds may a court avoid a binding precedent? (37–40)

INTERNET RESOURCES

European Court of Human Rights
   www.echr.coe.int
European Court of Justice
   www.curia.europa.eu
European Union Law
   www.europa.eu
Irish Constitution 1937
   www.constitution.ie
Legislation or Statute Law
   www.irishstatutebook.ie
   www.oireachtas.ie

chapter 2

THE DIVISION OF LAW – CIVIL AND CRIMINAL

Topics covered

- Civil proceedings
- Criminal proceedings

- Distinction between
  civil and criminal wrongs

Summary

In order to be able to understand fully the court system, it is first necessary to have an understanding of the classification of law. This chapter outlines the division of law into civil law and criminal law.

1. Law is the body of rules imposed by a State upon its members which is designed to regulate human conduct within that State.

2. The most fundamental distinction in the classification of law is that drawn between civil law and criminal law. The objectives of both, though closely connected, are clearly different.

• Civil proceedings

3. Civil law exists to deal with civil, or private, wrongs. The object of civil law is the resolution of disputes over the rights and obligations of individuals dealing with each other. The State has no role in such disputes. It is up to injured parties to commence a civil action to seek compensation for a loss which they have suffered.

4. In most civil cases, there will be a plaintiff (the aggrieved party) and a defendant (the offending party). The plaintiff sues the defendant, and the burden of proof shifts between both parties. A civil action must be proven on the balance of probabilities.

5. Civil cases use the names of the parties, the plaintiff's name being placed first, for example *Noonan* v. *Murphy* (1987). In some civil cases, there will not be a plaintiff and a defendant. For example, if an application were made to the court to interpret Murphy's will, the case would be known as *Re Murphy*.

6. Some of the many categories of civil law are:

(a) *Contract.* This determines whether agreements made by persons have given rise to obligations which are enforceable by law.

(b) *Tort.* This determines whether a wrong has been committed by one person against another, infringing a general duty imposed on them by law, e.g. the duty not to cause damage to a person's property, person or name.

(c) *Commercial law.* This covers contractual matters relating to negotiable instruments, agency, sale of goods and hire purchase.

(d) *Employment law.* This covers contractual relationships between the employer and the employee.

7. The general purpose of any judgment in civil proceedings is to impose a settlement on the matter, by ensuring that the injured party is compensated for any damage suffered by them. The concept of punishment does not exist. The main judicial remedies for civil wrongs are:

(a) an award of damages;

(b) an injunction to stop the defendant doing something (a prohibitory injunction) or to command the defendant to do something (a mandatory injunction);

(c) an order for specific performance, where the court compels the offending party to perform their obligations under a contract;

(d) a refusal of further performance, where there has been a breach of condition and the innocent party is relieved from further liability to perform their obligations.

• Criminal proceedings

8. Criminal law exists to deal with criminal, or public, wrongs. It is a set of standards imposed by a society on its individuals, breaches of which incur sanctions to punish the offender.

9. Criminal proceedings are started by the State against the offender through the office of the Director of Public Prosecutions. Although most crimes have specific victims, e.g. rape, the victim does not have a say in whether a prosecution is brought. Neither does the victim benefit from a conviction, since fines are payable to the State.

10. In a criminal trial, the accused is presumed to be innocent until proven to be guilty. The prosecution (i.e. the State) must prove the accused's guilt beyond reasonable doubt.

11. The general purpose of any judgment in criminal proceedings is to punish the guilty party. The main judicial remedies for criminal wrongs are:

(a) fines;
(b) imprisonment;
(c) binding of a party to keep the peace;
(d) community service orders, as an alternative to (b).

• Distinction between civil and criminal wrongs

12. The distinction between a civil and a criminal wrong is not found in the nature of the act or event itself, but in the legal consequences of it.

13. For example, a broken arm caused to a passenger of a taxi which has crashed is a single event which may give rise to a civil case (the passenger sues for compensation for pain and suffering caused by the wrong) and a criminal case (prosecution by the State for the offence of dangerous driving).

14. In some cases, therefore, the facts will indicate both a civil action and a criminal offence. In such cases, the victim will have to start a civil action separate from any prosecution brought by the State. The two sorts of proceedings are usually easily identified, however, since the procedures and terminology are different.

PROGRESS TEST

Numbers in brackets refer to paragraphs of this chapter

1. Explain the object of (a) civil, and (b) criminal law. (3, 8)
2. What is the standard of proof of civil proceedings? (4)
3. List four categories of civil law. (6)
4. What are the main judicial remedies for (a) civil, and (b) criminal wrongs? (7, 11)
5. Who starts criminal proceedings? (9)
6. What is the standard of proof of criminal proceedings? (10)
7. What is the distinction between civil and criminal wrongs? (12–14)

INTERNET RESOURCES

Director of Public Prosecutions
    www.dppireland.ie

chapter 3

ADMINISTRATION OF LAW

Topics covered

- The courts
- Personnel of the law

Summary

Having considered what law is and how it is created, it is now necessary to consider how it is enforced. This chapter explains the personnel of the law.

1. The law is made effective by the courts and the legal profession, supported by the State.

• The courts

2. The courts conduct an investigation into the liability or non-liability of a defendant in a civil litigation, or a fair trial into the guilt or innocence of the accused in a criminal case. The courts depend on the parties in dispute to do the bulk of the work. This saves the courts from having to make a full investigation into the facts in dispute and then drawing the appropriate conclusions.

3. In civil cases, the plaintiff makes a precise claim or claims against the defendant and the latter defends the action. The plaintiff must prove the action on the balance of probabilities. This is what is known as an adversary procedure – the courts are only concerned with ruling on the relevant issues brought to them for settlement and decision.

4. In criminal cases, the prosecution (the State) prepares its case precisely against the accused, and the accused attempts to counter it. The prosecution must prove the accused's guilt beyond reasonable doubt.

• Personnel of the law

5. The personnel of the law includes those people other than individual litigants who are responsible for carrying out the process of law in the courts, offices and in education.

Solicitors

6. The solicitor's profession has been regulated by the Law Society of Ireland since the nineteenth century. This controls entry to the profession, exercises disciplinary power over its members and protects the public against work by unqualified persons.

7. A solicitor often carries out routine legal work for the public where there is no dispute in hand. This includes the formation of companies and partnerships, the drafting of wills and contracts, and the conveyancing of property.

8. In addition, the solicitor carries out contentious office work, such as the preparation and/or settlement of issues in dispute. If the dispute goes to trial, the solicitor will gather the evidence, brief a barrister if necessary, conduct correspondence and attend preliminary hearings prior to the trial.

9. Solicitors are not involved exclusively in office work. A solicitor may, since 1971, also appear as an advocate without counsel's assistance. While entitled to appear before all the courts in Ireland, the solicitor tends to restrict appearance to lower courts where the special skills of the barrister may not be needed.

Barristers

10. The barrister's profession is regulated by the Bar Council. There are two types of barrister, senior and junior counsel. A junior counsel is 'called to the Bar' in the Supreme Court by the Chief Justice. After some years as an experienced and successful member of the profession, the barrister may be called to the 'Inner Bar' and become a senior counsel.

11. The barrister is first and foremost a specialist in the art of advocacy who presents a case in court on behalf of a client in a logical and effective manner. In some legal actions, the barrister can be essential to success because of the adversarial procedure applied in courts.

12. The barrister also drafts legal documents, such as pleadings, and is used as an expert on matters of legal opinion.

13. A lay client cannot engage a barrister directly. This must be done by a solicitor. This is known as a 'brief' – a formal document requesting the barrister's assistance. The barrister is expected, unless there is a good reason, to act on such a request.

14. In an important court action, the solicitor will gather the evidence, but will engage a barrister to draft the pleadings, to advise on the evidence and to present the case in court.

Judges

15. The judges of all courts are formally appointed by the President on the recommendation of the government in power when a vacancy arises. The Courts and Court Officers Act 1995 provided for the establishment of the Judicial

Appointments Advisory Board with the function of identifying and informing the government of the suitability of persons for appointment to judicial office.

16. Minimum periods of experience are a prerequisite. Under the Courts and Court Officers (Amendment) Act 2002, appointment to the District Court or Circuit Court requires at least ten years as a practising barrister or solicitor. A judge of the District Court is automatically eligible for appointment as a judge of the Circuit Court. Appointment to the High Court and Supreme Court is open to barristers or solicitors practising for at least twelve years, and for a continuous period of not less than ten years immediately before such appointment. In 2002, Michael Peart became the first solicitor to be appointed to the High Court.

17. Judges can only be removed from office for stated misbehaviour or incapacity, and then only by means of a resolution passed by both houses of the Oireachtas. Since the foundation of the State, no judge has actually been removed from office. In 2004, a motion to impeach a Circuit Court judge was launched in Dáil Éireann. He had been acquitted on charges of possession of child pornography when a Garda raid on his home had been done using an out-of-date search warrant. The Supreme Court subsequently upheld a challenge by the judge against a joint committee established by Dáil Éireann to consider the evidence. However, in November 2006, facing questioning by the committee, the judge resigned on health grounds and ended the impeachment process.

18. Judges' remuneration may not be reduced while in office, thereby guaranteeing their independence.

19. The function of the judge is to apply existing rules of law to the case before the court. The judge does not have a responsibility to investigate the total circumstances of the case. Instead, the judge must act as a neutral decision-maker, hearing facts and arguments presented by the parties, judging their merits, and applying the law accordingly.

20. Judges are capable, to a certain extent, of 'making law' through the interpretation of statutes and the doctrine of precedent.

The Director of Public Prosecutions
21. This office was established by the Prosecution of Offences Act 1974. The Director of Public Prosecutions is a civil servant, and is assisted by a staff of professional solicitors and civil service administrators.

22. The Director of Public Prosecutions' role concerns the prosecution of serious crimes in the name of the people. Proceedings may be initiated by this office when a case is referred to it by a government department or when the Director of Public Prosecutions considers that intervention is required.

23. The Director of Public Prosecutions is fully independent in the carrying out of the functions of the office. All decisions taken are final, and the reasons for the decision are not published.

The Attorney General

24. The office of Attorney General was created in 1924. It was preserved under Article 30 of the Constitution. The Attorney General is appointed by the President on the nomination of the Taoiseach. The Attorney General may be requested to resign, and will do so when the Taoiseach resigns.

25. The Attorney General is legal adviser to the government in matters of law and legal opinion, and institutes and defends proceedings to which the State is a party. The Attorney General's consent may be required by the Director of Public Prosecutions to bring proceedings in the criminal courts.

26. Additional responsibilities may be conferred upon the Attorney General by law. These include the scrutiny of extradition warrants and the enforcement of charitable trusts.

IMPORTANT STATUTES

Courts and Court Officers Act 1995
Courts and Court Officers Act 2002
Civil Liability and Courts Act 2004
Courts and Court Officers (Amendment) Act 2007

PROGRESS TEST

Numbers in brackets refer to paragraphs of this chapter

1. How does the court conduct an investigation in (a) civil, and (b) criminal cases? (2–4)
2. Describe the non-contentious office work performed by a solicitor. (7)
3. When is a solicitor likely to appear as an advocate? (9)
4. What are the functions of a barrister? (11–12)
5. Identify the minimum periods of experience required for judicial appointments. (16)
6. Describe the role of the Director of Public Prosecutions. (22)
7. How is the Attorney General appointed? (24)

INTERNET RESOURCES

Attorney General's Office
  www.attorneygeneral.ie
Bar Council
  www.lawlibrary.ie
Department of Justice, Equality and Law Reform
  www.justice.ie
Director of Public Prosecutions
  www.dppireland.ie
Law Society of Ireland
  www.lawsociety.ie

chapter 4

STRUCTURE OF THE COURTS

Topics covered

- Jurisdiction of the courts
- The District Court
- The Circuit Court
- The High Court
- The Court of Criminal Appeal
- The Supreme Court
- Additional courts

Summary

This chapter examines and describes the structure and jurisdiction of the courts to be found in the Republic of Ireland.

• Jurisdiction of the courts

1. Some courts deal only with civil cases and others only with criminal cases. Most, however, can deal with both. The jurisdiction of the courts can depend upon where the defendant lives, the type of legal problem involved, the seriousness of the offence and the amount of the claim or nature of the remedy sought.

2. The present structure of the Irish courts was first established by the Courts of Justice Act 1924. It now derives its authority from Article 34 of the Constitution, which states that: 'Justice shall be administered in courts established by law by judges appointed in the manner provided by this Constitution, and, save in such special and limited cases as may be prescribed by law, shall be administered in public.' The structure of courts that exists today was formally established by the Courts (Establishment and Constitution) Act 1961. No longer administered by the Department of Justice, the entire courts' system is now the responsibility of the Courts Service (an tSeirbhís Chúirteanna), an independent corporate organisation with its headquarters at Phoenix House, Smithfield, Dublin 7.

3. The court structure is organised on a hierarchical basis. At the bottom is the District Court, which has the narrowest jurisdiction. At the top is the Supreme Court, which is the final court of appeal. In the middle are the Circuit Court, the High Court and the Court of Criminal Appeal.

• The District Court

4. This, the lowest court within our legal system, is a unified court. The Courts and Court Officers (Amendment) Act 2007 provides that the number of judges of the District Court, in addition to the President, shall not be more than sixty. For the exercise of its duties, the country is divided into twenty-three districts to each of which one judge is permanently assigned, except in the case of the Dublin Metropolitan District and Cork, where the volume of cases requires the permanent assignment of a number of judges. Generally the venue at which a case is heard depends on where an offence was committed, or where the defendant was arrested or resides or carries out their business. Each District Justice sits alone.

5. The civil jurisdiction of the District Court covers a wide range of matters. It provides a cheap and quick forum for dealing with disputes of a local or relatively minor nature. In matters of contract and tort, the court has jurisdiction provided the amount claimed does not exceed €6,349. It can grant dance hall and liquor licences, and can order ejectment for non-payment of rent.

6. The criminal jurisdiction of the District Court covers summary offences and certain indictable offences. In either case, the offence must be a minor one.

7. A summary offence does not entitle a defendant to a trial by jury. It carries a maximum punishment of twelve months' imprisonment and/or a fine. An example would be driving a motor vehicle without insurance cover.

8. An indictable offence entitles a defendant to trial by jury. Providing the court considers the offence to be minor, and if the accused agrees to summary trial, the District Court can hear the case. In such cases, the maximum punishment is two years' imprisonment (i.e. two consecutive twelve-month sentences) or twelve months' imprisonment for one offence and/or a fine. An example would be serious assault.

9. In serious cases, such as murder, sexual offences and treason, the District Court may conduct a preliminary hearing to decide whether or not sufficient evidence exists to commit the accused for trial by jury before a higher court.

• The Circuit Court

10. This is a unified court which, in accordance with the Courts and Court Officers (Amendment) Act 2007, consists of a President and not more than thirty-seven ordinary judges. The country is divided into eight circuits. One Circuit judge is permanently assigned to each circuit, except under the provisions of the Courts and Court Officers Act 1995 whereby ten judges can be assigned to Dublin and three to Cork.

11. Civil cases in the Circuit Court are tried by a judge sitting without a jury. The civil jurisdiction is limited to €38,092, unless all parties to an action consent, in which case jurisdiction is unlimited.

12. An unsuccessful party in a District Court civil case can appeal to the Circuit Court, which will rehear the case and substitute its own decision, if different. This is final and cannot be appealed. Likewise, a defendant in a Circuit Court civil case has a right to appeal against the decision of the judge to the High Court. Finally, a Circuit Court judge may consult the Supreme Court on points of law.

13. The criminal jurisdiction of the Circuit Court covers indictable offences. In such cases, the Circuit Court consists of a judge and jury. Where the accused is found guilty, the Circuit Court judge may impose a punishment up to the maximum amount permitted by statute or common law.

14. A person convicted and punished in the District Court may appeal to the Circuit Court. The judge may completely rehear the case and reach independent conclusions, and may then decrease, let stand or increase the original punishment. The judge can only increase the punishment to the maximum which the District Court could have imposed.

• The High Court

15. The jurisdiction of the High Court extends to all matters whether of law or fact, civil or criminal. It also has exclusive jurisdiction in constitutional challenges to statutes. Article 34 of the Constitution provides as follows: 'The Courts of First Instance shall include a High Court invested with full original jurisdiction in and power to determine all matters and questions whether of law or fact, civil or criminal.'

16. The High Court consists of a President, who is a judge of the Supreme Court and a member of the Council of State and, in accordance with the Courts and Court Officers (Amendment) Act 2007, not more than thirty-five ordinary judges. The President of the Circuit Court and the Chief Justice are ex-officio additional judges of the High Court. Normally, the High Court hears cases with the judge sitting alone, but in certain cases three judges sit together.

17. A jury may be used by the High Court in civil cases. In such cases, a vote of nine out of twelve jurors is sufficient to award a judgment. The High Court can award unlimited damages.

18. When the High Court is hearing a criminal case it is known as the Central Criminal Court. It tries only serious crimes such as murder, attempted murder, conspiracy to murder or rape. It also tries cases which have been transferred from the Circuit Court to avoid trial before a local jury.

19. The High Court must use a jury in criminal cases where a plea of 'not guilty' has been made by the accused.

20. The High Court has a jurisdiction to give a ruling on the law as it affects the facts as stated by the District Court. The District Court, on its own behalf or on the application of one of the parties to the dispute, can submit the facts of a dispute in a formal document to the High Court. Having heard the arguments regarding the point of law, the High Court will decide upon the matter and will give an opinion and direction to the District Court, who must apply the decision accordingly. This is known as an appeal by way of 'case stated'.

21. Finally, the High Court also possesses supervisory jurisdiction over the inferior courts, state bodies and individuals. The High Court has power to issue an order of:

(a) *prohibition*, to prevent a person or body from exercising a power it does not legally have;
(b) *mandamus*, to compel a person or body to carry out a legal duty;
(c) *certiorari*, to stop a person or body who has exceeded their legal powers;
(d) *habeas corpus*, to require the person in custody and the detainer to attend before the High Court to explain the circumstances of, and justification for, detention.

• The Court of Criminal Appeal

22. This court hears appeals from the Circuit Court, Central Criminal Court or Special Criminal Court (the latter being a non-jury court which may be set up under Part V of the Offences Against the State Act 1939).

23. The court consists of three judges, one from the Supreme Court and two from the High Court. The court's decision is by majority.

24. Leave to appeal to the Court of Criminal Appeal will usually be given only where there is a dispute on a point of law. However, it may also be given in exceptional circumstances where new evidence becomes available which could not have been presented before the original court.

• The Supreme Court

25. This is at the top of the hierarchy of courts. It is the court of final resort for cases commenced in the High Court, as well as those cases which have made their way upwards to the High Court or which were directly appealed on a point of law to the Supreme Court.

26. There is no rehearing of the case in the Supreme Court as the record of the trial court is used.

27. The Supreme Court consists of the Chief Justice and seven ordinary judges. The President of the High Court is ex-officio an additional judge. The Supreme

Court may sit in two or more divisions and they may sit at the same time. Three judges will usually form a quorum but, in constitutional cases, five judges will constitute a court.

28. The Supreme Court has a consultative, as well as an appelative, jurisdiction. The President may consult it as to the constitutionality of a Bill which has been presented to the President for signature. The High Court and Circuit Court may consult it by way of 'case stated'.

• Additional courts

29. Apart from the civil and criminal courts operating in the Republic of Ireland, there are also other courts and tribunals which are of importance.

30. The European Court of Justice (see Chapter 29) and the European Court of Human Rights are just two of the extraterritorial courts whose decisions are binding when Ireland is a party to a dispute.

31. Administrative tribunals in Ireland act as courts in relation to taxation, social welfare benefits, planning, discrimination in employment and other administrative issues. Such tribunals are established by statute to settle disputes between individuals or between government agencies and individuals.

32. Examples of administrative tribunals include the Appeals Commissioners, the Social Welfare Appeals Office, An Bord Pleanála, the Labour Court and the Employment Appeals Tribunal.

33. The Employment Appeals Tribunal (EAT) hears claims of unfair dismissal or redundancy under the Unfair Dismissals Acts 1977–93. It consists of a legally qualified chair and vice-chair, together with an equal number of members nominated by the employers' organisations and the Irish Congress of Trade Unions (ICTU). A claim may come before the EAT from the employee directly or arising from the appeal, within six weeks, of a recommendation made by a Rights Commissioner. The EAT usually sits in a division consisting of either the chair or vice-chair and two members – one nominated by the employers' organisations and the other nominated by the ICTU. It hears the evidence from both parties to the dispute and issues a determination. If the EAT deems the dismissal to be unfair, it may specify one of the remedies listed in the Unfair Dismissals Acts 1977–2007, namely, reinstatement, re-engagement or compensation, which must be carried out by the employer within six weeks. If the remedy is not carried out within that time, the Minister for Enterprise, Trade and Employment may take the case to the Circuit Court on behalf of the employee. Either party may appeal a determination of the EAT, at their own expense, to the Circuit Court, within six weeks of the date of the issuing of the determination. The EAT also hears claims relating to written statements of the terms of employment under the Terms of Employment (Information) Act 1994–2001.

34. The advantages of administrative tribunals are that:

(a) they specialise in a particular field, and are composed of persons such as solicitors, judges and lay persons who have a specialised knowledge and experience in the field in question;
(b) they use more informal procedures than those familiar to courts;
(c) they are a less expensive method of resolving a dispute than a court action;
(d) they act more quickly than the courts, since they are able to meet by appointment when required.

35. On the other hand, the disadvantages of administrative tribunals are that:

(a) they may not, in certain cases, give reasons for their decisions;
(b) they may hear cases in private;
(c) they may not permit legal representation (at the initial proceedings, at least);
(d) they may not convince a party that a just and equitable hearing has been given to the case.

IMPORTANT STATUTES

Courts and Court Officers Act 1995
Courts and Court Officers Act 2002
Courts and Court Officers (Amendment) Act 2003
Civil Liability and Courts Act 2004
Courts and Court Officers (Amendment) Act 2007

PROGRESS TEST

Numbers in brackets refer to paragraphs of this chapter

1. How has the present structure of the Irish courts been established? (2)
2. Give examples of the types of cases tried in (a) a District Court, (b) a Circuit Court, and (c) the High Court. (5, 9, 11, 18)
3. What is a summary offence? (7)
4. Who staffs (a) a District Court, (b) a Circuit Court, (c) the High Court, and (d) the Supreme Court? (4, 10, 16, 27)
5. Describe the jurisdiction of the High Court. (15)
6. When are cases heard in the Central Criminal Court? (18)
7. What is 'case stated'? (20)
8. Explain the supervisory jurisdiction of the High Court. (21)
9. When will leave be given to appeal to the Court of Criminal Appeal? (24)
10. What matters does the Supreme Court deal with? (25, 28)

11. List (a) four advantages, and (b) four disadvantages of administrative tribunals. (34–5)

INTERNET RESOURCES

Employment Appeals Tribunal
  www.eatribunal.ie
Irish Courts Service
  www.courts.ie

Part 1: Introduction to the Study of Law

EXAMINATION QUESTIONS

1. There are four main sources of law in the Irish legal system. Describe each in detail.

   ICPA (Summer 2007)

2. You are employed as a marketing executive by a Japanese company which is expanding into Ireland. You have been asked to give a presentation of the main sources of law in Ireland to the board of directors. Outline the sources of law in Ireland, giving examples where appropriate, and in particular using examples relevant to the business environment.

   MII (May 2007)

3. (a) Write a note on the role of precedent in the legal system.
   (b) What are the 'maxims of equity' and discuss two maxims.

   IATI (Autumn 2007)

4. In relation to the Irish legal system, explain the doctrine of 'binding precedent', paying particular regard to:
   (a) the hierarchy of the courts; and
   (b) the advantages and disadvantages of the doctrine.

   ACCA (June 2007)

5. Outline the development of the body of law known as 'equity'. What remedies available in 'equity' were not available at 'common law'?

   IATI (Summer 2007)

6. What is 'common law' and explain how the law of equity developed?

   IATI (Autumn 2006)

7. It has been suggested that 'legislation' is the most significant source of Irish law in the modern context. Critically assess the statement. The answer should be supported by reference to examples of recent legislative measures which have a particular significance in the business context.

   MII (August 2006)

8. Discuss the sources of law in the Irish legal system.

   ICPA (Autumn 2006)

9. Analyse the development of the common law and equity as part of the law in Ireland.

ICPA (Autumn 2004)

10. What are 'maxims of equity'?

IATI (Summer 2006)

11. Discuss the extent to which the legislative provisions of the European Union, i.e. regulations, directives and decisions, are a source of Irish law. In answering the question, it is necessary to explain the extent to which such legislative measures are incorporated into Irish law.

MII (May 2006)

12. Examine each of the following legislative provisions of the European Union, both as to the policy objectives of such provisions and as a source of Irish law:
   (a) a regulation;
   (b) a directive;
   (c) a decision.

MII (May 2005)

13. Explain the divisions of law and explain the recent development of public law.

IATI (Summer 2006)

14. In relation to the Irish legal system, explain:
   (a) the meaning, scope and effectiveness of delegated legislation;
   (b) the powers of the courts to control such delegated legislation.

ACCA (June 2006)

15. Discuss the differences in the professions of barrister and solicitor as regards their functions in the Irish legal system.

ICPA (Summer 2006)

16. Outline the structure of the Irish courts in both civil and criminal jurisdictions.

IATI (Autumn 2006)

17. Discuss the structure and the operation of the civil courts in the Irish legal system.

ICPA (Summer 2005)

18. Which of the following statements is incorrect:
   (i) Common law and equitable principles can be applied by all the courts.
   (ii) A wrong committed by one person cannot result in both civil and criminal liability.

(iii) To be found guilty, the prosecution must prove beyond reasonable doubt that the accused committed the crime.
   A. (i) only
   B. (ii) only
   C. (i) and (iii) only
   D. (ii) and (iii) only

CIMA (November 2003)

ELEMENTS OF THE LAW
OF TORT

chapter 5

PRINCIPLES OF LIABILITY

Topics covered

- The nature of a tort
- General defences

Summary

A tort is defined as a civil wrong. This chapter outlines the principal rules and the general defences in tort.

• The nature of a tort

1. A tort is a civil, as opposed to a criminal, wrong for which the normal remedy is a common law action for unliquidated damages (i.e. damages determined by the court, and not previously agreed by the parties).

2. The wrongs dealt with by the law of tort include:

(a) causing physical injury to another intentionally or negligently (trespass to the person and negligence);

(b) interfering with another's land or goods (trespass to land, trespass to goods and nuisance);

(c) making a false statement about another (libel and slander).

3. While each individual tort has its own rules governing liability, in general plaintiffs must prove that:

(a) the defendant has infringed a right of theirs recognised by law; and

(b) some damage was caused to them by the tortious act.

4. In certain instances, however, the plaintiffs need not prove that they have suffered any damage or loss before a cause of action arises in tort. In such cases, all that the plaintiffs must show is that their legal right has been infringed. Examples of torts which are actionable *per se* include trespass and libel. In such cases, where there is an infringement of a legal right without harm, or *injuria sine damno*, the defendant will be found liable.

5. Furthermore, it does not necessarily follow that all actions which result in damage are actionable. The party suffering the damage must prove that some right recognised by law has been infringed. In cases where there is harm without the infringement of a legal right, or *damnum sine injuria*, the sufferer has no remedy.

• General defences

6. Defendants may try to refute an allegation that they have committed a tort. They need only argue a defence once the plaintiff has established the basic requirements of the tort.

7. There are a number of general defences in tort. These include:

(a) inevitable accident;
(b) consent of the plaintiff;
(c) necessity;
(d) statutory authority;
(e) limitation of actions.

Inevitable accident

8. Injury which could not be avoided by taking ordinary and reasonable precautions is not actionable. The defendant need only show that no reasonable precaution would have prevented the occurrence of an accident. The circumstances of the case will determine what is 'reasonable'.

Case: O'Brien v. Parker (1997)

The defendant lost control of his motor car and collided with the plaintiff's motor car, causing the plaintiff to suffer loss and damage. When the plaintiff sued seeking damages for negligence, breach of duty and breach of statutory duty, the defendant raised a defence of inevitable accident on the basis that the collision was the result of a sudden onset of temporal lobe epilepsy without any prior indication or warning, and that this had caused a state of unconsciousness in which he was left without control of his actions.

Held: There had to be total destruction of voluntary control on the defendant's part for automism, i.e. a state of unconsciousness, to be accepted as a successful defence in civil law. The defendant had been able to make the decision to drive and had failed to stop driving at a time when he was aware of a combination of unusual symptoms. Hence, the defence of inevitable accident had not been established on the balance of probabilities.

Case: Stanley v. Powell (1891)

The defendant fired his gun at a pheasant, but the bullet ricocheted off a tree and injured the plaintiff.

Held: Since the act could not have been avoided by reasonable precautions, the defendant was held to be completely blameless and not liable in negligence.

Consent of the plaintiff (volenti non fit injuria)

9. Those who undertake to run the risk created by the defendant cannot subsequently complain if, while doing so, they are injured – 'to the willing there can be no injury'. For example, a footballer could not sue as a result of a broken leg suffered in a match.

10. Mere knowledge of the risk does not necessarily imply consent. The defendant must show that the plaintiff appreciated the physical risk and consented to run that risk to the extent of surrendering legal rights. There must be no pressure on an employee to take the risk (e.g. the threat of loss of one's job).

Case: Regan v. Irish Automobile Club (1990)

The plaintiff was injured when struck by a racing car while officiating as a flag marshall at a motor race. She had signed a form prior to the race relieving the motor club from 'liability for accidents howsoever caused' in exchange for an insurance policy.

Held: The plaintiff, being aware of the risks involved, had waived her legal rights against the defendants in exchange for a valuable consideration, and was thereby unentitled to pursue the action.

Case: Bolt v. William Moss & Sons Ltd (1966)

The plaintiff was injured when falling off a painter's moveable scaffold which was moved while he remained on it. This was done despite his being expressly warned by his employer of the danger involved.

Held: *Volenti non fit injuria* was a good defence, because the task was undertaken entirely with full knowledge of the risk involved.

Case: Smith v. Charles Baker & Sons (1891)

The plaintiff, who was employed at a quarry, was injured when a stone fell from a crane which his employers negligently used to swing stones over his head.

Held: While it could be shown that the plaintiff knew of the risk, it could not be shown that he freely consented to run that risk. Since he may have continued to work under the crane through fear of losing his job, the plaintiff was entitled to recover damages.

Necessity

11. A tortious act, performed in order to prevent some greater evil, there being no reasonable alternative, is not actionable.

Case: Cope v. Sharpe (1912)

A fire broke out on the plaintiff's land. The defendant, a gamekeeper on adjoining land, set fire to heather on the plaintiff's land in order to create a fire-break so as to prevent the fire spreading to his employer's land. He was sued for trespass.

Held: Necessity was a good defence, since there was a real threat of a fire, and the defendant had acted reasonably.

Case: Lynch v. Fitzgerald (1938)

The plaintiff claimed damages for the death of his son, who was killed by the Gardaí when they opened fire on a demonstration which had evolved into a riot.

Held: Necessity was not a good defence, since such a course could only be considered necessary as a last resort to protect lives or property. Damages were awarded to the father of the youth.

Statutory authority

12. Where a statute has expressly authorised the action, or the action is a necessary consequence of what is authorised, this is a complete defence, provided the defendant can prove that any damage caused by the action did not arise as a result of negligence on the defendant's behalf.

Case: Smith v. Wexford County Council (1953)

The defendants, who had a statutory duty to keep rivers clear, deposited large amounts of soil and vegetable matter on the plaintiff's land. Some of his cattle ate the roots, which were poisonous, and died.

Held: The defendants could not reasonably have foreseen the poisonous nature of the roots. Statutory authority was, therefore, a good defence.

Limitation of actions

13. In accordance with the Civil Liability and Courts Act 2004, an action claiming damages in respect of personal injuries to an individual caused by negligence cannot be brought after the expiration of two years from the date on which the cause of action accrued, or the date of knowledge (if later) of the person injured.

Case: Bolger v. O'Brien (1999)

The plaintiff was involved in an accident on 22 March 1990, as a result of which he suffered personal injuries including cuts, bruises and a back injury. He was unable to return to work for three months, during which time he underwent a course of physiotherapy. On returning to work, he was unable to perform manual labour and could only engage in supervisory work. The plaintiff took a case on 27 October 1993 claiming damages against the defendants. The High Court held that the plaintiff was not aware of the significance of his back injury until October 1992, and that his claim was therefore not statute barred by s. 3(1), Statute of Limitations (Amendment) Act 1991. The defendant appealed.

Held: The date when the plaintiff first had knowledge that his injury was significant was the date when the plaintiff knew or reasonably ought to have known from facts observable or ascertainable by him that he had suffered a significant injury. The full significance of the effect of the injury was irrelevant once it was established that the plaintiff knew from the date of his return to work that he was not fit for manual labour.

Case: Kelly v. O'Leary (2001)

On 26 March 1998, the plaintiff sought damages in negligence in respect of physical and mental injuries arising from events alleged to have occurred between 1934 and 1947.

Held: The inordinate time that had elapsed between the alleged wrongful acts and the commencement of proceedings gave rise to a real and serious risk of an unfair trial.

IMPORTANT CASES

Numbers in brackets refer to paragraphs of this chapter

O'Brien v. Parker (1997) .... (8)
Stanley v. Powell (1891) .... (8)
Regan v. Irish Automobile Club (1990) .... (10)
Bolt v. William Moss & Sons Ltd (1966) .... (10)
Smith v. Charles Baker & Sons (1891) .... (10)
Cope v. Sharpe (1912) .... (11)
Lynch v. Fitzgerald (1938) .... (11)
Smith v. Wexford County Council (1953) .... (12)
Bolger v. O'Brien (1999) .... (13)
Kelly v. O'Leary (2001) .... (13)

PROGRESS TEST

Numbers in brackets refer to paragraphs of this chapter

1. Define a tort. (1)
2. Give three examples of the wrongs dealt with by the law of tort. (2)
3. Explain, using examples, what is meant by (a) *injuria sine damno*, and (b) *damnum sine injuria*. (4–5)
4. Name four defences in tort. (7)
5. When is inevitable accident a good defence? (8)
6. Is it possible to use consent as a defence if (a) it has been obtained by fraud or threat; or (b) it has not been expressed? (9–10)

REMEDIES

Topics covered

- Damages
- Injunction

Summary

This chapter sets out the different judicial remedies for tortious behaviour which may be sought, and the circumstances in which each will be given.

1. The most common judicial remedies for tortious behaviour available from the courts are damages or an injunction.

Damages

2. The main remedy for the victim of a tort is an award of damages. The measure of damages is the amount of money which will compensate the plaintiff for the damage caused or restore the plaintiff to their original position. Tort damages are always unliquidated, i.e. determined by the courts and not previously agreed by the parties.

3. There are three main types of damages which may be awarded by a court:

(a) *Real damages*. The purpose of real damages (also known as compensatory damages) is to compensate the plaintiff, so far as money can do, for the loss, injury or damage suffered. The award of damages must take future loss into account, since usually only one action can be brought.

(b) *Nominal damages*. Where a tort is actionable *per se*, and the plaintiff proves the elements of the tort without showing real damage, the court will award a small sum known as nominal damages. An example is a simple trespass onto another's property.

(c) *Exemplary damages*. Where the court wishes to punish the defendant in addition to compensating the plaintiff, an additional sum, known as exemplary damages, is awarded. An example is damages awarded against the publisher of defamatory material so as to ensure that such damages would exceed the profits of the publication.

Case: Doran v. Delaney (1999)

The plaintiffs purchased a site with planning permission in 1990 and began to build a house on it. Due to a defective title in part of the property sold, the plaintiffs were obliged to stop building and were ultimately forced to sell the property at a loss. They were financially unable to purchase an alternative site or house, and sought damages for breach of contract, negligence and misrepresentation on behalf of the defendants.

Held: The solicitor for the plaintiffs on the purchase was in breach of a duty of care to the plaintiffs for failing to ensure that the land being acquired was that shown on a map presented to the clients and that there was access to the land for the purposes of construction. Likewise, the vendors were in breach of duty for failing to disclose the existence of a conflicting claim to ownership of part of the property. Finally, the solicitors for the vendors were also in breach of duty for responding negligently to requisitions on title. Therefore, the plaintiffs were entitled to recover by way of special damages a sum which would allow them to purchase a house of the kind which they had intended to build, the measure of damages to be the same for each defendant.

Case: Kennedy and Arnold v. State (1988)

The plaintiffs, political journalists, sued the State for damages arising from an invasion of their constitutional right to privacy by way of the monitoring and recording of their telephone conversations.

Held: The plaintiffs were entitled to exemplary damages because the injury caused to them was serious and was premeditated.

• Injunction

4. An injunction is an equitable remedy. It is an order of the court which commands a party to do (a 'mandatory injunction'), or to refrain from doing (a 'prohibitory injunction') some particular deed. For example, an injunction may be granted by a court to prevent unlawful picketing.

5. An 'interlocutory injunction' is frequently granted to preserve the status quo until the action can come for trial. The court may then, if the facts warrant it, grant a 'perpetual injunction' which may take either of the two aforementioned forms.

6. An injunction will not be given where damages would be an adequate remedy or where the court could not properly supervise the enforcement of its decree.

Case: National Irish Bank Ltd v. Radio Telefis Éireann (1998)

The plaintiff was granted an interim injunction by the High Court on 30 January 1998 restraining the defendant from publishing confidential information relating to themselves and their customers. On 6 March 1998, the plaintiff applied for a similar interlocutory injunction, arguing that the dissemination of the information in question would breach the confidential relationship between them and their customers, and would cause them irreparable damage. The defendants claimed, however, that such publication was justified by the overriding requirements of the public interest. The application for this interlocutory injunction was denied and an appeal was made to the Supreme Court.

Held: There exists a duty and a right of confidentiality between banker and customer, and there is a public interest in the maintenance of such confidentiality for the benefit of society at large. However, there is also a public interest in defeating wrongdoing, and where the publication of confidential information could be of assistance in defeating wrongdoing, then the public interest in such publication may outweigh the public interest in the maintenance of confidentiality. In this case, the appeal was dismissed and the order of the High Court affirmed.

IMPORTANT CASE

Numbers in brackets refer to paragraphs of this chapter

Doran v. Delaney (1999) .... (3)
Kennedy and Arnold v. State (1988) .... (3)
National Irish Bank Ltd v. Radio Telefís Éireann (1988) .... (6)

PROGRESS TEST

Numbers in brackets refer to paragraphs of this chapter

1. What are the most common remedies for tortious behaviour? (1)
2. Explain what is meant by unliquidated damages. (2)
3. When are (a) compensatory, (b) exemplary, and (c) nominal damages awarded? (3)
4. What is a 'prohibitory injunction'? (4)
5. Why may an 'interlocutory injunction' be awarded? (5)
6. Identify two situations when an injunction would not be given as a remedy for tortious behaviour. (6)

chapter 7

NEGLIGENCE

Topics covered

- Nature of negligence
- Legal duty of care
- Breach of duty
- Consequential harm
- Personal Injuries Assessment Board

- Contributory negligence
- Occupiers' liability
- Vicarious liability
- Strict liability
- Civil Liability and Courts Act 2004

Summary

This chapter examines the basic components which must be present for a negligence action to be proved. It also considers the liability of an occupier of premises for injuries caused to persons while on those premises.

Nature of negligence

1. Negligence is the breach of a legal duty of care which causes loss or injury to the person to whom the duty is owed.

2. The duty of care may arise in a number of ways. It is owed, for example, by a motorist to all other users of the road, by a manufacturer to the consumers of the product, by an employer to the employees and by a professional to the clients.

3. To succeed in a negligence action plaintiffs must prove that:

(a) the defendant owed them a legal duty of care;
(b) the defendant has been guilty of a breach of that duty; and
(c) the plaintiffs suffered injury, damage or loss as a result of that breach.

Legal duty of care

4. Not everyone who is 'careless' will be liable in negligence. It is only in certain limited circumstances that the law imposes a duty of care. A duty of care is owed to any person who we can reasonably foresee will be injured by our acts or omissions. Such persons are known as 'neighbours'.

5. In *Donoghue* v. *Stevenson* (1932) the court ruled that a person could owe a duty of care to another with whom they had no contractual relationship.

Case: Donoghue v. Stevenson (1932)   Studiare

The plaintiff's friend purchased a bottle of ginger beer from a retailer and gave it to the plaintiff to consume. The bottle was opaque. The plaintiff drank a portion of the contents of the bottle, and then poured the rest into her glass. The remains of a small snail emerged from the bottle. The plaintiff subsequently became seriously ill and sued the defendant, the manufacturer, in negligence. The defendant argued that he did not owe a duty of care to the plaintiff since there was no contract between the defendant and the plaintiff (the purchaser having been the plaintiff's friend).

Held: The defendant had prepared the product in such a way as to show that he intended it to reach the ultimate consumer in the form in which it left him. He could reasonably foresee that somebody other than the original purchaser might consume the product, and, therefore, he was held liable to the plaintiff.

6. The existence of a duty of care to one's neighbour, defined by the House of Lords in the above case as 'all persons who are so closely and directly affected by my act that I ought reasonably to have them in contemplation as being so affected when I am directing my mind to the acts or omissions which are called into question', became known as the 'neighbour principle'. It has been applied in several other cases since.

Case: King v. Phillips (1952)

The defendant carelessly drove his car over a boy's bicycle. The boy, who was not on his bicycle at the time, screamed. The plaintiff, his mother, on hearing the scream, looked out the window and saw the mangled bicycle, but not her son. As a result, she suffered a severe shock and became ill. She sued the defendant for negligence.

Held: The defendant could only reasonably foresee that his carelessness would affect other road users, and not persons in houses. The defendant was held not liable to the plaintiff, since he did not owe her a duty of care.

Case: Dutton v. Bognor Regis UDC (1972)

An inspector, employed by the defendant council, examined the foundations of a house being built and passed them as fit. Three years later, after the plaintiff had purchased the house from its original owner, cracks began to appear and the internal walls started to subside. The plaintiff had the house surveyed independently and was told that his house was built on a rubbish tip, which was an unstable foundation. He sued the council for negligence.

Held: The professional person who provided an opinion as to the safety of the house owed a duty of care, not only to the owner at that time, but to all subsequent owners who might suffer injury or loss as a result of its use. The defendant council was held liable.

Case: Kelly and Others v. Haughey, Boland & Co. (1987)

The plaintiffs, directors of Cavan Crystal Ltd, contracted to buy another company, Royal Tara China Ltd, having examined the audited accounts for a number of years' trading, as certified by a partner of the defendant accountancy firm. They subsequently sued the defendants for negligence, claiming that the stock figure had been overstated and had resulted in the plaintiffs purchasing a company which was worth less than they had originally thought.

Held: Although the defendants had not taken reasonable care in the certification of the figures, they did not owe a duty of care to the plaintiffs, since they could not have foreseen that the company would be sold.

Case: Glencar Exploration Plc & Andaman Resources Plc v. Mayo County Council (2002)

The plaintiffs were granted licences by the Minister for Energy to explore for gold in the Westport area and had invested heavily in the mining activity for 24 years. In 1991, they set up a joint venture with an Australian company, Newcrest Mining Ltd, which collapsed when a mining ban was introduced by Mayo County Council in accordance with its 1992 draft county plan. The plaintiffs successfully challenged the mining ban in the High Court and sought to recover damages from Mayo County Council for breach of duty.

Held: Although the defendant had been negligent in adopting the ban, this did not give rise to any right to damages as there was an insufficient relationship of proximity between the parties.

Case: Breslin v. Corcoran and Motor Insurers Bureau of Ireland (2003)

The first-named defendant left his car unlocked and with the keys in the ignition whilst entering a shop to buy a sandwich. Coming out, he saw an unknown person enter his car and drive it off at speed. The plaintiff was struck by the car and injured as he crossed a street nearby. An action was brought alleging negligence in leaving the car unattended in the manner described.

Held: There was nothing to suggest that the first-named defendant should have anticipated as a reasonable probability that the car, if stolen, would be driven so carelessly as to cause injury to another user of the road such as the plaintiff. A car owner would not usually owe a duty of care to someone injured by a thief's negligent driving.

7.   The Liability for Defective Products Act 1991 implements the EC Directive on Products Liability and further strengthens the position of the consumer by imposing liability on a producer for a defect in a product regardless of whether the producer was negligent or not. As a consumer protection measure, the Act is not confined to a person who deals as a 'consumer', as that term is defined under the Sale of Goods and Supply of Services Act 1980 (see Chapter 26), thereby covering a potentially wider category of litigant. The Act covers defective products only,

and does not have relevance as far as services are concerned. With the exception of primary agricultural products and game which have not undergone initial processing, all moveables are considered as products under the terms of the Act. Injured parties only have to prove that there was a defect in the product and that it caused them the damage or injury. Damages are not recoverable for injury or damage to the product itself, but are confined to personal injuries or damage to the consumer's personal property in excess of €444.

Case: Delahunty v. Players & Wills (Ireland) Ltd and Gallaher (Dublin) Ltd (2006)

The plaintiff sued two tobacco companies for personal injuries allegedly caused by her addiction to their cigarettes over many years. The 80-year-old woman, a lifelong smoker suffering from cancer, alleged negligence, breach of duty and breach of statutory duty including, in particular, breaches of the Liability for Defective Products Act 1991 and of Council Directive 85/374/EEC. The defendants attempted to halt the plaintiff's claim on the grounds that it disclosed no responsible cause of action.

Held: The claim based on liability for defective products could not be dismissed at this stage and the plaintiff could bring proceedings against the tobacco companies.

8.   Some defences, as listed in section 6 of the Act, are available to the producer. The defendant will have a defence if it can be proven that:

(a) the defendant did not put the product into circulation;
(b) it is probable that the defect which caused the damage did not exist at the time the product was put into circulation;
(c) the product was not manufactured for a commercial purpose or in the course of business;
(d) the defect concerned is due to compliance by the product with any requirement imposed, or under any enactment required, by law of the European Union;
(e) the state of scientific and technical knowledge at the time when the producer put the product into circulation was not such as to enable the existence of the defect to be discovered;
(f) the defect was caused entirely by the design of the product in which the component has been fitted (in the case of the manufacturer of a component) or the raw material has been incorporated to the instructions given by the manufacturer of the product (in the case of the producer of raw material).

9.   Liability under the Act expires ten years from the date the product is put into circulation, unless proceedings have already been instituted.

• Breach of duty

10. Given the existence of a duty of care in any particular case, it is then necessary to establish whether the defendant took reasonable care in the circumstances. The question posed is whether the defendant exercised the care that a reasonable person would have exercised.

Case: S.E.E. Co. Ltd v. Public Lighting Services Ltd (1988)

The defendants sold eight floodlighting masts, which complied with British standards of safety, to the plaintiffs. The plaintiffs erected these masts on a sports ground, but one of them collapsed during the course of a storm. The plaintiffs sued for negligence.

Held: There was no evidence that there had been a lack of reasonable care taken by the defendants, since the masts complied with standards accepted and used in Ireland.

11. If the defendant is acting in a professional or skilled capacity, the care, skill and knowledge which could be reasonably expected from a member of that profession or trade – accountant, dentist, doctor, plumber, carpenter or electrician, as the case might be – must be exercised.

Case: Flynn v. O'Reilly (1999)

The plaintiff fell and fractured her wrist while taking part in a running backwards race held during her school's sports day. She claimed that the field had been dangerous, the activity ought to have been forbidden and that there had been negligence on the part of the school teachers in failing to supervise the plaintiff adequately.

Held: The duty of a school principal is to take such care of pupils as a careful parent would of their children. It is not necessary that normal healthy children be under constant supervision whilst in the playground. There is some risk attached to all forms of sport and imposing standards of care, approaching absolute liability, would be unreasonable in the circumstances.

12. A duty to take reasonable care to avoid a particular risk may vary with the magnitude of the foreseeable risk and the ease or difficulty of guarding against the risk involved.

Case: Latimer v. A.E.C. (1953)

The defendants' factory was flooded by a thunderstorm. This had the effect of making the floor slippery. Despite the defendants' efforts to clear the water and make the factory floor safe by the use of sawdust, the plaintiff slipped on one of these areas and injured himself. The plaintiff sued for negligence, alleging that the factory should have been closed.

Held: Economic factors had to be taken into account. The risk of injury did not justify the closure of the factory. The defendants exercised the care that a reasonable person would have exercised. They were not held liable.

Case: Paris v. Stepney Borough Council (1951)

The plaintiff, who had only one eye, a fact which was known to his employer, was employed by the defendant as a vehicle welder. He lost his other eye when a spark flew into it. The plaintiff sued his employer for negligence, claiming that goggles should have been provided.

Held: While goggles were not usually provided for two-eyed welders, the employer should have provided them in this situation because of the greater risk involved. The defendant, therefore, had not taken reasonable care and was held liable.

Case: Curran v. Cadbury (Ireland) Ltd (2000)

On the day in question, the plaintiff had been working at a conveyor belt which carried chocolate bars to her workstation, where they were packed by the plaintiff and her workmate. The machine feeding out the chocolate bars was stopped without notification to the plaintiff, and as she turned the machine back on she immediately became aware of the screams and shouts of a fitter repairing the machine from within. The plaintiff got an intense shock, thinking that she had killed or done serious injury to a fellow employee, and subsequently suffered a serious psychiatric illness. She sought damages for post-traumatic stress as a consequence of the defendant's negligence and breach of duty.

Held: The plaintiff was within the range of persons to whom a duty of care was owed. There had been a failure on the part of the defendant to take reasonable care for the safety of the employees in general and the plaintiff in particular. The plaintiff had suffered a compensatable injury, which was reasonably foreseeable in the circumstances, and was entitled to damages totalling €23,744 for the injury sustained.

Res ipsa loquitur

13. The burden of proving the tort of negligence rests on the plaintiff, except where the *res ipsa loquitur* (the thing speaks for itself) rule applies. Under this rule, the facts of a particular case may be such as to raise a presumption of negligence where there is no other obvious cause of the incident. The defendant must prove that, despite the facts, reasonable care was shown.

14. There is prima facie evidence of negligence when:

(a) the defendant has sole control of the incident;
(b) the defendant has knowledge denied to the plaintiff; and
(c) the damage is such that it would not normally have happened without some element of negligence by the defendant.

Case: Byrne v. Boadle (1863)

A barrel of flour fell from the defendant's warehouse on to a public place, injuring the plaintiff, a passer-by. The burden of proof was placed by the court on the defendant, who was obliged to show that he had not broken his duty of care.

Held: The defendant could not prove he had taken reasonable care to ensure that such an accident would not happen. He was held to be negligent.

Case: Macon v. Osborne (1939)

The plaintiff had a swab left in his body after an operation. Although he was unable to prove a breach of duty, since he was under anaesthetic at the time, he sued the surgeon for negligence.

Held: The presence of the swab in the patient's body provided prima facie evidence of a breach of duty. The surgeon was unable to prove that he had taken reasonable care. He was held liable.

Case: O'Loughlin v. Kearney (1939)

The defendant had a trailer coupled to his car. It became detached and injured the plaintiff, who sued for negligence. The court placed the burden of proof on the defendant, who had to show that he had not broken his duty of care.

Held: The cause of the detachment remained unknown. The defendant, however, successfully proved that there was no defect in the coupling, and was thereby held not to be negligent.

• Consequential harm

15. The plaintiff must show that some damage, loss or injury has been suffered as a result of the breach of duty. For the claim to be proved, the harm must be:

(a) caused to a large extent by the conduct of the defendant;
(b) sufficiently closely related to the negligent act; and
(c) either physical injury to the plaintiff's property, or economic loss consequential upon physical injury.

16. The court will then look at whether the harm which occurred was reasonably foreseeable, i.e. the defendant is only liable for the consequences of any act that a reasonable person could have foreseen.

Case: Overseas Tankship (UK) Ltd v. Morts Dock & Engineering Co. Ltd (*The Wagon Mound*) (1961)

An action was brought by the owners of a wharf against the owners of a ship, *The Wagon Mound*. The defendant's employees had spilt a large quantity of fuel oil into Sydney harbour, which had spread to another part of the harbour where the plaintiff was engaged in welding on his wharf. He had ceased welding until he had received expert advice that oil would not burn on water. The oil was ignited, however, by welding sparks which fell on cotton waste. Much damage was caused to the wharf.

Held: Harm to the wharf by fouling was foreseeable, but harm by fire was unforeseeable, since oil on water does not usually ignite. Damages were not awarded for harm caused by the explosion and fire.

• Contributory negligence

17. At common law, if the plaintiff was guilty of any negligent actions which contributed to the cause of the harm, the defendant could escape liability for negligence.

18. Since 1961, by virtue of the Civil Liability Act 1961, where a person suffers harm partly as a result of their own fault, and partly due to the fault of another, the damages recoverable will be reduced according to the share of the responsibility.

Case: O'Leary v. O'Connell (1968)

The defendant, a motorcyclist, knocked down the plaintiff who was walking across a road. As a result, the plaintiff's leg was broken.

Held: Both parties were negligent in not keeping a proper look-out. The degree of fault was apportioned 85 per cent to the defendant and 15 per cent to the plaintiff, and damages were awarded accordingly.

19. A person can be guilty of contributory negligence if their conduct, while in no way contributing to the accident itself, contributed to the nature and extent of their injuries.

Case: Sinnott v. Quinnsworth Ltd (1984)

The plaintiff, a passenger in a car owned by the defendant, was injured in a collision between the car and a bus. Evidence showed that the injuries would have been less serious if the plaintiff had been wearing his seat-belt.

Held: The plaintiff's damages would be reduced by 15 per cent.

• Occupiers' liability

20. Occupiers have a duty to exercise care towards persons who enter their premises, regardless of any contractual relationship between them. At common law, this liability was governed by the ordinary principles of negligence, and varied with the occupier's relationship to the visitor, who could be:

(a) an 'invitee', who comes on to the premises for some purpose in which the occupier has an interest;
(b) a 'licensee', who comes on to the premises with the express or implied consent of the occupier, but only does so for the licensee's benefit; or
(c) a 'trespasser', who comes on to the premises without permission and has no right to be there.

21. The Occupiers' Liability Act 1995 provides a firm statutory basis for the duty of care owed by occupiers to entrants on their property.

22. Under this Act, a duty of care is owed to:

(a) a 'visitor', who enters the premises at the invitation, or with the permission, of the occupier; as of right; or by virtue of an express or implied term in a contract;

(b) a 'recreational user', who enters the premises for the purpose of engaging in a recreational activity without a charge, whether this is with or without the occupier's permission or at the occupier's implied invitation;

(c) a 'trespasser', who is any user other than a visitor or a recreational user.

23. Visitors are owed a duty of care that they and their property do not suffer injury or damage by reason of any danger existing on the premises of the occupier. (s. 3)

Case: Duffy v. Carnabane Holdings Ltd (1996)

The plaintiff slipped on a dance floor and sprained his ankle whilst attending a disco held at the defendant's hotel. He later instituted proceedings against the defendant, giving evidence that there had been spillages and broken glass on the dance floor before the accident occurred. The defendant argued that it had warned people against taking glasses onto the dance floor, that it had sufficient staff available, and that mops and buckets had been placed at strategic places to clean up any spillages.

Held: Whilst an invitor is not an insurer for the safety of an invitee, the invitor owes a duty to the invitee to take reasonable care of all the circumstances to see that the premises are reasonably safe. There was evidence to support that there had been spillages and broken glass on the dance floor for an appreciable time prior to the accident, and therefore the plaintiff was entitled to recover damages.

24. Recreational users and trespassers are owed a duty of care that the occupier does not injure them intentionally or act with reckless disregard for them and their property. (s. 4)

Case: Weir-Rodgers v. S.F. Trust Ltd (2005)

The plaintiff was sitting near the edge of a cliff admiring a sunset. Upon standing up, she lost her footing and rolled down the cliff. She ended up in the sea and was rescued by her friend, but not before sustaining serious injuries. The plaintiff sued the landowner under the Occupiers' Liability Act 1995, claiming that there should have been an adequate fence and a warning sign.

Held: The fact that there was an old decayed fence did not impose any liability on the landowner. The duty of care owed to recreational users is to not injure them intentionally and to not act with deliberate or reckless disregard for their person or property. The defendant had no case to answer.

25. The occupier owes a duty of care to maintain in a safe condition any structure on the premises which is or has been provided for use primarily by recreational users. (s. 4)

26. Occupiers are entitled, in certain circumstances, to modify their duty of care by agreement or notice. (s. 4)

27. In all cases, warnings from occupiers may be sufficient to absolve them from liability to all persons entering their premises. (s. 5)

28. Occupiers are not liable for injury or damage unintentionally caused to persons entering their premises for the purpose of commiting an offence or who commit an offence while there, unless the court decides otherwise in the interests of justice. (s. 4)

• Vicarious liability

29. A person may be held liable by law by authorising another, either expressly or implicitly, to commit an action which causes injury or damage to a third party. Hence, the general rule is that a person is liable in tort for their own actions only, but in some exceptional cases they may also be answerable for the acts of others.

30. Vicarious, or indirect, liability arises most commonly in the relationship between employers, their agents and their employees. An employer is generally liable for torts committed by an agent acting within the scope of authority, or for torts of employees committed in the course of their employment. However, where an agent or employee has acted negligently or has committed some other tort, they will themselves be liable.

Case: Ilkiw v. Samuels (1963)

The defendant expressly instructed an employee not to allow anybody else to drive his lorry in any circumstances. Some time later it became necessary to move the lorry away from a conveyor belt, and the aforementioned employee allowed another person to drive it. This person was unable to stop the lorry and, as a result, injured the plaintiff, who sued the defendant for negligence.

Held: Although the employee had been negligent in allowing somebody else to drive the lorry, this negligence arose in the course of the employment. Accordingly, the defendant (i.e. the employer) was held to be vicariously liable.

• Strict liability

31. Liability is strict, i.e. it may arise without fault, where a person collects or stores non-natural things on their property which are likely to do harm if they escape from the property. The defendant need not have acted either negligently or intentionally for strict liability to apply.

Case: Rylands v. Fletcher (1868)

The defendant, a mill owner, employed independent contractors to construct a reservoir on his land for the purpose of supplying water for his mill. During the work, the contractors found disused mine shafts which, unknown to them, had an adjoining passageway with mine shafts on the plaintiff's neighbouring land. They did not fill in these shafts. When the reservoir was filled with water, the water escaped through the old mine shafts and flooded the plaintiff's land. The plaintiff sued for negligence.

Held: Although the defendant had not been negligent, since he had employed competent workmen and was himself unaware of the existence of the disused mine shafts, he was nonetheless personally liable, and not merely vicariously liable, for the contractors' negligence.

32. The rule in *Rylands* v. *Fletcher* has been applied to the escape of many non-natural things beyond the boundaries of the defendant's land such as water, gas, chemicals, animals, vibrations, explosives and fire.

Case: Berkery v. Flynn (1982)

The defendant built a slurry pit on his own land. An overflow of slurry entered the general water system and subsequently contaminated the contents of a well on the plaintiff's land. The plaintiff was dependant on supplies from this well for both farming and domestic purposes.

Held: The plaintiff was able to recover damages under the rule in *Rylands* v. *Fletcher* because he had an interest in the polluted well, and the loss was a sufficiently direct consequence of the escape of the slurry into the general water system.

33. Some defences to the rule are available. Defendants will have a defence if they can prove that:

(a) the escape was caused by:
    (i)   the action of the plaintiff;
    (ii) an act of God; or
    (iii) a third party over whom they had no control.
(b) the accumulation was made:
    (i)   with the express or implied consent of the plaintiff; or
    (ii) under statutory authority.

• Personal Injuries Assessment Board

34. The Personal Injuries Assessment Board is a statutory body established under the Personal Injuries Assessment Board Act 2003 with a view to reducing legal costs and other fees charged by experts involved in personal injuries claims and reducing the amount of time it takes to finalise a compensation claim. It provides an independent assessment of personal injury claims for compensation arising from workplace, motor and public liability accidents where the person or organisation responsible is not seeking a decision on liability, that is, where legal issues are not disputed. Injured persons must submit their claims for compensation for personal injury to the Board before being at liberty to issue proceedings in court if they or the respondent are ultimately dissatisfied with the value assessed by the Board for the injury.

35. Claims are assessed using all the medical evidence provided, having regard to the Book of Quantum published by the Board. This contains guidelines of compensation figures for specific injuries based on the nature and severity of an injury and existing levels of compensation. Normally an assessment comprises both general damages to compensate for pain and suffering resulting from injuries sustained and special damages to cover loss of wages, medical bills, out-of-pocket expenses and property damage. If either party rejects the award, the Board issues an authorisation entitling them to pursue their action through the court system.

• Civil Liability and Courts Act 2004

36. The Civil Liability and Courts Act 2004 introduces significant changes to court procedure in civil cases, restricting the latitude previously afforded to claimants under the law. A plaintiff must now serve a letter of claim on an intended defendant within two months of the event giving rise to the claim. All claims must be commenced by a personal injuries summons detailing in depth the circumstances of the accident, the medical consequences of the injury and the alleged legal wrongdoing of the defendants. Plaintiffs must provide full details of other personal injury actions they have been involved in upon the defendant's request, and must swear a verifying affidavit in respect of all documents filed to support the claim.

37. Either party may ask the court at any time before trial to direct the holding of a mediation conference with a view to settling the claim outside of court. In the event that the parties cannot agree on the appointment of a mediator, the court will appoint one and specify the time and location where the mediation is to take place. The mediator will provide a report to the court setting out whether the mediation conference happened and whether or not a settlement of the claim had been reached.

38. Both parties are required to make formal offers of terms of settlement with each other prior to the trial. Copies of the offers are lodged in the court but not communicated to the judge until after the judgment is given. The court, when addressing the cost issue, must consider the terms of the formal offers and the reasonableness of the parties making them. In deciding the level of compensation for an injury, the court is also obliged to give consideration to the Book of Quantum, the guide published by the Personal Injury Assessment Board.

39. Neither the Personal Injuries Assessment Board nor the Civil Liability and Courts Act 2004 change the underlying principles of negligence. The individual making a personal injury claim must be able to prove that the defendant owed them a legal duty of care, that the defendant has been guilty of a breach of that duty and that the plaintiff has suffered injury, damage or loss as a result of that breach.

IMPORTANT CASES

Numbers in brackets refer to paragraphs of this chapter

IMPORTANT STATUTES

Civil Liability Act 1961
Liability for Defective Products Act 1991

Personal Injuries Assessment Board Acts 2003 and 2007
Civil Liability and Courts Act 2004

PROGRESS TEST

Numbers in brackets refer to paragraphs of this chapter

1. Define negligence. (1)
2. List the basic components which must be present for a negligence action to be proven. (3)
3. To whom is a legal duty of care owed? (4–5)
4. What is the 'neighbour principle'? (6)
5. What is meant by *res ipsa loquitur*? (13–14)
6. Identify the factors which must exist for a claim of consequential harm to be proven. (15)
7. When can a person be guilty of contributory negligence? (19)
8. Describe the duty of care which occupiers of premises have towards (a) visitors, (b) recreational users, and (c) trespassers. (23–5)
9. What is meant by vicarious liability? (29–30)
10. What defences exist to the rule in *Rylands* v. *Fletcher*? (33)
11. On what basis are claims assessed by the Personal Injuries Assessment Board? (35)
12. When is a mediator appointed by the court in a civil liability case? (37)

INTERNET RESOURCES

Personal Injuries Assessment Board
  www.piab.ie

chapter 8

DEFAMATION

Topics covered

- Libel
- Slander
- Establishment of a case of defamation

- Innuendo
- Defences
- Mitigation and aggravation damages
- Press Council

Summary
The law guards a person's good name, more specifically, the interest in the person's reputation. This chapter examines the different forms of defamation and the factors which must exist for a plaintiff to succeed in such an action.

1. Defamation is the publication of a false statement which tends to injure the plaintiff's reputation, or causes the plaintiff to be shunned by ordinary members of society. Publication is defined as being the communication of the defamatory matter to some person other than the person about whom it is made.

2. There are two forms of defamation recognised by the Defamation Act 1961 and common law, namely, libel and slander.

• Libel
3. Defamatory matter is classed as libellous if it is in permanent form, or if it is for general reception, for example writing, pictures, films, records, television or radio.

4. Libel is actionable *per se*, i.e. without proof of actual damage suffered.

5. A libel which tends, or is likely, to cause a breach of the peace is a criminal offence as well as a tort. In such a case of criminal libel, however, publication to the defamed party alone is sufficient since such action may tend to cause a breach of the peace.

• Slander
6. Defamatory material is classified as slanderous if it is in a transient form, for example words or gestures.

7. Slander is not a crime. In most cases, slander is not actionable *per se*. Plaintiffs must prove that they suffered special damage, i.e. actual material loss capable of monetary evaluation. Examples of this would include loss of employment or loss of a contractual business advantage, and not mere loss of friendship or reputation.

8. Slander, like libel, is actionable *per se*, however, where it imputes:

(a) that the plaintiff has committed a criminal offence punishable with imprisonment;
(b) that the plaintiff is suffering from certain existing diseases, such as venereal disease or AIDS;
(c) unchastity, adultery or lesbianism in a woman;
(d) that the plaintiff is incompetent in any office, profession, trade or business held or carried on by them.

In each of these situations, the plaintiff need not establish any special damage in order to recover for slander.

- **Establishment of a case of defamation**

9. If plaintiffs are to succeed in defamation actions they must show:

(a) that the statement is defamatory. This would be so where the words would tend to lower the plaintiffs in the estimation of right-thinking members of society generally.

Case: Bennett v. Quane (1948)

The plaintiff, a solicitor, brought a case against a doctor who had said of him 'He brought an action to the Circuit Court instead of the District Court to get more costs for himself'.

Held: The words, which had suggested that the plaintiff had brought a case in a higher court merely to secure extra fees, were defamatory.

(b) that the statement refers to the plaintiffs, expressly or by implication, in such a way as to be reasonably understood by others as referring to them.
Prior to the Defamation Act 1961, even if a statement was true of someone else to whom it referred, plaintiffs could nonetheless recover if they showed that it also referred to them.

Case: Newstead v. London Express Newspapers Ltd (1939)

The defendants published a statement in their newspaper that 'Harold Newstead, a thirty-year-old Camberwell man' had been convicted of bigamy. There were, however, two Harold Newsteads living in the same area and of about the same age. So, while the statement was true in respect of a Camberwell barman of that name, it was untrue of the plaintiff.

Held: The plaintiff had been defamed because the words clearly, though innocently, referred to him, and he recovered damages.

(c) that it has been published by the defendant, i.e. communicated to at least one other person. Communication to the defendant's spouse, however, does not amount to publication.

Case: Coleman v. Kearns Ltd (1946)

The plaintiff was accused by an employee of the defendant of having stolen goods from the defendant's shop. This accusation was made in a public street in the presence of others.

Held: The accusation of theft in these circumstances was publication of a false statement and thereby defamatory.

Case: Berry v. The Irish Times (1973)

The plaintiff was a senior civil servant and the head of the Department of Justice which was the government department responsible for the administration and business of the public services connected with law, justice, public order and the police. The defendants published a photograph in their daily newspaper of a street scene which showed a man carrying a placard on which was written: 'Peter Berry – 20th Century Felon Setter – Helped Jail Republicans in England'. The plaintiff sued for damages for libel, complaining that the words were a slur on his character as a private citizen.

Held: The printing of the photograph amounted to publication. However, the words in the context in which they appeared in the photograph did not constitute defamation.

(d) that the statement is untrue.

In addition, as outlined above, in most cases of slander, i.e. where it is not actionable *per se*, plaintiffs must prove that they suffered special damage.

• Innuendo

10. Plaintiffs may succeed in an action for defamation even if the words used are not prima facie defamatory, i.e. defamatory in their ordinary meaning. To do so they must claim, and be able to prove an innuendo, i.e. by giving the words a certain meaning they are defamatory. An innuendo, therefore, is a statement by plaintiffs of the meaning that they attribute to the words.

Case: Fulham v. Associated Newspapers Ltd (1955)

The defendants were proprietors of a newspaper which had published an article stating that the plaintiff, a former renowned international footballer, 'had never used his right foot for anything except balancing on'. The plaintiff alleged that the article was defamatory in that it implied that he could not play with his right foot, that he had not been a competent footballer, and that he should not have been picked as an international footballer.

Held: The plaintiff had been the subject of defamation by innuendo, and was awarded damages in consequence.

• Defences

11. The common defences available in an action for defamation are:

(a) consent;
(b) justification;
(c) fair comment;
(d) absolute privilege;
(e) qualified privilege.

Consent

12. A person may consent to the publication of defamatory statements about themselves. This might, for example, be to enhance their career. The consent must be to the actual publication, however, in order to be effective as a defence to the tort of defamation.

Case: Green v. Blake (1948)

The decision of a complaint made against the plaintiff, a racehorse owner, was published in the *Racing Calendar*. The plaintiff argued that entry of a horse in a race did not amount to consent to the publication of such decisions.

Held: Such publication was defamatory. The mere submission to a set of rules was not sufficient consent for the publication of the decision.

Justification

13. If the statement is true in substance, the defence of justification is available. It is not necessary, therefore, to show that every detail of the statement is true.

Case: Alexander v. N.E. Railway Company (1865)

The plaintiff, a train passenger, was convicted of failing to pay his train fare. Subsequently, the defendant published a poster stating that his sentence was a fine or 'three' weeks' imprisonment. The alternative, however, should have been 'two' weeks' imprisonment.

Held: This was but a small inaccuracy. The statement remained true in substance, and the defence of justification was not defeated.

14. The law does not allow a person to recover damages in an action for defamation for an apparent injury to a character they either do not have, or ought not to possess.

Case: Cooper-Flynn v. RTE, Bird and Howard (2004)

Lasting 28 days, this was the longest ever libel trial in the history of the State. The plaintiff, a former financial adviser with National Irish Bank, alleged she was libelled in six RTE broadcasts in 1998 which reported that, as an employee of the bank, she had encouraged or assisted a number of persons in tax evasion. The High Court jury found that there was insufficient evidence that the plaintiff had induced the third-named defendant to evade tax, but accepted RTE's defence that the plaintiff had induced other named individuals to evade tax in the same way. It found that the plaintiff's reputation had suffered no material injury through the broadcasts by the defendants and awarded no damages. An appeal to the Supreme Court was launched by the plaintiff.

Held: In delivering a unanimous dismissal of the appeal, the Chief Justice approved an observation of the English law lord, Lord Bingham, that 'the tort of defamation protects those whose reputations have been unlawfully injured. It affords little or no protection to those who have, or deserve to have, no reputation deserving legal protection.' He then said: 'I am satisfied the same considerations apply to this case.'

15. The defence of justification is rarely used, because the onus of its establishment rests on the defendant. If this defence fails, the court may award exemplary damages to the plaintiff because the defendant has repeated, and continued to repeat during the trial, the defamatory statement.

Fair comment

16. Where a statement of opinion is a fair comment made in good faith on a matter of public interest, it is not actionable.

17. To be successful in this defence, it is necessary to prove:

(a) that the comment was based on facts which were true, or substantially true. No comment could be fair if it was based on false facts.
(b) that the comment was fair, and made in good faith, i.e. was an honest expression of the defendant's opinion. The comment, therefore, cannot be motivated by malice.
(c) that the subject matter commented upon was of public interest or concern. Examples of such matters are the conduct of politicians or the administration of justice.

Case: Cohen v. Daily Telegraph Ltd (1968)

The plaintiff alleged defamation in an article published by the defendants. The defendants pleaded a defence of fair comment on the grounds that the subject matter commented upon was of public interest. Furthermore, the defendants provided additional information to the court of events which had happened after the article had been published in an attempt to refute the allegation of defamation.

Held: The defence of fair comment was not open to the defendants as the facts which were in existence at the time the article was published could not be relied upon.

Case: Reynolds v. Times Newspapers Ltd & Others (1999)

The plaintiff resigned as Taoiseach following a political crisis. On the Sunday following his resignation, the defendants published an article on the crisis which failed to mention the plaintiff's explanation of events. The plaintiff brought libel proceedings against the publishers of the newspaper, its editor and the author, arguing that the article had claimed that he had deliberately and dishonestly misled the Dáil, his cabinet colleagues and the Tánaiste. At trial, the jury rejected a defence of justification, but found that the author had not acted maliciously. They awarded no damages to the plaintiff. However, the judge substituted an award of one penny and, in a subsequent argument over costs, rejected the defence of qualified privilege. The plaintiff appealed, arguing that the judge had misdirected the jury, whilst the defendants cross-appealed contending that any libellous statement made in the course of political discussion was free from liability if published in good faith.

Held: The subject matter was undoubtedly of public concern and interest in the United Kingdom, as the plaintiff had been one of the architects of the Northern Ireland peace process, but the article made serious allegations without mentioning the defendant's considered explanation. Hence, the allegations were not information that the public had a right to know, and thus the publication was not one which should, in the public interest, be protected by privilege in the absence of proof of malice. The appeal was dismissed in its entirety.

Absolute privilege

18. No action lies for defamation, however false or malicious the statement, if it is made in either House of the Oireachtas or is contained in official reports or publications of the Oireachtas. Absolute privilege also covers statements made in the course of judicial proceedings by judges, counsel, juries or witnesses. This includes statements made in connection with a trial, such as communications between clients and solicitors.

Case: Macauley & Co. Ltd v. Wyse-Power (1943)

An action for slander was taken against a Circuit Court judge because of remarks he had made during a case which seriously attacked the reputation and character of the plaintiff.

Held: The judge was protected by privilege, and the case was dismissed.

19. Absolute privilege is granted, therefore, in cases where complete freedom of expression is considered of paramount importance.

Qualified privilege

20. The defence of qualified privilege is available when a person makes a communication under some duty – legal, social, or moral – to a person who has some corresponding interest to receive it. This privilege will apply provided the communication is not made more widely than necessary, and provided it is not motivated by malice.

Case: Watt v. Longsdon (1930)

The plaintiff, a company employee, sued a director of the company for defamation because the director, on receipt of allegations of drunkeness, dishonesty and immorality by the plaintiff, had shown these allegations to the chair of the company and to the plaintiff's wife. Although the allegations were completely unfounded, the defendant believed them to be true. The defendant pleaded the defence of qualified privilege.

Held: Qualified privilege was a valid defence for the communication to the chair of the company, since both a duty to make the statement, and an interest in receiving it, were present. The defence of qualified privilege in respect of the communication to the plaintiff's wife failed, however, because the defendant had no legal, social or moral duty to communicate such allegations. The plaintiff, therefore, was entitled to damages.

• Mitigation and aggravation of damages

Mitigation

21. The defendant may mitigate payment of damages by:

(a) making an apology and an offer of amends. An offer of amends means that the defendant must offer to publish an appropriate correction of the words complained of, and a sufficient apology to the injured party;

(b) producing evidence of the plaintiff's bad reputation prior to the publication of the defamation;

(c) proving provocation by counter-defamation; or

(d) showing that the plaintiff had previously obtained compensation in respect of a similar defamation.

Aggravation

22. The defendant, however, may aggravate payment of damages by:

(a) pleading the defence of justification for the defamation which the court subsequently finds to be unfounded;

(b) the method used in communicating the defamatory material; or

(c) conduct throughout the trial.

• Press Council

23. In 2007, the media industry, honouring a commitment to independently regulate the newspaper and magazine sectors, established a Press Council, a Press

Ombudsman and a 10-point code of practice to:

(a) ensure protection of freedom of expression of the press;
(b) protect the public interest by ensuring ethical, accurate and truthful reporting by the press;
(c) maintain minimum ethical and professional standards among the press; and
(d) ensure the privacy and dignity of the individual is protected.

24. Members of the public with a complaint about the print media in Ireland are still asked to contact newspapers or magazines first. If dissatisfied, the next step is to contact the Office of the Press Ombudsman who, although having no power to levy a financial or other penalty on newspapers or magazines, can make them publish an apology or retraction in a prominent place. This office does not institute inquiries, get involved in proceedings that are before the courts or examine complaints based on matters of taste. Instead, it covers issues of accuracy, balance and fairness to which all journalists are expected to adhere. Finally, only major complaints or complaints unsatisfied at Ombudsman level are referred to the thirteen-member Press Council, which has a lay majority.

IMPORTANT CASES

Numbers in brackets refer to paragraphs of this chapter

IMPORTANT STATUTES

Defamation Act 1961

PROGRESS TEST

Numbers in brackets refer to paragraphs of this chapter

1. What is defamation? (1)
2. Distinguish between libel and slander. (3–8)
3. Discuss the things a plaintiff must show in order to succeed in an action for defamation. (9)
4. Can a plaintiff succeed in a defamation action even if the words used are not prima facie defamatory? (10)
5. When is consent a valid defence to the tort of defamation? (12)
6. Why is the defence of justification rarely used? (15)
7. Identify those factors which must be proven in a defence of fair comment. (17)
8. Distinguish between 'absolute' and 'qualified' privilege. (18–20)
9. How may a defendant mitigate payment of damages? (21)

INTERNET RESOURCES

Press Council of Ireland
    www.presscouncil.ie

Part 2: Elements of the Law of Tort

1. Explain what is meant by tort and describe general defences available in an action for tort.

   IATI (Autumn 2006)

2. Write a note on each of the following:
   (a) Nominal damages.
   (b) Real damages.
   (c) Exemplary damages.

   IATI (Summer 2007)

3. In a case of negligence, explain what four things a plaintiff must prove.

   IATI (Summer 2006)

4. Turbo Security Ltd (hereinafter Turbo) have contracted to provide night security patrols at the factory of Alpha Plc (hereinafter Alpha). Whilst on patrol a Turbo employee lit a small fire which got out of control and destroyed Alpha's factory and stock. Alpha has sued for breach of contract and Turbo seek to rely upon an exclusion clause which states that: 'Under no circumstances' are Turbo to be 'responsible for any injurious act or default of any employee unless such act or default could be foreseen and avoided by the exercise of due diligence on the part of Turbo as his employer; nor, in any event are Turbo to be held responsible for any loss suffered by Alpha through fire or any other cause except in so far as such loss is solely attributable to the negligence of Turbo's employees acting within the course of their employment. There is no allegation that Turbo were negligent in employing the employee involved. Discuss the likelihood of Alpha being successful in their action for breach of contract.

   ICPA (Summer 2007)

5. Critically examine the importance of the tort of negligence in today's business environment.

   MII (August 2007)

6. Discuss and analyse the duty of care in Irish tort law.

   ICPA (Autumn 2006)

7. Gasco, a gas excavation company, has been granted a licence by the Minister for Energy to explore for gas off the coast of County Clare. Gasco has spent

a considerable amount of money investing in equipment to excavate the gas. However, it has encountered a problem. Clare County Council has introduced a new environmental plan which forbids gas excavation off its coast. Gasco has suffered considerable damages as a result because it has lost the money it invested in the equipment. Clare County Council was not empowered to impose such a ban and was wrong in doing so. Advise Gasco as to whether Clare County Council owes it a duty of care.

ICPA (Autumn 2006)

8. Fiona is an avid member of a local hunt. During a recent hunt she lost control of her horse, Libertine, which bolted over a hedge and onto the public road. Peter, who was cycling along the road, was struck by the horse and injured. Peter has sued Fiona for negligence. Discuss the legal principles that apply.

IATI (Autumn 2007)

9. Mr Clever is a solicitor. When recently qualified, he gave advice to a client, Clare, when she was purchasing a property. Ten years later, Clare decides to sell her property, but to her horror discovers that there is a defect in the title, which means that she never actually owned the property in the first place. Clare is distraught and seeks your advice as to what she can do. Advise Clare.

ICPA (Autumn 2005)

10. In the area of product liability, critically examine how and to what extent the Liability for Defective Products Act 1991 (as amended) achieves a high level of consumer protection against damage caused to health or property by a defective product.

MII (May 2007)

11. Kevin recently bought a Supermatic Toaster Deluxe 2000. The manufacturer claims that the toaster, which has its own computer chip, can be set for up to six toasting cycles. Kevin has found that when he tries to use the Supermatic, it invariably incinerates his bread. He tried pressing a button on the side of the toaster to cut the toast cycle short but when this did not work he unplugged the toaster from the socket; in so doing he suffered a mild electric shock. Kevin attempted to rectify the problem by resetting the six toasting cycles. However, on the last occasion on which he used the Supermatic the bread he was toasting caught fire, was ejected with considerable force and set the curtains in his kitchen alight. When Kevin complained to the manufacturer about its product he was asked whether he had considered getting Venetian blinds for his kitchen window. The shop where Kevin bought the toaster has since closed down. Kevin wishes to take proceedings against the manufacturer and has asked that you outline and discuss the main provisions of the Liability for Defective Products Act 1991.

ICPA (Summer 2007)

12. (a) ABC Plc manufactures a form of patio heater. Unfortunately, due to inadequate assembly instructions, some of the heaters proved unstable when assembled and two have fallen on customers and caused injuries. The remaining heaters have been recalled by ABC Plc.

(b) Last year, due to high demand for hammocks, ABC Plc imported hammocks from China and sold them packaged as 'Quality outdoor leisure product from ABC Plc.' The fabric of the hammocks was faulty and Peter has sustained a back injury due to the fabric tearing and causing him to fall.

You are asked to explain any possible liabilities the company may face in the situations above under the Liability for Defective Products Act 1991.

MII (August 2007)

13. John was driving home on a dark and wet evening in hazardous driving conditions when his car was hit by a lorry, which skidded on the road due to travelling at high speed. As a result of the accident, John suffered serious physical injury and his car was destroyed. The lorry driver was not hurt nor was his lorry damaged in any way. The lorry driver claims that he is not responsible for the accident. Advise John as to any line of action that he might pursue and the type of compensation that he might be entitled to.

ICPA (Summer 2005)

14. In the context of the need to protect consumers from dangerous defective products, compare and contrast the basis of liability for such products as provided for by the law of negligence and the Liability for Defective Products Act 1991, as amended. The answer should indicate the possible advantages to a consumer of pursuing liability under either of the alternatives indicated above.

MII (August 2005)

15. Michael has purchased a new laptop computer. Whilst using it at home, it overheated and burnt Michael's new oak desk. Discuss the liability of the manufacturer and/or the retailer with reference to both common law and statute, and give examples of any defence that could be claimed.

IATI (Summer 2006)

16. (a) John and Anne bought tickets for a gig to hear their favourite band 'The Blades'. Whilst there, Anne fell over some exposed wiring and injured her arm. Advise the concert promoters as to their liability.

(b) Paul, on the other hand, did not buy a ticket but climbed over the back wall to get into the gig. On jumping down from the wall, he twisted his ankle falling onto a box. Advise the concert promoters as to their liability.

IATI (Autumn 2006)

17. (a) What is defamation?
    (b) Outline the difference between libel and slander.

IATI (Autumn 2007)

18. Explain the main differences between libel and slander in the tort of defamation and explain the defence of qualified privilege.

ICPA (Autumn 2004)

19. Mary was in negotiations for a contract to design a new building for a large multinational company. However, the company telephoned her yesterday to say they had changed their minds and told her that she should read the latest issue of 'Build It' magazine. In the magazine was an article naming her as having bribed clients to get work. Mary is furious, says it's a lie and wants your advice.

    (a) Advise Mary what the tort of defamation is.
    (b) Explain to her the difference between libel and slander.
    (c) Outline any defence the magazine may try to rely on.

IATI (Autumn 2006)

LAW OF CONTRACT

chapter 9

THE NATURE OF A CONTRACT

Topics covered

- The concept of a contract
- The essentials of a contract
- Void, voidable and unenforceable contracts

Summary

The law of contract is essentially based on enforcement of the freely negotiated agreement of the parties to a contract. This chapter sets out the essential characteristics of such a contract.

• The concept of a contract

1. A contract is an agreement enforceable at law between two or more parties whereby rights are acquired by one or more parties in return for certain acts or forbearances on the part of the other or others.

2. It has been described as the most important legal mechanism for business activity. Indeed, almost all transactions made by, or on behalf of, a business will be governed by the principles of contract. These include the sale of goods and supply of services, the purchase of materials and the hiring of employees.

3. The factor which distinguishes contractual from other legal obligations is the agreement of the parties. The parties to a contract may, within well-defined limits, make 'law' binding on themselves. Common law and statute law, however, are used in certain circumstances to interfere directly with freedom of contract in order to redress the balance in favour of the weaker party. Common law, for example, attempts to protect minors from onerous contracts, while statute law achieves its objectives by implying terms, in favour of the weaker party, into certain contracts regardless of the wishes of the parties.

• The essentials of a contract

4. For a contract to be valid, and therefore binding on the parties, there are certain essential requirements:

(a) there must be an agreement made as a result of an offer and an unequivocal acceptance of that offer;
(b) either the contract must be under seal or there must be consideration;
(c) there must be an intention to create legal relations;

(d) the parties must have capacity to contract;

(e) there must be genuine consent to the terms by all parties to the contract;

(f) the terms of the contract must be legal and capable of performance.

• Void, voidable and unenforceable contracts

Void contracts

5. A void contract is not a contract at all, and is but an agreement without legal effect. The expression usually describes a situation where the parties have attempted to contract, but the law will not give effect to their agreement because, for example, there is a common mistake on some major term, or it has been entered into by a minor for the supply of goods other than necessities. The parties are not bound by such an agreement, and if they transfer property under it they can sometimes recover such property from the person in possession.

Voidable contracts

6. A voidable contract is a contract in which the law allows one of the parties to withdraw from it if they wish, thus making it void. It remains valid, however, unless and until the innocent party chooses to terminate it. A contract might be voidable if one of the parties to that contract had been a minor or had been induced by undue influence or misrepresentation to enter that contract. If the parties transfer property before the avoidance of the contract, then such property is usually irrecoverable from a third party.

Unenforceable contracts

7. An unenforceable contract is a valid contract which will not be enforced by the courts because of the lack of legal evidence, e.g. the written evidence for a contract for the sale of land. If a contract is deemed to be unenforceable, therefore, and either party refuses to perform or to complete their part of the performance of the contract, the other party cannot compel them to do so. Any property transferred under an unenforceable contract cannot be recovered – even from the other party to the contract.

PROGRESS TEST

Numbers in brackets refer to paragraphs of this chapter

1. Define a contract. (1)
2. Distinguish between contractual and other legal obligations. (3)
3. Give six essential elements of a binding agreement. (4)
4. Distinguish between a void and a voidable contract. (5–6)

chapter 10

OFFER AND ACCEPTANCE

Topics covered

- Requirements of a valid offer
- Recognising an offer
- Termination of an offer
- Requirements of a valid acceptance

- Communication of acceptance
  – general rules
- Communication of acceptance
  – exceptions

Summary

A contract is based on the agreement or mutual consent of the parties involved. This chapter examines both the offer and the acceptance which lead to binding agreement.

1. The first essential of a valid contract is the agreement or mutual assent of the parties involved. In the event of a dispute about such agreement, the courts seek to discover whether there was *consensus ad idem* (agreement as to the essential point), i.e. whether the words and conduct of the parties are sufficient to lead a reasonable person to assume that they had reached agreement with respect to the same subject matter. The court may examine the negotiations surrounding the transactions to see if there was a definite 'offer' made by one party which was clearly accepted without qualification by the other party.

• Requirements of a valid offer

2. An offer exists where the offeror undertakes to be contractually bound if the offeree makes a proper acceptance. It is a definite promise to be bound on certain specific terms. The essentials of a valid offer are as follows:

(a) *The terms of an offer must be clear, certain and complete.* It cannot be vague. Otherwise, the court may hold that there was a failure to make a complete agreement.

Case: Gunthing v. Lynn (1831)

The offeror promised to pay a further sum for a horse if it was 'lucky'.
    Held: The offer was too vague. The court was unable to give effect to the alleged agreement, because no clear meaning could be determined.

(b) *The offer must be communicated to the other party.* An offer can be communicated to a particular person, a group of persons or to the public at large. It can be accepted by anybody who comes within the terms of the offer.

Case: Carlill v. Carbolic Smoke Ball Co. (1893)

The defendants undertook, in various advertisements, to pay £100 reward to anyone who caught influenza after having sniffed a smoke ball three times daily for two weeks. The plaintiff used the smoke ball as prescribed, and caught influenza after more than two weeks' treatment, and while still using the smoke ball. She then claimed her £100 reward.

Held: It was an offer to the public at large which the plaintiff could accept, and had accepted, by performance of the conditions in the offer. While an advertisement in a newspaper is not normally an offer but an invitation to treat (see para. 6), in this case, a sum of money was lodged in the bank by the company as a sign of their good faith, thereby providing consideration to support the offer.

(c) *The offer must be made by written or spoken words, or be inferred by the conduct of the parties.* It may be communicated by letter, telephone, telex or any means of communication which is appropriate and reasonable in the circumstances.

(d) *The offer must be intended as such before a contract can arise.* If it is not made with a view to a legal relationship, e.g. if the offer excludes recourse to the courts for its enforcement, then it will not constitute an offer.

• Recognising an offer

3. Only an offer in the proper sense, i.e. made with the intention that it shall become binding when accepted, may be recognised so as to form a binding contract. An offer must be distinguished from the following, which are not offers:

(a) the answer to a question or the supplying of information;
(b) an invitation to treat;
(c) a statement of intention;
(d) an option.

The answer to a question or the supplying of information

4. An offer must not be confused with the answer to a question or the supplying of information.

Case: Harvey v. Facey (1893)

The plaintiff telegraphed to the defendant 'Will you sell us Bumper Hall Pen? Telegraph lowest cash price'. The defendant telegraphed in reply 'Lowest price for Bumper Hall Pen £900'. The plaintiff regarded this as an offer and telegraphed 'We agree to buy Bumper Hall Pen for £900 asked by you'. The defendant made no further reply.

Held: No contract had been made. The second telegram was merely a statement of the price which the defendant would sell for, if and when he chose to sell his property. It was not an offer which the plaintiff could accept, but the supply of information in response to a question.

5. If, however, in the course of negotiations for a sale, the seller states the price at which the item will be sold, that statement may be an offer which can be accepted.

An invitation to treat

6. An invitation to treat is an invitation to another person to make an offer. An 'offer' can be converted into a contract by acceptance, provided the other requirements of a valid contract are present, but an 'invitation to treat' cannot be 'accepted'.

7. To advertise goods or to exhibit goods for sale in a shop window or on the open shelves of a self-service shop is to invite customers to make offers to purchase, or an 'invitation to treat'.

Case: Fisher v. Bell (1961)

A shopkeeper was prosecuted for 'offering for sale' offensive weapons by displaying flick-knives in his shop window.

Held: Although he had exhibited the flick-knives, accepted buyers' offers and sold the goods, he had not offered them for sale, because goods on display are not on offer for sale, but an invitation to treat.

Case: Minister for Industry and Commerce v. Pim Bros Ltd (1966)

A coat was displayed for sale in the defendants' shop window. It had a notice of the cash price and a weekly sum attached to it. The minister brought an action against Pim Bros Ltd on the grounds that they were in breach of the then legislation which made it an offence to offer for sale goods on credit terms without specifically stating these terms.

Held: This did not constitute an offer to sell which could be made a contract of sale by acceptance. It was simply an invitation to treat for the sale of the article with an indication that credit facilities were available.

Case: Pharmaceutical Society of Great Britain v. Boots Chemists (1952)

By statute, certain drugs containing poisons could only be sold 'under the supervision of a qualified pharmacist'. Boots operated a self-service shop, with the drugs displayed on open shelves and with a qualified pharmacist located at the check-out. The Pharmaceutical Society brought an action against Boots Chemists for being in breach of their supervisory requirements.

Held: The display of goods was only an invitation to treat – the selection and presentation of the goods by the customer was the offer and the taking of money by the pharmacist at the cash desk was the acceptance. Therefore, Boots Chemists did not commit an offence, because the sale took place at the check-out.

8. The publication of a prospectus by a company in respect of the issue of shares is an invitation to the public to make offers. The company has only a limited number of shares and cannot intend to allot whatever number the public may apply for.

9. The advertisement of an auction, or the putting up of items for bids, is an invitation to treat and not an offer to sell to the highest bidder. The offers come from successive bidders, and the fall of the auctioneer's hammer is the acceptance. A bidder may retract the bid until this happens. However, if the auction is advertised as being 'without reserve', this constitutes a firm offer to sell to the highest bidder.

10. A tender is an estimate submitted in response to a prior request. An invitation for tenders to supply goods or services is not an offer but an invitation to others to make offers. The tenders made, however, are normally recognised as legal offers which may lead to a binding contract if accepted. A tender must be accepted as tendered or there may be no agreement.

A statement of intention

11. If a person states that they intend to perform some act, and ultimately they do not carry out the stated intention, no rights may be conveyed on another party who may suffer loss due to non-performance. For example, were a father to state that one of his sons or daughters would be a beneficiary of his estate, this alone would not confer any contractual rights on the respective party.

An option

12. An option is the right to buy or sell something at a specified price. It is, in effect, a conditional contract. The person who is offered the option is not bound to take it up, i.e. they can fail to exercise their option. The person offering the option, however, is legally bound by it in the event of the option being exercised.

• Termination of an offer

13. There must be some duration for which an offer or counter-offer stands and is open to acceptance by the offeree leading to a contract. This duration must be at least long enough to give the offeree an opportunity to reply to the offer. An offer, however, does not continue indefinitely and can be terminated without maturing into a contract in any of the following circumstances:

(a) if the offeror has revoked (withdrawn) it;
(b) if it has expired by lapse of time;
(c) if the offeree has rejected it or made a counter-offer;
(d) if there is a failure of an express or implied condition;
(e) if the offeree or offeror dies.

Revocation

14. The offeror may revoke (withdraw) the offer at any time before it has been accepted. This is true even when the offeror undertakes that the offer shall remain open for acceptance for a specified time, unless by a separate contract (an 'option') the offeror is given consideration in return for keeping the offer open for the whole of the specified time.

Case: Routledge v. Grant (1828)

The defendant, in an offer to buy the plaintiff's house, laid down a requirement of his offer being accepted within six weeks. Within that period, he withdrew his offer.

Held: The offeror was entitled to revoke his offer at any time prior to acceptance because no option agreement existed.

15. Revocation of an offer is only effective if it is communicated to the offeree, either by the offeror or by any third party who is a sufficiently reliable informant.

Case: Dickinson v. Dodds (1876)

The defendant offered by letter to sell property to the plaintiff for £800, saying that 'this offer to be left open until Friday, 12 June, 9.00 a.m.' On Thursday, 11 June, the plaintiff delivered a letter of acceptance to an address at which the defendant was no longer residing so that the defendant did not receive it. The defendant sold the property on Thursday, 11 June, to another buyer. A Mr Berry, who had been an intermediary between the plaintiff and the defendant, informed the plaintiff of this sale. Mr Berry, nevertheless, delivered a duplicate of the plaintiff's letter of acceptance to the defendant at 7.00 a.m. on Friday, 12 June.

Held: There was no contract, the offer having been revoked before acceptance and communication by a third party being valid. An offer to sell a particular item is revoked by implication, therefore, if the item is sold to another person.

16. Revocation communicated by post only takes effect from the time of receipt and not from the time of posting.

Case: Byrne v. Van Tienhoven (1880)

The defendant, who resided in Cardiff, offered by letter dated 1 October to sell goods to the plaintiff, who resided in New York. On 8 October, the defendant wrote to the plaintiff revoking his offer. The plaintiff received the letter of offer on 11 October and telegraphed his acceptance of the offer. He confirmed this acceptance by letter dated 15 October. The letter of revocation was received by the plaintiff on 20 October.

Held: The letter of revocation had no effect until received; it could not revoke the contract made by acceptance of the offer on 11 October.

Lapse of time

17. An offer will terminate at the end of the time specified in the offer, or if no time-limit is specified, it will terminate after a reasonable time. What is reasonable depends on the nature of the contract and the circumstances of a particular case (on what is usual and to be expected).

Case: Walker v. Glass (1979)

The defendant offered to sell his house to the plaintiff, the offer to remain open until a specified date. The defendant wrote to the plaintiff before that date revoking the offer.

Held: The defendant was free to revoke his offer at any time before acceptance by the plaintiff.

Case: Ramsgate Victoria Hotel Co. v. Montefiore (1866)

The defendant offered in June 1864 to take shares in the plaintiff's hotel, and paid a deposit to the company's bank. The plaintiff did not reply, but in November 1864 the company sent him an acceptance by issue of a letter of allotment. The defendant refused to take the allotted shares and to pay the balance due on them, contending that his offer had expired and could no longer be accepted.

Held: The defendant's offer was for a reasonable time only. The courts considered that five months was much more than that. The refusal to take the shares was justified, therefore, since the plaintiff's delay had caused the defendant's offer to lapse.

Rejection of the offer or a counter-offer

18. An offer may be terminated if outright rejection is communicated to the offeror or if a counter-offer is made by the offeree. An attempt to accept an offer on terms, other than those contained in the offer, is a rejection accompanied by a counter-offer. A rejected offer cannot subsequently be accepted.

Case: Butler Machine Tool Co. v. Ex-Cell-O Corp. (1979)

The plaintiff, on request, sent a standard form offering to sell a machine to the defendant at a specified price, subject to a price variation clause to take account of inflation should there be a delay. The defendant placed an order for the machine on its own standard form, which excluded any price variation clause. When the machine was delivered, the defendant refused to pay an extra sum based on the price variation clause, and the plaintiff sued for payment of the full amount.

Held: The sending of the second standard form by the defendant represented a rejection of the original offer and the making of a counter-offer, which the plaintiff had accepted by delivering the machine. The price variation clause, therefore, was not a term of the contract between the parties.

Case: Hyde v. Wrench (1840)

The defendant offered to sell his farm to the plaintiff for £1,000. The plaintiff made a counter-offer in writing of £950, which the defendant rejected. The plaintiff then wrote accepting the original offer of £1,000. The defendant refused to sell, and the plaintiff sued for breach of contract.

Held: The counter-offer of £950 terminated the original offer of £1,000. Therefore, when the plaintiff purported to accept at £1,000, there was no offer in existence to be accepted, and no contract could be formed.

19. A request as to whether or not additional terms would be acceptable does not constitute a counter-offer and, therefore, does not, by itself, terminate an offer.

Case: Stevenson v. McLean (1880)

The defendant offered to sell iron to the plaintiff at £2 per ton cash. The plaintiff wrote and asked whether the defendant would agree to a contract providing for credit facilities. On receiving no reply, the plaintiff accepted the offer as made.

Held: There was a contract, since the enquiry was not a counter-offer but a request for information as to a variation of terms. It was not a rejection, and did not terminate the defendant's offer.

Failure of an express or implied condition
20. An offer cannot be validly accepted if it is made subject to an express or implied condition, and this condition fails.

Case: Financings Ltd v. Stimson (1962)

The defendant, who wished to purchase a car, signed a hire-purchase form on 16 March. The form stated that the agreement would only become binding when the plaintiffs signed the form. The car was stolen from the plaintiffs' premises on 24 March, and was recovered badly damaged. The plaintiffs signed the form on 25 March.

Held: The defendant was not bound contractually to take the car. There was an implied condition in the defendant's offer that the car would remain in the same condition until the moment of acceptance. The condition had failed.

Death of the offeree or offeror
21. Death of the offeree probably terminates an offer, because an acceptance can only be made by an offeree or an authorised agent.

22. Death of the offeror terminates the offer unless the offeree accepts it in ignorance of the offeror's death, and the offer is not of a personal nature requiring the skills of the deceased, e.g. singing in a concert. If the offer, therefore, can be completed equally well by the deceased's personal representatives, then they will probably be obliged to fulfil it upon acceptance by the offeree.

- ## Requirements of a valid acceptance

23. An acceptance takes place when an offeree unqualifiedly accepts an offer made by an offeror. In most cases there is little difficulty in deciding whether an offer is accepted. Where negotiations are complicated, however, the courts may be called upon to examine the correspondence and surrounding circumstances in order to establish whether, on a true construction, the parties agreed to the same terms.

The essentials of a valid acceptance are as follows:

(a) *Acceptance may be oral, written or implied from conduct.* An example of acceptance being implied from conduct would be the dispatching of goods in response to an offer to buy.

(b) *Acceptance must be clear and unqualified and must exactly match the offer.* A counter-offer or a conditional assent is insufficient and causes the original offer to lapse.

Case: Neale v. Merrett (1930)

The defendant made an offer to sell land to the plaintiff for £280. The plaintiff replied accepting the offer, enclosing £80 and promising to pay the balance in four monthly instalments.

Held: The proposal for deferred payment was a variation of the terms implicit in the offer. Since the normal terms of a contract for the sale of land are that the entire price is payable as a single sum at completion, it was held that there had been no acceptance.

(c) *Acceptance must be communicated to and received by the offeror.* Otherwise, no enforceable agreement will exist between the parties.

- ## Communication of acceptance – general rules

24. Acceptance must be communicated by the offeree, or by someone with their authority, to the offeror.

Case: Powell v. Lee (1908)

The plaintiff applied for the post of headmaster of a school. After being interviewed, the management passed a resolution appointing him, but made no decision as to how the appointment was to be communicated. One of the managers, without authorisation, informed the plaintiff that he had been appointed. The management subsequently appointed another candidate. The plaintiff sued for breach of contract.

Held: Since acceptance had not been properly communicated to the plaintiff, there was no valid contract.

25. The offeror may expressly or impliedly stipulate the method of communicating acceptance, but unless the offeror states that this is the only adequate method of acceptance, the offeree may accept by some other method, so long as the offeror suffers no disadvantage.

Case: Yates Building Co. v. R J Pulleyn & Sons (1975)

The defendants called for acceptance of their offer by registered or recorded delivery letter. The plaintiffs sent an ordinary letter containing their acceptance. This arrived without delay.

Held: The acceptance was valid, since the defendants had not stipulated that this was the only method of acceptance which sufficed. The method selected by the plaintiff was equally advantageous to the defendant.

26. There must be some act on the part of the offeree to indicate acceptance. The offeror cannot impose a condition, without the offeree's consent, that silence shall constitute acceptance.

Case: Felthouse v. Bindley (1862)

The plaintiff offered by letter to buy a horse stating that 'If I hear no more about him, I consider the horse is mine at £30 15s'. No acceptance was communicated, but the owner told the defendant, an auctioneer in whose possession the horse was at the time, not to sell the horse. When the horse was sold by mistake at auction to someone else, the plaintiff sued the defendant for conversion (a tort alleging wrongful disposal of the plaintiff's property).

Held: The offeror could not impose acceptance merely because the offeree had not rejected the offer. There had been no contract of sale and the plaintiff did not own the horse. Hence, the case for conversion failed.

27. Acceptance is not effective if communicated in ignorance of the offer. Acceptance may be effective, however, even though the offer was not the sole reason for it being made.

Case: R v. Clarke (1927)

The defendant offered a reward to anyone who found and returned his lost property. The plaintiff, not knowing about the offer, found the property and returned it of his own free will. He subsequently discovered the reward offer and sued to recover it.

Held: The plaintiff was not accepting the defendant's offer, since he was unaware of it. There was no contract and, therefore, there could be no contractual obligation to pay the reward.

Case: Williams v. Carwardine (1833)

The plaintiff, an accomplice in a crime, provided information which led to the arrest of criminals. She had been aware of the existence of a reward for the provision of such information, but was motivated primarily by remorse at her own part in the crime.

Held: A contract had been formed, even though the motive for acceptance was different than that contemplated by the offeror.

• Communication of acceptance – exceptions

28. Although as a general rule there cannot be a binding contract unless acceptance has been communicated to the offeror by the offeree, two exceptions to this general rule apply:

(a) where performance of an act or the conduct of a person is deemed to constitute acceptance;

(b) where acceptance is made by post, telegram or cable and such communication is lost or delayed.

Where performance or conduct constitutes acceptance

29. A 'unilateral contract' may be established whereby the offeror includes in the offer a term providing that complete performance or conduct by the offeree will constitute complete acceptance. There is no need to give advance notice of acceptance to the offeror.

Case: Kennedy v. London Express Newspapers (1931)

The publishers of an English newspaper offered a free accident insurance scheme to its registered readers. The plaintiff's wife had registered with a newsagent and on her being killed accidentally by a bus, her husband claimed the sum payable under the insurance scheme.

Held: The offer of the free insurance scheme represented a unilateral offer made to the world at large. Registration by the plaintiff's wife brought a valid contract into existence, and the publishers were legally bound by it.

Acceptance by letter or telegram

30. Whereas an offer only takes effect if and when received, an acceptance by letter takes effect when posted and an acceptance by telegram takes effect when given to the post office for transmission. Acceptance by telephone or telex follows the normal rule and is effective from the time received.

Case: Household Fire Insurance Co. v. Grant (1879)

The defendant applied for shares in the plaintiff company and enclosed a deposit for those shares. The company accepted his offer by posting a letter of allotment, which never arrived, to the defendant. The company later went into liquidation and the liquidator called upon the defendant to pay the balance due on the shares.

Held: The subscriber for shares was bound by an acceptance in a letter of allotment although the letter was never delivered.

31. S.19 of the Electronic Commerce Act 2000 provides that acceptance of an offer or any related communication (including any subsequent amendment, cancellation, revocation or acceptance of an offer) may, unless otherwise agreed by the parties, be communicated by means of electronic communication.

IMPORTANT CASES

Numbers in brackets refer to paragraphs of this chapter

IMPORTANT STATUTES

Electronic Commerce Act 2000

PROGRESS TEST

Numbers in brackets refer to paragraphs of this chapter

1. Identify the essentials of a valid offer. (2)

2. Is (a) a statement of the prices of goods, or (b) a display of goods, an offer which becomes a contract if accepted? (4, 7)
3. List five methods by which an offer may be terminated. (13)
4. When will lapse of time terminate an offer? (17)
5. Outline the essentials of a valid acceptance. (23)
6. What effect does the stipulation by the offeror of the method of communicating acceptance have? (25)
7. Is acceptance effective if communicated in ignorance of an offer? (27)
8. Explain the significance of (a) unilateral contracts, and (b) the postal rule. (29–30)

chapter 11

CONSIDERATION

Topics covered

- The nature of consideration
- Legal rules governing consideration

- The principle of promissory estoppel

Summary

All contracts, except those made by deed under seal, require consideration to pass between the parties before they can be said to be valid. This chapter examines the concept of consideration and the rules developed by the courts which govern it.

• The nature of consideration

1.   Consideration is required for all enforceable contracts, except those made by deed. A person cannot sue on a simple contract unless they can show that they gave, or promised to give, some advantage to the party they wish to sue, in exchange for what that party promised in return. A promise, therefore, is only legally binding if it is made in return for another promise or act, i.e. it is part of a bargain.

2.   In *Currie* v. *Misa* (1875), consideration is defined as 'some right, interest, profit or benefit accruing to the one party, or some forebearance, detriment, loss or responsibility given, suffered or undertaken by the other'. Such a benefit accruing or detriment suffered is, of course, in return for a promise received or given.

3.   The courts, therefore, do not recognise a bare promise. To prove that no consideration was given in return is a complete defence in a court action. A number of rules have been formulated by the courts in cases where the question as to the existence of consideration arises.

• Legal rules governing consideration

Consideration must be of some value, but it need not be adequate

4.   Anything of value which contributes to the bargain made is recognised in law as good consideration. It can be money, land, goods, services or any other undertaking which confers a benefit on one party or represents a loss to the other.

However, in the absence of fraud or unfair dealing, the court will not assess the relative value of the contributions made by each party. The law refuses to protect a person of full capacity who makes a bad bargain.

Case: Commodity Broking Co. Ltd v. Meehan (1985)

The defendant, the principal shareholder of a company, intimated that the company was insolvent, but promised to pay off the outstanding debt by monthly instalments of £1,000. He made two such payments, but then refused to pay any more.

Held: There had been no consideration for the defendant's promise to pay off the company's debts, so therefore the promise was unenforceable. The plaintiffs' reason for not suing the company was the intimation that it was insolvent – not that the defendant had promised to pay off the company's debts.

Case: Thomas v. Thomas (1842)

The plaintiff's husband expressed a wish before his death that the plaintiff, his widow, should have the use of his house throughout her life. After his death, the executors of the husband's will allowed the plaintiff to occupy that house in return for her undertaking to pay a rent of £1 per annum. They later argued that no consideration had been provided for the benefit of the use of the house.

Held: The promise of a payment of £1 per annum was valuable, but not adequate, consideration. Consequently, the contract was valid and enforceable.

Consideration must not be illegal, vague or impossible to perform
5.   The court will not enforce an illegal contract, such as an undertaking to pay a reward for a criminal act, because to do so would be contrary to public policy. A court may similarly refuse to enforce a contract where the consideration relied upon is vague or impossible to perform, because this would indicate that no real agreement was reached.

Consideration must be something which the promisee is not bound to do under the general law or under an existing contract with the other party
6.   Performance of an existing obligation imposed by statute is no consideration for a promise. However, if some extra service is given then that is sufficient consideration.

Case: Collins v. Godefroy (1831)

The plaintiff, a witness in a lawsuit, was promised expenses by the defendant in return for giving evidence. It turned out that the witness had already been subpoenaed, i.e. ordered to attend.

Held: The performance of an existing obligation was no consideration for a promise of expenses. The promise was, therefore, unenforceable.

Case: Glasbrook Bros Ltd v. Glamorgan CC (1925)

The owners of a colliery asked for, and promised to pay for, a special police guard on their mine throughout a time of industrial unrest. They later reneged on their promise, claiming that the police had only been performing their public duty.

Held: The police had provided more protection than was reasonably necessary and so there was something unique given which could be regarded as good consideration. The extra protection provided, therefore, did amount to consideration for the promise to pay.

7. A promise to do something which an existing contract already requires a person to do is no consideration. There is no extra obligation and no extra rights or benefits.

Case: Stilk v. Myrick (1809)

The plaintiff was a member of the eleven-man crew of a ship. During the voyage, two members deserted and the captain promised the rest of the crew that they would share the wages of the deserters if they would complete the voyage. On completion, the plaintiff requested his share, and was refused.

Held: The plaintiff was already contractually bound to complete the voyage and did not provide consideration for the promise of extra pay. The promise, therefore, was not binding.

Consideration must be provided by the promisee
8. Consideration is the price of a promise, so a person can only enforce a promise if they themselves provided the consideration.

Case: Tweedle v. Atkinson (1861)

The plaintiff's father and father-in-law exchanged promises that they would each pay a sum of money to the plaintiff following his marriage. The father-in-law died without making the promised payment, and the plaintiff sued his father-in-law's executor for the specified amount.

Held: The plaintiff had no enforceable rights under the agreement because he had provided no consideration for his father-in-law's promise.

9. As a general rule, only a person who is a party to a contract, i.e. has provided consideration, can sue on it. This is known as the 'privity of contract doctrine'. Any person not contributing to the consideration is not 'privy' to the contract and has no enforceable rights or obligations under it.

Case: Dunlop Pneumatic Tyre Co. Ltd v. Selfridge & Co. Ltd (1915)

The plaintiffs, a tyre manufacturer, supplied tyres to Dew & Co. Ltd on terms that Dew & Co. Ltd would not re-sell the tyres at less than the current list price, with the exception of sales to trade customers. If Dew & Co. Ltd sold the tyres wholesale to trade customers, they would have to get a written undertaking from those buyers not to sell the tyres below the current list price. The defendants purchased tyres on these conditions from Dew & Co. Ltd, and subsequently sold tyres to two customers at less than the minimum price. Dunlop Pneumatic Tyre Co. Ltd sued to recover damages.

Held: The plaintiffs could not recover damages under a contract to which they were not a party. The agreement had been between Dew & Co. Ltd and Selfridge & Co. Ltd and Dunlop Pneumatic Tyre Co. Ltd were, therefore, unable to enforce the contract since no consideration had passed from them to the defendants.

Consideration must not have been provided prior to the agreement
10. Past consideration is any act which has already been performed before a promise in return is given, and, as a general rule, is not sufficient to enforce the promise. The promisor is not getting anything in exchange for the promise, since they already have it, so unless the promisor chooses to recognise a moral obligation they can renege on the promise.

Case: Roscorla v. Thomas (1842)

The plaintiff purchased a horse from the defendant. After the sale was complete, the defendant promised that the horse was not vicious. This consequently proved to be wrong, as the horse did indeed turn out to be vicious.

Held: The act put forward as consideration, i.e. the payment of the price, was complete before the promise was made. The plaintiff gave no new consideration for the promise, and, therefore, the promise was unenforceable.

Case: Provincial Bank of Ireland Ltd v. Donnell (1932)

The defendant's husband was overdrawn in his account with the plaintiffs. The defendant subsequently had given the plaintiffs a guarantee, not under seal, that she would pay a specified annual premium in consideration of advances already made or that might thereafter be made by the plaintiffs to her husband. The defendant later refused to pay the premium, and pleaded lack of consideration for the guarantee.

Held: The case was dismissed on the grounds that there was no consideration for the wife's guarantee since the advance had already been made.

Exceptions to the past consideration rule
11. Past consideration will support bills of exchange (such as a cheque), since most of these are issued to pay existing debts.

12. Past consideration supports a later promise to pay for something done at the promisor's request. The contract is made when the 'past' consideration is requested, and the parties understand that payment will be made. The later promise to pay merely fixes the price to be paid – it does not create the agreement.

Case: Lampleigh v. Braithwait (1615)

The defendant, who had killed a man, asked the plaintiff to obtain a royal pardon for him. The plaintiff incurred expense and trouble in subsequently securing such a pardon, and the defendant later promised to pay the plaintiff £100 for his services. He broke his promise and the plaintiff sued him.

Held: An implied promise to pay could be related back to the defendant's initial request for help. The promise was, therefore, held to be binding as the later promise to pay £100 was merely fixing the amount. The plaintiff's subsequent efforts amounted to consideration for the defendant's promise.

Consideration must be given to enforce the waiving of a contractual obligation
13. If a party to a contract waives existing rights which it has under the contract, it is not legally bound by such a waiver unless it has received consideration for it. This is because the waiver leads to a new agreement which must be accompanied by consideration to make it enforceable.

Case: Foakes v. Beer (1889)

The defendant obtained a judgment against the plaintiff of £2,091, which attracted interest if not paid immediately. The plaintiff asked for time to discharge the debt, and they entered into a written agreement whereby the plaintiff would make an immediate payment of £500 and the remainder in agreed instalments. In return, the defendant agreed not to take 'any proceedings whatsoever' on the judgment. When the debt was paid off as agreed, the defendant sued for £360 interest which was due.

Held: The defendant was entitled to the debt with interest. No consideration had been given by the plaintiff in return for the promise to waive interest. Therefore, the claim was upheld.

14. There are a number of exceptions to the rule that the waiving of a contractual debt must be accompanied by consideration in order for the waiver to be binding:

(a) if the creditor accepts payment of a lesser sum in full settlement before the due date, the payment discharges the whole debt;

(b) if the creditor accepts anything different to which already entitled, e.g. goods instead of cash, even though the value of the goods may be less than the cash value;

(c) if the creditor accepts part payment in full settlement from a third party. The creditor will have received consideration from an individual against whom they had no previous claim;

(d) if a group of creditors arrange that they will each accept part payment in full settlement. This will be binding between themselves;

(e) if it can be enforced under the principle of 'promissory estoppel'.

• The principle of promissory estoppel

15. Equity mitigates the hardship that could be caused to a person who relies on a promise that a debt will not be enforced in full. Under the principle of promissory estoppel, where a person makes a promise, unsupported by consideration, to waive a debt or other obligation, and where the promisee acts on this promise, the promisor is estopped (prevented) from retracting the promise.

16. It is important to note, however, that the principle prohibits promisors from insisting on their strict legal rights when it would be unjust to allow them to do so. For example, if circumstances were to change, so as to remove the reasons for the promise, the original rights of the promisor would become enforceable again.

Case: Central London Property Trust v. High Trees House (1947)

In 1939, the plaintiff leased a block of flats to the defendant for ninety-nine years at an annual rent of £2,500. Due to the war, he was unable to sublet all of the flats, so the plaintiff agreed in writing to accept a reduced annual rent of £1,250. After the war, when the flats were fully let, the plaintiff claimed the rent arrears and a full rent for the future.

Held: The plaintiff was entitled to the full rent from the end of the war and for the future, but was estopped in equity from going back on his promise and claiming the full rent back to the start of the war.

17. Two limitations to the scope of promissory estoppel are:

(a) It only applies to a promise of waiver which is voluntary.

Case: D & C Builders v. Rees (1966)

The defendant owed the plaintiffs £482, and knowing that they were in financial difficulty offered them £300 in full settlement of the debt. The plaintiffs accepted a cheque for this amount, but later sued for the balance.

Held: The promise was not voluntarily given, as it was given under threat that if they did not take this sum they would receive nothing. The plaintiffs were entitled to the balance.

(b) It only applies to the waiver of existing rights. Any new rights or obligations must be supported by consideration in the usual way.

Case: Combe v. Combe (1951)

A husband promised his wife during divorce proceedings to pay her an annual allowance. As a result, she did not apply to the court for a maintenance order. Subsequently, the husband paid no maintenance and the wife sued to enforce his promise. The wife succeeded in the High Court on the basis of promissory estoppel, but this was appealed to the Court of Appeal.

Held: Promissory estoppel applies only when a person who promises not to enforce their legal rights or obligations retracts their promise. It does not apply to new contracts, which must be supported by consideration. Since the wife had not provided such consideration, her action failed.

IMPORTANT CASES

Numbers in brackets refer to paragraphs of this chapter

Commodity Broking Co. Ltd v. Meehan (1985) .... (4)
Thomas v. Thomas (1842) .... (4)
Collins v. Godefroy (1831) .... (6)
Glasbrook Bros Ltd v. Glamorgan CC (1925) .... (6)
Stilk v. Myrick (1809) .... (7)
Tweedle v. Atkinson (1861) .... (8)
Dunlop Pneumatic Tyre Co. Ltd v. Selfridge & Co. Ltd (1915) .... (9)
Roscorla v. Thomas (1842) .... (10)
Provincial Bank of Ireland Ltd v. Donnell (1932) .... (10)
Lampleigh v. Braithwait (1615) .... (12)
Foakes v. Beer (1889) .... (13)
Central London Property Trust v. High Trees House (1947) .... (16)
D & C Builders v. Rees (1966) .... (17)
Combe v. Combe (1951) .... (17)

PROGRESS TEST

Numbers in brackets refer to paragraphs of this chapter

1. Define consideration. (2)
2. If, in return for a promise, the promisee provides something which no longer has any value, is there sufficient consideration to make this promise binding? (4)
3. Is the performance of something which you already are required to do by (a) law, or (b) an existing contract, held to be valid consideration? (6–7)
4. Can a person enforce a contract if they are not a party to it? (8–9)
5. Is it true that 'past consideration is no consideration'? (11–12)
6. If a creditor accepts part payment of an existing debt in full settlement, may they still claim the unpaid balance? (13)
7. List five exceptions to the rule that the waiving of a contractual debt must be accompanied by consideration in order for the waiver to be binding. (14)
8. Explain the principle of promissory estoppel and identify two limitations to its scope. (15–17)

chapter 12

INTENTION TO CREATE LEGAL RELATIONS

Topics covered

- Intention to be legally bound
- Commercial agreements
- Domestic agreements
- Collective agreements

Summary
The parties to a contract must have intended to create a legally binding transaction before a contract can validly exist. This chapter examines a number of different types of agreements and how they fulfil such a requirement.

• Intention to be legally bound

1.   The law upholds agreements, not only because of the consideration involved, but also because the parties intended to create legal relations. Otherwise, there is no binding contract.

2.   What matters is not whether the parties intended in their minds to be bound by what they agreed to do, but the inferences that a reasonable person would draw from their words, conduct or the circumstances of the negotiations.

3.   An express statement by the parties of their intention not to create legal relations is conclusive. When phrases such as 'subject to contract', 'agreement in principle' or 'provisional agreement' are used, the usual assumption of the courts is that such phrases indicate that the parties did not intend to be legally bound prior to the signing of a formal contract.

Case: Rose & Frank Co. v. Crompton Bros Ltd (1925)

An agreement was made whereby the defendant, a British manufacturer of paper tissues, appointed the plaintiff to be its sole distributors in the United States. The agreement expressly stated that it was 'not subject to legal jurisdiction in the law courts'. The defendant terminated the agreement without giving the required notice.

Held: The agreement was binding in honour only and, therefore, was not enforceable as a contract.

4.   In most contracts, there is no express statement that the parties intend the agreement to be legally binding. In the absence of such an express intention, the courts have generally applied three presumptions to a case:

(a) commercial or business-type agreements are usually intended to be legally binding;

(b) domestic or social agreements are *not* usually intended to be legally binding;

(c) collective agreements are *not* usually intended to be legally binding.

• Commercial agreements

5. Where negotiations suggest that the agreement is of a commercial or business nature, it is presumed the parties intend to create legal relations. This is the normal situation and is rarely the cause of the dispute.

6. The presumption that a commercial or business agreement is legally binding needs to be expressly denied, as in *Rose & Frank Co.* v. *Crompton Bros Ltd* (1925).

Case: Jones v. Vernon Pools Ltd (1938)

The plaintiff claimed that he had sent a football pools coupon to the defendant on which the forecasts he had made entitled him to receive payment of a dividend. The agreement included a clause which stated that any transaction would be 'binding in honour only'.

Held: This clause expressly denied an intention to create legal relations, was a bar to an action in court and resulted in the contract being invalid.

• Domestic agreements

7. An agreement between husband and wife, relatives or friends is normally presumed not to contain an intention to create legal relations.

Case: Balfour v. Balfour (1919)

The defendant, an English civil servant stationed in Ceylon, promised the plaintiff, his wife, that he would pay her £30 per month to maintain her in England during his absence. The marriage subsequently ended in divorce and the plaintiff sued for the monthly maintenance allowance which the defendant no longer paid.

Held: Their agreement was unenforceable because the parties had not intended that it should be subject to legal consequences.

8. In some domestic agreements, however, the circumstances may establish that there had been an intention to create legal relations. This would be the case if the parties were in some way estranged, e.g. separated or divorced, or could be shown to have displayed 'mutuality of agreement'.

Case: Courtney v. Courtney (1923)

The married couple agreed to separate. The defendant agreed to pay his wife £150 and she agreed to return a watch and ring. The plaintiff sued her husband when he retracted his promise.

Held: In the circumstances, intention to create legal relations was to be inferred, as the parties were separated and intended to have no further dealings. The wife, therefore, succeeded in her action for breach of contract.

Case: Simpkins v. Pays (1955)

Three women who lived in the same house took part in a weekly competition run by a Sunday newspaper. They agreed to send their entries on a single coupon and to share any prize money. One week, they won £750, but the plaintiff was denied her share by the others.

Held: The agreement to share had been intended to be legally binding, and was an enforceable contract.

Case: Mackey v. Jones (1959)

The plaintiff laboured on his uncle's farm for no pay over a period of years. His uncle left the entire farm to another relative in his will. On the uncle's death, the plaintiff sued the personal representatives of his uncle, claiming that his uncle had verbally agreed to leave the farm to him.

Held: There was no contract to leave the farm to the plaintiff. The words of the deceased were no more than a statement of intention or wish.

• Collective agreements

9. Procedural agreements between trade unions and employers relating to a contract of employment are not usually legally binding, despite their elaborate and very legal contents. If the court finds, however, that the parties intended to create legal relations through such a collective agreement, it will hold that the contract is enforceable.

10. Whereas a trade union may be bound by such a collective contract, an individual member of the union or a non-union worker is not bound by the provisions of a collective agreement, unless they are expressly or impliedly incorporated into the employment contract.

Case: O'Rourke and Others v. Talbot (Ireland) Ltd (1983)

The defendant company had given an assurance in writing to 'guarantee' protection for four of its workers against compulsory redundancy up to 1984. When the plaintiffs were made redundant in 1980, they sued for breach of contract.

Held: Although the defendant company may not have intended the collective agreement with the four workers to create legal relations between both parties, this had not been made known to its workers. The High Court ruled that the plaintiffs, therefore, were entitled to damages for breach of contract.

IMPORTANT CASES

Numbers in brackets refer to paragraphs of this chapter

PROGRESS TEST

Numbers in brackets refer to paragraphs of this chapter

1. What is the effect of a 'subject to contract' statement in a commercial agreement? (3)
2. Identify three presumptions that courts have usually applied to a case in the absence of express intention by the parties for an agreement to be legally binding. (4)
3. Describe the circumstances under which a commercial agreement is not intended to be legally binding. (6)
4. What type of domestic agreement will the court regard as having been subject to an intention to create legal relations? (8)
5. Are trade unions and their members legally bound by collective agreements with employers? (9–10)

chapter 13

TERMS OF A CONTRACT

Topics covered

- Express terms
- Implied terms

- Conditions, warranties and exemption clauses

Summary

Once the prerequisites of a binding contract have been established, the terms of the contract, which determine the limits to which the parties are bound, fall for examination. This chapter considers the implications of the different classes of contractual terms.

1. The contents of a contract are its terms, which define the rights, obligations and rules by which the parties are to be bound in their agreement. Contractual terms may be either express or implied.

• Express terms

2. The express terms of a contract are the words used by the parties, whether written or spoken, during negotiations leading up to a contract, and by which they intended to be bound. Such terms must be distinguished from statements, called mere representations or non-contractual representations, which help to induce the making of the contract but which are not intended to be legally binding, e.g. 'it's the best bargain in the world'. The importance of the distinction is that different remedies are available when a term is broken than when a representation is untrue.

3. To resolve disputes concerning the express terms of a contract, the courts have formulated 'rules of construction'. The courts will not usually look beyond the words of an express term in a contract, presuming instead that the words are possessed of their ordinary literal meaning, while legal terms are possessed of their technical meaning.

4. Disputes concerning the contents of an oral contract can only be resolved by evidence produced before the courts.

5. If the parties have expressed the terms of a contract in writing, however, the introduction of oral evidence to add to, vary or contradict the document is

restricted. In certain exceptional circumstances, oral evidence may be given to assist the court in reaching a decision. Such evidence may be admitted:
(a) To explain the circumstances surrounding a term concerning trade practice or custom.
(b) To prove that the written agreement was not the whole agreement.

Case: De Lassalle v. Guilford (1901)

The plaintiff signed a written lease agreement on an assurance that the drains were in order. This term was not written into the lease agreement.

Held: The term was one of a collateral contract made at the same time but not incorporated into the written contract. The parties had, therefore, agreed that their written consent should not take place until the unwritten term had been satisfied.

(c) To correct a mistake in a written agreement drawn up subsequently. In order to rectify a mistake, it must be proven that:

   (i)   there was complete agreement between the parties on all important terms;
   (ii) the verbal agreement continued unchanged until it was reduced into writing;
   (iii) the writing did not express what the parties had agreed.

Case: Nolan v. Graves (1946)

An oral agreement was made at a public auction to purchase premises for £5,550. When drafting the memorandum of the agreement subsequently, this figure was mistakenly entered as £4,550.

Held: The memorandum of the agreement was to be corrected in favour of the seller.

6. If an express term in a contract is so ambiguous as to allow two different constructions, the court will generally choose the meaning unfavourable to the party who imposed the term. This is called the *contra proferentem* rule, and it is usually applied to contracts in a fixed form.

• Implied terms
7. The parties to a contract may not expressly state each term of the contract, but they may choose to agree to the main purpose of the contract and some basic terms, and leave the rest to be implied from the circumstances. Additional terms of a contract may be implied by law:

(a) to give effect to the presumed intentions of the parties;
(b) to supply a term normally implied in a particular type of contract; or

(c) to comply with statute law and the Constitution.

To give effect to the presumed intentions of the parties

8. Terms may be implied if the court decides that the parties intended these terms to apply and did not express them because they were taken for granted. The implied term must be a necessary inference from the expressed terms of the contract. The court will not imply a term simply because it is reasonable to do so. In such cases, the 'officious bystander' test must be used; if when the parties had been making the contract, an officious bystander intervened to remind the parties that they had not mentioned a certain point, they would have answered 'Naturally, we didn't bother to state that; it's too obvious'.

Case: Ward & Fagan v. Spivack Ltd (1957)

The plaintiffs were appointed sole agents, on a commission basis, for the defendants' products. On termination of the agency, the plaintiffs sought a declaration that they would continue to be entitled to commission on orders received from customers which they had introduced to the defendant company.

Held: To imply such a term in the contract, the court had to be satisfied that the parties would have agreed to the term had the matter been mentioned when the contract was originally being negotiated.

Case: Murphy, Buckley & Keogh Ltd v. Pye (Ireland) Ltd (1971)

The defendants appointed the plaintiffs to be sole agents for the purpose of finding a purchaser of their factory, and agreed to pay them a commission if they succeeded in effecting such a sale. The defendants subsequently negotiated a sale of the premises to a purchaser not introduced by the plaintiffs, and refused the plaintiffs' claim for commission on the sale.

Held: The plaintiffs' efforts as sole agents had not played any effective part in effecting the sale of the factory to the purchaser. To imply a term into the contract that the plaintiffs had to be paid commission on any sale would be in conflict with the express terms of the contract.

Case: Irish Welding v. Philips Electrical (Ireland) Ltd (1976)

The plaintiffs had been appointed sole agents for the defendants in Ireland. When the defendants tried to terminate the agreement, the plaintiffs claimed that it was not possible to terminate the agency at all within the terms of the contract.

Held: It had to have been within the contemplation of the parties involved that reasonable notice, in this case nine months, given by either party could terminate the agreement.

To supply a term normally implied in a particular type of contract

9. The reluctance of the court to imply terms does not apply to terms normally implied by reference to a custom or practice prevailing in the particular trade to which the contract relates. Such standardised terms are always implied unless a contrary intention is expressed.

Case: Les Affreteurs etc. v. Walford (1919)

It was expressly provided in an agreement for a charter of a ship, contrary to trade custom, that payment was to be made on signing the charter, and not at a later time.

Held: The contract was upheld. The express term superseded the term implied by custom.

To comply with statute law and the Constitution

10. The courts will also imply terms into contracts which have legal or constitutional connotations. Certain implied terms have been used so often by the courts that they have become formalised in statutes in an attempt to codify the law.

11. Implied terms are embodied in the Bills of Exchange Act 1882, Sale of Goods and Supply of Services Act 1980 and the Consumer Credit Act 1995, which we will examine in later chapters.

12. Some terms must also be implied to comply with the Constitution. For example, under Article 40 of the Constitution, an individual's right of free association or free disassociation is guaranteed. This may lead to courts implying terms into contracts of employment.

Case: Educational Company of Ireland v. Fitzpatrick (1961)

Some employees of the company, who were union members, picketed the premises in an attempt to force the employer to employ only trade union labour and to compel all employees to join the union.

Held: Picketing to coerce workers to join associations was unlawful. The courts implied a term into the employment contract that employees who when being employed were not required to belong to a union had the constitutional right to disassociate (i.e. to refuse to join a union).

• Conditions, warranties and exemption clauses

13. The terms of a contract may be classified into conditions, warranties, exemption from liability clauses or limitation of liability clauses. Where there is difficulty in classifying a term as a condition or a warranty, it is known as an 'innominate, or intermediate, term'.

Conditions

14. A condition is a vital term of a contract, breach of which entitles the injured party to rescind the contract, but allows the injured party the option to affirm it. In either case, the injured party may also recover damages for losses incurred.

Case: Poussard v. Spiers (1876)

The plaintiff contracted to sing in a London operetta throughout a series of performances. She failed to perform during the first week, due to an illness. A replacement was engaged, who insisted that her services be retained for the entire run. Thus, on the recovery from the illness, the producer of the operetta declined to accept the plaintiff's services for the remaining performances.

Held: Failure to sing for the first week of the operetta was a breach of condition which entitled the producer to rescind the contract.

15. A contract may be made subject to a 'condition precedent', whereby the contract will not come into being in the absence of a specified condition being fulfilled. Similarly, it may be made subject to a 'condition subsequent', whereby the contract will be dissolved without either party incurring any liability in the event of the specified condition occurring.

Warranties

16. A warranty is a minor term subsidiary to the main purpose of a contract, breach of which merely entitles the injured party to claim damages. The injured party is still bound by the contract.

Case: Bettini v. Gye (1876)

The plaintiff, an opera singer, contracted to sing in a series of performances. The contract included a clause whereby the plaintiff was obliged to attend rehearsals for six days before the opening performance. He missed the first three days, owing to illness, at which time he was informed that his services were no longer required.

Held: The singer had breached a warranty only, because the clause regarding rehearsals was subsidiary to the main purpose of the contract. The producer was obliged to accept the plaintiff's services and could not rescind the contract. He could, however, claim damages for failure to attend the six days' rehearsals, if he could prove any resultant loss.

Innominate terms

17. Instead of the traditional classification of terms into conditions and warranties, the tendency in recent years has been to consider a term of a contract in its context as to whether or not in itself it is vital to the existence of the contract. If a term is considered of such importance and is broken, the injured party is entitled to rescind the contract.

18. The significance of not classifying the relevant term until the seriousness of a breach can be judged is that a court will not be limited to a specific remedy due to a premature classification as a breach of condition (with a remedy of specific performance) or a breach of warranty (with a remedy of damages).

Exemption clauses

19. An exemption clause is a term of a contract which seeks to exempt one of the parties from a liability which might arise out of the adoption or performance of the contract, or which seeks to limit liability to a specific sum if certain events occur, such as a breach of warranty or negligence. These are also known as 'exclusion clauses'.

20. Exemption clauses are a legitimate device between parties negotiating their contract from positions of more or less equal bargaining strength. There has, however, been strong criticism of the use of exemption clauses by large organisations to abuse their bargaining power. The courts have developed various rules of case-law designed to restrain the effect of such clauses, and have adopted an approach which involves examining both the nature of the parties involved in the contract and the type of exemption clause in question. The courts will also scrutinise the position of the clause, the size and clarity of the print and the opportunity provided to the party contracted to read the clause.

21. An exemption clause may become a term of the contract by signature or by notice. If a person signs a contractual document, they are bound by the terms even if they do not read them, unless the other party misrepresented its terms.

Case: L'Estrange v. Graucob (1934)

The plaintiff, who was the owner of a cafe, purchased a cigarette vending machine. She signed, without reading, an agreement which contained conditions that excluded her normal rights under the Sale of Goods Act 1893. The machine proved defective, and the plaintiff sought a legal remedy.

Held: The conditions of the contract were binding of the plaintiff because she had signed the written agreement.

Case: Curtis v. Chemical Cleaning Co. (1951)

The plaintiff took her wedding dress to be cleaned. She was given a form to sign on which there were conditions by which the company disclaimed liability for all damage. Before signing it, she asked about its contents and was told that it excluded the cleaner's liability for damages to the beads and sequins. The dress was badly stained during the course of the cleaning process.

Held: The defendants could not rely on their exemption clause since they had misled the plaintiff as to the effect of the form.

22. Where contractual documents are not signed, an exemption clause will only apply if the party adversely affected by it knows of the clause, or if reasonable steps are taken to bring the clause to the party's notice before the contract is made.

Case: Thornton v. Shoe Lane Parking Ltd (1971)

The plaintiff took a ticket from a dispensing machine as he drove his car into an automatic car park. On his return to collect the car there was an accident and he was severely injured. The defendants argued that the ticket incorporated a condition exempting them from liability. In the bottom left hand corner in small print it was said to be 'issued subject to conditions . . . displayed on the premises'. On a pillar opposite the dispensing machine a set of printed 'conditions' was displayed in a panel, one of which stated that the garage would not be liable for any injury to the customer occurring when his car was on the premises.

Held: Notice of the contents of the exemption clause as specified on the ticket issued from the dispensing machine was too late, because the plaintiff had no option except to drive on into the garage. The defendants had not done what was reasonably sufficient to bring the exemption condition to the notice of the plaintiff, and therefore were not exempted from liability.

Case: Olley v. Marlborough Court (1949)

The plaintiff and her husband booked in at the defendant's hotel and paid for a room in advance. When they reached their bedroom they saw a notice on the wall by which the hotel disclaimed liability for articles lost or stolen unless they were handed to the management for safe keeping. The plaintiff left furs in the room, locked the door and handed in the key at the reception desk. The key was taken by a thief and the plaintiff's furs were stolen.

Held: The disclaimer of liability was too late, since the contract was completed at the reception desk when the room was booked and paid for. The hotel, therefore, could not rely on the notice disclaiming liability.

Case: Carroll v. An Post National Lottery Company Ltd (1996)

The plaintiff claimed he was entitled to €250,000 of a share of a Lotto jackpot because one of his playslips with winning numbers was not entered in the draw by a post office counterhand. At the bottom of the playslip was a blue arrow and underneath, printed in red, the words 'See instructions on reverse side'. These stated: 'Players acknowledge the Lotto agents are acting on their behalf in entering playslips into the National Lottery computer system. The National Lottery holds no responsibility for tickets cancelled in error or where the apparent numbers on a ticket disagree with numbers on file at the central computer for that ticket'. It was also stated: 'By playing the game, a player agrees to abide by the National Lottery rules and regulations in effect at the time the play is made.' Although he acknowledged that he knew there were rules regulating the lottery, the plaintiff argued that he was unaware of the rules on the back of the playslip.

Held: The plaintiff must have seen the words: 'See instructions on reverse side'. The risks involved in holding the National Lottery in the absence of such 'exemptions' (as stated on the back of playslips) would leave the company vulnerable to fraudulent claims, and it was entitled to reasonable protection from such circumstances. The plaintiff's action was dismissed.

23. If an exemption clause cannot be eliminated from a contract, the courts will strictly construe it against the party seeking to use it to avoid liability. For example, where there is a fundamental breach of contract (i.e. the fundamental obligation is not fulfilled), the party responsible cannot seek the protection of an exemption clause to escape liability.

Case: Clayton Love & Sons Ltd v. The B&I Steam Packet Company Ltd (1966)

The defendants contracted with the plaintiffs to transport by sea consignments of quick-frozen scampi in a refrigerated hold in their ship. One such consignment was loaded into the refrigeration hold at approximately atmospheric temperature, and by the time it was delivered to its destination a large part of the consignment had gone bad. The plaintiffs made a claim for damages for breach of contract, which the defendants rejected under the terms of their standard conditions of carriage whereby they exempted themselves from liability for any 'damage, loss, detention, deterioration, delay, misdelivery or non-delivery of or to the goods howsoever, whensoever, or wheresoever the same may have been caused'.

Held: The service the plaintiffs got was radically different from the service they had contracted for, and hence there had been a fundamental breach of contract which no exemption clause, no matter how well drafted, could cover. The defendants, therefore, were not entitled to avail of the general exemption provisions in their standard conditions of carriage to escape liability.

24. This approach to exemption clauses by the Irish courts has since been interpreted more widely by English courts, who now take the view that in contracts between business people negotiating on equal terms, there is no reason why the parties should not be free to agree on who should bear the risk for loss or damage arising from a fundamental breach of contract.

Case: Photo Productions v. Securicor Transport Ltd (1980)

The defendants contracted with the plaintiffs to provide a night security patrol service for their factory of four visits a night. The contract incorporated standard conditions which, amongst others, provided that the defendants would not be liable for any loss or damage to the premises 'by any employee of the company unless such act or default could have been foreseen and avoided by the exercise of due diligence on the part of the company as his employer'. This clause was agreed by the plaintiffs, who took out an insurance policy to cover damage or loss by fire or theft. One of the defendants' employees subsequently entered the factory on duty patrol and lit a fire which burned down the entire factory. The plaintiffs claimed damages based on breach of contract.

Held: Since the parties had bargained on equal terms and had made provisions for their respective risks according to the terms they chose to agree, the exemption clause covered even this serious breach of contract.

IMPORTANT CASES

Numbers in brackets refer to paragraphs of this chapter

PROGRESS TEST

Numbers in brackets refer to paragraphs of this chapter

1. Distinguish between the express terms of a contract and mere misrepresentations. (2)
2. Under what circumstances may oral evidence add to a written contract? (5)
3. When may additional terms, not expressed in the contract, be implied by law as part of the contract? (7)
4. Explain the 'officious bystander' test. (8)
5. Differentiate between a condition and a warranty. (14, 16)
6. What is the significance of an 'innominate' term? (18)
7. Compare a limitation of liability clause and an exemption of liability clause. (19)
8. List, and describe, the ways by which an exemption clause may become a term of a contract. (21–2)
9. Explain what is meant by strict construction of an exemption clause. (23)

chapter 14

FORM OF A CONTRACT

Topics covered

- Contracts which must be by deed
- Contracts which must be in writing
- Contracts which must be evidenced in writing
- The equitable doctrine of part performance

Summary

The form of a contract is generally a matter to be decided by the parties. This chapter considers a number of special cases in which the law requires a special form to be used.

1. The general rule is that there are no formalities required for creation of a contract; it may be made in writing, orally or even by implication from conduct. There are, however, some exceptional cases where the law demands some formality, without which the contract may still be valid but unenforceable.

2. The three categories of exceptions are:

(a) contracts which must be by deed (or under seal);
(b) contracts which must be in writing;
(c) contracts which must be evidenced in writing.

• Contracts which must be by deed

3. Certain contracts, such as those unsupported by consideration or the promise of a gift, are required to be in the form of a deed and may not be binding unless they are in that form. A deed is a written document, the essentials of which are that it be signed by the contracting parties, impressed with a seal and delivered by the person executing the deed. Other contracts, which need not be made by deed, may also be created under seal in this way to give them extra effect.

• Contracts which must be in writing

4. Some contracts, mainly commercial, are required by statute to be in the form of a written document, but not necessarily under seal. They are invalid if they are not in that form. This category includes:

(a) bills of exchange and promissory notes (Bills of Exchange Act 1882);

(b) share transfers (Stock Transfer Act 1963);
(c) leases greater than ones from year to year (Deasy's Act 1860);
(d) marine insurance contracts (Marine Insurance Act 1906); and
(e) hire-purchase agreements.

• Contracts which must be evidenced in writing

5. Certain contracts do not have to be in writing, but need only to be evidenced in writing to be enforceable in a court of law.

6. The Statute of Frauds (Ireland) Act 1695, section 2, provides that the following contracts must be evidenced in writing:

(a) a contract of guarantee, in which a person promises 'to answer for the debt, default or miscarriages of another person';
(b) a contract made in consideration of marriage;
(c) a contract relating to the sale of land or any interest in land;
(d) a contract which is not to be performed within the space of one year of it being made.

7. No legal action can be brought in a court of law to enforce these contracts 'unless the agreement upon which such action shall be brought, or some memorandum or note thereof, shall be in writing, and signed by the party to be charged therewith, or some other person thereunto by him lawfully authorised'.

8. The memorandum or note must contain the names or identities of both parties to the contract, the subject matter of the agreement and the consideration provided. It need not be prepared for the purpose of satisfying the statutory requirements – it can be any writing, made after the oral contract and before the action is brought, which sets out the terms of the agreement. If the memorandum consists of two or more documents, these must be joined together.

9. The memorandum must be signed by the person to be charged, or their authorised agent. The signature may be stamped or printed, or even initials will suffice.

Case: Hynes v. Hynes (1984)

The parties entered into an agreement to transfer a business from one brother to the other. The contract was not performed within a year, and the defendant attempted to avoid it on the grounds that some memorandum or note of the agreement in writing was required for it to be enforceable.

Held: The parties had intended at the time of contract that it should be completed within the space of a year. Hence, the contract remained enforceable, even in the absence of a memorandum or note in writing.

• The equitable doctrine of part performance

10. In some cases the Statute of Frauds caused hardship, particularly when an oral contract had been wholly or partly performed. Equity, therefore, developed the principle that if the plaintiff could prove that the defendant allowed them to do acts which were in part performance of a contract consistent with the one alleged, it would enforce the contract, even though there was not written evidence of it. The contract of part performance must point clearly to a contract consistent with the one the plaintiff seeks to enforce.

Case: Rawlinson v. Ames (1925)

The plaintiff agreed orally to lease a flat to the defendant. It was part of the agreement that the plaintiff would make several alterations to the flat, which he did under the defendant's supervision. The defendant then refused to take the lease. The plaintiff sued for specific performance.

Held: The defendant had requested and supervised the alterations, thereby indicating that she had agreed to take the lease. Although a written memorandum did not exist, the order for specific performance was made (i.e. the defendant had to take and pay rent under the lease).

IMPORTANT CASES

Numbers in brackets refer to paragraphs of this chapter

Hynes v. Hynes (1984) .... (9)
Rawlinson v. Ames (1925) .... (10)

IMPORTANT STATUTES

Statute of Frauds (Ireland) Act 1695

PROGRESS TEST

Numbers in brackets refer to paragraphs of this chapter

1. What are the three categories of exceptions where the law demands some formality for the creation of contracts? (2)
2. State the essentials of a valid deed. (3)
3. Give three examples of contracts which must be in writing in order to be valid. (4)
4. How may a contract for the sale of an interest in land be enforced? (7)

5. List the essentials of a valid memorandum. (8)
6. Explain the doctrine of part performance and the circumstances in which it may be applied to an otherwise unenforceable contract. (10)

chapter 15

MISREPRESENTATION

Topics covered

- Nature of misrepresentation
- Types of misrepresentation
- Loss of the right of rescission

Summary

Many statements are made during negotiations leading to the formation of a contract. This chapter looks at those false statements of fact which induce the other party to enter into a contract, and the different remedies available.

• Nature of misrepresentation

1. A misrepresentation is a false statement of material fact, made innocently or otherwise by one party to the other, before the contract is made, in order to induce the latter to enter into the contract, which is relied on by the party who was misled.

It must be a false statement of material fact

2. A false statement of opinion, intention, law or mere 'sales talk' is not a misrepresentation. It is not meant to be a legally binding statement. The extent of the speaker's knowledge, as much as the words used, determines the category to which the statement belongs.

Case: Bisset v. Wilkinson (1927)

The seller of a farm in New Zealand, which both parties knew had not previously been grazed by sheep, stated that it could support about 2,000 sheep. This proved to be untrue.

Held: This was merely a statement of opinion, which did not constitute misrepresentation.

3. It is usually necessary for the statement to be expressed, though silence can amount to a misrepresentation where there is a failure to reveal changes in circumstances relevant to the contract. Silence is not usually a misrepresentation except when a statement of fact made in the course of negotiations subsequently becomes false and is not corrected, or when silence distorts a literally true statement.

Case: With v. O'Flanagan (1936)

A doctor disclosed the turnover of his practice to a potential purchaser. Between the time of this disclosure and the eventual contract, there was a significant deterioration in the value of the practice, which the vendor failed to reveal.

Held: There was misrepresentation by way of omission or silence.

The false statement must have induced the person to enter into the contract, and must have been relied upon

4. To be actionable, a misrepresentation must have induced the person to enter into the contract. The injured party, therefore, cannot avoid the contract if they did not know there had been a misrepresentation, if they knew the statement was untrue or if they did not allow the statement to affect their judgment.

Case: Grafton Court Ltd v. Wadson Sales Ltd (1975)

The plaintiff had represented to the defendant, at the time of signing the lease for a unit in a shopping complex, that the other tenants in the complex would be 'of high quality'. The defendant later sought to avoid the contract on the basis that this had been a misrepresentation by the plaintiff.

Held: Since the defendant had known of all or most of the occupants in the shopping complex at the time of signing the lease, he could not therefore have relied on this representation in deciding on whether or not to enter into the contract.

Case: Stafford v. Keane Mahony Smith (1980)

The plaintiff contracted to purchase a certain property, but subsequently found it unsuitable for use as a residence and eventually resold it at a loss. He claimed damages from the defendants, partners in a firm of auctioneers, whom he alleged had represented to him that the property would be suitable as a residence and that it would be a sound investment in that it would be available for immediate resale at a profit. He claimed that these statements had induced him to contract to purchase the property. The defendants denied making the alleged representations to the plaintiff, and claimed that in fact they were acting exclusively for the brother of the plaintiff until the last moment upon the signing of the contract. They had then been retained by the plaintiff for the resale.

Held: There was no documentary evidence to indicate that the defendants had made representations to the plaintiff prior to his purchase of the property. Even assuming that the defendants had made the alleged representations to the plaintiff's brother, and the plaintiff had heard of such representations prior to purchasing the property, the defendants would not have been under a duty of care to the plaintiff since they could not reasonably have contemplated that he would have relied on that information.

5. The person to whom a misrepresentation is made is under no obligation to check upon its truth or relevance, even if given the opportunity.

• Types of misrepresentation

6. A misrepresentation may be classified as:

(a) fraudulent;
(b) innocent; or
(c) negligent

for the purpose of determining what remedies are available. The classification depends on the state of mind of the person making the false statement.

Fraudulent misrepresentation

7. A misrepresentation is fraudulent when a false statement is made knowingly, or without belief in its truth, or recklessly without regard to whether it is true or false.

Case: Donnellan & Donnellan v. Dungoyne Ltd (1995)

The defendant's letting agents had represented to the second named plaintiff that virtually all of the units of a shopping centre had been leased to tenants and would be occupied and trading before Christmas 1991. The first named plaintiff entered into a 35-year lease (with an initial rent-free period of five months) of a unit with the defendant, guaranteeing the performance of the second named plaintiff, his son, as a tenant. However, at no stage was the centre fully let or well on the way to being fully let. The plaintiffs subsequently claimed that the centre had attracted insufficient numbers of potential customers and as a result the plaintiffs' retail business had failed. They sought rescission of the lease, repayment of the deposit, damages for negligent and/or fraudulent misrepresentation and damages for breach of contract.

Held: The encouraging remarks attributed to the defendant's letting agents were well within the bounds of what was permissible in order to attract potential tenants to the shopping centre. Rescission of the lease was inappropriate because the first named plaintiff would have entered into a tenancy agreement even if he had known the truth. However, the plaintiffs were entitled to damages for negligent misrepresentation. These were awarded and calculated by reference to the additional rent-free period that the first named plaintiff would have been likely to negotiate if he had known the true position.

Case: Fenton v. Schofield (1966)

In selling a fishery, the vendor claimed that an average of three hundred fish had been caught in the previous four years. He also claimed that he had spent a large sum of money renovating the property.

Held: The vendor was guilty of fraudulent misrepresentation because both statements were false.

8. The party misled may:

(a) rescind the contract (since it is voidable);
(b) refuse to perform their part of the contract; and/or
(c) recover damages in tort for any loss suffered.

Innocent misrepresentation

9. A misrepresentation is innocent when a false statement is made in the belief that it is true, and with reasonable grounds for that belief.

Case: Smelter Corporation of Ireland v. O'Driscoll (1977)

The defendant was reluctant to contract to sell her land to the plaintiff. She did so eventually, after being told by an agent of the company that she had no real choice as her property would be otherwise acquired by compulsory purchase by the local authority. The plaintiff sued for specific performance.

Held: The agent of the company had believed what he said to be true, but it was, in fact, false. He was, therefore, liable for innocent misrepresentation. The court held that it would be unjust to order specific performance, and the defendant could refuse to perform the contractual obligations.

10. The party misled may:

(a) rescind the contract, subject to being awarded damages in lieu of rescission by the court; or
(b) refuse to perform their part of the contract.

Case: Gahan v. Boland (1984)

On inspection of the defendant's property, the plaintiff enquired as to whether a proposed motorway would affect the property in any way. The defendant assured him that it would not, and, based on this assurance, the plaintiff agreed to purchase the property. The plaintiff subsequently discovered that the motorway was in fact routed to pass through the property and sought to rescind the contract.

Held: By acting on the defendant's innocent misrepresentation, the plaintiff was entitled to rescind the contract.

Negligent misrepresentation

11. A misrepresentation is negligent when a false statement is made in the belief that it is true, but without reasonable grounds for that belief.

12. The misrepresentation must be in breach of a duty of care which arose out of a 'special relationship'. Anyone with special knowledge or skill, who applies it for the assistance of another, owes a duty of care to that person, or to persons likely to be affected by it. This duty exists only where the person who makes the statement foresees that it may be relied on.

Case: Hedley Byrne & Co. Ltd v. Heller & Partners Ltd (1964)

The plaintiffs, advertising agents, requested credit references from the defendants, bankers, on a mutual client, E. Ltd. The defendants stated that E. Ltd was a respectably constituted firm and was considered good, but they also stated that this statement was made without responsibility on their part. As a result of this statement, the plaintiff granted credit to E. Ltd on several advertising contracts. Shortly afterwards, E. Ltd went into liquidation, and the plaintiffs were unable to recover £17,000 owed to them. The plaintiffs, therefore, sued the defendants on their negligent statement.

Held: The defendants owed the plaintiffs a duty of care, because the plaintiffs relied on the skill and judgment of the defendants, and the defendants knew, or ought to have known, of this reliance. However, although the defendants had broken their duty, they were not held to be liable, because the reference was given with a disclaimer of responsibility.

13. The party misled may:

(a) rescind the contract, subject to being awarded damages in lieu of rescission by the court;
(b) refuse to perform their part of the contract; or
(c) recover damages in tort for any loss suffered.

• Loss of the right of rescission

14. Rescission allows the parties to a contract to be restored to their position as it was before the contract was made. This remedy is not available when:

(a) the party misled affirms the contract after discovering the true facts;
(b) a court awards damages in lieu of rescission;
(c) restoration to the pre-contract state of affairs is impossible;
(d) lapse of time, in the case of innocent misrepresentation, implies affirmation; or
(e) the rights of third parties, such as creditors of an insolvent company, would be prejudiced.

IMPORTANT CASES

Numbers in brackets refer to paragraphs of this chapter

PROGRESS TEST

Numbers in brackets refer to paragraphs of this chapter

1. Define a misrepresentation. (1)
2. Distinguish between a false statement of opinion and a misrepresentation. (2)
3. When may silence be construed as misrepresentation? (3)
4. Can a person avoid a contract if they did not know there had been a misrepresentation? (4)
5. Explain the difference between fraudulent and negligent misrepresentation. (7, 11)
6. What are the remedies available to a party who has been misled by innocent misrepresentation? (10)
7. Describe the circumstances which may lead to negligent misrepresentation. (12)
8. When may a party misled by misrepresentation be unable to rescind the contract? (14)

chapter 16

MISTAKE IN CONTRACT

Topics covered

- Mistake as to the identity of the subject matter
- Mistake as to the identity of the other party
- Mistake as to the existence of the subject matter
- Mistake as to the existence of a fundamental state of affairs
- Mistake as to the nature of a document

Summary

As a general rule, mistake will not justify rescinding a contract concluded under such a misapprehension. This chapter considers the circumstances under which a contract may be void or voidable for mistake.

1. In general, a mistake made by one, or both, parties to a contract will not affect its validity. Offer and acceptance establish the terms of the contract; what the parties think or intend should not override those terms. However, in certain restricted circumstances, a contract may be rendered void or voidable. This will only apply if the parties contract under a fundamental mistake of fact, such that there was never any real agreement between them.

• Mistake as to the identity of the subject matter

2. If 'A' believes that the contract refers to something, and 'B' believes it refers to something else of the same nature, then the contract is void, as the terms are uncertain.

Case: Raffles v. Wichelhaus (1864)

The plaintiff agreed, in London, to sell to the defendant a cargo of cotton, which was to arrive 'Ex *Peerless* from Bombay'. There happened to be two ships called *Peerless* with a cargo of cotton from Bombay; one in October and the other in December. The defendant intended the contract to refer to the October sailing, and the plaintiff to the December sailing.

Held: The defendant was able to show that there was ambiguity, and that he intended to refer to the October sailing. The contract was, therefore, void.

3. Mistake as to *quality* of subject matter does not make the contract void. If each party is unaware that the other intends subject matter of a different quality, they may perform their side of a contract according to their intention, regardless of the other party expecting something different.

Case: Smith v. Hughes (1871)

The plaintiff was shown a sample of oats by the defendant. Believing them to be old oats, he bought them. The defendant was, in fact, selling new oats, and he was unaware of the plaintiff's impression. When the plaintiff discovered his mistake, he refused to accept the new oats.

Held: The mistake was one of quality, and as such did not make the contract void. Although the parties were at cross-purposes, it was not to such an extent that there was no agreement. The defendant, therefore, was entitled to deliver and to receive payment for his oats.

Case: John O. Ferguson v. Merchant Banking Ltd (1992)

The plaintiff contracted to purchase land contained in certain folios from the defendant. The defendant, on discovering that the relevant folios contained a vacant site with development potential, a fact which had at all times been known to the plaintiff, attempted to rescind the contract on the grounds of mistake.

Held: There had been agreement as to what in substance was being sold. The plaintiff, therefore, was entitled to specific performance of the contract.

- **Mistake as to the identity of the other party**

4.   Unless identity of the parties is essential to the contract, mistaken identity does not render a contract void.

5.   Where a buyer fraudulently adopts the identity of another existing person known to the seller, with whom the seller intends to make the contract, the sale to the actual buyer is rendered void.

Case: Cundy v. Lindsay (1878)

The plaintiff received an order for handkerchiefs from a dishonest person called Blenkarn, who gave his address as 37, Wood Street. He signed the letter so that his name appeared to be Blenkiron & Co., a respectable firm known to the plaintiff, who traded at 123, Wood Street. The plaintiff dispatched the handkerchiefs to Blenkiron & Co. on credit at 37, Wood Street, where Blenkarn possessed them. Blenkarn sold the handkerchiefs to the defendant, and absconded with the proceeds, without paying the amount due to the plaintiff. The plaintiff subsequently sued the defendant to recover the value of the handkerchiefs.

Held: The plaintiff intended to deal with Blenkiron & Co. and, therefore, no title could pass to Blenkarn. So, he could not pass title to the defendant. The mistake over the address was considered reasonable, so the defendant was liable to the plaintiff for the value of the handkerchiefs.

6.   Where a buyer fraudulently adopts the identity of a non-existent person, the seller cannot make a mistake as to identity. The contract, therefore, is only voidable for fraud.

Case: King's Norton Metal Co. v. Eldridge, Merrett & Co. Ltd (1897)

The plaintiff received an order for wire from Hallam & Co., an alias for a dishonest person called Wallis. The letterhead indicated that Hallam & Co. had substantial premises and overseas branches. The plaintiff dispatched the wire on credit to Hallam & Co. Wallis possessed the wire and resold it to the defendant. The plaintiff sued the defendant for the value of the wire.

Held: The plaintiff had, in fact, intended to contract with the writer of the letter, since Wallis and Hallam & Co. were one and the same. Thus, the contract was only voidable for fraud. Wallis acquired title of the wire and passed it to the defendant before the contract between the plaintiff and Wallis was rescinded. The defendant, therefore, was not liable for the value of the wire.

7. Mistake as to identity cannot be made when the parties deal face to face. There is a presumption that the parties do intend to deal with each other. In such a situation, a person can only make a mistake as to the attributes of the other party. So, the contract will only be voidable for misrepresentation, and the aggrieved party must avoid the contract at the earliest opportunity or else suffer the loss.

Case: Lewis v. Averay (1972)

A dishonest person proposed to purchase a car from the plaintiff and to pay for it by cheque. He claimed to be a well-known television actor, and produced a false pass from the studios bearing a photograph which resembled the aforementioned actor. The plaintiff then accepted the cheque and allowed him to take away the car. When the cheque was dishonoured, the plaintiff attempted to recover the car from the defendant who had purchased it in good faith from the dishonest person.

Held: The plaintiff could not recover the car. The contract between the plaintiff and the dishonest person was not void, but only voidable, as a result of the fraudulently induced mistake. The dishonest person had transferred the voidable title to the defendant.

• Mistake as to the existence of the subject matter

8. If the parties make a contract relating to subject matter which unknown to them both does not exist, or which no longer exists, e.g. it has been destroyed prior to the contract, there can be no contract. It is void.

Case: Galloway v. Galloway (1914)

A man and woman entered into a separation agreement, believing that they were married. Neither of them knew that, at the time of their marriage ceremony, the man's wife was still alive.

Held: The separation agreement was void for mistake, because the 'marriage', which formed the basis of the agreement, was null and void.

Case: Couturier v. Hastie (1852)

The plaintiff made a contract in London with the defendant to purchase a cargo of corn, which was being shipped from Salonika. Unknown to either party, the cargo of corn had, in fact, been sold in transit at the time the contract was made, as it was deteriorating due to the weather.

Held: There was no contract between the plaintiff and the defendant, because it had related to non-existent subject matter.

9. A contract is also void if, by mistake, a party purports to buy their own property. In such cases, a contract is void because there is nothing to buy.

Case: Cochrane v. Willis (1865)

The defendant was entitled, under a family settlement, to inherit property on his brother's death. His brother had become bankrupt and, to prevent the property from being sold to a third party, the defendant agreed to buy the property from his brother's bankrupt estate. Unknown to the defendant and the plaintiff, his brother's trustee, the property had already passed to the defendant by inheritance, because his brother had died before the contract was made.

Held: The defendant could not buy what already belonged to him. The contract, therefore, was void.

• Mistake as to the existence of a fundamental state of affairs

10. If both parties are equally mistaken on some fundamental point, such that had this state of affairs not existed the contract would not have been made, the contract is void.

11. However, if both parties are equally mistaken concerning some quality in the subject matter bargained for, such contract is voidable rather than void, and may be set aside on such terms as the court sees fit.

Case: Grist v. Bailey (1966)

The plaintiff bought a house, which was occupied by a tenant, from the defendant for £850. Both parties believed the house to be subject to rent control. It later turned out that this was not the case, and so was worth £2,250.

Held: The contract was voidable. The defendant was entitled to rescind the contract, with the condition attached that the plaintiff should get first option to buy the house at the current market price.

12. Moreover, if subsequent facts become known which, although relevant, do not affect the subject matter of the contract when it was first made, the contract remains valid.

Case: Bell v. Lever Bros Ltd (1932)

The defendants wished to terminate the employment of the plaintiff, their managing director. The plaintiff negotiated a payment of £30,000 in consideration for the cancellation of his employment contract. At a later stage, the defendants discovered that the plaintiff had used inside information to make profits on his own account. This was serious misconduct, which would have entitled the defendants to dismiss him without compensation. The defendants claimed that there had been a mistake as to the existence of a fundamental state of affairs, since the employment contract for which they had paid £30,000 was, in fact, valueless to the plaintiff. They sued to recover the compensation paid.

Held: The defendants could not recover compensation paid to the plaintiff, because there was not a sufficiently fundamental mistake on the part of either party at the time of the contract.

• Mistake as to the nature of a document

13. In general, if a person signs a document, they are bound by it, even if they do not read or understand the document. However, if a contract is signed by one party in the mistaken belief that they are signing a document of a fundamentally different nature, such a mistake will render the contract void. The mistaken party will be able to successfully plead '*non est factum*' ('it is not my deed').

14. The following conditions must be satisfied in repudiating a signed document as '*non est factum*':

(a) the signature must have been induced by fraud;
(b) there must be a fundamental difference between the legal effect of the document signed and that which the person who signed it believed it to have; and
(c) the party who signed the document must prove that they acted with reasonable care.

Case: Foster v. Mackinnon (1869)

The defendant, an elderly man of feeble sight, was asked to sign a guarantee. The document put before him was a bill of exchange for £3,000, which he mistakenly signed as acceptor. The bill of exchange was subsequently negotiated to the plaintiff. The defendant repudiated it, raising a defence of '*non est factum*'.

Held: As the defendant was not negligent in endorsing the bill of exchange, and the document signed was so different from what he believed it to be, he was not liable.

Case: Lewis v. Clay (1897)

The defendant was asked to sign two documents as a witness. Apart from the spaces for the signatures, the rest of the documents were covered. The reason given to the defendant for this was that the documents were of a private nature. The defendant, in fact, signed two promissory notes, which he later repudiated, claiming a defence of '*non est factum*'.

Held: Although the defendant was unable to say what type of document he thought he had signed, the defence of '*non est factum*' applied. He was held not liable.

IMPORTANT CASES

Numbers in brackets refer to paragraphs of this chapter

Raffles v. Wichelhaus (1864) .... (2)
Smith v. Hughes (1871) .... (3)
John O. Ferguson v. Merchant Banking Ltd (1992) .... (3)
Cundy v. Lindsay (1878) .... (5)
King's Norton Metal Co. v. Eldridge, Merrett & Co. Ltd (1897) .... (6)
Lewis v. Averay (1972) .... (7)
Galloway v. Galloway (1914) .... (8)
Couturier v. Hastie (1852) .... (8)
Cochrane v. Willis (1865) .... (9)
Grist v. Bailey (1966) .... (11)
Bell v. Lever Bros Ltd (1932) .... (12)
Foster v. Mackinnon (1869) .... (14)
Lewis v. Clay (1897) .... (14)

PROGRESS TEST

Numbers in brackets refer to paragraphs of this chapter

1. Does mistake as to (a) identity, or (b) quality, of the subject matter render a contract void? (2–3)
2. What are the consequences of a buyer fraudulently adopting the identity of a non-existent person while entering into a contract with a seller? (6)
3. If the subject matter of a contract no longer exists, is agreement between the unsuspecting parties binding? (8)
4. Can a person contract by mistake to buy their own property? (9)
5. Explain what is meant by the defence of '*non est factum*' and outline the conditions which must be satisfied in order for such a claim to be successful. (13–14)

chapter 17

DURESS AND UNDUE INFLUENCE

Topics covered

- Duress
- Undue influence

- Unconscionable bargains

Summary

A contract may be voidable if the consent of one of the parties is not freely given. This chapter examines the circumstances under which force and pressure may render a contract voidable.

1. It is presumed in law that any agreement between contracting parties is made voluntarily. Consequently, if an agreement is brought about by improper force or pressure, this will undermine the agreement, making the contract voidable.

• Duress

2. Duress is the actual or threatened violence to, or the false imprisonment of, the contracting party, their spouse or partner, parents or children. Its effect, if proved, is that the contract is voidable.

Case: Cummings v. Ince (1847)

An old woman was induced to make a settlement of her property in favour of a relative by a threat of detention in a mental home.

Held: The contract was voidable on the grounds of duress.

Case: Griffith v. Griffith (1944)

A young man was induced into marrying a young woman he was alleged to have made pregnant. The woman's mother, his own father and the local priest pressed him into entering a contract of marriage. Under a threat of imprisonment, the young man agreed to the marriage. Later, it became known that he was not the child's father and he petitioned for a decree of nullity.

Held: The contract of marriage was void for duress, but would have been upheld were he the father of the child.

3. In older cases, a threat to a person's goods or property has been held to be insufficient grounds for duress. In some recent English decisions, however, the courts have set aside contracts made under economic duress.

Case: The Atlantic Baron (1979)

The parties reached agreement on the purchase price to be paid for a ship. Shortly afterwards, a currency devaluation prompted the seller to claim a 10 per cent increase in the original price. When the purchaser refused to pay, the seller threatened to terminate the contract. As a result of this threat, the purchaser reluctantly agreed to the price increase.

Held: The threat by the seller amounted to economic duress, thereby rendering the contract voidable.

Case: Universe Tank Ships of Monrovia v. International Transport Workers Federation (1982)

The defendants, a trade union, had demanded payment of a specified sum of money from the plaintiffs in order to avoid boycott of their vessels by the trade union's members. The plaintiffs had felt they had no option but to comply with the demand.

Held: The threat of boycott constituted economic duress and the plaintiffs were entitled to recover all sums paid.

- **Undue influence**

4. The equitable doctrine of undue influence enables a court to set aside contracts, where an agreement has been reached by excessive pressure, which falls short of duress, being brought to bear on an individual by a potential beneficiary or third party.

Case: Bank of Nova Scotia v. Hogan & Hogan (1997)

Margaret Hogan had created a mortgage on property she owned in favour of the plaintiff to secure her husband's indebtedness. Prior to this, a solicitor from the firm who acted for both defendants had advised her that she was under no obligation to create this mortgage but if she did so the plaintiff would be entitled to sell the property in the event of a default by her husband. The plaintiff subsequently brought proceedings to enforce the security. Margaret Hogan, in defence, argued that the security had been obtained by reason of an inequality of bargaining power between herself and the plaintiff and by reason of the exercise of undue influence over her by the plaintiff. She also argued that the advice she had received from the solicitors was inadequate because they had also acted for the plaintiffs.

Held: There was an absence of evidence as to the exercise of undue influence by her husband or that he had in any way misrepresented the situation to her. Likewise, the relationship between the bank and Margaret Hogan did not of itself give rise to a presumption of undue influence and there was no evidence to suggest that any dealings between them had raised an inference of any such wrongdoing. Hence the defendants had no right to have the transaction set aside.

5. There is a presumption of undue influence where the parties to a contract are in a special relationship with each other, such that one of them, by reason of the confidence placed in them, is able to take unfair advantage of the other. Undue influence is presumed in contracts between a parent and child, an accountant and client, a trustee and beneficiary, a doctor and client, a religious adviser and disciple, a guardian and ward, among others.

6. Where the presumption of undue influence is made, the onus of proof is on the person in the dominant position to show that the other party expressed free and independent judgment. The stronger party can do this by showing that the weaker party had independent legal advice, that there was a full disclosure of all the relevant facts and that the consideration was adequate.

Case: White v. Meade (1840)

The plaintiff, an 18-year-old girl, entered a religious institution as a lodger. The defendants induced the plaintiff to take vows, without taking guidance from her brother, and to transfer property to the religious order. The deed for the transfer of property was prepared by the legal adviser to the religious institution.

Held: The plaintiff was able to set aside the transfer of property.

Case: Croker v. Croker (1870)

A son transferred property in favour of his father and subsequently sought to have the transfer set aside.

Held: The father was unable to prove that his son had exercised free will in transferring the property, so the contract was set aside.

7. Even if the presumption of undue influence does not arise automatically, it is possible to prove from the conduct of the parties in their dealings that one, in fact, did have undue influence.

Case: Williams v. Bayley (1866)

A father mortgaged property to a bank because a bank official had hinted at prosecuting his son for forgery of promissory notes with the father's signature.

Held: There had been undue influence, and, as a result, the agreement to execute the mortgage was set aside.

• Unconscionable bargains

8. A court will intervene in a contract, or other transaction, in cases in which one party is in a position to victimise the weaker party. Where an advantage is taken of a weak, distressed or mentally deficient person in negotiating a contract, the court will give relief against such unconscionable bargains.

9. The party wishing to uphold the contract must justify its fairness. Otherwise, the court will regard it as an unconscionable bargain, and will set it aside.

Case: Grealish v. Murphy (1946)

An elderly, illiterate and mentally deficient man transferred his farm, after consulting a solicitor, at under its value in favour of a younger man, who was unrelated.

Held: The bargain was invalid, because it was so improvident that no reasonable person would have entered into it. The solicitor had not done everything to advise fully on the implications of the transaction, since he was unaware of all the material facts and of the extent of his client's mental deficiency.

Case: Smyth v. Smyth (1978)

A young man, with a drink problem, sold part of the property of his trust to his trustee. The sale took a long time to complete and one solicitor acted for both parties.

Held: The bargain was neither improvident nor unconscionable, because the seller first raised the question of sale, the consideration paid was adequate and the length of time to complete the sale gave the seller plenty of time for reflection. The contract was, therefore, valid.

Case: Noonan v. Murphy (1987)

The plaintiff, a 73-year-old farmer, had transferred half of his land to his nephew, upon whom he was totally dependent. The transaction had been completed without the plaintiff getting any independent legal advice whatsoever.

Held: The contract was invalid because the transfer of land was so improvident or unconscionable that no reasonable person could have entered into it had he understood its effects.

IMPORTANT CASES

Numbers in brackets refer to paragraphs of this chapter

PROGRESS TEST

Numbers in brackets refer to paragraphs of this chapter

1. What is the difference between duress and undue influence? (2, 4)
2. Explain how a presumption of undue influence is established. (5)
3. How can the dominant party prove that the other party expressed free and independent judgment in making the bargain? (6)
4. Describe how a court may grant relief against unconscionable bargains. (8–9)

chapter 18

CONTRACTS ILLEGAL OR CONTRARY TO PUBLIC POLICY

Topics covered

- Contracts void by statute
- Contracts illegal and void at common law

- Contracts in restraint of trade

Summary

The law refuses to give effect to a contract for an illegal purpose, or for a purpose which offends public policy. This chapter examines the different types of such contracts.

1. A court will not enforce some types of contract because they are invalidated by statute or because they are prohibited under common law, since these are contrary to public policy. The most important examples of the latter type are those in unreasonable restraint of trade.

• Contracts void by statute

2. Some contracts are proscribed by statute. The following examples provide a sample of such contracts:

(a) contracts of insurance which fail to disclose an insurable interest are void under the Insurance Acts 1909–2000;
(b) contracts of hire purchase which are not evidenced in writing are void under the Consumer Credit Act 1995;
(c) contracts by way of wagering or gambling are void under the Gaming and Lotteries Acts 1956–1986;
(d) contracts for the conveyance of the family home, without the prior consent in writing of the other spouse, are void under the Family Home Protection Act 1976.

• Contracts illegal and void at common law

3. Contracts which will not be enforced because they are contrary to public policy include:

(a) contracts to commit a crime, tort or fraud;
(b) contracts promoting sexual immorality;

(c) contracts which detract from the institution of marriage;

(d) contracts which impede the administration of justice;

(e) contracts which serve to defraud the Revenue Commissioners;

(f) contracts which serve to corrupt public officials;

(g) contracts in unreasonable restraint of trade.

Case: Ennis v. Butterly (1997)

The plaintiff and defendant were married but not to each other, although they cohabited together as though they were husband and wife. The plaintiff alleged that the defendant had asked her to marry him as soon as possible. He had also allegedly made representations to her regarding a share of a substantial amount of money that he was about to receive and a directorship in a company provided she discontinue her business and live at home full-time as a home-maker. She claimed that she had acted on these representations but that the plaintiff had failed to honour his commitments.

Held: Even before the Family Law Act 1981 abolished the action for breach of promise of marriage and provided that such contracts could not give rise to enforceable rights, the agreement by persons to cohabit and to marry when possible was unenforceable as a matter of public policy. This would give such agreements a status similar to that of marriage contracts.

Contracts to commit a crime, tort or fraud

4. Such agreements are obviously contrary to public policy.

Case: Everett v. Williams (1725)

Both parties to the contract were highwaymen who turned to the courts seeking assistance concerning a 'partnership' arrangement.

Held: The contract was originally illegal and, therefore, void.

Case: Daly v. Daly (1870)

The defendant had been declared bankrupt, but had obtained such an order by fraud. The plaintiff, one of his creditors, aware of this fact, agreed not to attempt to have the bankruptcy set aside on condition that his debt was paid in full. A cheque for the full amount was given to the plaintiff, but was subsequently dishonoured.

Held: The contract was contrary to public policy, as the consideration, i.e. the undertaking not to attempt to have the bankruptcy set aside, was illegal.

Contracts promoting sexual immorality

5. Even if the conduct contemplated by the contract is not in itself illegal, a contract which promotes sexual immorality will be held to be illegal.

Case: Pearce v. Brooks (1866)

The plaintiff hired out a carriage to a prostitute who, to the knowledge of the owner, intended to parade along the streets in the carriage as a means of soliciting clients, and would pay for the carriage out of her immoral earnings. She later refused to pay the agreed amount and the plaintiff sued to recover it.

Held: The plaintiff's knowledge of the immoral purpose behind the contract rendered the contract illegal and void.

Contracts which detract from the institution of marriage

6. The courts regard it as a matter of public interest to uphold the sanctity of marriage. This is enforced by Article 41 of the Constitution. Contracts in restraint of marriage, contracts for future separation and marriage brokerage contracts, whereby one person agrees to procure a marriage for a money payment, are void.

Case: Williamson v. Gihan (1805)

The plaintiff contracted to pay £500 to the defendant in return for assistance in helping a young lady to elope so he, the plaintiff, could marry her. The money was to be paid from his wife's estate, and when the plaintiff rescinded his promise, the defendant sued for the amount agreed.

Held: The plaintiff was not entitled to fetter his wife's property. In these circumstances, the contract was void because it was illegal at common law.

Contracts which impede the administration of justice

7. Contracts which serve to frustrate the administration of justice are not of themselves criminal, but they are illegal and cannot give rise to enforceable contractual obligations.

Case: Brady v. Flood (1841)

The plaintiff paid a sum of money to the defendant in return for a promise to have criminal charges of conspiracy against the plaintiff's son dropped. The plaintiff later sued to recover the amount.

Held: The judge refused to hear litigation on the transaction. He stated, 'I will not try this case. You are parties to an illegal contract and, whoever has got the money, I will allow him to keep it'.

Contracts which serve to defraud the Revenue Commissioners

8. The courts will not enforce a contract which defrauds the Revenue Commissioners through, for example, a misstatement of consideration, or a collective arrangement between an employer and an employee in order to reduce liability to PRSI contributions, because it is void as illegal at common law.

Case: Lewis v. Squash Ireland Ltd (1983)

The plaintiff brought an action for unfair dismissal against the defendants, his former employers. The employers and employee had been party to an agreement whereby the payment of salary was treated in the company's books as 'expenses', in an attempt to avoid the payment of income tax and social insurance contributions.

Held: The claim for unfair dismissal was not upheld because this collusive arrangement had been designed to defraud the Revenue Commissioners, and was consequently void as illegal at common law.

Contracts which serve to corrupt public officials

9. A contract to promote corruption in public life is void as being illegal at common law.

Case: Lord Mayor of Dublin v. Hayes (1876)

The defendant, on being appointed Marshall of the City of Dublin, a position which also gave him the post of Registrar of Pawnbrokers, agreed to accept a fixed salary and to hand over to the treasury of the plaintiff those fees he was entitled to collect. He was subsequently sued by the plaintiff for failure to comply with the arrangement.

Held: The promise to transfer the fees was void because the appointment was adjudged by the court to have been made in exchange for the defendant's promise to pay over the aforementioned monies, thereby promoting corruption among public officials.

Contracts in unreasonable restraint of trade

10. A contract in unreasonable restraint of trade is one whereby the action of one party to a contract restricts the other party from freely exercising their trade, profession or calling in such a way and with such persons as they choose. Such contracts are prima facie void, as they are contrary to public interest.

11. We shall now examine in detail the circumstances under which a restraint of trade can be justified and be enforceable.

• Contracts in restraint of trade

12. A restriction on the freedom of an individual to trade will be upheld if it is shown to be in the interest of both parties and the public. The onus of proof in any action in respect of contracts, or, more correctly, clauses in restraint of trade lies with the party trying to enforce it.

13. A restraint of trade clause may be justified and enforceable if:

(a) the person who imposes it has a genuine interest to protect;
(b) the restraint is reasonable between the parties as a protection of that interest; and
(c) the restraint is also reasonable to the public at large.

14. The main categories of contracts in restraint of trade which may be upheld as being reasonable are as follows:

(a) restrictions imposed on ex-employees;
(b) restrictions imposed on the sellers of a business;
(c) solus (exclusive dealing) agreements;
(d) resale price maintenance agreements.

Restrictions imposed on ex-employees

15. Any restraint imposed upon an employee's freedom to take up other employment, or to carry on business on their own account, after leaving the employer's service, will not be upheld unless it can be justified.

16. A restraint must be no wider than is necessary to protect the employer's trade secrets or business connections. Therefore, if a restraint is imposed on an employee who is not in a position to gain the confidence of the employer's customers or who has no access to the employer's secrets, it will be void. Furthermore, if it is excessive as regards the prohibited trades, the geographical area to which it applies, or the time for which the restraint is to last, it is also void. The reasonableness of the extent and duration of the restraint depends on the type of business to be protected.

Case: Mulligan v. Corr (1925)

The defendant, a solicitor's apprentice, agreed that on leaving the plaintiff's employment he would not practise within thirty miles of Ballina and Charlestown, and within twenty miles of Ballaghaderreen. The plaintiff sought an injunction to compel the plaintiff to abide by the terms of the agreement.

Held: Even if the severance of the restriction regarding practice within twenty miles of Ballaghaderreen were to take place, the geographical area was too large and went far beyond what was reasonably required for the protection of a solicitor's practice.

Case: Fitch v. Dewes (1921)

The defendant, a former law clerk, had qualified as a solicitor while being employed by the plaintiff. On the commencement of his employment he had contracted not to practise as a solicitor within seven miles of the Town Hall at Tamworth. The plaintiff sought an injunction to prevent the defendant from a breach of the employment contract.

Held: The restraint on the employee was reasonable in the above circumstances because, though unlimited as to the duration, it confined the restraint to a reasonable space.

Case: Macken v. O'Reilly (1978)

The plaintiff, an international showjumper, challenged a rule of the Equestrian Federation of Ireland which obliged competitors representing Ireland in international competitions to ride only Irish-bred horses.

Held: This rule was not an unreasonable restraint, since it was designed to protect the public interest, i.e. to protect the Irish-bred horse industry.

Case: ECI European Chemical Industries Ltd v. Bell (1981)

The defendant was an industrial chemist who, in the process of training and employment, acquired trade secrets from his employer. He had agreed that if he were to leave the employment, he would abstain from using these trade secrets for his own or another competitor's profit for a period of two years. After over six years, he gave notice of termination of his employment with the plaintiff and proposed to commence employment immediately with one of the plaintiff's competitors. The plaintiff sought an injunction to prevent this course of action.

Held: An interlocutory injunction was granted. The restraint of trade was prima facie valid, since the aforementioned interests were ones which an employer is entitled to protect.

Case: Hollis & Co. v. Stocks (2000)

The plaintiffs, a small firm of solicitors, sought an injunction to enforce a restrictive covenant in the defendant's contract of employment, namely, 'You will not, for 12 months from the termination of your employment, work within ten miles of the firm's office to include not advising or representing any clients whatsoever at Sutton-in-Ashfield or Mansfield Police Station or Mansfield Magistrates' Court.' The defendant argued that the covenant was void because it was wider than was reasonably required to protect the plaintiffs' interests in that it prevented him from carrying out any work whatsoever within the ten mile radius, not only work as a solicitor.

Held: The contract between the parties started with a definition of the defendant's employment as being that of a solicitor and all the terms of the contract were directed to that employment. The clause itself, although it did not specify so, plainly meant work as a solicitor. Both the area of 10 miles and the period of one year were deemed to be perfectly reasonable, and therefore an injunction was granted.

Restrictions imposed on the sellers of a business

17. A restraint on the seller of a business from doing business with old customers or clients will be more readily upheld in favour of the buyer, because goodwill has been paid for it. The restraint will only be effective if there is a genuine sale of the goodwill of the business and the restraint is not excessive.

Case: RGDATA v. Tara Publishing Co. Ltd (1995)

The plaintiff association sold its interest in the title and ownership of two publications, *Retail News* and *Retail News Yearbook*, to the defendant in 1985. The plaintiff agreed not to publish any other publications in the Republic of Ireland for a period of twenty years and also agreed that *Retail News* would be the only official publication of the plaintiff association. The plaintiff subsequently sought a declaration by the courts that this latter clause was rendered void by the Competition Act 1991. The defendant counter-claimed for damages, alleging that the plaintiff had broken the agreement by publishing a document, which had been described as 'An RGDATA publication'.

Held: The publication of the document with the above description constituted a breach of contract, and damages were awarded to compensate the defendant for the loss in advertising revenue arising from the unlawful competition. However, it was also held that the scope and duration of the agreement was restrictive and that the plaintiff was free to publish or assist in publications if, and only if, such publications were not described, represented or held out to be its official publications.

Case: Nordenfelt v. Maxim Nordenfelt Guns and Ammunition Co. Ltd (1894)

The defendants, owners of an armaments business, sold it to the plaintiff and agreed in writing not to carry on a similar business anywhere in the world for a duration of twenty-five years, except on behalf of the purchasers.

Held: The restraint was neither excessive nor contrary to public policy, and was, therefore, held to be valid.

Case: British Concrete Co. v. Scheiff (1921)

The defendant, who carried out a small business of making a single type of steel road reinforcement, sold his business to the plaintiffs, manufacturers of road reinforcements used throughout the UK. The defendant agreed in writing not to compete with the plaintiffs in the sale or manufacture of road reinforcements in any part of the UK.

Held: The restraint was too wide, because it attempted to protect the plaintiffs from more than what they bought. The restraint of trade was, therefore, void.

Solus (exclusive dealing) agreements

18. A solus agreement is the name given to a contract by which a trader agrees not to use goods except together with others made by the same manufacturer, or agrees not to buy or sell goods except from or to a particular person.

19. In general, such exclusive dealing agreements are valid since the parties bargain in a position of equal strength and do not create a market structure detrimental to the public. The duration, therefore, of such restraints is usually the most important factor in assessing the reasonableness of these agreements.

Case: McEllistrem v. Ballymacelligott Co-operative Agricultural and Dairy Society (1919)

The plaintiff was a member of a Kerry co-op, which had been formed to develop and improve dairy farming in the district. The members of the co-op were bound by its rules to supply all their milk to the co-op, and were precluded from supplying any other local creamery.

Held: The restraint of trade went further than necessary in protecting the supply of milk to the co-op. The contract was therefore invalid due to its unreasonableness.

Case: Continental Oil Company of Ireland Ltd v. Moynihan (1973)

The defendant, a petrol retailer, entered into a solus agreement in 1970, which provided that he would purchase all his petrol from the plaintiffs at their scheduled prices; he was to take the largest possible consignments, not less than 800 gallons; he would keep the station neat and clean; he would not reduce the number of pumps; the agreement would last for five years and he would purchase the petrol pumps on interest-free hire-purchase terms. The defendant later refused to take any further supplies when the plaintiffs changed their pricing arrangements. The plaintiffs sought an injunction.

Held: The agreement was reasonable and its enforcement was not against the public interest. An injunction was granted.

Resale price maintenance agreements
20. Agreements between producers or retailers, which keep the price of goods or services at a certain level, are valid unless such agreements are designed to produce a monopoly or the price level maintained is unreasonable.

Case: Cade & Sons Ltd v. John Daly & Co. Ltd (1910)

The members of the South of Ireland Mineral Water Manufacturers and Bottlers Trade Protection Association agreed that no member would sell alcohol or minerals below fixed prices for a period of six months, within sixteen miles of the city of Cork. The defendant, a member of the association, sought to have this arrangement overturned as being unreasonable.

Held: The restraint was binding on the defendant. The agreement was reasonably made with the intention of protecting local trade and, therefore, valid at common law.

IMPORTANT CASES

Numbers in brackets refer to paragraphs of this chapter

IMPORTANT STATUTES

Insurance Acts 1909–2000
Consumer Credit Act 1995
Gaming and Lotteries Acts 1956–1986
Family Home Protection Act 1976

PROGRESS TEST

Numbers in brackets refer to paragraphs of this chapter

1. Give three examples of contracts which are void by statute. (2)
2. What is the implication of a contract which serves to frustrate the administration of justice? (7)
3. Define a contract in unreasonable restraint of trade. (10)
4. What must be shown to justify and enforce a restraint of trade? (13)
5. How can a restriction imposed on an ex-employee's freedom to take up other employment, or to carry on business on their own account, be justified? (16)
6. Why will a restriction on the seller of a business from trading with old customers be more readily upheld in favour of the buyer? (17)
7. What is a solus agreement, and how is the doctrine of restraint of trade applied to such a contract? (18–19)
8. When will a price maintenance agreement be invalid? (20)

chapter 19

CAPACITY TO CONTRACT

Topics covered

- Minors
- Corporations

- Persons of unsound mind

Summary
The law seeks to protect certain persons by limiting their legal capacity to enter contracts. This chapter examines those legal persons who are unable to contract freely.

1. In order for an agreement to be a valid contract, both parties must have capacity to contract. In general, all persons have full capacity to enter into legally binding contracts. Different rules apply, however, to minors, corporations and persons of unsound mind. These have only restricted capacity and contracts made by them may be valid, voidable or void.

• Minors
2. A minor (or infant) is, by virtue of the Age of Majority Act 1985, a person who has not reached the age of eighteen.

Valid contracts of a minor
3. A minor may enter binding contracts for necessary goods and services, and they may enter beneficial contracts of employment or apprenticeship.

4. Necessary goods, or 'necessaries', are defined as goods suitable to the condition in life of the particular minor and to their actual requirements at the time of sale and delivery. The goods (or services) must, therefore, satisfy a double test of 'suitability' and 'need' if they are to be necessaries. The test in each case is what is reasonable for that particular minor, and the burden of proof rests with the seller.

5. The seller must first prove that the goods are capable of being necessaries. An item of 'mere luxury', for example a racehorse, cannot be a necessary. However, a luxurious item of utility, such as a gold watch, may be defined as such. This broad definition of necessaries has been adopted to give protection to suppliers who give credit to minors from wealthy families.

6. The seller must then prove that the goods are, in fact, necessary for the particular minor in question. Necessaries do not include goods with which the minor is already well supplied, and so does not need any more. Minors are not liable if they have an adequate supply of the goods, even if the supplier did not know this.

Case: Nash v. Inman (1908)

The plaintiff, a tailor, sued the defendant, a Cambridge undergraduate, for the price of clothes, including eleven fancy waistcoats, which he had supplied to the minor over a period of nine months.

Held: The clothes were suitable for the defendant's use, but the plaintiff was unable to show that the minor was not adequately supplied at the time. The clothes, therefore, were not necessaries, and the plaintiff could not recover the monies due to him.

7. Beneficial contracts of employment or apprenticeship are also binding on a minor if they may reasonably be regarded as for the benefit of the minor. If the terms, on the whole, are too harsh or oppressive, they will be invalid.

Case: Doyle v. White City Stadium (1935)

Jack Doyle, who was a minor, obtained a licence to compete as a professional boxer from the British Boxing Board of Control. The terms of the licence provided that should the licensee be disqualified for a foul blow (as, in fact, happened) his portion of the purse would be forfeited. The plaintiff challenged the terms of the licence, alleging that as the contract was not for his benefit, they could not bind him.

Held: The terms of the licence were beneficial as a whole, since it was generally in the plaintiff's interests that illegal blows be prohibited. This was true even though on this occasion the terms operated against him.

Case: De Francesco v. Barnum (1890)

A minor entered into an apprenticeship for stage dancing with the plaintiff. The terms of the contract provided that she was entirely at the disposal of the plaintiff; that she would only get paid if he actually employed her; that she could not get married during the apprenticeship and that his consent was required before she could accept any other professional engagement with the defendant. The minor subsequently accepted a professional engagement with the defendant, who was sued by the plaintiff in the tort of inducing a breach of contract.

Held: The contract was, on the whole, unreasonably harsh and oppressive and, as such, could not be described as being beneficial to the minor. It was held to be invalid.

Voidable contracts of a minor
8. Certain long-term contracts will be binding on both parties, unless they are

avoided by the minor before, or within a reasonable time after, reaching the age of eighteen. The other party cannot avoid the contract.

9. Contracts voidable by a minor are contracts whereby a minor acquires interests of a continuing nature and undertakes obligations incidental to them. These include:

(a) contracts involving land, e.g. leases;
(b) purchases of shares in a company;
(c) partnership agreements; and
(d) marriage settlements.

10. Although a minor may repudiate such contracts, the minor may not be able to recover money or property which has been paid or transferred under the contract, unless no consideration whatsoever has been received for it.

Case: Steinberg v. Scala (1925)

The plaintiff, a minor, applied for and was allotted shares in the defendant company. When she was requested to pay the balance of the purchase price, she attempted to avoid the contract and recover the money that she had already paid.

Held: The plaintiff had the right to rescind the contract and be removed from the register of members. However, she could not recover what she had already paid, because she had received some consideration, such as the right to receive dividends and the right to vote at company meetings.

Case: Blake v. Concannon (1871)

The defendant, a minor, had leased land from the plaintiff and enjoyed its use up until the time he reached the age of majority, whereupon he repudiated the contract and refused to pay rent due.

Held: The defendant was entitled to repudiate the lease, but was liable for the rent up to the date of the repudiation.

Void contracts of a minor

11. Certain types of contracts which are entered into by minors are held to be absolutely void. Such contracts cannot be confirmed by the minors nor enforced against them.

12. The Infants Relief Act 1874 states that the following contracts are absolutely void:

(a) contracts for the repayment of money lent, or to be lent, to an infant (minor);
(b) contracts for goods (other than necessaries) supplied, or to be supplied, to an infant.

13. The Betting and Loans (Infants) Act 1892 makes void any new agreement by a person after reaching the age of majority to repay a previous loan contracted during minority.

14. As with voidable contracts which are avoided, the minor cannot recover money or property under a void contract which has been performed, unless there has been total failure of consideration.

Case: Pearce v. Brain (1929)

The plaintiff exchanged his motor cycle and sidecar for the defendant's second-hand motor car. After being driven by the plaintiff for about seventy miles, the car broke down due to a defect in the back axle. The plaintiff immediately took an action for the recovery of the motor cycle and sidecar on the grounds that the contract was void under the Infants Relief Act 1874.

Held: The plaintiff was unable to show a total failure of consideration because he had used the car, albeit for only four days.

• Corporations

15. Companies formed under the Companies Acts and statutory corporations are limited by their constitutions, contained in the objects clause of the memorandum of association and incorporating statutes respectively, to entering only certain types of contracts. If they make contracts outside these limits, the contracts are said to be *ultra vires* (beyond the power) and void.

Case: Re Bansha Woollen Mill Co. Ltd (1888)

A shareholder and director loaned money to the company, which was empowered by its memorandum to borrow money but restricted by its articles as to the amount of such borrowing. He later sought the recovery of his money but was refused on the grounds that the company had been acting *ultra vires*.

Held: The party who loaned the money was privy to the activities of the company, and ought to have known the objects of the company. Since the shareholder and director, therefore, ought to have known that the company was acting *ultra vires*, he was not entitled to recover his money.

16. The harshness of the *ultra vires* doctrine preventing a third party, honestly dealing with a company, from being able to sue on a contract has led towards certain statutory reform.

17. Under s. 8, the Companies Act 1963, a company cannot defeat the claim of a third party contracting with it, unless it can be shown that the third party was actually aware that the company was acting *ultra vires*.

18. This provision has since been joined by the European Communities (Companies) Regulations 1973, whereby contracts made in good faith with directors of companies are deemed to be valid. Where the contract is *ultra vires*, it will still be binding on the company, but the directors will be personally liable to the company for any loss suffered as a result of entering into such a contract.

19. A contract may still be *ultra vires* and void where the third party is supplied with a copy of the memorandum and mistakenly believes it to authorise the transaction.

Case: Northern Bank Finance Corporation Ltd v. Quinn and Achates Investment Co. (1979)

The plaintiffs contracted to loan the first defendant money on the condition that an officer of the second defendant would guarantee the loan by the mortgage of some of the company's property. An officer of the plaintiffs inspected the memorandum and articles of association, but failed to appreciate that the company was not empowered to guarantee loans. When the first defendant defaulted, the company argued that the transaction, namely signature of a guarantee, was *ultra vires.*

Held: The plaintiffs were aware of the contents of the memorandum, but failed to appreciate their significance. The plaintiffs' action against the company was dismissed.

• Persons of unsound mind

20. If a person is insane or intoxicated when entering into a contract, the contract is voidable if it can be shown that:

(a) the person was at the time incapable of understanding the nature of the contract; and
(b) the other party knew, or ought to have known, of this disability.

21. The burden of proof is on the party suffering from the incapacity to prove the knowledge of the other party.

22. A contract made by a person of unsound mind may be ratified on recovery to a sober or lucid state, and thereby become completely valid.

Case: Mathews v. Baxter (1873)

The defendant, while in a drunken state, contracted to buy some houses from the plaintiff. He later ratified the contract when he became sober.

Held: The contract was binding on the defendant.

Case: Hassard v. Smith (1872)

The plaintiff leased property, which included land, a house and garden, to the defendant for a period of five years. The plaintiff later attempted to have the lease set aside on the grounds that he was of unsound mind at the date of the lease and had let the property at an undervalue.

Held: The contract was an honest and bona fide transaction, and was completely executed. Assuming that the plaintiff was insane at the time of the contract, there was no evidence to show that the defendant had any actual knowledge of this fact.

23. The Sale of Goods Act 1893 provides that when necessaries are supplied, with the intention of obtaining payment, to a person of unsound mind, they must pay a reasonable price for them in any case. Necessaries, as outlined before, are goods suitable to the condition in life of such a person and to their actual requirements at the time of sale and delivery.

IMPORTANT CASES

Numbers in brackets refer to paragraphs of this chapter

Nash v. Inman (1908) .... (6)
Doyle v. White City Stadium (1935) .... (7)
De Francesco v. Barnum (1890) .... (7)
Steinberg v. Scala (1925) .... (10)
Blake v. Concannon (1871) .... (10)
Pearce v. Brain (1929) .... (14)
Re Bansha Woollen Mill Co. Ltd (1888) .... (15)
Northern Bank Finance Corporation Ltd v. Quinn and Achates
    Investment Co. (1979) .... (19)
Mathews v. Baxter (1873) .... (22)
Hassard v. Smith (1872) .... (22)

IMPORTANT STATUTES

Age of Majority Act 1985
Infants Relief Act 1874
Betting and Loans (Infants) Act 1892
Sale of Goods Act 1893

PROGRESS TEST

Numbers in brackets refer to paragraphs of this chapter

1. Define a minor. (2)
2. When may a minor be bound to pay for goods? (3–6)

3. Under what circumstances may a minor be bound by a contract for employment or apprenticeship? (7)
4. Give three examples of contracts which are voidable by a minor. (9)
5. Explain the circumstances under which a contract entered into by a minor can be held to be absolutely void. Can a minor recover money or property under such a contract? (12–14)
6. What is the doctrine of *ultra vires*? (15)
7. When is a person of unsound mind not bound by a contract? (20)

chapter 20

DISCHARGE OF CONTRACT

Topics covered

- Discharge by performance
- Discharge by agreement
- Discharge by frustration
- Discharge by breach

Summary

Once the requirements of a valid contract have been established, the parties to the contract proceed to fulfil their obligations. This chapter considers the ways by which the parties may be discharged from those obligations.

1. There are four ways by which the rights and obligations of the parties to a valid contract may be terminated, i.e. extinguished, determined or discharged. These are, by:

(a) performance;
(b) agreement;
(c) frustration;
(d) breach.

• Discharge by performance

2. In general, when both parties have performed their contractual obligations, the contract is extinguished or discharged. The performance must be complete and be exactly in accordance with the terms of the contract. A party who does not precisely perform the contract will be in breach and may not be able to sue on the contract to recover payment or other benefits.

Case: Re Moore v. Landauer (1921)

A supplier of canned fruit contracted to supply 3,100 cases of the goods, packed thirty tins to a case. When he delivered the goods, the number of tins met the contract requirement, but about half the shipment was packed in cases of twenty-four tins each. The market value of the goods supplied was unaffected, but the buyer attempted to reject the entire consignment because of the failure to meet the contract description.

Held: The buyer was entitled to rescind the contract because the goods were not of the contract description. There had been a breach of contract, and so it was not discharged by performance.

Case: Coughlan v. Moloney (1905)

The plaintiff, a builder, agreed in July 1902 to build a house for the defendant for £200, and to have it completed by December 1902. The building was left incomplete at that date and, the following November, the defendant engaged another builder to finish the work. The original builder sued for the value of the work completed.

Held: The claim was dismissed because the contract was dependent on complete performance. The defendant had been left with no option but to accept a partially constructed house built on his own land.

3. Where prompt performance is an essential condition in a contract, it is said that 'time is of the essence', and that late performance will not discharge obligations.

4. Time will be of the essence where it is an express or implied term of the contract, or if time is vital considering the particular nature of the contract. However, even if time was not originally of the essence, either party to the contract could make it so, once the time of performance has been reached, by serving a notice to complete within a reasonable time on the other party.

5. There are a number of exceptions to the general rule that unless both parties have performed their obligations completely and exactly, the contract is not extinguished.

Partial performance
6. Where a contract may be divided into several parts, payment for parts that have been completed may be claimed. Or, if performance is by instalments, it is possible to recover payment for each instalment completed unless the intention of the parties is to treat the contract as an entire agreement.

Case: Taylor v. Laird (1856)

The plaintiff contracted to captain a ship up the River Niger. The terms of the contract allowed for him to be paid a wage of £50 per month, but when he abandoned the job before it was completed, the defendant refused to pay him any wages for the months completed.

Held: The contract had provided for performance and payment in monthly instalments, and the plaintiff was thereby entitled to payment for each complete month.

7. Where partial performance of the contract is accepted by both parties, then the contract is discharged. The law assumes thereby a willingness and intention to make a reasonable payment for the work done, and an action may otherwise be brought on a *quantum meruit* ('as much as he deserved', see Chapter 21, para. 26).

8. A person may also sue on a *quantum meruit* where completion of the contract is prevented by the other party.

Case: Planche v. Colburn (1831)

The plaintiff contracted to write a book to be published by instalments in the defendant's periodical. After the plaintiff had carried out some research, and written some of the book, the defendant ceased publication of his periodical.

Held: The plaintiff had been wrongfully prevented from performing the contract and could therefore recover on a *quantum meruit* for the work he had carried out under the contract.

Substantial performance
9. The doctrine of substantial performance states that where a contract has been performed as completely as a reasonable person could expect, the person is entitled to sue on the contract for the contract price, less a reduction for the cost of rectifying any defects. This removes the inequity of depriving a person, who has substantially performed what they contracted to do, of all remuneration.

Case: Hoenig v. Isaacs (1952)

The plaintiff undertook to decorate the defendant's flat for a price of £750, to be paid in instalments as the work was being completed. The defendant made regular payments, totalling £400, in the course of the execution of the contract, but then, in objection to the quality of work which had been performed, refused outright to pay the outstanding amount. It was estimated at the trial that the cost of making good any defective work and completing the job was £56.

Held: The plaintiff was entitled to receive the balance outstanding of the total contract price, less a deduction of £56 damages to cover the costs of rectifying the defects.

• Discharge by agreement
10. A contract being formed by agreement may also be varied or terminated by agreement. It may be discharged by the agreement of the parties to the contract by:

(a) conditions contained in the contract;
(b) waiver of the contract;
(c) release of one of the parties;
(d) novation of the old contract.

Conditions contained in the contract
11. A condition precedent, designed to prevent a contract coming into effect prior to the condition being met, and a condition subsequent, whereby a contract will no longer remain in effect following the later happening of an event, are means by which the contract may include provisions for its own discharge.

12. Examples of conditions subsequent are to be found in some contracts of a continuing nature, such as franchise or employment contracts, which may be discharged by agreement when the required notice is given by one or other of the parties.

Waiver of the contract

13. Where the contract remains wholly unperformed by either party, they may agree to cancel the contract by a simple waiver. However, this agreement to discharge the contract is itself a new contract which must be accompanied by consideration. Under this type of discharge by agreement, the consideration will be the waiving of rights and obligations by both parties to the contract. This is a bilateral discharge.

Case: McKillop v. McMullen (1979)

The defendant contracted to sell land to the plaintiff before a specified date, subject to the plaintiff acquiring planning permission and the defendant acquiring a right of way over a road to be built on the land. Although the planning permission had not been acquired by the specified date, the defendant did not rescind the contract. Planning permission was eventually acquired, but shortly afterwards the defendant attempted to rescind the contract.

Held: The defendant was not allowed to rescind this particular contract, because he had implicitly waived his right to terminate the contract for failure to acquire planning permission by the specified date. The court also held, however, that this waiver need not be unqualified and that the right to terminate the contract could still be exercised upon giving reasonable notice of a new date.

Release of one of the parties

14. One party to the contract who has wholly or partly performed their obligations may discharge the contract by releasing the other party from their obligations. This unilateral discharge also requires consideration so as to make it effective. This usually takes the form of a cancellation fee, which is termed 'accord and satisfaction' for the obligations foregone.

Novation of the old contract

15. Where the parties to an unperformed contract substitute it with a new one, this is referred to as novation of the old contract. The necessary consideration is provided in the new contract. An example of novation would arise in an agreement to transfer one party's obligations to some other third party, thereby replacing the old contract with a new one.

• Discharge by frustration

16. If some event occurs during the course of the contract, without the fault of either party, which renders the contract fundamentally different in its nature from the contract originally entered into by the parties, it may be discharged by frustration.

17. A contract may be discharged by frustration owing to:

(a) destruction of the subject matter of the contract;
(b) non-occurrence of an event upon which the contract is dependent;
(c) incapacity to perform a contract for personal services;
(d) government intervention or subsequent illegality.

Destruction of the subject matter of the contract
18. Where the subject matter of the contract is destroyed, and this renders the contract impossible to perform, the contract may be discharged by frustration.

Case: Taylor v. Caldwell (1863)

The defendant let a music hall for a number of concerts to take place on specified dates. The hall was completely destroyed by fire before the first of these, and the plaintiff sued the owner of the music hall for damages arising out of breach of contract.

Held: The contract was discharged by frustration: performance of the contract was impossible due to the destruction of the subject matter and, therefore, the defendant could not be held liable for damages.

Non-occurrence of an event upon which the contract is dependent
19. Where further performance of a contract would be in appearance only, as the real or substantial purpose cannot be fulfilled, the contract may be discharged by frustration.

Case: Krell v. Henry (1903)

The defendant rented a room overlooking the route of the coronation procession of Edward VII for the day of the ceremony so as to view the procession. Upon cancellation of the ceremony, due to the illness of the King, the defendant refused to pay on request and was subsequently sued by the plaintiff in an attempt to recover the agreed fee.

Held: The coronation procession was the sole occasion of the contract, and the non-occurrence of this event thereby frustrated the contract. In such circumstances, the defendant was held not liable for payment for the room.

Incapacity to perform a contract for personal services
20. A contract to perform personal services may be frustrated by illness (where personal incapacity is established), death, imprisonment or a call-up for military service. If vicarious performance is possible, however, there will be no frustration.

Case: Condor v. Barron Knights (1966)

The plaintiff, under contract to perform as a drummer with the defendant pop group, became seriously ill and was advised by his doctor to restrict his performances to four nights per week. His contract was terminated.

Held: Personal incapacity did not allow the plaintiff to perform his duties in the manner as originally envisaged by the parties, and the contract was therefore correctly discharged by frustration.

Government intervention or subsequent illegality

21. A contract may be frustrated where a government intervenes to restrain or suspend its performance, or where a subsequent change in the law renders the contract illegal.

Case: O'Crowley v. Minister for Justice (1934)

The plaintiff made a claim in respect of pension rights relating to a judicial office which had been abolished by statute.

Held: The contract was frustrated by the intervention of the legislature in suspending its performance.

22. There will, however, be no frustration, where:

(a) the contingency has been provided for in the express terms of the contract;
(b) the event was foreseen, or reasonably foreseeable, so that it should have been covered by a contractual term;
(c) mere inconvenience, hardship or loss has arisen; or
(d) an alternative means of performance is still possible.

Case: Davis Contractors v. Fareham Urban District Council (1956)

The plaintiffs had entered into a contract in July 1946 to build seventy-eight houses for the defendants for a fixed sum within a period of eight months. Due to unexpected circumstances, adequate supplies of labour were not available and the work took twenty-two months to complete. It also cost much more than the agreed price. The plaintiffs claimed that the contract had been frustrated owing to the scarcity of labour, and sought damages on a *quantum meruit* basis.

Held: The plaintiffs were not entitled to treat the contract as frustrated. The fact that there had been an unforeseen event which made the contract more onerous than had been contemplated was not sufficient grounds for relieving the contractors of the obligation they had undertaken.

Case: McGuill v. Aer Lingus and United Airlines (1983)

The plaintiff booked a holiday with the defendants. Due to strike action by the defendants' employees, the plaintiff was carried on another flight by a different airline, but at a higher price. The plaintiff sued for breach of contract, and the defendants argued that the contract had been frustrated by the strike.

Held: The defendants were aware of the possibility of a strike, but entered into the contract without including an exemption clause to safeguard their position in the event of a strike taking place. Consequently, the defendants were not able to use a defence of frustration and were liable for breach of contract.

23. When a contract is discharged by frustration, the parties may recover payments made under the terms of the contract to the extent that there has been a total failure of consideration. If either party, however, has received a valuable benefit (other than money) under the contract, prior to it being discharged, the court may order them to pay all or part of that value to the other party.

• Discharge by breach
24. A contract may be terminated by:

(a) actual breach; or
(b) anticipatory breach.

Actual breach
25. If a party to a contract breaks a condition, the injured party may treat the contract as discharged. We have already seen in *Poussard* v. *Spiers* (1876) (see Chapter 13, para. 14) that breach of a condition is sufficiently serious to entitle the injured party to repudiate the contract. Mere breach of warranty is not enough.

Case: Robb & Co. v. James (1881)

The plaintiffs purchased fabrics at an auction held by the defendants. A condition of the contract was that the price be paid and the goods collected within twenty-four hours. A dispute arose as to the price to be paid, and the plaintiffs refused to pay the requested amount and remove the goods. The defendants sold the fabrics to a third party, and the plaintiffs sued for breach of contract.

Held: The plaintiffs had failed to perform the most essential term of the contract, i.e. to pay for and remove the fabrics within twenty-four hours. The defendants, therefore, were perfectly entitled to treat the contract as abandoned by the plaintiffs, and to detain and resell the goods.

26. The injured party, on the other hand, may prefer to ignore the breach and to tender performance on their own part, and merely claim damages for the loss suffered.

Anticipatory breach
27. A party to a contract may break a condition merely by declaring in advance that they are unable or unwilling to fulfil their obligations under the contract. In

such circumstances, the other party may take this as 'anticipatory breach' of contract, thereby allowing them to treat the contract as discharged and to bring an action for damages immediately, even before the time agreed for performance.

Case: Hochster v. De La Tour (1853)

The plaintiff was employed as a courier to accompany the defendant on a tour commencing on 1 June. The defendant, however, wrote to the plaintiff on 11 May, saying that his services were no longer required. The plaintiff immediately commenced legal proceedings on 22 May for breach of contract, to which the defendant objected on the grounds that the breach was not actionable until 1 June.

Held: Although the previously agreed commencement date of employment was in the future, the plaintiff was entitled to instigate legal proceedings once the anticipatory breach had happened on 11 May.

28. The injured party has the option to ignore the anticipatory breach and, instead, allow the contract to continue until such a time as there is an actual breach. Under such circumstances, the opportunity is afforded to the party guilty of anticipatory breach to change their mind and fulfil their obligations under the contract after all.

IMPORTANT CASES

Numbers in brackets refer to paragraphs of this chapter

PROGRESS TEST

Numbers in brackets refer to paragraphs of this chapter

1. List the ways by which the rights and obligations of the parties to a valid contract may be terminated. (1)
2. Under what circumstances will late performance of a contract fail to discharge obligations? (3–4)
3. When may a party to a contract be entitled to payment without having performed their obligations completely and exactly? (6–9)
4. How can a contract be discharged by agreement? (10)
5. Differentiate between a condition precedent and a condition subsequent. (11)
6. When will a contract be discharged 'in accord and satisfaction'? (14)
7. List and describe the circumstances under which a contract may be discharged for frustration. (17–23)
8. What is anticipatory breach? What options does it offer the injured party on its occurrence? (27–8)

chapter 21

REMEDIES FOR BREACH OF CONTRACT

Topics covered

- Damages
- Rescission
- Specific performance

- Injunction
- *Quantum meruit*

Summary
Where a contract has been breached, the injured party may seek a legal remedy from the court for the loss incurred by not having the contract performed. This chapter examines the remedies available to the injured party and the circumstances under which each will be used.

1. When one party to a contract breaches the agreement, the injured party may apply to the court for a legal remedy for the loss incurred by not having the contract performed, provided application is made without delay.

2. The right to a legal remedy for breach of contract is subject to time-limits. Under the Statute of Limitations 1957, the right to sue for breach of a simple contract becomes statute-barred after *six* years from the date when the cause of action arose, or after *twelve* years where the contract was by deed. An action consisting of or including damages for personal injuries, however, must be commenced within *three* years.

Case: Behan v. Bank of Ireland (1998)

The plaintiff decided in 1981 to sell between forty and seventy acres of his farm to eliminate or substantially reduce his indebtedness to the defendant. He alleged that his bank manager persuaded him at a meeting on 18 May 1981 not to sell any land on the basis that there would be a cyclical change in the market leading to a decrease of his cash flow problems. He also alleged that the bank manager had assured him that he would be provided with all necessary financial facilities to tide him over, which ultimately exceeded £200,000. On 23 December 1983, the defendant agreed to convert the plaintiff's liabilities into a rescue package loan, and informed the plaintiff that no additional financial facilities would be offered to him. Despite the restructuring package, the plaintiff's financial position deteriorated further, so much so that by July 1985 the indebtedness to the defendant was £213,891. At this point it was agreed that a sum of £165,000, financed from the sale of most of the plaintiff's land, would be paid to the defendant in full settlement of the debt. In July 1990, the plaintiff made a claim for damages relating to negligence, breach of duty and breach of contract.

Held: The plaintiff must have been aware in 1983, if not earlier, that the advice he had allegedly received from the defendant was bad advice. The cause of action had arisen on that date, and the claim was statute barred under the Statute of Limitations 1957 and the Statute of Limitations (Amendment) Act 1991.

3. The limitation period may be extended where the plaintiff is a minor or under some other contractual disability, such as being of unsound mind, or where the breach was not discovered by the plaintiff because of fraud, concealment or mistake.

4. The following remedies may be applied for to the court on the occasion of a breach of contract:

(a) damages;
(b) rescission;
(c) specific performance;
(d) injunction;
(e) *quantum meruit.*

• Damages

5. Damages are a common law remedy, the purpose of which is to put the injured party, by an award of monetary compensation, into the same position they would have been in if the contract had been performed.

6. Every breach of contract gives rise to an action for damages. Where there is a breach of *warranty*, but the injured party sustains no loss, only nominal damages will be awarded so as to acknowledge that legal rights have been infringed. However, where there is a breach of *condition*, the injured party may regard the contract as discharged or reduce the breach to a breach of warranty, claim damages and continue with the contract. If the injured party opts for a discharge of the contract, they will be unable to take an action for damages, but will be able to sue for reasonable expenses incurred prior to the date of breach of the condition.

7. The parties to a contract may agree in the contract itself that, in the event of a breach of contract, damages shall be fixed at a sum certain or to be calculated in a certain manner. Such *liquidated damages* will only be enforced by the courts if it is a genuine pre-estimate of loss, and not merely a penalty to secure performance. An amount could be held to be a penalty where the specified sum is extravagant compared with the conceivable loss, where the same sum is to be paid irrespective of the nature of the breach or number of the breaches, or where the specified sum is greater than a money debt due under the contract. In such cases, the penalty intends to frighten a party into compliance with the terms of the contract, and will be void and unenforceable.

Case: Toomey v. Murphy (1897)

The defendant agreed to pay 'a penalty as liquidated damages' of £5 per week if construction work which he had undertaken was not completed by a specified date. Due to the work being incomplete at the end of the agreed duration, the plaintiff subsequently sued for damages relating to thirty-two weeks.

Held: This was a valid liquidated damages clause, and the defendant was obliged to pay the £160.

Case: Kemble v. Farren (1829)

The defendant, an actor, had agreed to pay the plaintiff, his manager, a sum of £1,000 in the event of a breach of contract by him. The plaintiff subsequently sued for such 'liquidated damages'.

Held: Since the actor's daily fee was less than £4, the specified sum was extravagant in comparison with the greatest loss that could result from the breach, and was but a penalty clause. The sum of £1,000, therefore, was not recoverable.

8. Where a contract makes no provision for the quantification of damages on the occasion of a breach, or where such a sum is void as a penalty, then the injured party will sue for *unliquidated damages*, and the court will decide what losses resulting from the breach are compensatable.

9. Damages may be recovered from the court for losses, financial or non-financial, resulting naturally from the breach of contract, or which may reasonably have been in the minds of the parties on making the contract, as likely to result from a failure to complete the contract.

10. As a general rule, the amount awarded as damages by a court is assessed on the basis of what is considered as a reasonable and fair estimation of the injured party's loss due to non-performance of the contract. This amount may be arrived at by a comparison with market prices. Furthermore, the injured party may be compensated for incidental expenses arising out of the breach, as well as for normal loss of profits, but under no circumstances may be compensated for special unspecified profits. Finally, the injured party may also be entitled to damages for physical inconvenience, such as loss of enjoyment or mental distress, arising from the breach of contract.

Case: Hadley v. Baxendale (1854)

The plaintiffs owned a flour mill. When the crankshaft of their steam engine broke, they had to dispatch it for repair. The defendants, carriers, promised delivery by a certain date, but were unreasonably late in returning it to the plaintiffs. The flour mill was unable to operate without the crankshaft, and was stopped for the entire duration. The plaintiffs sued the defendants for damages arising out of the loss of profits caused by the delay.

Held: The plaintiffs were not entitled to damages, since the consequences of the breach of contract had not been made known to the defendants who might, had they contemplated them, have wished to have made arrangements under the contract.

11. In assessing the amount of damages, the courts assume the injured party will have taken any reasonable steps to moderate or 'mitigate' their loss. Otherwise, the amount of compensation will be reduced.

12. Other factors may influence the amount of damages awarded. The court may take inflation into account where inflationary loss was a foreseeable consequence of the breach of contract. It may also reduce the amount to take account of sums claimed for out of which taxation would have been paid.

Case: Hickey & Co. Ltd v. Roches Stores (Dublin) Ltd (1980)

The plaintiffs contracted in 1969 to sell retail fashion fabrics in the defendants' store on a profit-sharing basis. In 1972, the defendants broke the contract on the assumption that, even after paying agreed compensation for breach of contract, they would profit from continuing the business alone. The assessment of damages was not finalised until 1980. Consequently, the plaintiffs sought an upward adjustment of the amount to account for inflation, and the defendants sought a downward adjustment to account for the burden of taxation on it.

Held: The defendants were not liable to compensate the plaintiffs for the consequences of inflation, since the parties could not have reasonably foreseen the delay in the award of damages at the time the contract was originally entered into. Furthermore, as the damages receivable by the plaintiff are chargeable to tax, it was not appropriate to make any deduction from the total amount.

• Rescission

13. The injured party may rescind a contract upon breach of a condition. This remedy terminates the rights and obligations of both parties to the contract at the time of rescission, unlike as in the case of misrepresentation where the contract is held never to have existed if rescission is allowed.

14. An application to the court for an order of rescission may be made by the injured party to establish entitlement, to be relieved from further liability to perform obligations, or to effect the return of a deposit.

Case: Grist v. Bailey (1966)

The plaintiff bought a house, which was occupied by a tenant, from the defendant for £850. Both parties believed the house to be subject to rent control. It later turned out that this was not the case, and so was worth £2,250.

Held: The contract was voidable. The defendant was entitled to rescind the contract, with the condition attached that the plaintiff should get first option to buy the house at the current market price.

15. Where rescission is allowed by the court, any benefits received must be restored by the parties to the contract, unless it is given as a guarantee of performance. If the injured party is unable to restore the benefits received under the contract, the right of rescission may be lost and the injured party may have to be content with damages.

16. The injured party will be entitled to claim in addition for damages, whether or not the contract is rescinded.

• Specific performance

17. Specific performance is a court decree ordering a contracting party to perform the duties under a contract. It is an equitable remedy and will not be ordered in circumstances where:

(a) the common law remedy of damages is adequate;
(b) the contract is of a personal nature;
(c) performance is over a long duration and the court could not properly supervise its enforcement;
(d) one of the parties is a minor; or
(e) restoration to the pre-contract state of affairs is impossible.

18. Contracts for the sale of land are enforced by an order for specific performance, because the land may be needed for a particular purpose and the loss of the bargain could not be adequately compensated by an award for damages.

Case: O'Brien v. Kearney (1995)

The defendant agreed at auction to purchase thirty-three acres of land and an associated milk quota from the plaintiff. The brochure issued by the auctioneers contained a map which was inaccurate and which omitted to disclose a possible claim to a right of way over the lands sold. On discovery of this, the defendant refused to complete the contract and the plaintiff initiated proceedings seeking specific performance and damages.

Held: Specific performance was ordered, with the defendant being entitled to a reduction of £2,500 in the purchase price for the loss suffered by him as a result of the various defects in the title.

19. Contracts for the sale of goods, however, are not usually enforced in this way, unless the goods in question are rare and unique (such as a rare stamp), and, therefore, no substitute is available.

20. A decree for specific performance will not be made to enforce a contract of a personal nature, such as a contract of employment or of personal service, since such a decree would require performance over a period of time, and the court could not properly supervise its enforcement.

Case: Rawlinson v. Ames (1925)

The plaintiff agreed orally to lease a flat to the defendant. It was part of the agreement that the plaintiff would make several alterations to the flat, which he did under the defendant's supervision. The defendant then refused to take the lease. The plaintiff sued for specific performance.

Held: The defendant had requested and supervised the alterations, thereby indicating that she had agreed to take the lease. Although a written memorandum did not exist, the order for specific performance was made, i.e. the defendant had to take and pay rent under the lease.

21. Since an order for specific performance is an equitable remedy, such a decree will not be made unless the injured party has behaved fairly. Where the injured party has been in default of their obligations, or where the contract involves an attempt to defraud the revenue authorities, specific performance will be refused.

22. Damages may be awarded as well as, or instead of, a decree for specific performance.

Case: Vandeluer & Moore v. Dargan (1981)

The plaintiffs contracted to sell land for £320,000 to the defendant, who subsequently refused to complete the sale. The defendant had only paid a deposit of £20,000, and the plaintiffs sought and obtained an order for specific performance of the contract. The defendant failed to comply with this order, and the plaintiffs sought to collect damages in lieu of specific performance.

Held: The plaintiffs were entitled to apply to the court for enforcement of the court order, or to apply to the court to dissolve the order and ask the court to discharge the contract. Upon discharge of the contract, the plaintiffs would be entitled to damages appropriate for a breach of contract.

• Injunction
23. An injunction is another example of a discretionary court decree, ordering a party to a contract to perform, or not to perform, a certain act. It may be mandatory, prohibitory or interlocutory.

24. A mandatory injunction is a court decree for a party to the contract to perform a definite act, while a prohibitory injunction is a court decree restraining a party to the contract from doing something which is unlawful. Both are suitable in contracts of an ongoing nature. Finally, an interlocutory injunction is a court decree which preserves the status quo between the parties to a contract pending a court hearing.

25. An injunction will not be ordered by the court, however, where damages would be an adequate remedy, or where it would be unfair to the parties to the contract. It will normally only be granted in circumstances in which a decree for specific performance might have been made, except in a case to enforce a contract of personal service, for which a request for a decree for specific performance would be refused by the court.

Case: Lumley v. Wagner (1852)

The defendant agreed to sing at a series of concerts organised by the plaintiff, and undertook that she would not sing for anyone else during the period of the agreement without the plaintiff's written consent. The plaintiff subsequently sued for an injunction to restrain the defendant from breaking this undertaking.

Held: The injunction was granted, since it did not force her to sing for the plaintiff, but rather encouraged her to do so. Similarly, it did not prevent her from obtaining different types of work.

Quantum meruit

26. Where a contract is discharged because of breach by one of the parties, the injured party may make a claim on a *quantum meruit* ('as much as he deserved') for the work done, or services provided, in performance of the contract, as an alternative to the remedy of damages.

Case: Hoenig v. Isaacs (1952)

The plaintiff undertook to furnish and decorate the defendant's flat for a price of £750, to be paid in instalments as the work was being completed. The defendant made regular payments, totalling £400, in the course of the execution of the contract, but then, in objection to the quality of work which had been performed, refused outright to pay the outstanding amount. It was estimated at the trial that the cost of making good any defective work and completing the job was £56.

Held: The plaintiff was entitled to recover on the basis of a *quantum meruit* the balance outstanding of the total contract price, less a deduction of £56 damages to cover the costs of rectifying the defects.

Case: Cutter v. Powell (1795)

The defendant agreed to pay the plaintiff's husband a wage of thirty guineas for acting as second mate upon a ship sailing from Jamaica to Liverpool. The plaintiff's husband died at sea while the ship was approximately nineteen days short of its destination, and his widow sued in respect of the work he had done during the previous forty-nine days of sailing from Jamaica.

Held: She was unable to recover on a *quantum meruit* a proportionate part of the agreed wages, because her husband had failed to do what he had expressly agreed to do.

27. Similarly, if the contract is unenforceable either because it was only partially completed by the plaintiff, or because it did not comply with the Statute of Frauds, but the defendant accepted the work done, a claim may be made on a *quantum meruit*. Such an award would be in restitution for the work done, as opposed to being in compensation.

IMPORTANT CASES

Numbers in brackets refer to paragraphs of this chapter

IMPORTANT STATUTES

Statute of Limitations Act 1957
Statute of Limitations (Amendment) Act 1991

PROGRESS TEST

Numbers in brackets refer to paragraphs of this chapter

1. When may the right to sue for breach of contract become statute-barred? (2–3)
2. What remedies are available for breach of contract? (4)
3. Under what circumstances will a court refuse to enforce liquidated damages? (7)
4. How is the amount awarded by a court as damages assessed? (10–12)
5. What are the implications of rescission as a remedy for breach of contract? (15–16)

6. A decree of specific performance will not usually be used to enforce what types of contracts? (17, 19, 20)

7. Differentiate between mandatory, prohibitory and interlocutory injunctions. (24)

Part 3: Law of Contract

EXAMINATION QUESTIONS

1. (a) What are the requirements for a valid contract?
   (b) What are the remedies available to an aggrieved party for a breach of contract?

   IATI (Autumn 2006)

2. State and explain the remedies available for breach of contract.

   ACCA (June 2007)

3. Explain the rules of offer and acceptance in the formation of a binding contract.

   ICPA (Summer 2006)

4. David agreed to sell his motorbike to Anne but when they signed the agreement they had not fixed a price. They later disagree on what the price should be. What is the legal position of this contract?

   IATI (Summer 2007)

5. In relation to the acceptance of an offer in contract law, explain the meaning and effect of:
   (i)   a counter-offer;
   (ii) acceptance subject to contract;
   (iii) the postal rule.

   ACCA (December 2006)

6. Michael heard that Paula wanted to sell her car and telephoned her to see how much she wanted for it. Paula said she would take €5,000 but that Michael had to make his mind up by the weekend. On the Thursday before the weekend, Michael's friend, John, rang to say he'd just heard Paula had sold the car to someone else. Michael instantly texted Paula saying he'd take the car at the €5,000 offered. Advise Michael.

   IATI (Autumn 2007)

7. Ace Ltd had been having difficulties in developing software for its new Internet service Brag.com. As the time for delivering the service, 1 May 2007, approached, Ace Ltd placed the following notice in the January edition of its company journal: '€10,000 reward to any employee who can design a solution to the Brag problem before 1 April.' The journal was distributed to all employees of Ace Ltd, but was also made available on their website. Cid, a self-employed computer expert, who was married to an employee of Ace

Ltd, read the journal and thought that he could solve the problem so started work on it. Dan, who was employed on the Brag.com project, did not see the advert, but nonetheless was working on trying to find a solution in his own time. Ed, a computer software expert employed by Ace Ltd, but not involved with the Brag.com project, saw the advert and decided to work on it in his own time after reading the journal. Fran, who had no links with Ace Ltd, read the notice on the company's website and also decided that she could solve the problem. However, before anyone could solve the problem, Ace Ltd decided to cancel the Brag.com project and placed a note in the March edition of its journal cancelling the reward for overcoming the Brag.com problems.

Required: Analyse the scenario from the perspective of contract law and advise Cid, Dan, Ed and Fran, each of whom managed to solve the Brag.com problem after the cancellation of the reward but before the original deadline.

ACCA (June 2007)

8. On Monday morning, Adam sent a letter to Sean offering to buy 500 tonnes of wood pellets at current market prices. Sean received the letter on Wednesday and he immediately posted a letter accepting Adam's offer. Later on Wednesday, Carl contacted Sean offering to buy 500 tonnes at a higher price. Sean immediately phoned Adam and told him he was 'unable to supply due to distribution problems' and then revoked his acceptance. He then sold the quantity to Carl at the higher price. The acceptance letter was received by Adam the next day, Thursday.

Advise Adam, giving reasons for your answer, whether or not he had a contract with Sean and any action he could take.

MII (August 2007)

9. Explain the following requirements for consideration in the law of contract:
   (a) consideration need not be adequate but must be sufficient;
   (b) consideration must not be past;
   (c) consideration must move from the 'promisee'.

IATI (Autumn 2007)

10. What is the doctrine of privity of contract and what are the exceptions to this doctrine?

IATI (Summer 2007)

11. Deirdre offered to sell her car to Michael for €5,000 on Monday. Michael replied: 'I will buy it if I can raise the money.' Deirdre promised that she would not sell to anyone else before Saturday, and added that Michael could collect the car at any time before noon on Saturday. On Thursday, Deirdre was visited by John who said that he would pay €6,000 for the car. Deirdre

accepted the offer and sold the car to John. On Saturday, Michael arrived at 10 a.m. with the €5,000 to take collection of the car. He has informed Deirdre of his intention to sue her for breach of a contract for the sale of the car. Advise Deirdre as to her legal position.

MII (May 2006)

12. Explain the differences between duress and undue influence in the law of contract.

ICPA (Autumn 2006)

13. In the area of contract law, explain the concept of misrepresentation, including the possible effects on a contract if one party makes a misrepresentation.

MII (May 2007)

14. Discuss the concept of 'fraudulent', 'negligent' and 'innocent' misrepresentation in contract law.

IATI (Autumn 2007)

15. Explain the various types of misrepresentation in the law of contract, outlining the types of action available to the wronged party in each instance.

ICPA (Autumn 2006)

16. What is 'misrepresentation' in the law of contract, and when can a contract be rescinded for misrepresentation?

IATI (Summer 2006)

17. By analysis of appropriate case law, explain the approach of the courts to the incorporation of an exclusion clause into a contract in the following circumstances:
    (a) where the clause is contained in a signed document; and
    (b) the clause is contained in a ticket or receipt.

MII (August 2006)

18. Alan has purchased a microwave oven from Powers Ltd. After a month of using it, the microwave blew up and gave him a nasty shock. He took it back to the shop and demanded his money back. The shop refused to give him his money and told him he should complain to the manufacturer. On checking the manufacturer's condition of sale, Alan discovered it had a clause excluding the manufacturer from liability in respect of any condition or warranty concerning the quality of the microwave oven. Advise Alan.

IATI (Summer 2007)

19. Art has operated his own Internet business since 1995 and ever since then he

has used Bling Ltd to provide for all his computer requirements. On the five previous occasions he upgraded his computer network, the contract with Bling Ltd was in writing and contained a clause stating that: 'Bling Ltd is not liable for any financial or other losses caused through the installation, or use, of any equipment supplied by it, whether as a result of negligence or otherwise of the company or its staff.' In October 2005, Art once more contacted Bling Ltd with an urgent request for them to upgrade his computer system before the expected rush of business before the Christmas period. On this occasion, although the terms of the contract were amicably agreed over the phone, due to the need for speed, the contract was not reduced to a written document. However, when Bling Ltd's workers arrived to install the new computers, the foreman handed Art a delivery note which detailed the number and cost of the new computers and related software. On the back of the document was printed the usual exclusion clause, as stated above. Art only checked the front of the document and did not notice the statement on the reverse. On the first occasion that Art tried to use the new computers, a wiring fault caused a fire to break out and as a result, not only was Art severely burned, but his premises suffered €50,000 worth of damage. As a result, he was not able to supply any goods for Christmas, which caused him to lose a further €100,000. Bling Ltd admits that the fire was caused by the negligence of its workers, but is relying on the exclusion clause to deny any liability for the damage caused.

(a) Advise Art whether the exclusion clause was incorporated into his contract with Bling Ltd.
(b) Assuming the clause has been incorporated into the contract, advise Art whether it covers all the damages suffered as a result of Bling Ltd's admitted negligence.

ACCA (December 2006)

20. Explain the meaning and legal effect of 'contracts in restraint of trade' with particular regard to their application to contracts of employment.

ACCA (June 2006)

21. In relation to contract law, explain the meaning and operation of the doctrine of 'promissory estoppel'.

ACCA (June 2006)

22. In relation to the law of contract, explain the rules relating to:
    (i)   the remoteness of damages;
    (ii) the measure of damages;
    (iii) the duty to mitigate losses.

ACCA (December 2006)

Part 4

COMMERCIAL LAW

chapter 22

NEGOTIABLE INSTRUMENTS

Topics covered

- Choses in action
- Definition of a negotiable
  instrument

- Negotiability of an instrument

Summary

Negotiable instruments are transferable commercial documents conferring a title to money or property. This chapter outlines the means by which such a document can be freely transferred, and in respect of which a transferee can acquire a better title to it than the transferor.

• Choses in action

1. A chose in action is a property right which cannot be reduced into physical possession, but which can only be enforced by legal action. It is, therefore, an intangible form of personal property, such as a debt, patent, copyright or share.

2. Owners of such property usually have some document of title to prove that they have such a valuable right and to facilitate the transferability of their title. Such documents of title are known as 'instruments', and these include cheques, bills of exchange, promissory notes, share certificates, debentures and dividend warrants.

3. The transfer of a chose in action is referred to as an 'assignment'. At common law, a chose in action was non-transferable, though, in time, equity allowed transfer subject to two restrictions:

(a) Notice in writing of the assignment had to be given to the person against whom the right operated; to the debtor, for example, in the case of a debt. Otherwise, if this person paid the assignor (the original creditor), they could not be called upon to pay the assignee.
(b) The assignee could obtain no better rights than the assignor. The assignment was, therefore, subject to whatever defects existed at the time of the transfer. For example, the debtor might dispute liability to the original creditor. Investigation of the past history of the debt was, therefore, required by the assignee, so as to avoid uncertainty as to their own rights.

4. These restrictions were disliked by the business community, however, who needed an unrestricted means of giving credit, and of transferring debts as a method of paying for goods and services. The practice has grown through custom and usage, therefore, whereby certain types of choses in action have evolved to which these restrictions do not apply. These are known as 'negotiable instruments'.

• Definition of a negotiable instrument

5. A negotiable instrument is defined in the Bills of Exchange Act 1882 as: 'a chose in action, the full and legal title to which is transferable by mere delivery of the instrument with the result that complete ownership of the instrument and all the property it represents passes free from equities to the transferee, provided the latter takes the instrument in good faith and for value'.

6. The essential characteristics of a negotiable instrument are:

(a) title is passed by delivery (if the instrument is payable to 'bearer'), or by delivery and a signature (endorsement) of the previous holder on the back of it;

(b) transferees have an unqualified right to payment of the full amount. The transferees can obtain a good title even though the transferor had no title or a defective title, provided the instrument was in a negotiable state and the transferees took it in good faith, for value and without notice of any defect in title;

(c) transferees are entitled to sue on the instrument in their own name.

• Negotiability of an instrument

7. The negotiability of certain instruments has been established by statute and custom, i.e. by proof that they are universally regarded as such by mercantile usage. Negotiable instruments, therefore, include:

(a) bills of exchange;
(b) cheques;
(c) promissory notes, including bank notes;
(d) debentures payable to bearer;
(e) share warrants; and
(f) banker's drafts.

8. Negotiable instruments, however, do not include IOUs (which are merely acknowledgments of a debt), postal orders or money orders.

IMPORTANT STATUTES

Bills of Exchange Act 1882

PROGRESS TEST

Numbers in brackets refer to paragraphs of this chapter

1. Define a chose in action. (1)
2. Explain what is meant by an 'assignment'. (3)
3. Identify the restrictions under equity of the transfer of a chose in action. (3)
4. What are the essential characteristics of a negotiable instrument? (6)
5. Is an IOU a negotiable instrument? Why? (8)

chapter 23

BILLS OF EXCHANGE

Topics covered

- The purposes of a bill of exchange
- Definition of a bill of exchange
- Types of bills of exchange
- Acceptance of a bill of exchange
- Negotiation and endorsement of a bill of exchange
- Holder of a bill of exchange
- Liabilities of the parties to a bill of exchange
- Dishonour of a bill of exchange
- Discharge of a bill of exchange

Summary

The Bills of Exchange Act 1882, which codified the existing common law rules, distinguished a bill from other negotiable instruments. This chapter examines how a bill of exchange works in practice, and sets out the obligations of the parties to this instrument.

• The purposes of a bill of exchange

1. Nowadays, the use of bills of exchange in domestic transactions is comparatively uncommon. Cheques (which are a particular type of bill of exchange) are, of course, widely used both in commercial and in consumer transactions, but these only developed in popularity in the twentieth century.

2. The Bills of Exchange Act 1882, therefore, is mainly concerned with a different kind of financial document, which is now most frequently used in foreign trade. The purposes of a bill of exchange can best be illustrated by an example.

3. If O'Brien, in Dublin, supplies goods to Smyth, in London, who requires a sixty-day credit period, O'Brien will draw a bill of exchange on Smyth, ordering him to pay in sixty days.

4. The bill of exchange may be drawn as follows:

€5,000	Dublin 1 June 2008
Sixty days after date pay to my order the sum of five thousand euros (€5,000) value received.	
To John Smyth London	Patrick O'Brien Ltd

5. If Smyth agrees to the terms of this bill of exchange, he shows his acceptance by signing his name on the face of it and returning it to O'Brien.

6. O'Brien may keep the bill of exchange until the agreed date, i.e. until maturity, and then present it to Smyth for payment. Alternatively, O'Brien may sell (i.e. negotiate) it to a bank, or anyone else, at its face value less a small discount, because the buyer will have to wait until maturity to collect the money. The buyer is said to have 'discounted' the bill of exchange.

7. The bill of exchange may be negotiated many times before payment. This is done by the holder simply signing their name on the back of the bill of exchange. This is referred to as 'endorsement'.

8. Therefore, O'Brien has his money, while Smyth has credit for sixty days as requested. O'Brien has the facility of transferring the bill of exchange to another party, so that when it matures the holder may seek payment from Smyth, who hopefully will have the funds to make the payment.

• Definition of a bill of exchange
9. The Bills of Exchange Act 1882 defines a bill of exchange as: 'an unconditional order in writing, addressed by one person to another, signed by the person giving it, requiring the person to whom it is addressed to pay on demand, or at a fixed or determinable future time, a sum certain in money, to, or to the order of, a specified person, or to bearer'.

10. The definition refers to, and requires that there shall be, three parties to a bill of exchange:

(a) The *drawer* is the person who orders money to be paid.
(b) The *drawee* is the person to whom the order to pay is addressed. If, and when, the drawee signs their name on it, they become the acceptor.
(c) The *payee* is the person to whom payment is ordered to be made. If no payee is specified, the order may be expressed to be payable to 'bearer', and so it is payable to any person in possession of it.

11. To comply with the definition, the instrument must fulfil the following conditions:

(a) it must be an order and not a mere request;
(b) the order must be unconditional as between the drawer and the drawee;
(c) the order must be in writing;
(d) the order must be addressed by one person to another;
(e) the order must be signed by the drawer;
(f) the order must be to pay on demand or at a fixed or determinable future time;

(g) the order must be in respect of a sum certain in money;

(h) the bill must be payable to, or to the order of, a specified person or to the bearer.

It must be an order and not a mere request

12. A bill of exchange must be phrased imperatively. However, words of courtesy or politeness, such as 'please pay', are permissible.

The order must be unconditional as between the drawer and the drawee

13. If payment under the document is to be made only on either the occurrence of a contingency or the fulfilment of a condition, the document will not qualify as a bill of exchange.

Case: Bovins & Simms v. London & South Western Bank (1900)

The order contained an instruction to pay 'provided the receipt form at the foot hereof is duly signed'.

Held: The order to the drawee was conditional, and was therefore not a bill of exchange.

Case: Nathan v. Ogdens (1905)

At the foot of the document, an instruction stated 'the receipt on the back must be signed'.

Held: This was a valid bill of exchange. Such an order was addressed to the payee, rather than the drawee, who was ordered to pay unconditionally.

The order must be in writing

14. 'Writing' includes printing or typing. It also includes orders made by pencil, although payment is frequently refused in practice, since this obviously facilitates fraudulent alterations. The writing may be done on any substance which is capable of delivery. For example, a cheque, which is a type of bill of exchange, need not necessarily be drawn on a pre-printed numbered form issued by a bank. It could be written on any piece of paper, but must, of course, be stamped.

The order must be addressed by one person to another

15. The word 'person' includes legal persons, and not merely individuals. It includes both limited companies and partnerships.

16. The drawer and the drawee, however, may be the same person. For example, a bank may address an order to itself, known as a banker's draft. This is frequently used to pay for a purchase of land, because the amount of money involved is such that the seller would not be prepared to accept a cheque. As the order is signed by the bank itself, this makes it a safer means of payment than an order signed by any other person.

17. Similarly, when a cheque is drawn payable to the drawer by name or 'self', the drawer and the payee will be the same person.

Case: North & South Insurance Corporation v. National Provincial Bank Ltd (1936)

A cheque was drawn with the words 'pay cash or order' on it. The defendants refused to honour it, saying that it was not a valid bill of exchange.

Held: The document remained a valid order to the banker to whom it was addressed, even though the words 'pay cash or order' deprived it of its character as a bill of exchange.

The order must be signed by the drawer
18. The drawer need not sign at the time the bill of exchange is drawn, but until such a time as this is done, the bill of exchange will be of no effect.

19. The statutory requirement of a signature may be interpreted liberally. As well as an ordinary signature, the initials or mark of the drawer or a mechanically produced signature will also be acceptable.

20. The drawer may also have an order signed by a duly authorised agent. Where an agent signs a bill of exchange in their own name, they are personally liable on the bill unless they add words to indicate that they sign in the capacity of agent. For example, if they sign the bill of exchange:

> Sean Farrell, Director
> For and on behalf of Patrick O'Brien Ltd

they will be exempt from personal liability.

21. However, if they merely specify their position:

> Sean Farrell, Director
> Patrick O'Brien Ltd

they will be treated as signing in a personal capacity, and will be liable accordingly.

The order must be to pay on demand or at a fixed or determinable future time
22. A bill of exchange is payable on demand if it is so expressed, or if nothing is written on it to establish a time for payment.

23. A bill of exchange may also be made payable at a fixed future time after the date of the bill or after the date of presentation for acceptance (the latter being referred to as the period 'after sight' of the bill of exchange).

24. Finally, the bill may be made payable on or at a fixed period after the occurrence of a specified event which is certain to happen, though the time of happening may be uncertain.

25. For example, an order to pay a bill of exchange three months after a person's death will be valid, because this person's death is inevitable, but an order to pay a bill of exchange three months after a person's marriage will be invalid, because occurrence of the event is not certain.

The order must be in respect of a sum certain in money
26. Where the order demands that anything be done other than pay a sum of money, it will not qualify as a bill of exchange.

27. A bill of exchange may provide for payment of a sum certain in money, even if it is required to be paid by stated instalments, with interest, or according to a stated or ascertainable rate of exchange.

28. The sum payable need only be expressed in figures. Where, however, the sum payable is expressed in both words and figures, and there is a discrepancy between the two, the sum denoted by the words is the amount payable.

The bill must be payable to, or to the order of, a specified person or to the bearer
29. The payee must be named or indicated with reasonable certainty, unless the bill of exchange is payable to bearer. A bill may be payable to two or more persons jointly, to the holder of a particular office, e.g. 'Collector General', or to a person by the name under which they trade, e.g. 'Irish Commercial Academy'.

30. The bill of exchange is payable to the bearer if it is drawn as such, or if the only or last endorsement is in blank, which is where the endorser merely signs their own name without specifying the endorsee.

- **Types of bills of exchange**

Order bill
31. An order bill is one payable to order, or which is expressed to be payable to a particular person, and does not contain words prohibiting transfer. For example, 'Pay Orla' or 'Pay Orla or order' means that Orla is entitled to payment but she may, if she wants, order (by endorsement) that payment shall be made to someone else.

Bearer bill

32. A bearer bill is one payable to bearer originally, or an order bill on which the only or last endorsement is an endorsement in blank.

33. A bearer bill is also one payable to a fictitious or non-existent person. It may appear to be an order bill, but in reality it is not.

34. The essential distinction between a bearer bill and an order bill is that a bearer bill is negotiated (transferred) by delivery alone, whereas an order bill can only be negotiated by an endorsement by the holder coupled with delivery. Delivery without endorsement does not transfer ownership – only possession.

Inchoate bill

35. Where a bill of exchange is lacking in any material particular, the person in possession of it has prima facie authority to fill up the omission in any way they think fit.

36. Moreover, where a person signs a blank piece of paper with the intention that it may be converted into a bill of exchange, it can operate as authority to complete it for any amount, using the signature already on it as that of the drawer, endorser or acceptor.

• Acceptance of a bill of exchange

37. The drawee is under no liability on a bill of exchange, unless they accept it by signing their name on the front of the bill and, as is usual but not legally necessary, by adding the word 'accepted' and possibly the date.

38. In general, it is not necessary for the holder to present the bill of exchange for acceptance. This duty of presentation for acceptance only arises when the holder receives a bill of exchange which has not already been accepted. The holder usually presents such a bill to the drawee for acceptance, and presents it again when payment falls due. However, if the bill of exchange is one payable on demand, it can never be presented for acceptance, since, by its nature, it is due for payment as soon as it is presented.

39. Presentation of a bill of exchange for acceptance is only necessary in three specific cases:

(a) where the bill is payable at a specified time 'after sight';
(b) where the bill expressly requires that it be presented for acceptance; or
(c) where the bill is drawn payable elsewhere than at the place of business or residence of the drawee.

40. An acceptance may be either general or qualified. A *general* acceptance assents without qualification to the bill of exchange as drawn. A *qualified* acceptance varies in some way the effect of the bill of exchange as drawn. There are five types of qualified acceptance:

(a) conditional acceptance: this makes a condition of acceptance (e.g. by writing 'accepted, provided goods delivered by 1 June 2008');
(b) partial acceptance: acceptance is made in respect of only part of the amount of the bill (e.g. on a €1,000 bill, by writing 'accepted for €800 only');
(c) local acceptance: acceptance is made for the bill to be paid in one particular place, and not elsewhere (e.g. by writing 'accepted, to be paid in Galway only');
(d) acceptance qualified as to time: acceptance is made for payment at a time different from that expressed in the bill of exchange (e.g. by writing 'accepted, payable in sixty days', whereas the bill specified thirty days);
(e) acceptance by some, but not all, of the drawees: acceptance for a bill drawn on two or more persons jointly is made by one or more of the drawees, but not all of them.

41. On receiving a qualified acceptance, the option to take or refuse it rests with the holder.

42. Where the holder assents to a qualified acceptance, notice should be given to the drawer and any endorser. They are discharged from liability, unless they have assented to the qualification. Moreover, they are deemed to assent if, within a reasonable time after notification, they do not dissent.

43. Where the holder does *not* assent to a qualified acceptance, the bill of exchange may be regarded as dishonoured (rejected) by non-acceptance.

• Negotiation and endorsement of a bill of exchange
44. A bill of exchange may be negotiated when it is transferred from one person to another so as to constitute the transferee the legal holder of the bill.

45. If the bill of exchange is payable to bearer, it may be negotiated by delivery, but if it is payable to order, it may be negotiated by endorsement of the holder coupled with delivery.

46. The endorsement must be written on the bill of exchange itself. It must be signed by the endorser. An endorsement of the entire amount is required to operate as a negotiation. A partial endorsement, which attempts to transfer to the endorsee part of the sum payable, will not qualify as a negotiation.

47. The four main types of endorsement are:
(a) endorsement in blank;

(b) special endorsement;

(c) restrictive endorsement;

(d) conditional endorsement.

Endorsement in blank

48. An endorsement in blank is a simple signature of the holder on the bill of exchange, without the endorsee being specified. For example,

(signed) Nuala Perry

49. An order bill so endorsed becomes payable to bearer, since it authorises payment to anyone to whom the bill of exchange is delivered.

Special endorsement

50. A special endorsement includes both the signature of the holder plus instructions to pay a particular person, known as the endorsee. For example,

Pay Audrey McDonnell
(signed) Nuala Perry

51. The bill remains an order bill. If the bill of exchange is delivered to Audrey McDonnell, she becomes the holder and may in turn negotiate the bill to another person by endorsement (special or in blank) plus delivery. If the bill of exchange comes into possession of anyone other than Audrey McDonnell, that person is not the holder. The bill is not payable to the possessor alone, nor is it payable to bearer.

Restrictive endorsement

52. A restrictive endorsement prohibits further negotiation of the bill of exchange, or merely gives directions, without transferring ownership. For example,

Pay Audrey McDonnell only

or

Pay Audrey McDonnell for the account of Louise Tierney

Conditional endorsement

53. A conditional endorsement makes the transfer of the property in a bill of exchange subject to the fulfilment of a specified condition. For example,

> Pay Jude O'Neill, if she delivers the goods on order

54. Such a condition will exist between the endorser and endorsee alone. It can be disregarded by the payer, and payment to the endorsee will be valid whether the condition has been fulfilled or not.

• Holder of a bill of exchange

55. A holder of a bill of exchange is the payee or endorsee in possession of it, or the bearer of a bearer bill. The holder will usually be the person legally entitled to possession of the bill, although a thief or finder of a bearer bill is technically also a holder. The rights of a holder will depend on whether they are a holder for value or a holder in due course.

Holder for value

56. A holder for value is a holder who has given, or is deemed to have given, valuable consideration for a bill of exchange.

57. For example, if Anne issues a cheque to Richard in respect of a supply of goods, then Richard gives, and Anne receives, value. If Richard then endorses the cheque and delivers it to Mary as a present, Mary, who has given no value herself for the bill of exchange, is nonetheless a holder for value.

58. A holder for value receives no better title to a bill of exchange than that of the immediate transferor. Therefore, although a holder for value is entitled to sue in their own name to enforce a bill of exchange against those liable on it, the holder for value's enforcement rights may be defeated, since the title to the bill will have been taken subject to any defects in title arising because of fraud or illegality.

59. For example, if John steals a bearer bill, for which value has been given, and delivers it to Fiona as a present, Fiona, as a holder for value, has no better title than John, i.e. no title at all.

60. The rights of a holder for value are against the latest party to the bill of exchange who received value, and all parties previous to that latest party, whether or not they received value.

61. For example, suppose Anna gives a cheque to Barry as a gift, and Barry negotiates it for value to Ciara. Ciara then negotiates it for value to Declan, and

Declan gives it to Eithne as a gift. If the cheque is not paid, Eithne can sue Anna, Barry or Ciara, but not Declan, who has received no value from her. Anna is liable because value, although not received by herself, was given after she issued her cheque.

Holder in due course

62. A holder in due course is a person who has taken a bill of exchange which is complete and regular on the face of it, before it is overdue, without notice of any previous dishonour, in good faith, for value, and without notice of any defect in the title of the person who negotiated it.

(a) *The bill of exchange must be complete and regular on the face of it.* It will not be complete and regular if the name of the payee or signature of the drawer is absent, if it has an alteration which is apparent or if it has an endorsement which is irregular.

(b) *The bill of exchange must not be overdue for payment.* The bill of exchange may be negotiated when overdue for payment, but will be subject to any defects of title which existed at the date of maturity.

(c) *There must be no notice of any previous dishonour or a defect of title of the person who negotiated it.* Only when some irregularity is established in the history of the bill of exchange must the holder show that they had no knowledge or strong grounds of suspicion of the facts in question.

(d) *The bill of exchange must be taken in good faith.* As long as the bill of exchange is taken honestly, it is irrelevant as to whether or not there was any negligence.

(e) *The bill of exchange must be taken for value.* The value given for a bill need not be equal to the full amount of the bill. It is usually money or property, but it may take any other form.

63. A holder in due course holds a bill of exchange free from any defect of title of previous parties. In other words, the holder in due course can sometimes take a better title than the transferor had to it.

64. Finally, a holder in due course may negotiate enforcement rights to any person, other than one who was a party to a fraud, illegality or other unlawful act on the bill.

Differences between a holder for value and a holder in due course

65. Certain distinct differences exist between a holder for value and a holder in due course, the most important of which are:

(a) A holder for value takes the bill of exchange 'subject to equities', with the same rights as the transferor had. A holder in due course takes the bill of exchange 'free of equities', enforceable against previous parties.

(b) A holder for value is the holder of a bill of exchange for which value has at some time been given, but not necessarily by the holder. A holder in due course must have given value for the bill of exchange.

(c) A holder for value can enforce the bill of exchange against previous parties down the sequence as far as the last to receive value. A holder in due course has rights against all previous parties.

- ## Liabilities of the parties to a bill of exchange
66. By signing a bill of exchange as drawer, acceptor or endorser, a person becomes a party to whom special liabilities apply.

Liabilities of the drawer
67. By issuing a bill of exchange ordering payment, the drawer undertakes that the bill will be accepted and paid at the due date, and that, if it is dishonoured, the drawer will compensate the holder or any endorser who is compelled to pay it, provided the necessary proceedings on dishonour are taken.

68. The drawer may not deny payment to a holder in due course on the grounds that the payee does not exist or because of the lack of capacity.

Liabilities of the drawee
69. The drawee is the person to whom the order in the bill of exchange is given. The drawee, will, however, only have liability as a party to the bill after acceptance, thereby becoming acceptor.

70. The acceptor undertakes that the bill of exchange will be paid in accordance with the terms of the acceptance.

71. The acceptor may not deny payment to a holder in due course on the grounds that the drawer does not exist, that the drawer's signature is a forgery or because of the drawer's lack of capacity or authority to issue the bill of exchange.

Liabilities of the endorser
72. A person who endorses a bill of exchange undertakes that it will be accepted and paid at the due date, and that, if it is dishonoured, the endorser will compensate the holder or any person who endorses the bill subsequent to that endorser who is compelled to pay it.

73. An endorser may not deny payment to a holder in due course on the grounds of invalidity of the drawer's signature and all previous endorsements.

74. Neither may the endorser deny to an immediate or subsequent endorser that the bill of exchange was valid at the time of the endorsement.

• Dishonour of a bill of exchange

75. A bill of exchange can be dishonoured (rejected) by:

(a) non-acceptance;

(b) non-payment.

76. A bill of exchange will be treated as dishonoured by *non-acceptance* when the drawee fails, for whatever reason, to accept the bill when presented for acceptance.

77. A bill of exchange will be treated as dishonoured by *non-payment* either when it is presented for payment at the proper place and is not paid, or when presentment for payment is excused and the bill is overdue and unpaid.

78. In case of dishonour by non-acceptance or non-payment, the holder of the bill of exchange must give notice of the dishonour to the drawer and every endorser whom the holder of the bill may wish to hold liable within a reasonable time of dishonour (normally within twenty-four hours). Otherwise, they are discharged.

79. No special form of notice is required. It may be oral or in writing, so long as it clearly identifies the bill of exchange which has been dishonoured.

80. The duty to give notice of dishonour is dispensed with in a number of specified circumstances:

(a) when after the exercise of reasonable diligence, notice cannot be given (e.g. the drawer or endorser cannot be found);

(b) where the person entitled to notice has waived it;

(c) where the drawer has countermanded payment;

(d) where the drawee is a fictitious person; or

(e) where the drawee has insufficient contractual capacity.

81. When a foreign bill (i.e. one which is either drawn or payable outside Britain or Ireland) is dishonoured by non-acceptance or non-payment, formal notice of dishonour must be given by the procedure of 'noting' and 'protesting'. Noting involves a public notary re-presenting the bill of exchange for payment, and if it is again dishonoured, noting the relevant facts on the bill. Protesting, thereafter, involves the formal declaration by the notary of what has been done on a certificate of dishonour referred to as the 'protest'.

82. Either the drawer or any endorser may insert on the bill of exchange a 'referee in case of need' to whom the holder may apply for payment, should the drawee fail to accept the bill of exchange. This is an 'acceptance for honour', and serves to maintain the reputation of the drawer and any endorsers.

• Discharge of a bill of exchange

83. A bill of exchange is said to be discharged when all rights of action on it are extinguished. This will be so when nobody has any outstanding claims arising from it.

84. A bill of exchange is discharged:

(a) by payment in due course by, or on behalf of, the drawer or acceptor. 'Payment in due course' means payment is made at, or after, the maturity of the bill of exchange to the holder of the bill in good faith and without notice of any defect in the title;

(b) where the acceptor of a bill of exchange is, or becomes, the holder of the bill at, or after, its maturity;

(c) where the holder renounces in writing the rights against the acceptor, or delivers the bill of exchange to this person at, or after, its maturity;

(d) where the holder, or agent, intentionally makes a cancellation of the bill of exchange which is 'apparent';

(e) where there is a material alteration of the bill of exchange, without the consent of all the parties liable on it (e.g. alteration to the date, time of payment or sum payable).

IMPORTANT CASES

Numbers in brackets refer to paragraphs of this chapter

Bovins & Simms v. London & South Western Bank (1900) .... (13)

Nathan v. Ogdens (1905) .... (13)

North & South Insurance Corporation v. National Provincial Bank Ltd
    (1936) .... (17)

IMPORTANT STATUTES

Bills of Exchange Act 1882

PROGRESS TEST

Numbers in brackets refer to paragraphs of this chapter

1. Define a bill of exchange. (9)
2. Who are the parties to a bill of exchange? (10)
3. List and describe three types of bills of exchange. (31–6)

4. What is the difference between general and qualified acceptance of a bill of exchange, and how may acceptance be qualified? (40)
5. Identify the four main types of endorsement. (47)
6. Explain the differences between a holder for value and a holder in due course. (65)
7. Outline the specific liabilities of a drawer (67–8), a drawee (69–71) and an endorser (72–4) of a bill of exchange.
8. How may a bill of exchange be dishonoured? (75) Will notice of dishonour always be required? (80)
9. Describe five ways by which a bill of exchange may be discharged. (84)

chapter 24

CHEQUES AND PROMISSORY NOTES

Topics covered

- Definition of a cheque
- Crossing a cheque
- Relationship between banker and customer
- Protection of banks
- Differences between cheques and other bills of exchange
- Promissory notes

Summary

The Bills of Exchange Act 1882 defines cheques and promissory notes. This chapter examines their unique features and the obligations of the parties to these instruments.

- **Definition of a cheque**

1. A cheque is a bill of exchange drawn on a banker payable on demand.

2. Combined with the definition of a bill of exchange (see Chapter 23, para. 9), a cheque may be further defined as: 'an unconditional order in writing addressed by one person *to a bank*, signed by the person giving it, requiring *the bank* to pay *on demand* a sum certain in money to, or to the order of, a specified person, or to bearer'.

3. Suppose Angela O'Connor, in Dublin, supplies goods to John Kelly, in Limerick, who does not wish to pay by cash; she may accept a cheque drawn as follows:

South Western Bank Ltd Patrick St, Limerick	1 June 2008
Pay Angela O'Connor, or order	€500.00
	John Kelly

4. When Angela O'Connor, or her endorsee, wishes to get payment of this cheque, she may present it at the South Western Bank Ltd, Patrick St, Limerick, and get payment across the counter. Alternatively, she may lodge the cheque in her own bank, which will present the cheque to the South Western Bank Ltd for payment.

5. If John Kelly has funds in his bank account, or he has permission to overdraw on his account, the South Western Bank Ltd will pay on the cheque, debit John Kelly's account and cancel the instrument. The bank which has collected payment will then credit the bank account of Angela O'Connor, or her endorsee.

• Crossing a cheque

6. A cheque is crossed so as to convey instructions to the drawer's bank that it is to be paid in a particular manner. This is done through a bank, thereby making fraud more difficult.

7. If a bank fails to obey the instructions and makes payment in a manner other than that demanded, this may leave the bank open to an action by the drawer.

General crossing

8. A general crossing is made by drawing two parallel lines across the face of the cheque with, or without, the addition of the words 'and company', or any abbreviation thereof (e.g. '& Co.'), between the lines.

9. The effect of a general crossing is to make the cheque payable only through a collecting bank, and not across the counter.

10. In addition to the ordinary general crossing, two common general crossings are often used:

(a) if the words 'not negotiable' are inserted between the traverse lines, the person into whose hands the cheque may come does not have (and cannot give to the transferee) any better title than that which the transferor had. The cheque is still transferable, but it is not negotiable;

(b) if the words 'account payee' or 'account payee only' are inserted between the traverse lines, they serve as an instruction to the collecting bank (i.e. the bank holding the account of the payee to the cheque) to credit the payee's bank account alone with the proceeds of the cheque.

Special crossing

11. A special crossing is made by an addition of the name of a bank across the face of the cheque, with or without the addition of two traverse lines.

12. The effect of a special crossing is that the cheque should only be paid to the bank named in the crossing (or another bank with authority to act as an agent for the named bank).

• Relationship between banker and customer

13. The relationship between a banker and a customer is a simple contractual relationship of debtor and creditor. Many of the terms of the contract are not expressed, but are implied by banking practice.

Duties of the banker

14. A banker, therefore, has an obligation to customers:

(a) to honour their cheques; and
(b) to maintain secrecy over their affairs.

Duty to honour the customer's cheques

15. A banker owes a duty to a customer (but not to a holder) to pay on a cheque presented for payment, provided the customer's account is in credit or within the overdraft limits allowed by the banker.

Case: Dublin Port & Docks Board v. Bank of Ireland (1976)

A drawer drew cheques on his bank in favour of the plaintiffs. At that time, his account was in credit. When the cheques were presented for payment, there were insufficient funds in the drawer's account and the bank refused to honour the cheques. The plaintiffs sued for amounts owing to them.

Held: The banker was completely entitled to refuse to honour the cheques, since it owed no duty to the payee, but to the customer alone.

16. If, however, a banker wrongly refuses to honour a cheque, the customer, if a *trader*, can claim damages, without proof of the actual loss, for breach of contract. A *private customer*, however, can only claim nominal damages, unless they can prove actual loss. The bank may also be liable to pay damages for the tort of defamation as a result of injuring the customer's reputation.

17. The banker's duty to honour the customer's cheques will be ended by notice of:

(a) countermand of payment being given to the correct branch of the bank on which the cheque is drawn;
(b) an act of bankruptcy on the part of the customer;
(c) a petition for compulsory liquidation, or a resolution for voluntary liquidation, of a company customer;
(d) the customer's death or insanity;
(e) a court order, whereby the customer's bank balance is frozen.

Case: Reade v. Royal Bank of Ireland (1922)

The plaintiff issued a cheque in payment of a gambling debt. He notified the defendants by telegram, before presentment, that he wished to have the cheque cancelled. The defendants, however, chose to ignore this instruction and paid the cheque on presentment. He sued the defendants for breach of duty.

Held: The plaintiff was entitled to recover the amount of the cheque, as the defendants had failed to follow his instructions.

Duty to maintain secrecy over the customer's affairs

18. A banker owes a general duty to the customer to keep information about the customer's affairs secret. This duty extends to include all information acquired in the position as banker, and not just the state of the bank account. It continues even after the closure of the account.

19. The duty of secrecy does end, however, where disclosure is:

(a) under compulsion by law;
(b) in the public interest;
(c) in the interest of the bank, such as when the bank sues a customer on an overdraft;
(d) by express or implied consent of the customer, such as when the customer gives the banker's name to a third party as a reference.

Duties of the customer

20. The customer owes a duty to the banker:

(a) to take those precautions in drawing a cheque which are usual, such as writing a cheque in ink and not in pencil;
(b) to inform the bank of any forgeries of which the customer is aware.

• Protection of banks

21. A bank has no authority to pay a cheque (and if it does so may not debit the customer's account) if:

(a) its authority has been terminated;
(b) the apparent signature of the drawer has been forged; or
(c) the cheque is void for material alteration.

22. Banks process a huge volume of cheques each day, and this means that each cheque cannot be given the careful scrutiny in the light of their knowledge of customers' affairs.

23. Therefore, both the paying bank and the collecting bank are given statutory protection against liability subject to certain conditions.

Protection of the paying bank

24. A paying bank is deemed to have paid a cheque in due course, i.e. to the person entitled, in spite of any forged, unauthorised or irregular endorsement, or the absence of any endorsement provided the bank pays:

(a) in good faith; and
(b) in the ordinary course of business.

25. A payment will be made *in good faith*, so long as it is made honestly, whether or not it has been made negligently.

26. A payment will be made *in the ordinary course of business*, so long as normal banking procedure is followed, even though there was negligence in doing this. However, for example, a payment outside banking hours, or a payment of a large sum to a suspicious person not known to the banker, could not be classified as being made in the normal course of business, and, therefore, statutory protection against liability could not be provided.

Protection of the collecting bank
27. A collecting bank is protected from liability where it receives payment for a customer who has no title, or a defective title, provided it acts:

(a) in good faith; and
(b) without negligence.

28. *Negligence* by a collecting bank has been established in cases where:

(a) an account was opened for a previously unknown customer without proper enquiry;
(b) payment was obtained for a customer of a cheque for an abnormally large amount in relation to their circumstances;
(c) payment was obtained for a customer of a cheque drawn by their employer in favour of a third party, or drawn by a third party in favour of their employer, and in either case endorsed over to the customer, without enquiring as to the customer's title to that cheque;
(d) payment was obtained for a customer of a cheque drawn as agent for a third party, but payable to the customer, without enquiring as to the customer's title to that cheque.

• Differences between cheques and other bills of exchange
29. The rules governing cheques and other bills of exchange, subject to some exceptions, are identical. However, there are a number of important differences:

(a) a cheque must always be drawn on a bank;
(b) a cheque must always be payable on demand;
(c) cheques are rarely negotiated;
(d) cheques may be crossed;
(e) delay in presenting a cheque for payment does not discharge the drawer, unless loss is suffered by that delay;
(f) bankers are protected against a forged or unauthorised endorsement of a cheque drawn on them (Cheques Act 1959).

• Promissory notes

30. A promissory note is an unconditional promise in writing made by one person to another, signed by the maker, engaging to pay, on demand or at a fixed or determinable future time, a sum certain in money to, or to the order of, a specified person or to bearer.

31. A promissory note may be drafted as follows:

Dublin
1 June 2008

I promise to pay Mary White or order (or bearer) the sum of five thousand euros (€5,000) on 1 December 2008, value received.

Signed: Anne Browne

---

32. The main differences between promissory notes and bills of exchange are that:

(a) whereas a promissory note has two parties to it – the promissor (maker) and the promisee (payee) – a bill of exchange has three parties to it – the drawer, the drawee and the payee;
(b) a promissory note is a promise to pay, while a bill of exchange is an order to pay;
(c) a promissory note is not complete until such a time as it is delivered to the promisee, whereas a bill of exchange is complete once it has been drafted and signed.

IMPORTANT CASES

Numbers in brackets refer to paragraphs of this chapter

Dublin Port & Docks Board v. Bank of Ireland (1976) .... (15)
Reade v. Royal Bank of Ireland (1922) .... (17)

IMPORTANT STATUTES

Bills of Exchange Act 1882
Cheques Act 1959

PROGRESS TEST

Numbers in brackets refer to paragraphs of this chapter

1. Define a cheque. (1–2)
2. Differentiate between a general and a special crossing. (8–12)
3. What are the duties of a banker to a customer, and under what conditions may such duties end? (14–19)
4. Identify those duties owed by a customer to a banker. (20)
5. Describe the statutory protection against liability given to (a) the paying bank (24–6), and (b) the collecting bank. (27–8)
6. List six differences between cheques and other bills of exchange. (29)
7. Define a promissory note. (30)
8. What are the main differences between promissory notes and bills of exchange? (32)

chapter 25

AGENCY

Topics covered

- Definition of agency
- Classification of agents
- Creation of agency
- Duties of an agent

- Rights of an agent
- Effects of contracts made by agents
- Termination of agency
- Special types of agents

Summary

Business activities are frequently conducted through the medium of agents. This chapter examines the distinctive characteristics of the persons who are used to effect contractual relations between principals and third parties.

• Definition of agency

1. Agency is the relationship which arises when one person, called an 'agent', has legal authority to bind another person, called a 'principal', by entering into contracts with others on the principal's behalf.

2. The legal usage of the word 'agent' must be distinguished from its usage in everyday language. For example, the word 'agent' is often used to describe a person who buys and sells a particular manufacturer's products. These are merely traders on their own account who buy and sell a particular manufacturer's goods under a special contract know as a 'franchise' or 'concession'. Such traders cannot usually contract with their customers so as to create legal relations between the customers and the manufacturer. Therefore, they cannot be known as agents of the manufacturer in the narrow legal sense, and the manufacturer cannot be described as their principal.

3. An agent, therefore, is a person employed to bring the principal into contractual relations with a third party. The most important feature of the relationship is that the agent has the power to make a binding contract between the principal and a third party without the agent becoming a party to the contract.

4. Since agents do not contract on their own behalf, they need not possess full contractual capacity. The agent may, for example, be a minor. However, the principal must have full capacity to enter into contractual relations.

• Classification of agents

5. There are many different types of agent. All agents, however, fall into one of three main categories:

(a) general agents;
(b) special agents;
(c) universal agents.

General agent

6. A general agent has implied authority to enter into any contracts which are normally within the scope of the trade, business or profession the agent has been appointed to by the principal.

7. The principal, therefore, appoints the general agent as a representative in all matters of a particular kind. For example, an agent appointed to manage a public house would have implied authority to enter into contracts on behalf of the principal to purchase alcohol, cigarettes and cigars.

Special agent

8. A special agent has authority to enter into any contracts relating to one specific purpose. For example, an estate agent may be appointed to find a purchaser for the principal's house.

Universal agent

9. A universal agent has unlimited authority to enter into any contracts for which the principal has contractual capacity. The agent can even execute a deed on the principal's behalf. This type of agency is very rare, although it may be used where a person is going to live abroad for some considerable time.

10. A universal agent is appointed by a deed known as a 'power of attorney'.

• Creation of agency

11. Agency may be created in the following ways:

(a) express authority;
(b) implied authority;
(c) ratification (retrospective);
(d) necessity (operation of law);
(e) estoppel.

Express authority

12. Agency is usually created under a contract of agency. This determines the rights and duties of the principal and agent, and is enforceable between them.

13. To create agency by express authority, no particular formalities are legally necessary. The agent may be appointed orally or in writing. But if the agent is to execute a deed on behalf of the principal, then the agent must be appointed by a power of attorney, which is itself a deed.

14. The extent of the agent's express authority depends on the true construction of the words of the appointment. The principal may be bound by these words, if they are vague or ambiguous, in the event of the agent interpreting them in a sense not intended by the principal.

Implied authority
15. Agency may be created from the conduct or relationship of the parties.

16. The express appointment of the agent need not define the authority in express terms. Every agent has implied authority, in the absence of express provisions to the contrary, to make those contracts which are a necessary or normal incident of the agent's activities. The principal may, of course, limit this implied authority by express definition, but any such restrictions are only effective if the principal communicates them to those with whom the agent deals on their behalf.

Case: Watteau v. Fenwick (1893)

The defendant, an owner of a public house, employed the previous owner, H, to manage it. He expressly forbade H to purchase cigars on credit, but H ignored this and proceeded to purchase cigars from the plaintiff, who believed that H still owned the public house. H was unable to pay for the cigars.

Held: The purchase of cigars on credit was within the implied usual authority of a manager of a public house, and it was this authority upon which the plaintiff was entitled to rely. The defendant was therefore bound by the contract.

17. At common law, a wife has implied authority to pledge her husband's credit for necessaries, i.e. goods or services appropriate to the lifestyle of the spouses. This is based on a presumption that the wife is expressly or by implication the agent of her husband for this purpose, but is restricted as follows:

(a) The husband and wife must be living together, or if they live apart, it must not be through any fault on the wife's part. Since cohabitation is the legal basis, this implied authority extends also to a man's mistress or housekeeper.
(b) Agency will not be implied for purchases by the wife which, although perhaps 'necessary', such as a motor car, are not usually under the wife's control as manager of the household.
(c) The husband may rebut this presumption of implied agency by:

    (i)   telling traders not to supply goods to her on his credit;
    (ii) forbidding her to pledge his credit in this way;

(iii) providing her with the means to pay without having to pledge his credit, such as a housekeeping allowance or joint bank account.

Ratification

18. If an agent exceeds authority, or a person having no authority purports to be an agent, the principal will not be bound by the contract. The third party could, therefore, take action against the agent.

19. Alternatively, the principal may retrospectively give the agent the authority or status lacking, by ratification of the contract. The contract then takes effect, and is binding from the time when the agent makes the contract. Ratification, therefore, is a case of express authority given after the contract has been made.

20. A contract can only be ratified if:

(a) The agent expressly informed the third party that they were contracting as an agent, and named the principal.

Case: Keighley Maxsted & Co. v. Durant (1900)

An agent had authority to buy wheat at 45s 3d per quarter from the defendant, who would not sell for less that 45s 6d. The agent contracted to buy at the latter price, without disclosing that he was buying for the principal, i.e. the plaintiffs. The plaintiffs later purported to ratify the contract. When they failed to pay the agreed price, the defendant sued for breach of contract.

Held: The undisclosed principal could not adopt and ratify the contract. It was, therefore, the agent who was personally liable to pay for the wheat.

(b) The principal existed, and had contractual capacity, at the date of both the contract and the ratification.

Case: Kelner v. Baxter (1866)

The defendant, purporting to be an agent of a company which was about to be formed, contracted to buy wine from the plaintiff. The company, when formed three weeks later, took over and sold the wine, but refused to pay the plaintiff.

Held: The defendant was personally liable to pay for the wine, because the company could not by ratification bind itself to a contract made before it existed.

(c) The principal has full knowledge of all material terms of the contract, or is prepared to ratify in any event.

(d) The principal ratifies the contract within the time period specified under the purported contract, or within a reasonable time after the agent has made the contract for the principal.

(e) The principal ratifies the whole contract, and not merely parts of it.

Necessity
21. An agency of necessity will be created, in certain circumstances, whereby the law will automatically confer an authority on one person to act as the agent of another, without requiring the principal's consent. This rule is of very restricted application, and will usually only apply to a party who acts to save the property of another, or to perform some obligation of another.

22. The courts will only uphold the actions of an agent by necessity provided:

(a) There was an emergency, which necessitated the agent taking the action.

Case: Prager v. Blatspiel (1924)

The defendant purchased skins as agent for the plaintiff, but was unable to send them to the plaintiff, because of prevailing war conditions. The defendant then sold the skins before the end of the war without communicating with the plaintiff.

Held: There was no real emergency, since the defendant could have stored the skins until the end of the war. The defendant, therefore, was not an agent of necessity.

(b) It was practically impossible to get instructions from the principal.

Case: Springer v. Great Western Railway (1921)

The defendant found a consignment of fruit, which it was carrying on behalf of the plaintiff, to be going bad, and sold it locally instead of delivering it to its ultimate destination.

Held: The defendant could have obtained new instructions from the owner of the fruit, and consequently was not an agent of necessity. The defendant, therefore, was personally liable in damages to the plaintiff.

(c) The agent acted in good faith in the principal's interests, and not merely for their own convenience.

Case: Walsh v. Bord Iascaigh Mhara (1981)

The engine of a trawler belonging to the defendants failed off the coast of Kerry. The trawler began to drift towards rocks in stormy conditions. A distress signal was transmitted, which was responded to by the crew of the Valentia lifeboat. They immediately put to sea and towed the trawler to safety. The plaintiffs claimed for a salvage award which would remunerate them fairly for their services.

Held: Although the crew of the Valentia lifeboat were unable to communicate with the defendants, so as to obtain their instructions within the time available, they had taken action which was reasonable to protect the defendants' interests. The plaintiffs were, therefore, deemed to be agents of necessity, and were entitled to a salvage award for the services rendered to the defendants whose trawler they had saved from destruction or serious damage.

Estoppel

23. Agency by estoppel may be created where a person, by words or conduct, represents to a third party that another person is agent to make contracts on their behalf, even though in fact no agency really existed.

24. The alleged principal will be bound by such contracts as if the person had expressly authorised them, i.e. the principal is 'estopped' from denying the existence of an agency.

Case: Kett v. Shannon (1987)

The defendant was given the use of a car by a garage owner whilst his own car was being repaired. On returning the car, and discovering that his own was still unavailable, the defendant obtained the use of a different car from a mechanic, an employee of the aforementioned garage owner. The defendant subsequently collided with the plaintiff, a pedestrian, who sued him for damages. The defendant argued that the garage owner's insurance should cover any expense involved.

Held: The defendant had been driving without the consent of the owner. There was no evidence to suggest that the garage owner had represented that the mechanic had been given express or implied authority to lend a car to the defendant. Therefore, the defendant was not covered by the garage owner's insurance and was personally liable for damages.

Case: Pickering v. Busk (1812)

The plaintiff, a merchant, employed a broker to buy hemp on his behalf. The broker, at the request of the plaintiff, retained the purchased hemp at his own wharf, but later sold it to the defendant.

Held: The plaintiff had represented that the agent had authority to act for him. The plaintiff, therefore, was estopped by his conduct from denying the existence of an agency, and the defendant was held to have obtained a good title to the hemp.

• Duties of an agent

25. An agent is a person appointed by a principal to arrange transactions between the principal and a third party. Since an agent is in a position to injure the principal by commitment to overambitious obligations, or by abusing the position to their own advantage, the law has prescribed various general duties which the agent owes the principal:

(a) The agent must 'perform' an agreed task in accordance with the principal's instructions, unless acting gratuitously (i.e. without reward).

Case: Turpin v. Bilton (1843)

The defendant, an insurance broker, was engaged as an agent, in return for a fee, to arrange insurance on the plaintiff's ships. The defendant failed to do so, and a ship was subsequently lost at sea.

Held: The defendant was personally liable to make good the loss suffered by his principal.

(b) An agent for payment must maintain a standard of 'skill and care' expected of a person in their trade or profession. An unpaid agent must display the standards of skill and care which people ordinarily use in managing their own affairs.

Case: Chariot Inns Ltd v. Assicurazioni Generali SPA (1981)

The plaintiffs employed insurance brokers as agents, who advised their principal not to disclose information regarding a previous loss on a proposal form for insurance. After a fire in the plaintiffs' premises, the defendant insurance company avoided the policy.

Held: The insurance company was entitled to avoid the contract, and the agent insurance brokers were later held liable in negligence.

(c) An agent must not delegate the performance of their duties, unless the principal expressly or impliedly authorises the agent to appoint a sub-agent. This is sometimes referred to as the maxim *delegatus non potest delegare* (a delegate cannot delegate). An agent, however, is not deemed to be delegating by instructing their own employees to perform necessary acts in connection with the performance of the agent's own duty.

Case: John McCann & Co. v. Pow (1974)

The defendant employed the plaintiff firm of estate agents as 'sole agents' to find a purchaser for his flat. The plaintiffs passed details of the flat to another firm of estate agents, who advised a Mr Rudd that the flat was for sale. When Mr Rudd went to see the flat, the defendant enquired as to whether he had been referred to him by the plaintiffs, and was told that he had not. The defendant and Mr Rudd agreed a sale between themselves. The plaintiffs subsequently sued the defendant for commission for introducing the purchaser of the flat.

Held: The claim for commission failed, since the plaintiffs were not entitled to delegate the agency without the express or implied authorisation of the defendant.

(d) An agent must both disclose all material information to the principal of their agency transactions and provide accounts, when requested, for all moneys arising from such transactions. An agent should keep their principal's property and money separate from their own, so that they will be easily identifiable.

(e) An agent must not let their own interests conflict with those of their principal. An agent who is appointed to sell cannot sell to themselves, and an agent appointed to buy cannot buy from themselves, in the absence of full disclosure to their principal.

Case: Armstrong v. Jackson (1917)

The defendant, a stockbroker, was employed by the plaintiff to buy shares for him. The defendant sold his own shares to the plaintiff, who subsequently sued to have the contract rescinded.

Held: The stockbroker, as agent, had a conflict of interest and duty. His interest as seller was to sell at the highest possible price, while his duty as agent was to buy at the lowest possible price. As a result, the contract was set aside.

(f) An agent must not make a secret profit or accept an inducement to do business with one person rather than another, without the principal's permission. A principal, on discovering that an agent has accepted a bribe, may dismiss the agent, recover the bribe, refuse to pay the agent the agreed remuneration, rescind the contract and sue the third party who paid the bribe to recover damages for any loss.

Case: Boston Deep Sea Fishing & Ice Co. v. Ansell (1888)

The defendant, who was employed as managing director of the plaintiff company, contracted with a shipbuilding company for the supply of ships, taking a secret commission from the suppliers. This was duly discovered by the plaintiffs, who dismissed the defendant and sued to recover the commission.

Held: The defendant's action was a breach of his duty to his principal. The company was therefore justified in dismissing him and was entitled to recover the amount of the commissions from him.

(g) The agent must not disclose or misuse confidential information regarding their principal's affairs.

• Rights of an agent

26. An agent is entitled to be paid any agreed commission or remuneration for their services by their principal. If it is agreed that an agent is to be remunerated, but the amount has not been settled, the agent is entitled to what is customary in the particular business, or in the absence of custom, to a reasonable amount.

Case: Way v. Latilla (1937)

The plaintiff undertook to provide information on gold mines in West Africa to the defendant. He later sued the defendant for remuneration.

Held: Agreement that there should be remuneration was inferred by the court in these specific circumstances, and an amount of £5,000 was awarded as being reasonable.

27. An agent is also entitled to be indemnified by the principal for losses and liabilities incurred in the course of the agency. If an agent acts negligently, or outside the limits of their authority, they lose this entitlement. However, if an agent makes a payment on behalf of their principal, which is not legally enforceable by the third party, but which is made as a result of some moral pressure (e.g. payment of a betting wager), they may reclaim this expense from their principal.

• Effects of contracts made by agents

28. The legal consequences of a contract made by an agent will depend on whether:

(a) the agent discloses the identity of the principal;
(b) the agent discloses the existence, but not the identity, of the principal;
(c) the agent does not disclose the existence of the principal;
(d) the principal is non-existent.

Identity of the principal disclosed by the agent

29. When an agent discloses to the third party that they (the agent) are acting for a principal whose identity is also disclosed, the agent will generally have no liability under the contract and no right to enforce it. The agent drops out of the transaction and privity of contract exists between the principal and the third party.

30. An agent may be liable, however, in some such cases:

(a) if the agent executes a deed or a negotiable instrument without indicating that it is being done on behalf of a principal;
(b) if trade custom makes the agent liable;
(c) if the agent contracts personally and is liable as the principal.

Existence, but not identity, of the principal disclosed by the agent

31. When an agent discloses to the third party that they (the agent) are acting for a principal whose identity is not disclosed, again the general rule is that the agent can neither sue nor be sued on the contract.

32. However, the agent may still be personally liable, regardless of whether or not the principal is identified, in the exceptional circumstances identified above (para. 30).

Existence of the principal not disclosed by the agent

33. When an agent enters into a contract with a third party apparently on their own behalf, but actually on behalf of a principal, the undisclosed principal may sue and be sued on the contract, provided:

(a) the agent was authorised to make the contract;

(b) the third party cannot show that they wanted to deal with the agent for reasons personal to the agent, such as skill, or that they would not have contracted with the agent if they knew who the agent was acting for;

(c) the contract made by the agent cannot be construed as having an express term in it that the agent is really the principal.

34. On discovering the principal, the third party may elect to treat the agent as the other party to the contract. However, the third party cannot sue both the agent and the principal, but must elect for one or the other. The commencement of legal proceedings against either does not necessarily amount to a conclusive election so as to bar proceedings against the other, but if the third party obtains judgment against one on the breach of contract they are barred from suing the other.

• Termination of agency

35. Agency may be terminated by:

(a) acts of the parties;

(b) operation of law.

Acts of the parties

36. Agency ends when the purpose for which it was created, such as the purchase of a house, is completed. Similarly, agency for a fixed period ends with the expiry of the period.

37. The parties may at any time mutually agree to end the contract, or the principal may revoke the agent's authority, subject to the following restrictions:

(a) if the agent has been given an authority coupled with an interest, such as where the agent is authorised to collect debts on behalf of the principal and retain a part of the sum collected, the principal cannot withdraw authority;

(b) if the agent is also an employee of the principal, then proper notice must be given to terminate the agent's contract of employment;

(c) if the principal does not give notice of the revocation to third parties with whom the agent has dealt, the principal will be estopped from denying the capacity of the agent, should the agent make subsequent contracts with these third parties.

38. Agency will be terminated without notice if an agent commits a serious breach of an express or implied duty. The principal may also be entitled to sue for damages.

Operation of law

39. Agency is automatically terminated in any one of the following circumstances:

(a) death, insanity or bankruptcy of the agent or principal;
(b) frustration or intervening illegality of the subject matter or operation of the agency agreement.

• Special types of agents

Auctioneer

40. An auctioneer is an agent employed to sell property at a public auction. The auctioneer is primarily an agent for the seller, and has authority to sell to the highest bidder.

41. If the seller fixes a reserve price (i.e. a minimum price below which the auctioneer is not authorised to sell), but nothing is said to the bidders, and if the auctioneer accepts a bid below the reserve price, the seller is contractually bound.

42. But, if the bidders are informed that the auction takes place 'subject to reserve', and the auctioneer accepts a bid below the sale price, then the seller is *not* contractually bound since notice has been given that the agent has only limited authority. The auctioneer, however, may be sued by the successful bidder for breach of warranty of authority in accepting the final bid with the implication that the auctioneer had the authority to sell at that price.

43. On the sale of the property by auction, an auctioneer has an implied authority to accept payment of the price and to sign the memorandum of sale on behalf of both the seller and the buyer.

Broker

44. A broker is an agent who is employed to buy or sell goods in the principal's name, but does not have possession of the goods or of documents of title to them. The compensation paid to such agents for their services is known as 'brokerage'.

45. A stockbroker is a member of the stock exchange who has an implied authority to make contracts for their principals, subject to the rules of the exchange. These rules bind the principals, irrespective of whether or not they are aware of them, as long as they are neither unreasonable nor illegal.

Factor

46. A factor is an agent entrusted with possession of goods or documents of title to them for purposes of sale in either their own name or their principal's name.

47. A factor also has a lien (i.e. the right to retain possession of goods until the contract price has been paid; see Chapter 26, para. 82) on the goods for their charges, and has an insurable interest in the goods.

Estate agent

48. An estate agent negotiates the purchase or sale of land or buildings on behalf of their principal. An estate agent has no usual or implied authority to conclude a sale for their principal, or to prepare a memorandum of sale. The estate agent will only be entitled to receive commission from the principal upon having done exactly what the estate agent was employed to do.

Del credere agent

49. A *del credere* agent undertakes to indemnify their principal should the third party purchasers of the principal's goods fail to pay for them. The *del credere* agent usually receives a higher commission than normal in return for this indemnity.

50. The *del credere* agent does not guarantee, however, that a buyer will accept delivery of the goods. In the event of the buyer not accepting delivery of the goods, the agent incurs no personal liability to the principal.

IMPORTANT CASES

Numbers in brackets refer to paragraphs of this chapter

PROGRESS TEST

Numbers in brackets refer to paragraphs of this chapter

1. Define agency. (1)
2. List three main categories under which the different types of agents may be classified. (5)
3. How may agency be created? (11)
4. In what circumstances may a person retrospectively give authority to another who has purported to contract on their behalf? (20)
5. When will the courts uphold the actions of an agent by necessity? (22)
6. What are the general duties which an agent owes a principal? (25)
7. When may an agent be liable for a contract made on behalf of a disclosed principal? (30)
8. How may agency be terminated? (35–9)
9. Differentiate between: (a) an auctioneer and an estate agent; and (b) a broker and a factor. (40–48)

chapter 26

SALE OF GOODS

Topics covered

- Contract for the sale of goods
- Terms of the sale of goods contract
- Transfer of property in the goods to the buyer
- Performance of the sale of goods contract
- Remedies for breach of a sale of goods contract
- Supply of services
- National Consumer Agency

Summary

A contract for the sale of goods is like any other contract, except that statutory provisions may apply to it. This chapter examines how the ordinary principles of contract law apply to such contracts, and how the statutory provisions, for the most part, merely set out the rules which will apply when some detail of the contracting parties' arrangement is not covered by express agreement.

1. A sale of goods is the most common type of commercial transaction. A contract for the sale of goods is regulated by the principles of contract law as modified by the Sale of Goods Act 1893 (the 1893 Act) and the Sale of Goods and Supply of Services Act 1980 (the 1980 Act).

2. A contract for the sale of goods, therefore, is like any other contract in law where, in addition to the statutory rules, the ordinary principles of contract law, e.g. the rules relating to offer, acceptance, mistake and misrepresentation, still apply. Statutory rules for the most part will merely apply where some detail of the contracting parties' arrangement has not been covered by express agreement.

• Contract for the sale of goods

3. The 1893 Act defines a contract for the sale of goods as 'a contract whereby the seller transfers or agrees to transfer the property in goods to the buyer for a money consideration called the price'.

4. The definition of a contract for the sale of goods includes two distinct transactions: a 'sale' and an 'agreement to sell'.

(a) Where ownership (called 'property' in the 1893 Act) is transferred immediately from the seller to the buyer, the contract is called a 'sale'. (s. 2(4))

(b) Where ownership of the goods is to be transferred at a future time, or subject to some condition later to be fulfilled, the contract is called an 'agreement to sell'. (s. 2(5))

5. The distinction is important because several consequences follow from the passing of property:

(a) Unless otherwise agreed, the risk of accidental loss or damage passes with the property.
(b) Once the property has passed to the buyer, the seller can sue for the price, even if there has been no delivery, i.e. no transfer of possession.
(c) If the property has passed to the buyer, the buyer may claim the goods if the seller becomes a bankrupt, or a company goes into liquidation.
(d) If the seller resells the goods after the property has passed to the buyer, no title is acquired by the second buyer unless protected by one of the exceptions to the *nemo dat quod non habet* ('one cannot give what one does not have') rule (see para. 52 below).

6. A contract for the sale of goods must be one for 'goods' which are defined as 'all chattels personal other than things in action and money'. Things in action include debts, shares, patents, cheques, bills of exchange and promissory notes.

7. 'Consideration' in a contract for the sale of goods must include money. If the consideration is goods alone, then the contract is one of exchange or barter and the Act will not apply. However, the consideration need not be exclusively money, and a contract for the sale of goods will be valid if the consideration is partly goods and partly money.

Formation of a contract for the sale of goods
8. The ordinary rules of contract govern the formation of a contract for the sale of goods. There must be agreement between the parties to the contract, an intention to create legal relations and consideration.

9. The 1893 Act provides that, subject to statutory exception, the contract may be made by deed, in writing, by word of mouth, by the conduct of the parties, or a mixture of these. (s. 4)

10. The 1980 Act provides that the Minister for Enterprise and Employment may order that contracts relating to goods of a specified type must be in writing.

11. Where goods are valued at £10 or over, the contract cannot be enforced unless one of the following conditions is fulfilled:

(a) there has been acceptance and receipt of part of the goods by the buyer;

(b) the buyer has given something in earnest (i.e. as a deposit) to bind the contract or in part payment; or

(c) there is a written note or memorandum containing the essential terms of the contract, and signed by the party to be sued or their agent.

Terms of the sale of goods contract

12. The contents of a contract for the sale of goods are determined by the normal principles of contract law. Statements will become terms of a sale of goods contract if the maker of them, expressly or by implication, warrants them to be true. A sale of goods contract, therefore, like all contracts, may contain both express and implied terms.

Express terms

13. Typically, the parties to a sale of goods contract will agree orally and/or in writing on the basic terms of their agreement. Such terms will normally include the amount and quality of the goods, the price to be paid and maybe the time and method of delivery. However, in the absence of express agreement some of these terms are governed by the 1893 Act.

14. The parties to a contract need not expressly agree to the price, provided they agree on a feasible method of fixing the price, such as the ruling market price on the day of the delivery. If a price is not determined as above, then the buyer must pay a price which is found to be reasonable in the circumstances of the case. (s. 8)

Implied terms

15. The Sale of Goods Acts 1893 and 1980 imply certain conditions and warranties into contracts for the sale of goods. These give extensive protection to the buyer, and cannot, except in certain circumstances, be excluded.

16. A condition is a vital term, breach of which normally entitles the innocent party to repudiate the contract and claim damages. A warranty is a subsidiary term, breach of which only entitles the innocent party to damages. However, a buyer may waive a breach of condition by the seller, or elect to treat it as a breach of warranty.

Title (seller's right to pass good title to the goods)

17. Under s. 12(1) of the combined Acts, there is an implied *condition* that the seller has, or will have at the time when property in the goods is to be transferred, a right to sell the goods. If a buyer purchases goods from a seller who has not a good title to the goods, the buyer must generally return the goods to the true owner. The buyer, however, may recover the entire price paid for the goods, without any allowance for the use of the goods, on the grounds that there has been a total failure of consideration.

Case: Rowland v. Divall (1923)

The defendant sold a car, which unknown to him had been stolen, to the plaintiff, who subsequently sold it to a third party. The true owner of the car later recovered it from the third party, who was fully reimbursed by the plaintiff. The plaintiff then sued the defendant to recover the full price originally paid by him, but the defendant argued that allowance should be made for the use of the car before it had been returned to the true owner.

Held: The plaintiff was entitled to recover the whole purchase price, without any set off for the use of the car. Since the contract was for the transfer of ownership of the car and not merely the right to use it, there had been a total failure of consideration.

18. Under s. 12(2) of the combined Acts, there is an implied *warranty* that the goods are free from any charge in favour of a third party which was not made known to the buyer either before, or at the time the contract was made, and that the buyer shall enjoy quiet possession of the goods, except so far as it may be disturbed by any person entitled to the charge disclosed.

Description (goods to correspond with description)
19. Under s. 13(1) of the combined Acts, there is an implied *condition* that where goods are sold by description, then the goods shall correspond with that description.

20. The courts tend to construe this condition widely. A sale may be 'by description' even if the buyer inspects the goods before buying them, provided the buyer relies essentially on the description, and any discrepancy between the description and the goods is not apparent. Moreover, if the buyer asks for the goods by stating their requirements and the seller then supplies them to those requirements, this is also the case.

Case: T. O'Regan & Sons Ltd v. Micro-Bio (Ireland) Ltd (1980)

The plaintiffs informed the defendants that they required a product in order to vaccinate day-old broiler chickens against infectious bronchitis. The defendants recommended that the plaintiffs purchase a vaccine, called H-120, from them. The plaintiffs subsequently purchased and administered the vaccine, only to discover that a large number of the treated chickens had died. Tests later proved that the vaccine supplied by the defendants had in fact been H-52, a much stronger product used to vaccinate adult fowl.

Held: There had been a breach of the condition as to description, since the vaccine sold did not correspond with that description because of its greater potency.

21. Under s. 13(2) of the combined Acts, there is also an implied *condition* that where goods are sold by sample, as well as by description, then it is not sufficient that the bulk of the goods shall correspond with the sample, if the goods do not correspond with the description.

Merchantable quality

22. Under s. 14(2) of the combined Acts, there is an implied *condition* that where goods are sold *in the course of a business*, the goods shall be of a reasonable standard and suitable for the purpose or purposes for which goods of that kind are commonly bought, and as durable as is reasonable to expect having regard to any description applied to them, the price (if relevant), and all other relevant circumstances.

Case: McCullough Sales Ltd v. Chetham Timber Co. (Ire.) Ltd (1983)

The plaintiffs sold a man-made building material, known as Celuform, to the defendants. This plastic substance, designed as an alternative to timber, was supplied with special nails to affix the material to masonry. The nails proved unsuitable to be applied to concrete walls in the Republic of Ireland, and the defendants refused to pay for those materials supplied.

Held: The plaintiffs were familiar with the purpose for which the defendants required the materials. The materials supplied were not of merchantable quality and not fit for the purpose for which they were required.

Case: Egan v. McSweeney (1956)

The plaintiff purchased coal from the defendant. When ignited, some of the coal exploded and the plaintiff was struck by flying particles, which led to the loss of her right eye. She sued the defendant for damages.

Held: The goods did not meet the implied condition of merchantable quality in that the coal was not fit for its ordinary use, i.e. to burn in a domestic fire. The defendant was therefore liable to compensate the plaintiff for personal injuries suffered by her.

23. The condition that the goods supplied under a contract sale are of merchantable quality is *excluded* if:

(a) any defects are brought specifically to the buyer's attention before the contract is made; or
(b) the buyer examines the goods before the contract is made as regards defects which that examination ought to reveal.

Fitness of goods for a disclosed purpose

24. Under s. 14(3) of the combined Acts, there is an implied *condition* that where goods are sold *in the course of a business*, and the buyer expressly, or by implication, makes known to the seller any particular purpose for which the goods are being bought, then the goods supplied under the contract shall be reasonably fit for that purpose, whether or not that is a purpose for which such goods are commonly supplied.

25. There is no such implied condition of fitness of goods for a disclosed purpose where the circumstances show:

(a) that the buyer did not rely on the seller's skill and judgment; or
(b) that it would have been unreasonable for the buyer to rely on the seller's skill and judgment.

26. Where there is only one obvious purpose for which the goods are required, it need not be made known expressly to the seller since it is clearly implied. But if the goods can be used for more than one purpose or there are special circumstances which affect their suitability, there is no breach of an implied condition of fitness unless the buyer has made an express disclosure.

Case: Godley v. Perry (1960)

The plaintiff purchased a catapult from the defendant. It broke whilst being used by the plaintiff and resulted in him losing an eye.

Held: The purpose of the purchase was known by implication. Because it was not an effective catapult, it was in breach of s. 14(3).

Sale by sample
27. Under s. 15 of the combined Acts, there are implied *conditions* that:

(a) the bulk shall correspond with the sample in quality;
(b) the buyer shall have a reasonable opportunity of comparing the bulk with the sample; and
(c) the goods shall be free from any defect rendering them unmerchantable, which would not be apparent from a reasonable examination of the sample.

Case: Nichol v. Godts (1854)

The plaintiff entered into a contract to purchase from the defendant 'foreign refined rape oil warranted only equal to sample'. However, the sample had not been 'foreign refined rape oil' in the first place, so although the bulk corresponded with the sample when delivered, it did not meet the plaintiff's described requirements. He sued the defendant for breach of condition.

Held: The defendant was in breach of s. 13(2) and s. 15 of the combined Acts in that the bulk did not correspond with the plaintiff's description and meet his specified requirements. The plaintiff was therefore not liable to pay the price.

Sale of motor vehicle
28. Under s. 12 of the 1980 Act, there is an implied *warranty* in a contract for the sale of a motor vehicle, except where the buyer is a person whose business it is to deal in motor vehicles, that the seller will make available for the specified period if any, such spare parts and 'adequate aftersale service' as are stated in any offer, description or advertisement given by the seller, or given on behalf of the

manufacturer. The Minister for Enterprise and Employment is empowered to define by order what a reasonable period will be in relation to any class of goods.

29. Under s. 13 of the 1980 Act, there is an implied *condition* in a contract for the sale of a motor vehicle, except when the buyer is a dealer, that at the time of delivery the vehicle is free from any defect which would render it a danger to the public, including persons travelling in the vehicle. This condition is not implied when, in a fair and reasonable agreement, the parties agree that the vehicle is not intended for use in the condition in which it is to be delivered to the buyer, and a certificate to that effect is signed by the seller, or someone on their behalf, and the buyer, and given to the buyer prior to, or at the time of, delivery.

Exclusion of implied terms

30. The 1893 Act permitted that the implied conditions and warranties could be excluded, or limited, in contracts for the sale of goods. Therefore, one of the parties to a contract was able to exclude or diminish their liability by way of an exemption clause, thereby rendering these valuable protections meaningless.

31. It is no longer possible for a seller of goods to totally exclude the statutory implied conditions and warranties from a contract for the sale of goods.

32. Under s. 55 of the combined Acts, any term in a contract for the sale of goods which excludes all or any of the provisions of s. 12, concerning the seller's title to the goods, is void.

33. Under s. 55(4) of the combined Acts, any term in a contract for the sale of goods which excludes all or any of the provisions of s. 13, concerning the description of the goods, s. 14, concerning the quality and fitness of the goods and s. 15, concerning the sale of goods by sample, is void where the buyer deals as a consumer, and in any other case will be unenforceable unless such exclusion is shown to be fair and reasonable.

34. A 'consumer' is defined as a party who does not make the contract in the course of a business, while the other party does, and the goods sold are of a type ordinarily sold for private use or consumption.

Case: O'Callaghan v. Hamilton Leasing (Ire.) Ltd (1983)

The plaintiff, owner of a take-away restaurant, leased a drink-dispensing machine from the defendants. The machine produced drinks which were dispensed by the plaintiff to the customer. After two payments, the machine proved defective and the plaintiff sued for breach of condition.

Held: The plaintiff had not dealt as a 'consumer' within the meaning of the Sale of Goods and Supply of Services Act 1980. The defendant, therefore, could not be held liable for a breach of condition.

35. In considering whether a term is to be judged 'fair and reasonable', it is up to the court to have regard to the circumstances which were, or ought reasonably to have been known to, or in the contemplation of, the parties when the contract was made. Particular regard should be taken of the relative bargaining power of the parties, any inducement received by the customer to agree to the term, the customer's knowledge of the existence and extent of the term and whether any of the goods supplied were manufactured, processed or adapted to the special order of the customer.

Guarantees

36. Section 15 of the 1980 Act defines a guarantee as any document, notice or other written statement, however described, supplied by a manufacturer or other supplier, other than a retailer, in connection with the supply of any goods and indicating that the manufacturer, or other supplier, will service, repair or otherwise deal with the goods following purchase.

37. Under s. 16 of the 1980 Act, it is an offence for a manufacturer or supplier who provides a guarantee to fail to make it clearly legible or to fail to state clearly the name and address of the person supplying the guarantee (i.e. the guarantor), the duration of the guarantee from the date of purchase, the procedure for presenting a claim, what the manufacturer, or other supplier, precisely undertakes to do in relation to the goods, and the charges, if any, to be met by the buyer.

38. Section 18 of the 1980 Act provides that a guarantee is not an alternative to the implied rights given by the statute, but instead is an addition to them. A guarantee which purports to exclude or limit the buyer's statutory or contractual rights is void.

39. Under s. 19 of the 1980 Act, the buyer of goods may sue a manufacturer (or importer, where the goods are imported) or other supplier who fails to observe the terms of the guarantee, as if they had sold the goods to the buyer and had committed a breach of warranty. The courts may enforce the observance of the terms of the guarantee or may award damages to the buyer. This liability extends to all persons who acquire title to the goods within the duration of the guarantee.

• Transfer of property (ownership) in the goods to the buyer

40. The 1893 Act is not concerned with the contract for the sale of goods alone, but also deals with the property (ownership) problems associated with a sale. Property and possession must be distinguished because the property in goods sold may pass to the buyer although the seller retains possession of the goods. Similarly, although the buyer is in possession of the goods, the seller may still be the owner of them.

41. The importance of distinguishing whether property in the goods remains with the seller or has been transferred to the buyer is outlined in para. 5 above and, because of its relevance, is repeated here.

(a) Unless otherwise agreed, the risk of accidental loss or damage passes with the property.
(b) Once the property has passed to the buyer, the seller can sue for the price, even if there has been no delivery, i.e. no transfer of possession.
(c) If the property has passed to the buyer, the buyer may claim the goods if the seller becomes a bankrupt, or a company goes into liquidation.
(d) If the seller resells the goods after the property has passed to the buyer, no title is acquired by the second buyer unless protected by one of the exceptions to the *nemo dat quod non habet* rule (see para. 52 below).

42. The time when property is transferred from seller to buyer depends partly on whether the goods are specific, ascertained or unascertained.

(a) *Specific goods* are those identified and agreed upon at the time when a contract of sale is made. For example, if a seller shows a buyer a suite of furniture, and the buyer agrees to purchase that suite, that is a sale of specific goods.
(b *Unascertained goods* are those defined by description only, and not identified until after the contract is made, for example 2 lb of tomatoes.
(c) *Ascertained goods* are those identified and agreed upon after a contract of sale is made; for example, a contract to sell a greyhound pup from a litter not yet born is one for unascertained goods, but when the buyer chooses one upon the birth of the pups, the goods become ascertained.

43. Where there is a contract for the sale of unascertained goods, no property in the goods is transferred to the buyer unless and until the goods are ascertained. (s. 16)

44. If the contract is for the sale of specific or ascertained goods, property in the goods is transferred to the buyer at such time as it appears the parties *intended* it to be transferred. Their intention may be deduced from the conduct of the parties, the terms of the contract and the circumstance of the case. (s. 17)

45. Where the intention of the parties at the time of contracting is not clear, the following rules of s. 18 shall be applied to decide the time at which property in the goods shall pass.

Rule 1
Where there is an unconditional contract for the sale of specific goods, which are in a deliverable state, property in the goods passes to the buyer when the contract is made, and it is immaterial whether the time of payment or delivery, or both, is postponed.

Case: Clarke v. Reilly & Sons (1962)

The parties entered into a contract for the sale of a new car to the plaintiff, who agreed that he would trade in his old car and pay the balance of the purchase price in cash to the defendants. Pending delivery of the new car which he had purchased, the plaintiff was allowed to use the traded-in car. He was involved in an accident and seriously damaged the traded-in car. The sellers attempted to repudiate the contract.

Held: Ownership of the traded-in car passed to the defendants as soon as the contract was made. The plaintiff was merely a bailee of the car and had taken reasonable care of it. The defendants were obliged to bear the loss.

Rule 2

Where there is a contract for the sale of specific goods and the seller is bound to do something to put the goods in a deliverable state, property in the goods does not pass to the buyer until the seller has done what is required and the buyer is notified to this effect.

Case: Underwood v. Burgh Castle Brick and Cement Syndicate (1922)

The defendants contracted to purchase an engine, which at that time was imbedded in a concrete floor. The engine was damaged whilst being detached from its base and loaded on to a rail wagon. The defendants refused to accept it and the plaintiff sued for the price.

Held: The engine had not been in a deliverable state when the contract was made. It was still in the plaintiff's ownership at the time of the damage, and so at his risk.

Rule 3

Where there is a contract for the sale of specific goods in a deliverable state, but the seller is bound to weigh, measure or test them for the purpose of determining the price, property in the goods passes to the buyer when the seller has done so and has notified the buyer to this effect. This rule only applies when it is the seller who must weigh, measure or test the goods. If the buyer is to do the act, the property in the goods passes when the contract is made.

Rule 4

Where goods are delivered to a prospective buyer 'on approval' or on 'sale or return' terms, property in the goods passes to the buyer when:

(a) the buyer signifies approval or acceptance to the seller;
(b) the buyer does any other act, such as pawning the goods, thereby adopting the transaction; or
(c) the buyer retains the goods beyond the time agreed for their return without giving notice of rejection, or if no time was agreed, if the buyer retains the goods beyond a reasonable time.

Case: Poole v. Smith's Car Sales (1962)

The plaintiff gave his car to the defendants in August 1960 on a 'sale or return' basis. Having made several requests for the return of his car, the plaintiff finally recovered it in a badly damaged state in November 1960. The plaintiff sued for the price.

Held: Property in the car had passed to the defendants, since it had not been returned within a reasonable time. The defendants were obliged to pay the price agreed.

Rule 5

Where there is a contract for the sale of unascertained goods, property in the goods passes to the buyer when goods of that description and in a deliverable state are unconditionally appropriated to the contract by one party, with the express or implied assent of the other.

Case: Pignataro v. Gilroy (1919)

The plaintiff contracted to purchase 140 bags of rice from the defendant, who sent a delivery order for 125 bags at a warehouse to the plaintiff, and asked him to collect the remaining fifteen bags from the defendant's own premises. The plaintiff took no action for a month, within which time the fifteen bags were stolen through no fault of the defendant. The plaintiff sued to recover the price paid for the fifteen bags.

Held: The defendant's appropriation of the goods for the contract, without the plaintiff's objection, constituted the transfer of ownership and risk to the plaintiff. The goods, therefore, belonged to the plaintiff when they were stolen.

Reservation of title to the goods by the seller

46. Where there is a contract for the sale of specific goods, or where goods are subsequently apportioned to the contract, the seller may, by the terms of the contract or appropriation, reserve the right of disposal of the goods until certain conditions are fulfilled. (s. 19)

47. The inclusion of a 'reservation of title' clause in a contract provides a seller of goods with a means of protecting their interest in goods which have not been paid for, or their interest in the proceeds of resales, in the event of a buyer becoming insolvent.

Case: Aluminium Industrie Vaassen BV v. Romalpa Aluminium Ltd (1976)

The defendants purchased aluminium from the plaintiffs on terms that ownership of the material would only be transferred to the purchasers when they had paid to the suppliers all money owing to them. After having taken delivery of a consignment of aluminium, the defendants went into receivership. The plaintiffs, who had not received the purchase price, sought to enforce the above provision so as to secure payment before distribution of the defendants' assets.

Held: The aluminium, though in the possession of the defendants, did not belong to them. The plaintiffs were entitled to recover the remaining stock of aluminium and the money held by the receiver, representing the proceeds of sales of aluminium to the defendants' customers.

48. However, a reservation of title clause may not apply:

(a) unless it is registered as a charge (where the buyer is a company) or as a bill of sale (where the buyer is an individual); or
(b) if the goods are subjected to some process, whereby they become 'mixed' with other goods.

49. Therefore, in order to ensure that a straightforward reservation of title to goods still in the buyer's possession will remain effective, it is advisable that the supplier require that the goods in question be kept separate from the buyer's other stock.

Transfer of title by a non-owner

50. The common law maxim *nemo dat quod non habet* ('one cannot give what one does not have') provides that a seller, or an agent acting for the seller, can give no better title to goods than the seller has.

51. This is reflected in s. 21 of the 1893 Act, which provides that where goods are sold by a person who is not the owner, the buyer acquires no better title than the seller has, unless:

(a) the seller has the authority or consent of the owner; or
(b) the owner is precluded by conduct from denying the seller's authority to sell.

52. However, there are a number of exceptions to this general rule, so as to protect an honest buyer from having nothing except an action against the seller. These exceptions fall under rules relating to:

(a) sale by mercantile agents;
(b) estoppel;
(c) sale under a common law or statutory power;
(d) sale in market overt;
(e) sale under a voidable title;
(f) disposition by seller who remains in possession after sale;
(g) disposition by buyer who obtains possession after agreement to sell;
(h) disposition under a hire-purchase agreement;
(i) sale under a court order.

(a) Sale by mercantile agents

If an ordinary agent sells goods without actual or apparent authority, there is usually no transfer of title to the buyer. But if a mercantile agent, i.e. an agent whose business is selling goods for others, has possession of goods (or documents of title to them) with the owner's consent, and sells them in the ordinary course of business to a buyer who buys in good faith, and without notice that the agent has no authority to sell (or was exceeding authority), the buyer then acquires title to the goods. (s. 21)

Case: Folkes v. King (1923)

The plaintiff gave his car to a motor dealer for sale at not less than £575. The dealer sold the car to the defendant for £340, and the plaintiff sued to recover his car.

Held: The motor dealer was a mercantile agent for the plaintiff. In the circumstances, therefore, the plaintiff was bound by the sale.

(b) Estoppel

If the true owner of goods, by their conduct, leads a buyer to believe that the person who makes the sale owns the goods, the true owner is later estopped (prevented) from denying the seller's authority to sell. (s. 21)

Case: Central Newbury Car Auctions v. Unity Finance (1957)

A third party was allowed by the plaintiffs to take possession of a car, and its registration book, pending completion of arrangements to buy it from a finance company on hire purchase. The finance company refused the application for hire purchase, but the third party had sold the car in the meantime to the defendants. The plaintiffs sued for recovery of the car.

Held: The plaintiffs were not estopped from denying that the third party to whom they had given possession of the car and registration book had authority to sell the car. Mere transfer of possession is not a representation that the transferee is the owner.

(c) Sale under a common law or statutory power

If a non-owner is entitled to dispose of the goods as if they were the true owner, at common law or under statute, a buyer will acquire good title to the goods. For example, at common law, a finder of goods, who makes a reasonable effort to find the true owner, is entitled to keep the goods and pass a good title to them. Under statute, various persons such as pawnbrokers, hotel proprietors, sheriffs, among others, have specific powers of sale of goods which come into their possession.

(d) Sale in market overt

A market overt is one established by statute, charter or long-standing custom. It takes place between sunrise and sunset, and concerns goods of a kind usually sold in the market. If goods are sold in market overt according to the usage of the market, the buyer acquires good title, provided they buy in good faith and without notice of any defects in the seller's title. (s. 22)

(e) Sale under a voidable title

If a seller of goods has a voidable title, but this title has not been avoided at the time of sale, a buyer acquires a good title to the goods, provided they buy in good faith and without notice of the seller's defect in title. This applies only to contracts which are voidable, such as for fraud or misrepresentation, and not those which are void, such as for mistake. (s. 23)

Case: Lewis v. Averay (1972)

A dishonest person proposed to purchase a car from the plaintiff and to pay for it by cheque. He claimed to be a well-known television actor, and produced a false pass from the studios bearing a photograph which resembled the aforementioned actor. The plaintiff then accepted the cheque and allowed him to take away the car. When the cheque was dishonoured, the plaintiff attempted to recover the car from the defendant who had purchased it in good faith from the dishonest person.

Held: The plaintiff could not recover the car. The contract between the plaintiff and the dishonest person was not void, but only voidable, as a result of the fraudulently induced mistake. The dishonest person had transferred the voidable title to the defendant.

(f) Disposition by seller who remains in possession after sale

If a seller of goods, or a mercantile agent acting on the seller's behalf, continues in possession of the goods, or documents of title to them, and sells the same goods to a person who receives them in good faith and without notice of the previous sale, the transaction is as valid as if authorised by the true owner. (s. 24)

Case: O'Reilly v. Fineman (1942)

The plaintiff purchased a suite of furniture from the defendant. However, that suite had already been sold to a third party, and when the mistake was discovered, the defendant refused to deliver the goods. As a result, the plaintiff sued for specific performance.

Held: An order for specific performance was not awarded, but damages for loss of bargain were, since there had been a breach of the implied condition as to title. However, had the plaintiff acquired possession of the goods in good faith and without notice of the previous sale, the first buyer would have been obliged to seek a remedy against the seller instead.

(g) Disposition by buyer who obtains possession after agreement to sell

If a buyer, or a person who has agreed to buy, obtains possession of the goods (or documents of title), with the seller's consent, and resells or otherwise disposes of the goods to a person who receives them in good faith and without notice of the other seller's rights, title passes to that person, but only if the original buyer acts as a mercantile agent in the ordinary course of business.   (s. 25)

Case: Newtons of Wembley v. Williams (1965)

The plaintiffs sold a car to a third party, who paid for it by cheque. The third party was allowed to take possession of the car, on condition that title in the car should not pass before the cheque was cleared. The cheque was dishonoured, but in the meantime the car had been sold in a second-hand car market to the defendant. The plaintiffs sued for the recovery of the car.

Held: The defendant had acquired good title to the car, because the third party from whom he had bought it was a buyer in possession with the sellers' consent at the time of sale, and the transferor acted as a mercantile agent in the ordinary course of business.

(h) Disposition under a hire-purchase agreement
If a hirer of goods is a dealer in goods, and sells those hired in the ordinary course of business to a buyer who acts in good faith, and without notice that the hirer had no authority to sell, the sale shall be valid as if the hirer were expressly authorised by the true owner to make the sale.

(i) Sale under a court order
If goods are the subject of legal proceedings, rules of court authorise the court to order their sale, such as in the case of perishable goods.

• Performance of the sale of goods contract
53. It is the duty of the seller to deliver the goods and of the buyer to accept and pay for them in accordance with the terms of the contract for sale. (s. 27)

54. Unless otherwise agreed, delivery of the goods and payment of the price are concurrent terms, i.e. the seller must be ready and willing to give possession of the goods to the buyer in exchange for the price, and the buyer must be ready and willing to pay the price in exchange for possession of the goods. (s. 28)

Delivery

Method
55. Delivery is the voluntary transfer of possession from one party to another. There are five possible ways of effecting delivery:

(a) physical transfer of possession;
(b) physical transfer of the means of control (e.g. by giving the buyer the key of the warehouse);
(c) physical transfer of a document of title (e.g. a bill of lading);

(d) attornment (i.e. by arranging that a third party who holds the goods acknowledges to the buyer that they are held on their behalf);

(e) alteration in the character of the seller's possession (e.g. if the seller agreed to hold the goods until the buyer wanted them).

Place

56. Except where there is a provision in the contract, the place of delivery is the seller's place of business, if there is one, and if not, the seller's residence: provided that, if the contract is for the sale of specific goods, which to the knowledge of both parties when the contract is made are in some other place, that place is the place of delivery. (s. 29)

Case: Board of Ordnance v. Lewis (1855)

The defendant contracted to supply coal to several different locations specified by the plaintiffs. The defendant failed to comply with the agreement, and delivered different quantities than those specified to individual locations.

Held: The defendant was in breach of contract.

Time

57. In the absence of an agreed date of delivery, the seller is bound to make delivery within a reasonable time and at a reasonable hour. (s. 29)

Case: McAuley v. Horgan (1925)

The defendant contracted to sell wool to the plaintiff, but no date was set for delivery. The wool ordered was never dispatched and the plaintiff sued for damages.

Held: The defendant was not entitled to avoid the contract on the grounds that no cheque was sent or money tendered by the plaintiff. The defendant had broken the contract and was liable for damages.

Costs

58. Unless otherwise agreed, the expenses of, and incidental to, putting the goods into a deliverable state must be borne by the seller. (s. 29)

Delivery of incorrect quantities

59. If the seller delivers *less* than the quantity that they contracted to sell, the buyer may reject them, or accept the lesser quantity and pay for them at the contract rate.

60. If the seller delivers *more* than the quantity that they contracted to sell, the buyer may reject the whole amount, accept the contract quantity and reject the excess, or accept the whole amount and pay for them at the contract rate.

Case: Wilkinson v. McCann, Verdon & Co. (1901)

The defendants contracted to purchase flags worth £28 from the plaintiff. In fact, flags worth £65 were delivered to the defendants, who refused to take delivery of them. The plaintiffs sued for the price of the flags.

Held: The defendants were justified in rejecting the whole amount.

61. If the seller delivers the contract quantity mixed with other goods which are not ordered, the buyer may either reject the whole amount or accept the goods contracted for and reject the rest. The buyer cannot accept the incorrect goods. (s. 30)

Delivery by instalments

62. Unless otherwise agreed, a buyer is not bound to accept delivery by instalments.

Case: Norwell & Co. Ltd v. Black (1931)

The defendants, a Dublin firm of furniture retailers, contracted to purchase a consignment of carpets and furniture from the plaintiffs. On arrival of the goods, which did not sufficiently correspond with the order, the defendants refused to accept delivery on the grounds that the whole order had not been tendered together in one lot. They subsequently accepted goods which had formed part of the original consignment, but this was, in effect, a new contract. The plaintiffs sued for breach of contract.

Held: The defendants had been entitled to refuse delivery by instalments.

63. Where a contract provides for delivery in stated instalments, which are to be separately paid for, the contract is severable. If one or more deliveries of instalments are defective, this may amount to a repudiation of the whole contract or merely give a right to claim compensation for the defective deliveries only. It depends on the ratio of defective to correct deliveries and the degree of probability that the defectiveness will be repeated in future instalments. (s. 31)

Case: Tarling v. O'Riordan (1878)

The defendant, a retail dealer, contracted to purchase clothes from the plaintiff in two instalments. The first instalment was received in perfect conformity with the order and was accepted. Part of the second instalment was not in accordance with the order, and the defendant rejected all the clothes of the second instalment.

Held: The defendant was entitled to reject the whole instalment.

Delivery through a carrier

64. Delivery of goods to a carrier, whether named by the buyer or not, for the purpose of transmission to the buyer, is prima facie deemed to be a delivery of the goods to the buyer.

65. However, if in fact the carrier is the agent of the seller, delivery of the goods to the carrier is not deemed to be a delivery to the buyer.

Case: Michel Frères Société Anonyme v. Kilkenny Woollen Mills (1961)

The plaintiffs, a French manufacturing firm, contracted to sell yarn to the defendants. A delivery date, but not a place of delivery, was specified in the agreement. The plaintiffs consigned the yarn to a carrier before the delivery date, but it did not reach Ireland until after that date. The defendants refused to accept the yarn, and the plaintiffs sued for damages for breach of contract.

Held: The defendants were entitled to refuse to accept the yarn when it arrived in Ireland. Delivery of the goods to the courier was not delivery to the defendants in accordance with the contract.

66. The seller must make a reasonable arrangement with the carrier, having regard to the nature of the goods and the other circumstances of the case.

67. Unless otherwise agreed, where goods are sent by the seller by a route involving sea transport, under circumstances in which it is usual to insure, the buyer must have notice in time to insure them during their sea transit, and, if the seller fails to give such notice, the goods shall be deemed to be at the seller's risk during the sea transit. (s. 32)

Acceptance

68. Where goods are delivered to a buyer, which the buyer has not previously examined, they are not deemed to have accepted them until they have had a reasonable opportunity of examining them to see if they are in conformity with the contract. (s. 34)

69. The buyer is deemed to have accepted the goods when they:

(a) inform the seller that they accept the goods;
(b) do any act in relation to the goods which is inconsistent with the ownership of the seller, e.g. resell them or convert raw materials into finished goods; or
(c) retain the goods, after the lapse of a reasonable time, without informing the seller that they have rejected them. (s. 35)

70. Where a buyer rightfully rejects the goods, the buyer does not have to see to their return, unless otherwise agreed, but need only inform the seller. (s. 36)

71. Where a buyer wrongfully refuses to take delivery of the goods within a reasonable time, the buyer becomes liable to the seller for any loss caused, and for storage during the period the seller was forced to retain the goods on the buyer's behalf.

Payment

72. Unless otherwise agreed, stipulations as to time of payment are not deemed to be of the essence of a contract of sale, i.e. a default of payment does not entitle the seller to repudiate the contract.

- ## Remedies for breach of a sale of goods contract

73. As with other contracts, the parties to a contract for the sale of goods are entitled to the usual common law and equitable remedies. The seller, however, has also statutory rights under the sale of goods legislation.

Buyer's remedies against the seller

74. Where a seller is in breach of a condition of a contract, a buyer may reject the goods and rescind the contract, unless the buyer has lost the right to do so by accepting the goods, or part of them, under s. 35. The buyer may, in addition, sue for damages.

75. Where a buyer has paid the price, but the consideration for it has failed (e.g. if a seller has no title), the buyer may sue for the return of the price. (s. 54)

76. Where a seller is in breach of a warranty of a contract, or if a buyer is obliged, or chooses, to treat a breach of condition as a breach of warranty, a buyer may sue for the loss or reduce the amount paid to the seller by an allowance for the breach of warranty.

77. Where a contract is for specific or ascertained goods, a buyer may sue for an order of specific performance. The court, however, would only be likely to order specific performance where damages would be inadequate, e.g. where the goods are unique in some special way.

78. Where a seller wrongfully neglects or refuses to deliver the goods, a buyer can claim damages for non-delivery. The measure of damages is the difference between the contract price and the market price on the date fixed for delivery, or if no date was fixed, at the time of refusal to deliver.

Seller's remedies against the buyer

79. A seller may sue a buyer for the contract price if:

(a) ownership of the goods has passed to the buyer, and the buyer wrongfully refuses to pay according to the terms of the contract; or

(b) the contract price is payable on a certain day and the buyer wrongfully neglects or refuses to pay it, regardless of delivery of the goods.

80. A seller may sue a buyer for damages for non-acceptance if the buyer wrongfully neglects or refuses to accept and pay for the goods. Once again, the measure of damages is the difference between the contract price and the market price on the date fixed for acceptance, or if no date was fixed, at the time of refusal to accept.

Seller's remedies against the goods

81. Either, or both, of the seller's remedies against the buyer may be of little value to the seller if the buyer is insolvent (i.e. the buyer has ceased to pay debts in the ordinary course of business or cannot pay debts as they fall due). The sale of goods legislation, however, gives an 'unpaid seller' (i.e. one to whom the whole price has not been paid or tendered, or who has received conditional payment, e.g. by cheque or bill of exchange, which has been dishonoured) the following rights in respect of the goods:

(a) a lien on the goods, so long as they are in the seller's possession;
(b) a right of stoppage in transit if the goods are in the hands of a carrier; or
(c) a right of resale.

Lien

82. A lien is the right to retain possession of goods (but not to resell them) until the contract price has been paid. Even if part of the goods have been delivered to the buyer, the unpaid seller has a lien on the remainder, unless part delivery indicates an agreement to give up the lien altogether.

83. In order to exercise a lien, one of the following conditions must be satisfied:

(a) the goods must have been sold without any stipulation as to credit;
(b) the goods have been sold on credit but the credit period has expired; or
(c) the buyer has become insolvent.

84. The unpaid seller loses a lien:

(a) when delivering the goods to a carrier for transmission to the buyer without reserving a right on their disposal;
(b) when the buyer or their agent lawfully obtains possession of the goods; or
(c) when the seller waives the lien. (s. 43)

Stoppage in transit

85. A seller has a right to stop goods in transit when a buyer becomes insolvent and to repossess the goods until having received payment of the contract price.

86. The goods cease to be in transit, and the seller's right of stoppage in transit ends:

(a) on delivery to the buyer or agent (whether at the agreed destination or before);

(b) if, on reaching the agreed destination, the carrier acknowledges to the buyer that the goods are being held on the buyer's behalf; or

(c) if the carrier wrongfully refuses to deliver the goods to the buyer or agent. (ss. 44–5).

Resale

87. Generally, a right of lien or stoppage in transit does not give an unpaid seller any right to resell the goods. An unpaid seller may do so, however, in the following exceptional circumstances:

(a) when the goods are of a perishable nature;

(b) when the seller has expressly reserved a right of resale under the terms of the contract; or

(c) when the buyer, having been given notice of the unpaid seller's intention to resell the goods, does not pay for them within a reasonable time period.

88. If an unpaid seller resells the goods, the second buyer acquires good title, even if the seller is not entitled to resell. The original buyer will not be able to recover the goods, although they may in that case sue the seller for damages.

• Supply of services

89. The 1980 Act introduced statutory implied terms into contracts for the supply of services, where the supplier is acting in the course of a business, as follows:

(a) that the supplier has the necessary skill to render the service;

(b) that the supplier will supply the services with due skill, care and diligence;

(c) that, where materials are used, they will be sound and reasonably fit for the purpose for which they are required; and

(d) that, where goods are supplied under the contract of service, they will be of merchantable quality. (s. 39)

90. Any implied term of a contract for the supply of services may be negotiated or varied by an express term of the contract, unless the recipient of the service deals as a consumer, in which case it must be shown that such an express term is fair and reasonable and has been specifically brought to the consumer's attention.

• National Consumer Agency

91. The Consumer Protection Act 2007 gives effect to the EU Unfair Commercial Practices Directive. It establishes the National Consumer Agency with a specific mandate to enforce a wide range of consumer protection laws on deceptive trading practices, consumer credit, package travel, unfair contract terms, pyramid promotional schemes, timeshare arrangements, consumer safety, food and textile labelling, unit pricing and price displays. It also aims to defend and promote consumer rights through forceful advocacy, targeted research, consumer information, and awareness programmes.

92. The Agency has a range of enforceable tools including prohibition notices, undertakings from traders, compliance notices, on-the-spot fines for offences relating to price display, and the power to 'name and shame' with the publication of the names of non-compliant traders.

IMPORTANT CASES

Numbers in brackets refer to paragraphs of this chapter

IMPORTANT STATUTES

Sale of Goods Act 1893
Sale of Goods and Supply of Services Act 1980
Consumer Protection Act 2007

PROGRESS TEST

Numbers in brackets refer to paragraphs of this chapter

1. Distinguish between a 'sale' and an 'agreement to sell', and explain the importance of this distinction. (4–5)
2. What is the implied condition as to the seller's right to pass good title to the goods? (17)
3. In what circumstances is it an implied condition that the goods correspond with the description? (19–21)
4. When is there an implied condition that goods sold be of a merchantable quality? (22–3)
5. Explain the implied condition that the goods shall be fit for the disclosed purpose. (24–6)
6. What is a sale of goods by sample, and what is implied in such a sale? (27)
7. Can a seller of goods exclude the statutory conditions and warranties from a contract for the sale of goods? (30–35)
8. What protection does a guarantee afford a buyer of goods? (36–9)
9. Differentiate between (a) specific, (b) unascertained, and (c) ascertained goods. (42)
10. Briefly outline the statutory rules which determine when property (ownership) in goods passes to the buyer. (43–5)
11. Explain what is meant by a 'reservation of title' clause, and the steps which should be taken to ensure its effectiveness. (46–9)
12. Describe, briefly, five exceptions to the *nemo dat quod non habet* common law maxim. (52)
13. When is a seller deemed to have delivered goods? (55)
14. State the implied terms of contracts for the supply of services, as introduced by the 1980 Act. (89)

INTERNET RESOURCES

Consumers' Association of Ireland
   www.consumerassociation.ie
European Consumer Centre (Ireland)
   www.eccdublin.ie
National Consumer Agency
   www.nca.ie

chapter 27

HIRE PURCHASE AND LEASING

Topics covered

- Nature of hire purchase
- Statutory requirements of hire-purchase agreements
- Implied terms
- Termination of agreement

- Restrictions on the owner's rights
- Transfer of ownership
- Credit sales
- Leasing

Summary

Sale is only one method of acquiring or distributing goods. This chapter examines the alternative methods of obtaining ownership or use alone of goods, and the statutory protection afforded to customers who avail of such methods.

• Nature of hire purchase

1. The possession and use of goods can be obtained without purchase by means of a hire-purchase or lease agreement, under which the owner of the goods allows another person to use them in return for rental payments.

2. A hire purchase is a bailment (i.e. a delivery of possession) of goods under which the bailee *may* buy the goods, or under which the property in the goods will, or may, pass to the bailee.

3. The bailee has an option to buy the goods, but is not bound to exercise that option. The bailee does not 'agree to buy' the goods at the time of the contract. Therefore, if the bailee sells the goods to another person before exercising the option to purchase, ownership in the goods is not passed.

Case: Helby v. Matthews (1895)

The plaintiff hired a piano to a third party, on the agreement that he should pay monthly instalments, he could terminate the agreement by delivering the piano to the plaintiff, and if he paid all the instalments punctually he would become the owner of the piano, but until such time, the piano would remain the property of the plaintiff. Before he had completed paying all of the instalments, the third party pledged the piano with the defendant, a pawnbroker, as security for a loan. The plaintiff sued for recovery of the piano.

Held: The plaintiff was entitled to recovery, because the third party had sold the piano before exercising his option to purchase by paying all of the instalments, and therefore could not pass good title to the defendant.

4. Irish hire purchase law is governed by the Consumer Credit Act 1995 (the 1995 Act), the single largest piece of consumer protection legislation in the history of the State, which implemented two EU Directives and extended the rights and protection of consumers in the area of credit well beyond the requirements of these directives. It is augmented by the Sale of Goods and Supply of Services Act 1980 (the 1980 Act).

5. A hire-purchase agreement may be made between a dealer and a consumer, but more commonly a finance company provides the credit. In the latter situation, the consumer negotiates with the dealer for the goods and, if the consumer requires hire-purchase facilities, the consumer will be asked to fill in an application form by the dealer. This is an application to a finance company who, when they have established the creditworthiness of the consumer, purchase the goods from the dealer. The finance company then lets them on hire purchase to the hirer, who has originally been the customer of the dealer.

6. At common law, the hirer's only recourse, in the case of defective goods, was against the finance company. The hirer had got the goods from the finance company as owners, and had no right of action against the dealer.

7. Under s. 80 of the 1995 Act, where goods are let under a hire-purchase agreement to a hirer dealing as a consumer, the person by whom the negotiations were conducted prior to the hiring shall be deemed to be a party to the agreement, and that person and the owner shall be answerable to the hirer for any breach of the agreement.

• Statutory requirements of hire-purchase agreements

8. Hire-purchase agreements are subject to the usual rules relating to the formation of a contract. There must be agreement between the parties, an intention to create legal relations, consideration, etc. However, certain statutory requirements also apply.

Notification of cash price

9. Section 57 of the 1995 Act requires the owner to notify the hirer of the cash price of the goods, before the agreement is made. The owner may do this:

(a) by informing the customer in writing;

(b) by having a ticket or label, which clearly states the cash price, attached to the selected goods; or

(c) by having the cash price clearly stated in any catalogue, price list or advertisement from which the goods have been selected.

Note or memorandum of the agreement

10. A hire-purchase agreement must be in writing, signed by the hirer and by, or on behalf of, all other parties to the agreement. Under s. 58 of the 1995 Act, the note or memorandum must contain:

(a) a statement of the hire-purchase or total purchase price;

(b) the cash price;

(c) the amount of each instalment and the dates of payment;

(d) a list of the goods to which the agreement applies;

(e) the words 'Hire Purchase Agreement' in a prominent position;

(f) the names and addresses of all parties to the agreement at the time of its making;

(g) any costs or penalties for breach of the agreement;

(h) a statement that the hirer has the right to withdraw from the agreement within 10 days of receiving a copy of the agreement;

(i) a statement that the hirer must inform the seller as to the whereabouts of the goods (when a written request to do so is received from the seller).

11. A copy of the note or memorandum must be delivered or sent to the hirer (and any guarantor) within 10 days of making the agreement.

12. If no note or memorandum of the agreement is made and signed, or if there is a failure to include the specified details or to send a copy to the hirer, the agreement, whilst remaining a valid one, will be unenforceable. However, a court has the discretion to waive the requirements if it is satisfied that non-compliance has not prejudiced the hirer and that it would be just and equitable to grant relief. (s. 59)

Case: Mercantile Credit Co. of Ireland Ltd v. Cahill (1964)

The plaintiffs gave a car on hire purchase to the defendant. When the parties signed the hire-purchase agreement, the required particulars were not filled in, and the terms included in the copy of the agreement sent to the hirer differed materially from those originally agreed. The defendant refused to pay any instalments and the plaintiffs sued him to recover the full amount due.

Held: The defendant was lawfully in possession of the car under an agreement that was unenforceable against him. It would not be just and equitable to dispense with the statutory requirements, and therefore, no order was made for the return of the car and a claim for the full amount was dismissed.

Case: British Wagon Credit Corp. v. Henebry (1963)

The defendant entered into a hire-purchase agreement with the plaintiffs for a tractor. He had signed a proposal form at the time of the agreement, but the required statutory details were not filled in at that time. The tractor proved defective, and the defendant refused to pay any further instalments.

Held: The defendant was lawfully in possession of the tractor under an agreement that was unenforceable against him.

• Implied terms

13. Sections 74-77 of the 1995 Act imply extensive conditions and warranties relating to the owner's title, the merchantable quality and fitness for purpose of the goods.

Title

14. Under s. 74, there is an implied *condition* that the owner has, or will have at the time when property in the goods is to be transferred, a right to sell the goods, unless the hire-purchase agreement states that the owner should transfer only such title as the owner or a third party may have.

15. There is also an implied *warranty* that the goods are free from any charge in favour of a third party which was not made known to the hirer either before, or at the time the hire-purchase agreement was made, and that the hirer shall enjoy quiet possession of the goods, except so far as it may be disturbed by any person entitled to the charge disclosed.

Description

16. Under s. 75, there is an implied *condition* that where goods are to be let by description, then the goods shall correspond with that description.

17. There is also an implied *condition* that where goods are let by sample as well as by description, then it is not sufficient that the bulk of the goods shall correspond with the sample, if the goods do not correspond with the description.

Merchantable quality

18. Under s. 76, there is an implied *condition* that where goods are let *in the course of a business*, the goods shall be of a reasonable standard, and suitable for the purpose or purposes for which goods of that kind are commonly let, and as durable as is reasonable to expect having regard to any description applied to them, the price (if relevant), and all other relevant circumstances.

19. Such a condition is *excluded* if:

(a) any defects are brought specifically to the hirer's attention before the agreement is made; or
(b) the hirer examines the goods before the agreement is made, as regards defects which that examination ought to reveal.

Case: Butterly v. United Dominions Trust (Comm.) Ltd (1963)

The plaintiff took delivery of a motor car on hire purchase from the defendants, and soon became aware of several defects. The car broke down completely after a short while. The plaintiff sued for breach of condition.

Held: The motor car was not of merchantable quality or fit for the purpose for which it was required. The plaintiff was entitled to rescind the contract, and to have his deposit and instalments returned.

Fitness for purpose
20. Under s. 76(3), there is an implied *condition* that where goods are let *in the course of a business*, and the hirer expressly, or by implication, makes known to the owner any particular purpose for which the goods are being hired, then the goods supplied under the agreement shall be reasonably fit for that purpose, whether or not that is a purpose for which such goods are commonly supplied.

21. There is no such implied condition if:

(a) the hirer did not rely on the owner's skill and judgment; or
(b) it would have been unreasonable for the hirer to rely on the owner's skill and judgment.

Sale by sample
22. Under s. 77, there are implied *conditions* that:

(a) the bulk shall correspond with the sample in quality;
(b) the hirer shall have a reasonable opportunity of comparing the bulk with the sample; and
(c) the goods shall be free from any defect rendering them unmerchantable, which would not be apparent from a reasonable examination of the sample.

Exclusion of implied terms
23. Under s. 79, any term in a hire-purchase agreement which excludes all, or any of the provisions of s. 74, concerning the owner's title to the goods, is void.

24. Any term in a hire-purchase agreement which excludes all, or any of the provisions of ss. 75, 76 and 77 is void where the hirer deals as a consumer, and in any other case will be unenforceable unless such exclusion is shown to be fair and reasonable.

• Termination of agreement

25. Under s. 63, a hire-purchase agreement may be terminated before the last instalment falls due, because the hirer either decides not to continue with it, or defaults under the agreement.

Termination is done by the hirer so notifying in writing the owner, or the person authorised to receive payments under the agreement.

26. When a hirer terminates the agreement, the hirer becomes liable to pay all outstanding sums, and any such further sum, which will bring the total payments up to one-half of the hire-purchase price (which may include installation charges), or such lesser sum as specified in the agreement.

27. If the hirer has not taken reasonable care of the goods whilst in possession, the hirer will be liable (in addition to the sums payable above) to pay compensation to the owner.

28. The hirer must, of course, allow the owner to retake possession of the goods. If, on termination of the hire-purchase agreement, the hirer wrongfully retains possession of the goods, the court may, in an action for repossession, order the hirer to deliver the goods to the owner, without giving the hirer the option to retain them by paying the value of the goods, unless it is satisfied that this would not be just and equitable.

29. Any provision in a hire-purchase agreement which excludes or restricts the hirer's right to terminate an agreement, or which imposes any liability, in addition to that outlined in the 1995 Act, for terminating the agreement, is void.

30. Similarly, any provision in a hire-purchase agreement which imposes a greater liability on a guarantor than that allowed by statute is void.

• Restrictions on the owner's rights

Entry to premises
31. Under s. 62 any term in a hire-purchase agreement which authorises an owner of goods to enter any premises, for the purpose of recovering goods let under that agreement, is void.

32. This restriction does not apply to a hire-purchase agreement for a motor vehicle. A term may be included which authorises an owner of a hired motor vehicle, or their agent, to enter premises, other than a dwelling house, in order to recover the motor vehicle.

33. The owner of the goods can, of course, enter the premises and recover the goods with the hirer's consent.

Recovery of goods

34. Under s. 64(1), where one-third or more of the hire-purchase price has been paid or tendered by the hirer or the guarantor, the owner cannot enforce any right to recover possession of the goods other than by a court action (except for a limited right in relation to motor vehicles).

35. If the owner seizes the goods without a court order:

(a) the hire-purchase agreement is terminated;
(b) the hirer or guarantor can recover all sums already paid; and
(c) the hirer or guarantor is released from all liability.

Case: McDonald v. Bowmaker (Ire.) Ltd (1949)

The plaintiff hirer, having paid in excess of one-third of the hire-purchase price on a lorry, fell into arrears with his payments. The defendants terminated the hire-purchase agreement, and demanded return of the lorry. They accompanied this with a threat of legal proceedings. The plaintiff returned the lorry voluntarily and sued for a return of the instalments paid.

Held: The plaintiff was not entitled to recover the amount already paid in instalments under the hire-purchase agreement. He had chosen to waive the provisions enacted for his protection by returning the lorry voluntarily to the defendants.

Recovery of motor vehicles

36. Under s. 64(3), if one-third of the hire-purchase price of a motor vehicle has been paid, and it is abandoned, or left unattended, in circumstances which have resulted, or are imminently likely to result, in damage or undue depreciation, the owner may still enforce a right to recover, provided the owner has commenced an action to recover possession of the vehicle.

The owner's remedies

37. Upon breach of a condition of a hire-purchase agreement by the hirer, the owner of the goods is entitled to rescind the contract, and also may:

(a) repossess the goods, where less than one-third of the purchase price has been paid, provided the owner does not enter premises without authority;
(b) claim return of the goods or their value, as well as damages for failure to take reasonable care of the goods;
(c) claim damages where the hirer fails to return the goods or has transferred them to another party; or

(d) claim arrears of instalment payments instead of rescinding the contract.

The court's discretion

38. Under s. 66, after one-third of the hire-purchase price has been paid, the court, in dealing with an action by an owner to recover possession of goods from a hirer, may:

(a) order the hirer to deliver the goods to the owner;
(b) order the hirer to deliver the goods, but with a postponement to allow the hirer, or any guarantor, to pay the unpaid balance of the price in such a manner, and subject to such conditions, as the court thinks just; or
(c) apportion the goods, if possible, between the owner and hirer, subject to such terms as to further payments, if any, as the court thinks is justified.

39. The court may, on an application by the owner for judgment, apportion the goods into parts, where they are divisible. It is then the duty of the owner to furnish evidence of the value of the parts into which the goods may be divided. Otherwise, the court may give the hirer the option to retain the entire goods on payment of the balance due under the agreement, where this is relatively small.

• **Transfer of ownership**

40. A hirer under a hire-purchase agreement is merely a bailee of the goods, and has no property in these goods until they exercise the option to purchase them. Therefore, a third party who acquires the goods from the hirer will not usually get a good title to them, under the *nemo dat quod non habet* rule that nobody can acquire a better title to the goods than that which the transferor had.

41. Under s. 70, such a sale will be valid, however, if:

(a) it is a sale in market overt; or
(b) the hirer is a dealer in the type of goods hired, and sells the goods in the ordinary course of business, provided the third party buys in good faith and without notice of the hirer's lack of authority to transfer property in the goods

• *Credit sales*

42. The 1995 Act deals not alone with hire-purchase agreements but also with credit-sale agreements, which are contracts for the sale of goods under which the purchase price or part of it is payable in installments and the property in the goods passes to the buyer immediately upon the making of the agreement.

43. The difference between the two types of agreements is that in the case of a credit-sale agreement, property in the goods passes as soon as the contract is made, whereas in the case of a hire-purchase agreement, the property *may* pass at some future date.

44. Credit-sale agreements are subject to the same formalities prescribed for hire-purchase agreements under hire-purchase legislation. However, since credit sales are *sales* of goods, the terms implied in a sale of goods contract apply.

45. The buyer of goods under a credit-sale agreement becomes the owner when the contract is made. The goods, therefore, unlike as in the case of a hire-purchase agreement, cannot be recovered by the seller unless there is a reservation of title clause. The seller can only sue the buyer for the balance outstanding.

• Leasing

46. The use of goods may also be acquired without purchase by means of a leasing agreement, under which the owner of goods allows a third party to use them in return for rental payments. Such agreements, therefore, are merely bailments of goods for reward, and no property in the goods passes, or is ever intended to pass, to the third party acquiring use of the goods.

47. Leasing agreements vary from short-term leases to long-term financial and operating leases.

48. In a *financial* lease, the lessor or owner is *not* responsible for repair and maintenance of the goods. The rental payments usually cover the initial capital cost of the goods leased, and the profit of the lending institution. Therefore, the goods are frequently re-let to the lessee at a nominal rent, once the primary lease period is completed, or sold to the lessee at a negotiated price.

49. In an *operating* lease, the lessor or owner *is* responsible for repair and maintenance of the goods. The leasing period will usually be less than that of the expected life of the goods, so rental payments will not normally cover the initial capital cost of the goods leased. The goods, therefore, are usually sold off by the owners on completion of the lease.

50. The 1995 Act protects a person acquiring goods by lease to virtually the same extent as it protects the hirer of goods. Leasing agreements are also subject to the statutorily implied terms as regards title, description, merchantable quality, fitness for purpose and, where applicable, terms as regards spare parts and aftersale service.

51. Any term in a leasing contract which excludes all, or any, of these implied terms is void where the lessee deals as a consumer, and in any other case will be unenforceable, unless such exclusion is shown to be fair and reasonable.

IMPORTANT CASES

Numbers in brackets refer to paragraphs of this chapter

IMPORTANT STATUTES

Consumer Credit Act 1995
Sale of Goods and Supply of Services Act 1980
Consumer Protection Act 2007

PROGRESS TEST

Numbers in brackets refer to paragraphs of this chapter

1. Define a hire purchase. (2–3)
2. In the case of defective goods, what recourse is available to the hirer? (6–7)
3. How may the owner notify the hirer of the cash price of the goods? (9)
4. List the requirements relating to a note or memorandum of the hire-purchase agreement. (10–11)
5. Briefly outline the implied conditions and warranties applicable to hire-purchase contracts. (13–22)
6. What will a hirer's liability be upon termination of a hire-purchase agreement before the last instalment falls due? (26–7)
7. What restrictions exist on the owner's right to recover goods? (34–6)
8. Identify those remedies available to an owner upon breach of a condition of a hire-purchase contract by a hirer. (37–9)
9. Distinguish between credit-sale and hire-purchase agreements. (43–5)
10. Explain the difference between (a) a financial lease, and (b) an operating lease. (48–9)

INTERNET RESOURCES

Financial Regulator
    www.financialregulator.ie
Financial Services Ombudsman
    www.financialombudsman.ie

chapter 28

INSURANCE

Topics covered

- The insurance contract
- Principles of insurance
- Types of insurance contract

Summary

Insurance exists to offset the loss suffered by an individual, or business concern, on the happening of some unforeseen event. This chapter examines the conditions under which the insured party may be so covered upon such an occurrence.

• The insurance contract

1. An insurance contract is one whereby the insurer, in return for repayments called premiums, agrees to pay a sum of money to the insured on the happening of a specified event, or agrees to indemnify the insured against any loss caused by the risk insured against.

2. Therefore, three elements are essential to an insurance contract:

(a) *consideration* must pass to the insurer. This usually takes the form of periodic payments, called premiums;
(b) there must be some degree of *uncertainty* as to whether the event insured against will happen, or if it is bound to happen, as to when it will happen; and
(c) the event, if or when it happens, must be *adverse* to the interest of the insured.

Formation of an insurance contract

3. An insurance contract is formed in the same way as other contracts, i.e. by agreement, consideration and an intention to create legal relations.

4. The person seeking insurance usually completes a proposal form, which generally requires particulars of the proposer, details of the cover sought and any other information considered necessary to enable the insurer to assess the risk involved.

5. The completed proposal form is then sent directly to, or through an agent of, the insurance company. If it is rejected, that is the end of the matter and no contract will come into effect.

6. If the proposal is accepted, the insurer will issue a policy conforming with the proposal. Normally, however, the proposal will be met with a statement that the policy will not become operative until the first premium is paid. Thus, either party is free to withdraw from their commitment between the time that the proposal form is submitted and the first premium is paid.

Case: Carna Foods Ltd & Mallon v. Eagle Star Insurance Co. (Ireland) Ltd (1997)

The defendant wrote to the plaintiffs stating that it would not be renewing three policies, and cancelling two existing policies, which were not up for renewal. The plaintiffs instituted proceedings to secure a disclosure of the reasons for the cancellations.

Held: There was no basis for the claim that an implied term in the defendant's contract was that reasons must be given in the event of a declinature or a cancellation of an insurance policy.

7. Pending a decision to accept or refuse a proposal, an insurance company may provide the proposer with temporary cover. This may be done orally, but is usually done by the issuing of a cover note. This is a short-term contract which is operative for a specified period, unless in the meantime the proposal is rejected. It is distinct from the insurance policy.

8. The person seeking insurance may go to an insurance broker or agent of the insurance company. If the role of the broker extends to filling up the proposal, they are an agent of the insurance company. However, if the role of the broker does not extend to filling up the proposal, and they nonetheless do so, they become the agent of the proposer. In such a case, were the company to avoid the contract, the insured might have recourse against the broker.

Case: Connors v. London & Provincial Assurance Co. (1913)

The plaintiff signed his name on a proposal form, and a broker for the defendants, with full knowledge of the true facts, completed the document incorrectly. When the defendants discovered the true facts, they sought to avoid the policy claiming that the broker's authority to act was confined by the defendants to the submission of proposal forms. The plaintiff initiated an action to prevent them from doing so.

Held: The defendants were not bound by any statement or representation of the broker and were entitled to avoid the policy, since the broker's authority was confined to the submission of the proposal form.

- ## Principles of insurance

Utmost good faith (uberrimae fidei)

9. All insurance contracts are *uberrimae fidei* (of utmost good faith). Unless a full disclosure is made to the insurer of all material facts which are known, or ought to have been known, to the insured at the time of making the contract, then the contract is voidable at the option of the insurer.

10. A fact is material if it would influence the judgment of a prudent insurer in deciding whether to accept such risk and, if so, what premiums and conditions to impose.

Case: Chariot Inns Ltd v. Assicurazioni Generali SPA (1981)

The plaintiff, when seeking fire insurance for its licensed premises, had to answer a series of questions contained in a proposal form. The answer given to the question, 'Material Damage: Give claims experience for loss over the last five years', was 'None'. The plaintiff had in fact been paid two years earlier on a claim for material damage suffered to property belonging to it, which had been stored in the premises of an associate company. An insurance policy was issued to the plaintiff. The licensed premises were subsequently damaged by fire. The defendants sought to avoid the contract of insurance because of the non-disclosure of the previous fire.

Held: The defendants were entitled to avoid the contract. Non-disclosure of the previous fire was material to the risk which the defendants had been asked to incur.

11. If an insurance policy is voidable due to fraudulent misrepresentation, the insurer may avoid the insurance contract, whether or not damage has resulted from the breach, without having to return any premiums paid.

Case: Griffin v. Royal Liver Friendly Society (1942)

The plaintiff, when seeking a life assurance policy, filled in a proposal form containing the following question: 'Is the proposed in good health and nature of last illness?' He answered 'None', while he had in fact been suffering from tubercular illness for some years. The defendants sought to avoid the policy, on discovering the true facts, and the plaintiff initiated an action to prevent them from doing so.

Held: The defendants were entitled to avoid the policy.

12. If the policy is voidable due to innocent misrepresentation, the premiums can be recovered by the insured, unless the policy itself provides that if it is found to be void, then any premiums paid cannot be recovered.

13. A duty of disclosure is not at an end when a proposal form is completed, but continues up to the moment the proposal is accepted, or later, depending on the circumstances.

Case: Harney v. Century Insurance Co. Ltd (1983)

The plaintiff, when seeking a health insurance policy, completed a proposal form, containing the following statement: 'The office must be notified of any changes in the health and circumstances of the life to be insured prior to the assumption of risk'. He signed the form on 23 May. He then attended his doctor on 9 August with a head cold, received antibiotics and continued working. The insurance policy was issued after this date, with a clause stating that the 'date risk assumed' was 31 August. The plaintiff's condition subsequently deteriorated, and when he claimed disability benefit under the policy, the defendants sought to avoid the policy on the grounds that they had not been informed of material facts affecting the risk, prior to the date of its assumption.

Held: Non-disclosure of the head cold was not material to the risk. Consequently, the defendants were not entitled to avoid the insurance policy.

14. The *contra proferentem* rule may be applied to insurance contracts in order to ease the duty of disclosure in special circumstances. Where a term of an insurance contract is so ambiguous as to admit to two different constructions, the court will choose the meaning unfavourable to the party who drew up the contract, to the benefit of the other party.

Case: Re Sweeney and Kennedy's Arbitration (1950)

A motor insurance policy contained a condition that drivers covered by the policy were not under twenty-one years of age, or had less than twelve months' driving experience. When the policy had been issued, that was factually correct, but subsequent to this, the insured employed his son in his business. The son was involved in an accident while driving one of the company's motor vehicles, before having reached twenty-one years of age. The insurer attempted to avoid the contract.

Held: The insurer had used ambiguous expressions, which had to be construed *contra proferentem*. The policy, therefore, was correct in so far as it related to the facts which existed when the policy was issued, and the court held the insurer liable to indemnify the insured for the loss suffered.

Insurable interest
15. An insurance contract is void unless the insured person has an insurable interest in the subject matter of the insurance, or the life assured. The insured person must benefit by its continued existence or be prejudiced (i.e. suffer) by its destruction or loss.

Case: O'Leary v. Irish National Insurance Co. Ltd (1958)

The plaintiff sought car insurance from the defendants. He filled out a proposal form which contained a question as to the owner of the car. He stated that he was the owner of the car – which was in fact untrue. After the plaintiff was involved in an accident, the defendants repudiated the policy and the plaintiff sued to enforce it.

Held: No valid contract of insurance had ever existed, since the plaintiff had no insurable interest in the car.

16. Any policy in which the insurer has no insurable interest is a wager, and void under the Gaming and Lotteries Act 1956.

17. Under the Life Assurance Act 1774 (applied to this country by the Life Assurance Act 1886), insurance cannot be taken out by a person on the life of another unless they have an interest in the life of that other.

18. A person has an insurable interest in their own life, as has one spouse in the other's life. However, an insurable interest is not assumed in the relationship of parent and child, brothers and sisters or more distant relatives. It *may* exist, however, in certain circumstances, such as when the child is supporting the parent, or vice versa.

19. Where a person has a pecuniary or legally enforceable interest in the life of another, they are deemed to have an insurable interest. A creditor has an interest in a debtor's life, an employer has an interest in an employee's life, etc.

20. Such an insurable interest need only exist at the date on which the policy is made. For example, a creditor who has taken out life assurance up to the amount of the debt on the life of the debtor, may claim on that policy at its maturity date, even if the debt has been honoured in full before that date.

21. The insurable interest in property is the loss which the insured would suffer on the occurrence of the risk. For example, an owner, a tenant, a mortgagee and a prospective purchaser may all have an insurable interest in the same piece of real property.

22. The insurable interest in fire and other types of property insurance, such as theft, must exist both at the date on which the policy is made and at the date of loss.

Indemnity
23. An indemnity is an undertaking to give protection against damage or loss. Insurance contracts, other than insurance of the person, are contracts of

indemnity, i.e. the insurer undertakes to make good (indemnify) the insured's actual loss, so far as it does not exceed the sum insured. It follows, therefore, that the insured is not allowed to profit from the policy, and a number of rules have been established to enforce this principle.

Amount recoverable

24. An insurance contract will usually provide that the insurer will pay the sum insured, or the amount of the actual loss suffered, whichever is the lesser. For example, a person insures his house for €30,000 and it is burnt down. If €20,000 will restore it, then he may claim €20,000 and no more. If it will cost €40,000 to restore it, then he may claim €30,000.

25. The measure of indemnity is:

(a) in the event of total loss, not the cost price, but the market value of the property at the time and place of the loss; or
(b) in the event of partial loss, the cost of repairs.

Case: St Alban's Investment Co. v. Sun Alliance & London Insurance Co. Ltd (1983)

The plaintiffs insured a premises against fire with the defendant insurers. When the premises was destroyed by fire, the plaintiffs entered a claim for the cost of rebuilding the damaged premises.

Held: The plaintiffs were entitled to the market value of the premises at the time of its destruction, and not the cost of rebuilding.

26. If the property is not insured for its full market value, the insurers are still liable for a partial loss up to the full limit of the sum insured. It is common, therefore, for the insurers to include a 'subject to average' clause, whereby if the amount insured is less than the value of the property, the insurers are only liable for that proportion of the actual loss which the sum insured bears to the value of the property. For example, if property with a market value of €10,000 is only insured for €5,000 under a policy containing a 'subject to average' clause, and damage is caused which totals €2,000, the insurer will only be liable for €1,000.

27. One exception to the rule that an insured cannot recover more than their actual loss arises under a 'valued policy'. With such a policy, the measure of indemnity is agreed at the time when the policy is issued. The insured can recover the agreed value if the loss is total, even though it may exceed the insured's actual loss. If the loss, however, is partial, the insured can recover such proportion of the agreed value as it is represented by the depreciation in the actual value.

Subrogation

28. Subrogation entitles an insurer, who has paid an indemnity to an insured, to all the rights of the insured against any third party liable in respect of the loss. This ensures that the policy holder obtains no more than a full indemnity.

29. The insurer brings the action in the name of the insured, who is compelled, under the terms of the policy, to lend their name to the proceedings in return for a promise that they will not be liable for costs. Once the insurer has been indemnified, any surplus belongs completely to the insured.

30. An insured, who renounces or compromises any right of action they have against a third party, without the consent of the insurer, must repay to the insurer the benefit of which they have thereby deprived them.

Contribution

31. The risk may be covered against with more than one insurer. This is called 'double insurance'. However, where two or more insurance contracts cover the same interest in a common subject matter in respect of the same risk, the law does not allow the insured to recover under each and so make a profit on their loss.

32. An insured may recover the total loss which is covered from any one of the insurers. In such an event, however, the insurer who pays the total sum acquires an implied right to 'contribution', i.e. a right to claim from each of the other insurers covering the same loss a rateable proportion of the amount paid out to the insured.

33. The insurance contract may contain a 'rateable proportion' condition, which obliges the insured to claim against all the joint insurers for a *pro rata* payment on any loss arising.

34. Finally, some insurance policies may contain a clause which excludes all liability if another policy exists which covers the same risk.

• Types of insurance contract

Life assurance

35. This is a contract by which the insured person agrees to pay a lump sum or annual payments to the insurer, over a specified period, in return for an undertaking by the insurer to pay a definite sum:

(a) on the insured's death;
(b) on the insured's death, if it occurs within a specified time; or
(c) on the insured reaching a specified age, or on their death if sooner.

36. The insurable interest necessary in such contracts is outlined in paras. 17 and 18.

37. A life assurance policy may be 'assigned'. An assignment is a transfer of the right to receive the policy money from the person originally entitled to a third party, called the assignee. In practice, this is often done to secure a loan.

38. A legal assignment is effected by an endorsement on the policy itself, or by a separate document evidenced in writing. The assignee must give notice in writing to the insurer in order to protect their interest in the policy. The assignee, thereafter, has a right to sue the insurer in their own name, if necessary, for the policy money.

39. An equitable assignment may be effected by an oral or written agreement, or by mere delivery. No special form is required, once it is clear that the insured has intended to assign the policy. An insurer will require a joint discharge from both the assignor and the assignee of an equitable assignment upon making payment under the policy.

Fire insurance
40. This is a contract which indemnifies the insured in the event of injury or loss caused by fire to specified property during a definite period of time.

41. An insurable interest must exist for the insured, not only when the contract is made, but also when the loss occurs.

42. If damage is caused by the wilful act of the insured, such as deliberately setting fire to the insured property, then they cannot recover on the loss. If, however, the damage is merely caused by their negligence, this will not defeat their claim.

Motor vehicle insurance
43. Under the Road Traffic Acts 1961–2006, a motorist must insure against any liability they may incur as a result of causing the death or injury of a third party by negligent use of the vehicle in a public place.

44. If the user of a motor vehicle is not insured against liability for causing injury to third parties, both the owner and the user are guilty of a criminal offence.

Theft insurance
45. The principles applicable to life and fire insurance also apply to theft.

Accident insurance
46. Personal injury to a policy holder is usually covered by life assurance policies. If a person does not have a life assurance policy, they may still insure themselves

against personal injury. They may also insure against liability arising from injuries to third parties.

IMPORTANT CASES

Numbers in brackets refer to paragraphs of this chapter

Carna Foods Ltd & Mallon v. Eagle Star Insurance Co. (Ireland) Ltd
(1997) .... (6)
Connors v. London & Provincial Assurance Co. (1913) .... (8)
Chariot Inns Ltd v. Assicurazioni Generali SPA (1981) .... (10)
Griffin v. Royal Liver Friendly Society (1942) .... (11)
Harney v. Century Insurance Co. Ltd (1983) .... (13)
Re Sweeney and Kennedy's Arbitration (1950) .... (14)
O'Leary v. Irish National Insurance Co. Ltd (1958) .... (15)
St Alban's Investment Co. v. Sun Alliance & London Insurance Co. Ltd
(1983) .... (25)

IMPORTANT STATUTES

Life Assurance Act 1886

PROGRESS TEST

Numbers in brackets refer to paragraphs of this chapter

1. Describe the three essential elements of an insurance contract. (2)
2. Differentiate between a 'proposal form' and a 'cover note'. (4, 7)
3. What is meant by *uberrimae fidei*, in relation to an insurance contract? (9–14)
4. Under what circumstances is an insurable interest in the subject matter of the policy assured by statute? (18–19)
5. Explain what is meant by the principle of indemnity. (23)
6. How do the rules relating to (a) subrogation, and (b) contribution, enable the enforcement of the principle of indemnity? (28–34)
7. Briefly outline the difference between life assurance and fire insurance. (35–42)

Part 4: Commercial Law

1. What are the characteristics of a negotiable instrument?
   IATI (Summer 2007)

2. Explain and outline the characteristics of negotiable instruments, distinguishing in particular between bills of exchange and cheques.
   ICPA (Summer 2005)

3. What is a bill of exchange?
   IATI (Summer 2007)

4. Explain what an 'agent' is and the ways in which the relationship of agency may be created and terminated.
   IATI (Summer 2007)

5. The relationship between principal and agent has an important role in commercial activity. Explain how the relationship of principal and agent arises.
   ICPA (Summer 2007)

6. You are employed by a company based in China, which is considering appointing a number of agents in Ireland. Explain the following principles of Irish agency law:
   (a) the definition of an agent;
   (b) express and apparent authority;
   (c) the duties of an agent;
   (d) the termination of an agency.
   MII (August 2007)

7. In relation to the law of agency:
   (a) explain the meaning of implied authority;
   (b) explain the extent of the implied authority of a company secretary.
   ACCA (June 2007)

8. Give explanations of the concepts of 'principal' and 'agent', and illustrate these concepts by reference to appropriate case law and examples.
   MII (May 2007)

9. With respect to the contractual relationship of a principal and an agent, explain each of the following:
   (a) the rights of the agent; and

(b) the duties of the principal.

MII (May 2006)

10. Dermot has agreed to become an Irish agent for New Age Clothing, a fashion house based in California which sells surf wear. Dermot isn't sure what being an agent involves and asks for your advice. Explain to him what an 'agent' is and the ways in which the relationship of agency may be created and terminated.

IATI (Summer 2006)

11. The relationship of principal and agent normally arises from agreement between the parties, but exceptions exist in the interest of commercial efficiency and to avoid injustice to a third party or the agent. In this context, discuss the following:
    (a) agency by estoppel; and
    (b) agency arising from necessity.

MII (August 2006)

12. (a) You have been asked to organise and market an organic produce fair. Explain the obligations of the sellers of organic produce at the fair with regard to the description and quality of the goods under the Sale of Goods Acts.
    (b) Outline the range of rights and remedies of consumers if there is a breach of the Sale of Goods Acts.

MII (May 2007)

13. Explain the implied conditions and warranties of a contract for the sale of goods in the Sale of Goods legislation.

IATI (Autumn 2007)

14. S Ltd manufactures high quality tweed coats. It sells them to retail outlets and also sells them directly from its own factory shop. You are employed in the Marketing and Customer Relations division and have been asked to provide a written summary of important aspects of the Sale of Goods Acts.
    (a) Explain the implied terms which apply when S Ltd sells its products.
    (b) Explain the remedies which a buyer has in the event of a breach of these terms.
    (c) Consider whether, and if so, to what extent S Ltd can exclude liability for breach of the implied terms as regards: (i) consumers who buy goods from the factory shop, and (ii) business retailers who order stocks from S Ltd.

MII (August 2007)

15. Critically analyse the elements that are contained in the implied terms that

goods must be of merchantable quality and reasonably fit for their purpose, as provided for by the Sale of Goods and Supply of Services Act 1980. An adequate answer to this question can only be provided by reference to appropriate illustrative case law.

MII (August 2006)

16. Barry saw an advertisement in his local paper placed by Technico Ltd, advertising for sale a second-hand DJ stereo system. The advertisement stated that the system was a top-of-the-range system, in excellent condition, that it was a 2004 system and available for only €800. Barry is a music enthusiast who considers himself to be an excellent DJ. He visited the Technico shop and was shown the system. The shop assistant confirmed that the system was in top order and that it was just under two years old. Barry, impressed by the system, decided to buy it. However, on setting up the system, Barry discovers that the speakers are faulty, the decks belong to an older model and the amplifier has been replaced on a number of occasions. After just three weeks, the system fails to work. Barry now wishes to return the system and recover the €800 that he paid for it. Advise him as to any rights he might have under the Sale of Goods Acts.

ICPA (Summer 2006)

17. (a) Explain the terms implied in a 'supply of services' contract under the Sale of Goods and Supply of Services Act 1980.
    (b) Describe the extent to which these implied terms may be excluded or varied.

MII (May 2007)

18. Angus bought a new mobile phone from Get Connected, a mobile phone retailer. Two weeks later, the mobile phone's screen cracked. Get Connected have refused to take the phone back or repair it. Advise Angus as to his rights under the Sale of Goods legislation.

IATI (Summer 2006)

19. Discuss what a hire purchase agreement is and how it differs from a credit sale contract and a conditional sale contract.

IATI (Summer 2007)

20. What are the statutory requirements as to the form of hire purchase agreements?

IATI (Autumn 2007)

21. Jack has bought a new sports car from a nearby car dealer. He has signed a hire-purchase agreement with Kerry Kar Finance to fund the purchase. Jack never received any documentation from Kerry Kar Finance who, after three

years of repayments, claim that the agreement was for repayments over four years. They have also threatened to take the car from Jack if he doesn't pay the balance. Jack is worried and seeks your advice.

IATI (Summer 2006)

22. Discuss and analyse the principle of 'utmost good faith' in insurance law.

ICPA (Summer 2006)

EUROPEAN UNION LAW

chapter 29

EUROPEAN UNION LAW

Topics covered

- Historical background
- Institutions of the European Union
- Sources of European Union law

Summary

This chapter examines the legal and institutional structures of the European Union and their implications for law in Ireland.

• Historical background

1. The idea of a closely knit association of European States did not find political expression to any great degree until after the Second World War. Only after Europe had yet again been devastated by war was the futility of constant national rivalry truly appreciated. Subsequent moves towards co-operation sprang from two main factors:

(a) Europe's realisation of her own weakness. The USA and Soviet Union now had far greater military, political and economic power than any of the individual European States could achieve, thereby displacing Europe from its position at the centre of the world stage.

(b) The need to prevent renewed military conflict. The two world wars, both of which had seen Europe as the main battlefield and principal sufferer, gave rise to this becoming the guiding principle of all political action.

2. On 18 April 1951, six countries (France, Germany, Italy, Belgium, the Netherlands and Luxembourg) ratified the Treaty of Paris which brought the European Coal and Steel Community (ECSC) into existence. The Treaty, which entered into force on 23 July 1952, had an objective of pooling the coal and steel production of the Member States under a joint High Authority. It was responsible for ensuring the most rational distribution of coal and steel with the maximum of efficiency. Unlike other later Treaties, the Coal and Steel Community Treaty had a limited life of fifty years. It expired on 22 July 2002. A Protocol to the Treaty of Nice 2001 provided for winding up arrangements.

3. Further attempts at economic integration led to the Six signing Treaties in Rome on 25 March 1957, aimed at establishing the European Atomic Energy

Community (Euratom) and the European Economic Community (EEC), which entered into force on 1 January 1958. These had an objective of creating a union of European States, bound together by common economic goals, namely, the harmonious development of economic activities, continuous economic expansion and a faster rise in the standard of living. Together, the three Communities were commonly referred to as the European Community (EC).

4. Ireland, Britain and Denmark joined all three Communities by ratifying treaties on accession in 1972, which came into force on 1 January 1973. In order for Ireland to do so, it was necessary to amend the Constitution to allow laws of the Community made externally, and not by organs established under the Constitution, to be part of our domestic law. A referendum, on 10 May 1972, adopted the necessary constitutional amendment.

5. On 1 January 1981, Greece became the tenth member of the Community, while on 1 January 1986, Spain and Portugal duly became the eleventh and twelfth members of the Community, after the signing of accession treaties and their ratification by the Member States and the applicant countries.

6. The Single European Act was signed on 17 February 1986 and came into effect on 1 July 1987. It contained widespread amendments and additions to the original Treaties, which finally dismantled all internal borders to establish a single market. These provisions covered the Community institutions, the internal market, economic and monetary co-operation, social policy, research and technological developments, foreign policy co-operation and the environment.

7. With the collapse of the Berlin Wall, followed by German unification in 1990, liberation from Soviet control and subsequent democratisation of the countries of Central and Eastern Europe and the disintegration of the Soviet Union in 1991, the Member States determined to strengthen their ties and negotiated a new treaty. The Treaty on European Union, signed in Maastricht in 1992 and entered into force in November 1993, conferred greater legislative powers on the European Parliament, introduced new decision-making procedures, and committed the Member States to working towards monetary union by 1999, common foreign and security policies, European citizenship and other new common policies.

8. On 1 January 1995, the European Union, which came into existence on 1 November 1993, was further enlarged with the accession of Austria, Finland and Sweden. The signing of the Treaty of Amsterdam in June 1997 strengthened and extended the powers of the European Parliament. Its assent was now needed for decisions on the accession of new Member States, association agreements with third countries, the conclusion of international agreements, a uniform procedure for elections to the European Parliament, the right of residence for Union citizens, the organisation and goals of the Structural Funds and the Cohesion Funds and the tasks and powers of the European Central Bank. On 2 May 1998, the Council of the European Union unanimously decided that 11 Member States (Germany, France, Ireland, Belgium, Spain, Luxembourg, the Netherlands, Austria, Portugal, Italy and Finland) fulfilled the necessary conditions for the adoption of the single currency on 1 January 1999. Greece became the twelfth member of the eurozone, following a proposal to this effect by the European Commission on 3 May 2000. These countries participated in Stage 3 of European Monetary Union (EMU) from the outset, appointing the President, Vice-President and four other members of the Executive Board of the European Central Bank. They irrevocably fixed their currencies to the euro from 1 January 1999, after which national currencies were phased out during a three-year transition period. In the biggest monetary changeover in history, euro banknotes and coins were introduced on 1 January 2002, the original currencies being no longer accepted in transactions after 28 February 2002. At that time, Denmark, Great Britain and Sweden were the only EU countries that had not adopted the euro. Under the Treaty of Nice 2001, new Member States are obliged to pursue the high degree of sustainable convergence required for the adoption of the euro, but it does not specify the timetable to achieve this. Slovenia was admitted in 2007, with Cyprus and Malta also joining in 2008. The dates that the remaining States are anticipated to enter the third stage of the EMU and adopt the Euro vary: 2009 for Slovakia; 2010 for Bulgaria, Latvia, Lithuania and Estonia; 2011 for Poland; 2012 for the Czech Republic; 2014 for Romania; and Hungary has yet to finalise a targeted date.

9. The Treaty of Nice provided the necessary legal framework for the enlargement of the European Union through the accession of up to twelve new Member States. It prepared the institutions of the Union to function effectively in an enlarged Union. The three central areas of change were related to the size and composition of the Commission, the weighting of votes in the Council and the extension of qualified majority voting. Ireland was the last Member State to ratify the Treaty, following a second referendum on 19 October 2002, leaving the way open for Cyprus, the Czech Republic, Estonia, Hungary, Latvia, Lithuania, Malta, Poland, the Slovak Republic and Slovenia to join the European Union on 1 May 2004. Bulgaria and Romania joined in 2007. Croatia hopes to join in 2009, however, the Commissioner for Enlargement has said 2010 is a more likely accession date. It has been recognised that Turkey's ultimate future is bound up with the European Union, and it is stepping up its efforts to fulfil the economic and political conditions (known as the 'Copenhagen criteria') necessary to enter negotiations for accession.

10. A Treaty establishing a Constitution for Europe, commonly referred to as the European Constitution, was rejected in referenda in France and the Netherlands in 2005. In June 2007, the European Council reached an agreement on the framework of a new treaty, which it hoped would be ratified by all Member States ahead of the 2009 European Parliament elections. In the event of this not happening as scheduled, it would come into force on the first day of the month following the last ratification. The Reform Treaty, now known as the Treaty of Lisbon, was formally signed by European leaders on 13 December, 2007. It retained most of the innovations agreed upon in the European Constitution such as a permanent EU president, a foreign minister (renamed 'High Representative of the Union for Foreign Affairs and Security Policy'), a reduced number of commissioners, a single legal personality for the EU thereby allowing it to sign international treaties, and the Charter of Fundamental Rights becoming legally binding. However, critics of the proposed changes argued that the treaty transferred too much power to EU institutions through the surrender of vetoes, new powers for the European Court of Justice, institutional changes and variations in the voting system used by Member States. With only Ireland obliged to have a referendum on the treaty, the remaining Member States aimed to have it ratified by their national parliaments by the end of 2008. However, the rejection of the Treaty of Lisbon by the Irish electorate on 12 June 2008 casts doubt on its ultimate fate.

• Institutions of the European Union
The European Commission
11. This is the executive body, or civil service, of the European Union. The Commission is an independent body appointed by the Member States to act as the neutral guardian of their shared interests. It is headed by the mutual agreement of the Member States. It is provided by the existing treaties that each of the twenty-seven Member States must have a national on the Commission. Under the proposed Treaty of Lisbon, this would be reduced in size, with the total number of Commissioners being two-thirds of the number of Member States.

12. Throughout their five-year term of office, Commissioners must remain independent of the governments of the Member States and of the Council of Ministers. The Council cannot remove a Commissioner from office. The European Parliament is consulted before the Member States appoint the President of the Commission, and the full Commission has to be approved by Parliament before it too is formally appointed. Provisions also exist for the Parliament to pass a motion of censure by a two-thirds majority compelling the Commission as a body to resign, in which case it would continue to handle everyday business until the Commission's replacement.

13. The President, with the approval of the Commission, may appoint Vice-Presidents from among its members. The President has the responsibility to allocate tasks among the Commission members, and may re-allocate portfolios among Commissioners at any point during their term of office. Finally, a member of the Commission must resign if asked to do so by the President, but the President must have the agreement of the Commission before making such a request.

14. Each Commissioner has a personal staff, called a cabinet, which helps them prepare their contributions to the work of the Commission, and their contacts with the services, with the other institutions, with the Member States and with the general public. In addition, the Commission has a large staff that comprises a secretariat-general, a legal service, a statistical office, directorates-general and a small number of specialised services.

15. Each Commissioner has special responsibility for one or more portfolios or broad areas of European Union activity, such as agriculture, energy, transport, external relations. Despite this autonomy, however, the Commission is bound to act with collective responsibility. It must adopt the various measures incumbent on it under the Treaties as a body. The Commission, headed by a President and currently with five Vice-Presidents, meets at least one day each week for this purpose.

16. When particularly sensitive matters are being discussed, the Commission sits alone, the only official present being the Secretary-General. In other cases, the officials responsible may be called in. Although its decisions can be taken by majority, many are in fact unanimous. Where a vote is taken, the minority abides by the majority decision, which becomes the position of the full Commission.

17. The Commission has been assigned a wide range of duties under the Treaties. It is required to:

(a) act as guardian of the Treaties;
(b) serve as the executive arm of the European Communities;
(c) initiate European Union policy and defend the European Communities' interest in the Council of Ministers;
(d) issue proceedings against Member States;
(e) make proposals; and
(f) fine individuals and companies.

18. The Commission has to see to it that the provisions of the Treaties and the decisions of the European Communities' institutions are implemented properly. It investigates a presumed infringement either on its own initiative or on the strength of complaints from governments, companies or private individuals. Once an infringement has been established, the Commission requests the Member State in question to submit its comments within a specified time period, generally two months. If the disputed practice is allowed by the Member State to continue, and it is unable to satisfy the Commission, then the Commission will issue a reasoned opinion, which the Member State must comply with before a specified deadline. If it does not do so, the Commission may refer the case to the European Court of Justice, whose judgment is binding on both parties.

19. The Commission has been conferred with wide executive powers by the Treaties and the Council of Ministers. It has particularly extensive legislative powers to issue decisions and regulations implementing certain Treaty provisions or Council of Ministers' acts. It applies Treaty rules to specific cases (involving governments or companies), administers safeguard clauses in the Treaties, and administers appropriations for the European Communities' public expenditure and the four major funds: the European Agricultural Guidance and Guarantee Fund, the European Social Fund, the European Regional Development Fund and the Cohesion Fund.

20. The Commission initiates European Communities policy by submitting proposals to the Council of Ministers and the European Parliament for consideration. This is known as the 'co-decision procedure'. When drafting its proposals, the Commission takes the often widely varying interests of the individual Member States into account in order to establish where the general interest lies. Once a proposal is lodged, and comments have been received from the European Parliament, a dialogue takes place between the ministers in the Council, who put their national points of view, and the Commission, which seeks to uphold the interest of the European Communities as a whole and find European solutions to common problems. Because of its non-partisan position, the Commission acts as a mediator between the Member States through the negotiations within the Council of Ministers in order to find an acceptable compromise without sacrificing the European Communities' interest.

21. The Commission also represents the European Union in dealing with non-Member States and other international organisations, such as GATT and the UN. It is also the Commission which examines applications for membership of the European Union.

The Council of Ministers
22. The Council consists of representatives at ministerial level of the governments of the Member States. They are authorised to commit the governments of each of those Member States. Although the 'main' representative for each is its Foreign Minister, membership of the Council varies with the subject down for discussion. Meetings are thus often attended by the ministers responsible for the subject area in question (e.g. agriculture, finance, transport, science). Presidency of the Council rotates every six months.

23. While the Council of Ministers represents the sovereignty of the Member States, and considers and protects national interests, it is also obliged to take the European Union interest into account. It is required to take decisions necessary for the attainment of the goals laid down in the Treaties. Some of its responsibilities include:

(a) co-ordinating the general economic policies of the Member States;
(b) adopting the main decisions relating to the common policies;

(c) defining common foreign and security policies; and

(d) drawing up conventions and arranging joint actions in the case of justice and home affairs.

24. The Council of Ministers is formally the legislative body for the European Union, since no major proposals can be implemented without its consent. The Commission drafts proposals concerning European Union policy and development for the Council of Ministers to discuss.

25. The Treaties specify whether the Council of Ministers is to take its decisions by unanimous agreement of all members, by qualified majority vote (QMV) or by simple majority (in the case of simple procedural issues). The Single European Act, the Treaty on European Union and the Treaty of Nice have substantially extended the Council's scope for taking qualified majority decisions. Under the proposed Treaty of Lisbon, a new version of qualified majority rules would apply from 2014.

26. While unanimity is required in some very sensitive areas of national policy-making, such as foreign policy and taxation, decisions on most issues are taken by qualified majority vote. The areas in which Council decisions are taken by qualified majority vote rather than by unanimity is considerably extended by the Treaty of Nice. Qualified majority voting is now applied to some thirty additional Treaty articles, including such issues as trade in services and commercial aspects of intellectual property rights (Article 133.5), economic, technical and financial co-operation with third countries (Article 181a) and the appointment of the President and members of the Commission (Article 214).

27. When the Council is required to act by a qualified majority, the votes of Member States is weighted as follows:

Austria	10	Latvia	4
Belgium	12	Lithuania	7
Bulgaria	10	Luxembourg	4
Cyprus	4	Malta	3
Czech Republic	12	Netherlands	13
Denmark	7	Poland	27
Estonia	4	Portugal	12
Finland	7	Romania	14
France	29	Slovenia	4
Germany	29	Slovakia	7
Greece	12	Spain	27
Hungary	12	Sweden	10
Ireland	7	United Kingdom	29
Italy	29		

28. Where the Council decides to adopt a proposal from the Commission, a qualified majority is constituted by 255 votes out of 345, cast by a majority of the Member States. In all other cases, a qualified majority is constituted by 255 votes, cast by at least two-thirds of the Member States. Finally, a member of the Council may request verification that the Member States constituting the qualified majority represent at least 62 per cent of the total population of the Union.

The European Council

29. In December 1974, the Heads of State or Government of the Community countries decided to meet regularly within a 'European Council' with their Foreign Ministers and the President and one of the Vice-Presidents of the Commission, with a view to defining new objectives and giving a fresh stimulus to European integration. This was formally incorporated into the Community's institutional framework by the Single European Act.

30. Meetings of the European Council are free of institutional formalities. It is simply a meeting of politicians, with neither civil servants nor experts present. In recent years, such meetings have provided political impetus in areas such as economic and monetary union, direct elections to the European Parliament, reform of agricultural policy, social policy measures and the accession of new members.

31. Although having no specific authority and currently unrecognised as an official institution, the European Council is considered as the supreme political body of the Union. The importance of the European Council in the workings of the European Union has steadily increased – a trend which is likely to continue as the authority of the Heads of State or Government grows stronger.

32. Meetings of the European Council take place in the country holding the Presidency of the Council of Ministers or in Brussels. The chair of the European Council continues to be held by the Member State holding the Presidency of the Council of Ministers. Under the proposed Treaty of Lisbon, the six-month rotating position of chair would be replaced by a President elected by EU leaders to serve a renewable term of two and a half years.

The European Parliament

33. On 7 and 10 June 1979, direct elections to the European Parliament were first introduced, with each Member State using its own national electoral system. These elections are held every five years, the next being in 2009.

34. The Treaty of Nice reached agreement on the re-allocation of seats for the 2004–9 term of the European Parliament. Depending on ratification of the proposed Treaty of Lisbon, the number of representatives elected from each

Member State in the 2009 elections will be modified as follows:

Member State	2007	2009 Nice	2009 Lisbon	Member State	2007	2009 Nice	2009 Lisbon
Austria	18	17	19	Latvia	9	8	9
Belgium	24	22	22	Lithuania	13	12	12
Bulgaria	18	17	18	Luxembourg	6	6	6
Cyprus	6	6	6	Malta	5	5	6
Czech Republic	24	22	22	Netherlands	27	25	26
Denmark	14	13	13	Poland	54	50	51
Estonia	6	6	6	Portugal	24	22	22
Finland	14	13	13	Romania	35	33	33
France	78	72	74	Slovenia	7	7	8
Germany	99	99	96	Slovakia	14	13	13
Greece	24	22	22	Spain	54	50	54
Hungary	24	22	22	Sweden	19	18	20
Ireland	13	12	12	United Kingdom	78	72	73
Italy	78	72	73				
					785	736	751

35. Parliament is presided over by a President, assisted by fourteen Vice-Presidents. Elected members organise themselves into groups based on political, social and economic philosophies, regardless of nationality. The largest of these are the European People's Party and European Democrats (EPP-ED), the Party of European Socialists (PES) and the Alliance of Liberals and Democrats for Europe (ALDE).

36. The European Parliament operates by way of twenty standing committees. Each committee specialises in some particular aspect of the European Communities' activity, such as agriculture, energy, monetary affairs. The appropriate member of the Commission, or their representative, appears before the committees to give an account of the decisions taken by the Commission, the proposals presented to the Council of Ministers and the position adopted by the Commission *vis-à-vis* the Council of Ministers. Committee work, therefore, takes up most of a Member of European Parliament's time. Eleven plenary sessions of one week's duration, involving the entire European Parliament, are also held each year.

37. The European Parliament shares legislative powers with the Council of Ministers. Legislation is proposed by the Commission, with the European Parliament and the Council of Ministers sharing the power to enact it. Under the Single European Act 1986, a co-operation procedure was introduced which required two readings of legislative proposals by the European Parliament and the Council of Ministers with the active participation of the Commission. Legislative powers were increased by the Treaty on European Union 1992, with a new co-decision procedure being introduced which gives the European Parliament the power to adopt regulations and directives on an equal footing with the Commission in legislation relating to the single market, social policy, economic and social cohesion, research, trans-European networks, consumer protection, education, culture and health. The Treaty of Nice extended further the Parliament's role by adding to the list of Articles where co-decision applies, including issues relating to movement of third country nationals (Article 62.2(a)), immigration (Article 63.3(b)), and judicial co-operation (Article 65). Parliament has now also a right to initiate action under the new procedure provided for in Article 7, dealing with situations where there is a risk of serious breach of fundamental principles, including human rights. Finally, there is an expanded role for the European Parliament in the area of enhanced co-operation, including in relation to the new provisions in the area of Common Foreign and Security Policy.

38. The supervisory function of the European Parliament extends to the Commission, which is obliged to defend and justify its position in public debates before the European Parliament. It votes on the Commission's programme and the Commission must also present an annual general report on the activities of the European Communities for discussion. Parliament thus keeps constant watch on the Commission's doings, making sure that it represents the European Union interest, ready at any time to call it to order if it gives the impression of yielding to the lobbying of governments. Ultimately, therefore, the Commission is responsible to the European Parliament and it can even be forced to resign by a motion of censure carried by a two-thirds majority.

39. The Treaty on European Union empowered the European Parliament to appoint an ombudsman to handle complaints concerning issues of maladministration in the activities of any of the European Communities' institutions.

40. The European Parliament also has widespread budgetary powers. It votes on the adoption of the annual budget and oversees its implementation. In certain cases it may not alone reallocate, but also increase, expenditure up to specified limits. It has the right to reject a budget as a whole, which it did with the 1980 and 1985 budgets. This has allowed the European Parliament to impose its point of view on the Council of Ministers on a number of occasions.

The Court of Justice and the Court of First Instance
41. The Court of Justice, based in Luxembourg, consists of twenty-seven judges, and is assisted by eight advocates-general. Judges are appointed by common accord of the governments of the Member States, and hold office for a renewable term of six years. Every three years, fourteen and thirteen judges are replaced alternately, thereby ensuring continuity of the Court's decisions.

42. The Treaty of Nice stipulates that the Court of Justice consist of one judge from each Member State and the Court of First Instance comprise of at least one judge from each Member State. The full Court sits with all judges present only in exceptional cases. A 'Grand Chamber' of thirteen judges hear most other cases, and the Court of Justice is also allowed to form chambers of three and five judges as appropriate.

43. Judges are chosen from persons whose independence is beyond doubt, and who are qualified to hold the highest judicial offices in their respective Member States. They select one of their number to be President for a renewable term of three years. The President directs the work of the Court of Justice.

44. Advocates-general are appointed on the same terms as judges, and have to satisfy the same criteria with respect to independence and training. Until recently, they were all nationals of the larger European Union countries. Lately, however, there have been appointments of nationals of the smaller Member States.

45. An advocate-general does not participate in the Court of Justice's deliberations. Instead, at a separate hearing some weeks after lawyers have addressed the Court, the advocate-general comments on the various aspects of the case in an unbiased manner, weighs up the provisions of European Union law, compares the case in point with previous rulings, highlights its possible implications for future development within the European Union and ultimately proposes an appropriate legal solution to the dispute. Decisions of an advocate-general are not binding, but are very persuasive.

46. The general tasks of the Court of Justice consist of the interpretation, application and development of European Union law. Thus, the Court of Justice has jurisdiction in:

(a) actions brought by the Commission or by Member States for an infringement of the Treaties by a Member State;
(b) actions brought by Member States, corporate bodies or private individuals against the Commission and the Council of Ministers, or by one of the latter European Communities institutions against the other on the grounds of lack of competence, infringement of the Treaties, violation of a procedural requirement or abuse of power;
(c) preliminary rulings on the interpretation of the Treaties, or on the validity of any of the European Communities' institutions.

47. The Court of Justice reaches its judgment by majority vote. However, no dissenting opinion is made public. Those judges participating in the deliberation sign the single judgment, which is then pronounced at a public hearing. The Court of Justice's decision is binding on the Member States. There is no right of appeal against such decisions. If a Member State does not comply with the ruling, new proceedings may be brought for a declaration by the Court that the obligations arising from its first decision have not been complied with. While the Treaties do not provide any sanctions where a Member State fails to give effect to a judgment, the experience has been that Member States have complied, sooner or later, with the Court of Justice's judgment.

48. The Single European Act 1986 has allowed the Council of Ministers, acting unanimously at the request of the Court of Justice and after consulting the Commission and European Parliament, to attach to the Court of Justice a Court of First Instance.

49. The composition of the Court of First Instance is determined by the Council of Ministers. Like the judges of the Court of Justice, they must satisfy specified criteria with respect to independence and training. They too are appointed by common accord of the governments of the Member States, and hold office for a renewable term of six years. Membership is partially renewed every three years, thereby ensuring continuity of the Court's decisions.

50. Not all classes of actions may be heard by the Court of First Instance. Actions brought by officials of the European Communities, actions for damages and competition cases may be dealt with by the Court. Decisions on such actions, however, may be appealed to the Court of Justice on points of law. The Treaty of Nice gave a higher status to the Court of First Instance, expanded its role and gave it jurisdiction to provide 'preliminary rulings' on issues regarding the interpretation of the Treaties or the validity of a Community act or an act of the European Central Bank as referred to it by national Courts.

51. Judicial panels, attached to the Court of First Instance, were established by the Treaty of Nice to hear and deal with specific classes of action. It was proposed that the first such panel deal with disputes between the Communities and members of its staff. There is a right of appeal from decisions of such panels to the Court of First Instance on points of law only, unless the decision establishing the panel has also provided for an appeal on matters of fact.

The Court of Auditors
52. The Court of Auditors consists of a national from each Member State, appointed for a six-year term by the Council of Ministers acting by qualified majority, after having consulted with the European Parliament. It has been in operation since October 1977, but the Treaty of Nice provides for the more effective operation of the Court of Auditors, particularly in the context of enlargement.

53. The functions of the Court of Auditors include:

(a) auditing the accounts of the European Communities and of the European Communities' bodies;

(b) examining whether revenue and expenditure have been properly and lawfully received and incurred;

(c) checking that financial management has been sound; and

(d) reporting back to the European Communities' institutions.

54. The Treaty on European Union 1992 conferred full institutional status on the Court of Auditors and gave it an additional responsibility, namely, to provide the European Parliament and the Council of Ministers with a statement of assurance as to the reliability of the accounts and the legality and regularity of the underlying transactions. The Treaty of Nice enables the Court of Auditors, with the approval of a qualified majority of the Council, to set up internal chambers to adopt certain types of reports or opinions without needing a full meeting of the Court.

The Economic and Social Committee

55. The Economic and Social Committee consists of members representing the various sectors of economic and social life of the European Communities. These are divided into three groups: employers, workers and other interests. It assists the Council of Ministers and the Commission, and must be consulted before decisions are taken on a large number of subjects. It is also free to submit opinions on its own initiative. This process ensures that the various interest groups are actively involved in the development of the European Communities. The Treaty of Nice limits the number of seats that each Member State can have to twenty-seven, with the total number of seats not exceeding 350. Ireland will continue to nominate nine members to the Committee as at present.

The Committee of the Regions

56. The Committee of the Regions was established by the Treaty on European Union 1992. As with the Economic and Social Committee, the Treaty of Nice limits the number of seats that each Member State can have to twenty-seven, with the total number of seats not exceeding 350. Ireland has nine members on the Committee at present. Members and alternates are appointed by the Council of Ministers based on nominations from Member States, and the Treaty of Nice stipulates that representatives must be members of a regional or local authority, or be politically accountable to an elected assembly. The Committee of the Regions must be consulted by the Council of Ministers or the Commission in a number of areas where regional interests are involved, such as education, youth, culture, public health, economic and social cohesion, and trans-European transport, telecommunications and energy networks. As well as meeting in plenary session five times a year, the work of the Committee is carried out by eight commissions and four subcommissions.

- ## Sources of European Union law

✗ *Treaties*

57. The 'primary legislation' of the European Union has been created directly by the Member States. It consists of the Treaties establishing the European Communities and Union themselves, including the annexes, schedules and protocols attached to the Treaties, and the subsequent additions and amendments thereto.

58. These written sources of European Union law include:

(a) Treaty establishing the European Coal and Steel Community of 18 April 1951 (otherwise known as the 'Treaty of Paris').
(b) Treaty establishing the European Atomic Energy Community (Euratom) of 25 March 1957 (otherwise known as the 'first Treaty of Rome').
(c) Treaty establishing the European Economic Community (EEC) – now EC – of 25 March 1957 (otherwise known as the 'second Treaty of Rome').
(d) Treaty establishing a single Council and a single Commission of the European Communities (Merger Treaty) of 8 April 1965.
(e) Treaty concerning the accession of Ireland, Denmark and Britain to the EEC and Euratom of 22 January 1972.
(f) Treaty creating a European Union combining three Communities moving towards economic and monetary union with intergovernmental co-operation in certain areas (otherwise known as the Treaty on European Union of 1992).
(g) Treaty strengthening and extending the powers of the European Parliament (otherwise known as the Treaty of Amsterdam of 1997).
(h) Treaty providing the necessary legal framework for the enlargement of the European Union through the accession of up to twelve new Member States to join the existing fifteen (otherwise know as the Treaty of Nice of 2001).

59. The Treaties set out broad objectives to be achieved by the European Union. The specific details are left to the Council of Ministers and the Commission, who have limited law-making powers which they may exercise in accordance with the provisions of the Treaties.

60. The primary law of the European Union takes precedence over national law. A legal consequence of this precedence is the fact that any provision of national law which conflicts with the European Union law is invalid. In theory, however, European Union law and national constitutional law are separate. In some Member States (e.g. The Netherlands and the Republic of Ireland) the precedence of European Union law has been provided for in the national constitution. Friction between Community policy and Irish constitutional law resulted from the Supreme Court's refusal in 1987 to permit the government to proceed with ratification of the Single European Act without the specific permission of the population by referendum. This delayed the entry into force of the Act by six months and served as a warning that Ireland's membership of the European Communities and ratification of the Single European Act did not rule out the possibility that referenda would be required again for further developments. This was the case with the referendum in 1992 which allowed the State to ratify the Treaty on European Union, commonly known as the Maastricht Treaty. Indeed, it took two referenda before the Treaty of Nice was eventually ratified by Irish voters on 19 October 2002.

European Union legislation

61. The legal acts which the Council of Ministers and the Commission have at their disposal when carrying out the tasks conferred on them are enumerated and described under Article 189 of the EEC Treaty 1957. This 'secondary law' of the European Union consists of:

(a) *Regulations.* These are used mainly to secure uniformity of law throughout the European Community and Euratom (e.g. Regulation No. 17 on restrictive practices of 6 February 1962 and Regulation No. 1612/68 on freedom of movement of 15 October 1968). They have general application, are binding in their entirety and are directly applicable in all Member States without the need for further legislation. They confer rights and impose obligations on those to whom they are addressed.

(b) *Directives.* These also have general application, but do not have immediate binding force. They are addressed to Member States and lay down the result to be achieved, but leave the choice of the form of the measures and methods used in the implementation of the directives to the individual national authorities. Once the Council of Ministers adopts a directive which has been placed before it by the Commission, then the Member States have until a specified date to incorporate the provisions of the directive into their own national laws. For example, the Eighth Directive on harmonising the qualifications for auditors, as well as dealing with their education and training, was adopted in April 1984. Member States had until 1988 to implement it, and until 1990 before its provisions needed to be applied.

(c) *Decisions.* These are the usual means whereby the European Community and Euratom institutions deal with individual cases, and in the competition field, for example, have had a far-reaching impact on the behaviour of undertakings. They may be addressed by the Council of Ministers or Commission to a Member State, or to one or more individuals in the Member States. Their content may be expressed in either concrete or abstract terms. Decisions are immediately binding in their entirety upon those to whom they are addressed.

(d) *Recommendations and opinions.* These are not legally binding and give rise to no legal obligation on the part of the addressees, who are for the most part Member States. Recommendations are usually made on the initiative of the

European institution issuing them, suggesting that the addressees take a specific course of action without legally obliging them to do so. Opinions, on the other hand, are delivered as a result of an initiative of one or more persons, and contain a general assessment of certain facts or prepare the ground for subsequent legal proceedings. Because of their lack of binding force, the importance of recommendations and opinions is primarily political and psychological.

PROGRESS TEST

Numbers in brackets refer to paragraphs of this chapter

1. What treaty established the EEC, and what were its immediate and long-term aims? (3)
2. Describe the composition of the Commission. (11, 14)
3. List the functions of (a) the Commission, (b) the Council of Ministers, (c) the European Parliament, and (d) the Court of Justice. (17, 23, 37–40, 46)
4. What are the primary sources of European Union law? (57–8)
5. Distinguish between (a) regulations, (b) directives, and (c) decisions, in European Union law. (61)

INTERNET RESOURCES

Committee of the Regions
  www.cor.europa.eu
Council of the European Union
  www.consilium.europa.eu
Economic and Social Committee
  www.eesc.europa.eu
European Central Bank
  www.ecb.europa.eu
European Commission
  www.ec.europa.eu
European Court of Auditors
  www.eca.europa.eu
European Court of Justice
  www.curia.europa.eu
European Ombudsman
  www.ombudsman.europa.eu
European Parliament
  www.europarl.europa.eu

Part 5: European Union Law

EXAMINATION QUESTIONS

1. (a) Write a note on the sources of European Union law.
   (b) Distinguish between a regulation and a directive in European Union law.

   IATI (Summer 2007)

2. There are five secondary sources of European Community law. Discuss each of these.

   ICPA (Summer 2007)

3. Outline the sources of European Community law.

   IATI (Autumn 2006)

4. Identify and explain the various sources of European Union law, referring in your answer to the nature of these sources.

   ICPA (Autumn 2006)

5. Define each of the following types of legislative provision of the European Union and explain how each type becomes part of the domestic law of this State:
   (a) a directive;
   (b) a regulation;
   (c) a decision.

   MII (Autumn 2007)

6. Write a note on the institutions of the European Community.

   IATI (Autumn 2007)

7. In European Community/European Union law, list the principal institutions and outline the structure and function of two of these institutions.

   IATI (Autumn 2005)

8. Explain in detail the functions of the Commission and the Council of Ministers as European Institutions.

   ICPA (Autumn 2005)

9. (a) Outline the functions of the EU Commission.
   (b) Explain the role of the Court of Justice of the EU.

   IATI (Summer 2005)

10. Explain in detail the role of the European Court of Justice in the legal system

of the European Community, referring in your answer to the Court of First Instance also.

ICPA (Autumn 2006)

11. (a) Outline the duties and powers of the Court of Justice of the European Union.
    (b) Explain what a 'regulation' and a 'directive' are in EU law and distinguish between the two.

IATI (Summer 2006)

12. Distinguish between, and explain the roles of, the following courts in relation to Irish law:
    (a) the European Court of Justice;
    (b) the European Court of Human Rights.

ACCA (December 2006)

Part 6

EMPLOYMENT LAW

EMPLOYMENT LAW

Topics covered

- Contract of employment
- Terms of the contract
- Common law duties of the employee
- Common law duties of the employer
- Statutory regulation of the terms of the contract
- Termination of the contract

Summary

A contract of employment forms the basis for a relationship between an employer and an employee. This chapter examines how this contract is, like other contracts, governed by the ordinary principles of common law but, unlike other contracts, is modified by statute and is a dynamic agreement, the terms of which may be regularly altered by the consensus of the parties involved.

• Contract of employment

1. An employment has been held to exist when a person is working under a 'contract of service'. The person is employed to provide labour or skill in whatever way their employer dictates in return for wages. The work is done subject to the employer's detailed control. The relationship between the employer and employee is regulated by a contract of employment or 'service'.

2. A contract of employment is governed by the ordinary principles of contract law. It is, however, a dynamic agreement which may be modified by statute.

Case: Tierney v. An Post (2000)

The plaintiff had been appointed postmaster of a sub-post office. The contract consisted of a document called 'Appointment of Postmaster', which stated that the position did not entitle the plaintiff to medical attendance, sick pay or annual leave, that the premises were to be kept to a certain standard, and that certain facilities were to be provided to the public at the sub-post office. However, the postmaster was stated to be under the control of the defendant's regional manager, and permission from the Head Postmaster was required before hiring an assistant. Following customer complaints and a subsequent investigation regarding the standard of accounting at the sub-post office, the defendant terminated the contract. The plaintiff, who had not been provided with the full evidence against him, argued that fair disciplinary procedures under employment law had not been completed, whilst the defendant claimed that the contract was not of service but was a contract for services.

Held: Although the degree of control exercised by the defendant was a factor to be considered, the plaintiff was in fact an independent contractor and not an employee.

Formation of the contract

3. A contract of employment may be created orally or in writing, or may be implied by the conduct of the parties. Generally, no formality is required, except that a contract for the employment of a seaman or a contract of apprenticeship in specified industries must be in writing.

4. Under the Irish Statute of Frauds 1695, a contract of employment which is not to be performed within one year is unenforceable unless it is evidenced by writing.

• Terms of the contract

5. As with other types of contracts, the terms of the contract of employment may be expressed or implied.

6. The *express* terms are those which are agreed orally or in writing between the employee and the employer (or their agent). These may include details of pay, hours of work, holidays, sick leave, etc.

7. Not all of the terms of the contract of employment will be expressly agreed between the parties. A term may be *implied in fact*, because it lends business efficacy to the contract. It may be *implied by custom and practice* in the trade, industry or locality provided those customs are well known and reasonable. Finally, some terms may be *implied at common law or by statute*, which are included in the implied duties of an employee or employer.

• Common law duties of the employee

8. Employees have been held to have the following implied duties towards their employers:

(a) *To give personal service.* Employees must attend and be available to do the work which they have been contracted to do, during agreed working hours. The employees must not, without the permission of the employer, delegate the performance of duties to another.

(b) *To obey lawful orders.* The employees must obey all orders given by the employer to them, provided these orders are within the terms of the contract, and do not place them in personal danger.

(c) *To exercise reasonable care and skill.* The employees must exercise due care and skill in the performance of their work. Where employees claim to have the skill and experience to perform the work undertaken, their tasks must be carried out diligently and efficiently.

(d) *To act in good faith.* The employees must act honestly and in the interests of the employer, when dealing with the employer's property or in exercising any trust placed in them. They must not accept bribes or make secret profits. They must disclose all inventions made using the facilities of the employer.

(e) *To maintain secrecy.* The employees must not disclose confidential information obtained by them in the course of, and as a result of, their employment. Neither must they exploit their employer's trade secrets or customer contacts. However, the employees may disclose information if it is such that it is in the public interest to do so, or if it is disclosed to someone who has a proper interest to receive it.

(f) *To indemnify their employer.* Employees may be liable to compensate their employer for any loss suffered as a result of a wrongful act. However, this rarely happens unless there is evidence of collusion or wilful misconduct on the employee's part.

• Common law duties of the employer

9. In the absence of any specific provisions in the contract of employment, the employer has the following implied duties towards an employee:

(a) *To provide work (in some cases).* In general, there is no duty on an employer to provide work for employees to do, so long as the employer continues to pay the agreed wages. There are, however, some exceptions:

    (i)   if employment is essential to provide a reputation for future employment, e.g. acting or journalism;

    (ii) if remuneration depends upon the amount of work performed, e.g. if the person is employed on a commission basis or to do piece work;

    (iii) if an employee is employed to perform a particular task, or to fill a particular post, the employer is in breach of contract if the post is abolished or the employee is removed from it.

(b) *To pay wages or remuneration.* The employer has a duty to pay the employees the agreed remuneration or what is reasonable in the circumstances.

Case: McEvoy v. Moore (1902)

The plaintiff was instructed to go to the defendant's premises with a view to being employed as a stableman. The period of employment and associated remuneration were not discussed. The plaintiff subsequently sued for payment of wages.

Held: The plaintiff was entitled to remuneration at the normal rate for work of that type.

(c) *To provide for the safety of the employees.* The employer owes a special duty of care towards employees. This duty may arise in tort, or it may be implied in the contract of employment. The employer has a duty:

   (i)   to employ competent employees who are not a danger to their fellow employees;

   (ii) to provide, and maintain, a safe place of work for the benefit of the employees;

   (iii) to provide, and maintain, proper equipment so as not to subject the employees to unnecessary risk; and

   (iv) to devise a system of working which is reasonably safe for employees.

Case: Everitt v. Thorsman Ireland Ltd (2000)

The plaintiff, in the course of his employment, attempted to open the lid of a bin with a lever provided for that purpose. The lever snapped, causing the plaintiff to fall and sustain an injury. The lever was found to have a latent defect. The plaintiff claimed that the employer owed him a common law duty of care to provide proper equipment and that the defendant had been negligent in this regard.

Held: The employer's duty of care had been discharged when he had purchased the tool, whose latent defect he had no means of discovering, from a reputable source. However, in finding for the plaintiff, the Court decided that under work safety legislation any employee injured through no fault of his own by using defective equipment should not be left without a remedy, and that the employer might seek indemnity from the third party who supplied the equipment.

(d) *To indemnify employees.* The employer must indemnify employees in respect of all losses, liabilities and expenses incurred whilst acting on the employer's behalf, except where:

   (i)   the employee knew that the act was unlawful; or

   (ii) the employee knew that the employer had no right to give the order.

• Statutory regulation of the terms of the contract

Terms of Employment (Information) Acts 1994–2001

10. These Acts give employees the right to have information about the terms of their employment set out in writing within two months of the date of commencement of employment. They must also be notified of any changes in the particulars as given in the statement not later than one month after the change comes into effect.

11. The provisions apply to any person:

   (a) working under a contract of employment or apprenticeship;

    (b) employed through an employment agency, or

    (c) in the service of the State (including members of the Garda Síochána and the Defence Forces, civil servants and employees of any local authority, health board, harbour authority or vocational education committee).

12. The Protection of Employees (Part-Time Work) Act 2001 removed the exclusion relating to persons who worked for an employer for less than eight hours a week.

13. However, the Acts do not apply to a person who has been in the continuous service of the employer for less than one month.

14. The employment agency or client company is the employer in the case of agency workers, and is responsible for providing the written statement of the employee's terms of employment.

15. The following particulars of the terms of employment must be included in the written statement:

    (a) full name of the employer and employee;

    (b) address of the employer;

    (c) place of work;

    (d) job title or nature of the work;

    (e) date of commencement of employment;

    (f) expected duration of employment, if contact is temporary;

    (g) date on which employment ends, if contract is for fixed term;

    (h) rate of pay or method of calculating pay;

    (i) pay reference period for purposes of National Minimum Wage Act 2000;

    (j) whether pay is to be weekly, monthly or otherwise;

    (k) details of hours of work and overtime;

    (l) holiday entitlements;

    (m) sick pay entitlements and pension schemes, if any;

    (n) period of notice of termination to be given by each party;

    (o) expiry date of contract, if employment is for a fixed period, and

    (p) details of any collective agreements which affect the terms of employment.

16. Where an employee is required to work outside the State for a period of not less than one month, the employer is obliged to add the following particulars to the written statement:

    (q) the period of employment outside the State;

    (r) the currency in which the employee is to be paid in respect of that period;

    (s) any benefits in cash or kind payable to the employee in respect of the employment outside the State; and

    (t) any terms and conditions governing the employee's repatriation.

17. The statement must be signed by or on behalf of the employer, and must be retained by the employer throughout the employment and for one year after the cessation of employment.

18. Moreover, even if the employee leaves the employment within the two-month period stipulated for providing a written statement, it must still be given to the ex-employee.

19. Employers are required to provide employees under the age of eighteen with a copy of the official summary of the Protection of Young Persons (Employment) Act 1977.

20. An employee has a right of complaint to a Rights Commissioner where an employer fails to provide a written statement in accordance with the terms of the Acts or fails to notify the employee of changes to the particulars contained in the Acts. The Rights Commissioner will send a copy of the notice of complaint to the employer. After hearing the parties, the Rights Commissioner will issue a written recommendation. Either party may appeal a recommendation of the Rights Commissioner to the Employment Appeals Tribunal.

Payment of Wages Act 1991

21. The main purpose of this Act is to establish a range of rights for all employees relating to the payment of wages, which include:

(a) a readily negotiable mode of wage payment;
(b) a written statement of gross wages and deductions; and
(c) protection against unlawful deductions from wages.

22. The Act applies to any person:

(a) employed under a contract of employment or apprenticeship;
(b) employed through an employment agency or through a sub-contractor; or
(c) in the service of the State.

23. Employees may be paid wages, otherwise than in cash, by:

(a) cheque;
(b) bank draft;
(c) postal or money order;
(d) credit transfer; or
(e) any other such method as specified in regulations made by the Minister for Enterprise, Trade and Employment.

24. Employers must give a written statement to each employee with every payment of wages, detailing the gross amount of wages payable to the employee and itemising the nature and amount of each deduction. Where wages are paid by credit transfer, the statement of wages should be given to the employee as soon as possible after the credit transfer has taken place.

25. Employers are required to take such reasonable steps as are necessary, not only to ensure that the statements are treated as confidential until they become the property of the employees, but also to ensure that the information which is contained in the statements is treated as confidential by those who are privy to it.

26. The Act restricts employers from making deductions from wages or receiving payment from their workers unless:

(a) required or authorised by law, such as PAYE or PRSI;
(b) required or authorised by a term of the employee's contract, such as certain occupational pension scheme contributions, breakages, or till shortages; or
(c) consented to in writing in advance by the employee, such as trade union subscriptions or VHI scheme premiums.

27. Employees have a right of complaint to a Rights Commissioner against any unlawful deductions or payments from wages. Either party may appeal a recommendation of the Rights Commissioner to the Employment Appeals Tribunal.

28. Transitional arrangements apply to employees who, when the Act came into operation, were paid their wages in cash or by a mode other than cash in accordance with an agreement under the Payment of Wages Act 1979.

Organisation of Working Time Act 1997
29. The Act sets out the statutory rights for employees in respect of maximum working time, rest and holidays.

30. Employees are only permitted to work, in each period of seven days, a maximum of on average forty-eight hours over a four month duration, except in cases where the work is subject to seasonality, or where employees are directly involved in ensuring continuity of service or production, in which case the maximum working week can be averaged over six months.

31. Employees who normally work at least three hours of their daily working time between midnight and 7 a.m. the following day, and whose annual number of hours worked between these times equals or exceeds fifty per cent of annual working time, are only permitted to work a maximum of on average eight hours in each period of twenty-four hours, calculated over a period that does not exceed two months or where a collective agreement permits a greater length of time.

However, for night workers whose work involves special hazards or heavy physical or mental strain, an absolute limit of eight hours work in each period of twenty-four hours is permitted.

32. Employees are generally entitled to a weekly rest break of twenty-four consecutive hours. Statutory provision is also made for eleven consecutive hours daily rest in each twenty-four hour period, with a break of at least fifteen minutes for each work period of four-and-a-half hours, or a break of at least thirty minutes for each work period of six hours.

33. The Act permits exemptions from the rest provisions in the event of exceptional, unusual or unforeseeable circumstances. Likewise, any sector or business may, by collective agreement, negotiate exemptions from statutory rest times. Finally, certain categories of employees, such as those involved in the provision of ambulance, fire and civil protection services are exempted by regulation from the rest provisions. This is subject to equivalent compensatory rest being made available to the employee.

34. This Act also lays down a minimum, legally enforceable entitlement, for employees working the required number of hours, to four weeks' annual holidays (with *pro rata* entitlements for periods of employment of less than a year) and to public holidays.

35. The Worker Protection (Regular Part-Time Employees) Act 1991, as amended by the Protection of Employees (Part-Time Work) Act 2001, provides that part-time employees who were not covered by the Organisation of Working Time Act 1997, are to get annual leave at the rate of six hours for every hundred hours worked.

36. Employees who are not covered by the Act include:

(a) outworkers;
(b) seafarers;
(c) lighthouse and lightship employees;
(d) fishermen;
(e) non-industrial State employees and established civil servants; and
(f) employees living with an employer who is a relative.

37. Employees are entitled to annual holidays of four working weeks in a leave year in which the employee works at least 1,365 hours (unless it is a leave year in which they change employment), or one-third of a working week per calendar month that the employee works at least 117 hours, or 8% of the hours an employee works in a leave year (but subject to a maximum of four working weeks).

38. If an employee is ill while on annual leave, and provides a medical certificate to that effect, that period covered by the medical certificate will not be counted as part of annual leave.

39. The time at which annual leave may be taken is determined by the employer, so long as the employee or trade union is consulted at least one month beforehand, and that the annual leave is taken either during the current leave year or within six months after its end.

40. The pay for annual leave must be at the normal weekly rate and must be given in advance.

41. Upon termination of employment, employees must be compensated for annual leave due.

42. The Act provides entitlement to nine public holidays:

(a) 1 January (New Year's Day), if falling on a weekday or, if not, the next weekday;
(b) 17 March (St Patrick's Day), if falling on a weekday or, if not, the next weekday;
(c) Easter Monday;
(d) the first Monday in May;
(e) the first Monday in June;
(f) the first Monday in August;
(g) the last Monday in October;
(h) 25 December (Christmas Day), if falling on a weekday or, if not, the next weekday;
(i) 26 December (St Stephen's Day), if falling on a weekday or, if not, the next weekday.

43. In respect of each public holiday, an employee is entitled to a paid day off on the holiday, or a paid day off within a month, or an extra day's annual leave, or an extra day's pay – as the employer may decide.

44. The employer may substitute a Church holiday for a public holiday (except Christmas or St Patrick's Day) provided that the employee is given notice of the substitution at least fourteen days beforehand. The following Church holidays may be substituted:

(a) 6 January (the Epiphany), except when it falls on a Sunday;
(b) Ascension Thursday;
(c) Corpus Christi;
(d) 15 August (the Assumption), except when it falls on a Sunday;

(e) 1 November (All Saints' Day), except when it falls on a Sunday;

(f) 8 December (the Immaculate Conception), except when it falls on a Sunday.

Safety, Health and Welfare at Work Act 2005

45. The Act places broad obligations in safety, health and welfare matters upon employers, employees and the self-employed at all places of work. The emphasis is on preventing accidents and ill-health from occurring by identifying workplace hazards and putting appropriate safeguards in place.

46. Employers are obliged to provide a safe place of work, safe plant, safe systems of work, appropriate information, appropriate training, adequate supervision, appropriate protective clothing or equipment, adequate emergency plans, and arrangements and facilities for welfare. Employers are required, as far as reasonably possible, to prevent any improper conduct or behaviour likely to put the safety, health and welfare of employees at risk. Employers should have established grievance procedures for dealing with complaints of harassment and bullying in the workplace and deal with such complaints immediately.

47. Employers (and the self-employed) must prepare a written safety statement based on a systematic evaluation of all the potential hazards to workplace health and safety, an assessment of the risks involved, and details of appropriate safety measures put in place. Employers are required to appoint a competent person as the organisation's Safety Officer, and the statement must identify the people in the workforce who are responsible for safety issues. Employees must be informed about the content of the Safety Statement at least annually, upon recruitment and whenever there is a change made to it.

48. Employees (including full or part-time, permanent or temporary) are obliged to take reasonable care for the safety and health of others, by making proper use of all machinery, tools and any personal protective equipment supplied for their safety. They have a duty not to be under the influence of drink or drugs in the workplace and, in addition, are required to undergo any reasonable medical or other assessment if requested to do so by the employer. Employees are entitled to appoint a safety representative to liaise with employers on any matters dealing with their health and safety in the workplace.

49. The Health and Safety Authority was established under the 1989 Act to provide an effective system of enforcement of occupational safety and health legislation, and to supply information, advice and guidance on the prevention of accidents and ill-health at work. The board of the Health and Safety Authority consists of representatives of employers' organisations, trade unions and the State.

Employment Equality Acts 1998–2007

50. The Employment Equality Acts specifically outlaw discriminatory practices in relation to and within employment. They prohibit both direct and indirect discrimination:

(a) by employers with regard to access to employment, conditions of employment, training and promotion;

(b) in collective agreements with regard to access to and conditions of employment and equal pay for like work;

(c) in job advertising or advertising that might reasonably be understood as indicating an intention to discriminate;

(d) by employment agencies against any person seeking employment or other services of the agency;

(e) in the provision of vocational training or any instruction needed to carry on an occupational activity; and

(f) by certain bodies such as trade unions, as well as professional and trade associations, as regards membership and other benefits.

51. Direct discrimination is defined as treating one person in a less favourable way than another person has been or would be treated because of:

(a) *Gender:* that they are of different genders, be it a woman, a man or a transsexual person. Specific protection also applies where, arising from her pregnancy or maternity leave, a woman employee is treated less favourably than another employee.

(b) *Marital Status:* that they are of different marital status, be it single, married, separated, divorced or widowed.

(c) *Family Status:* that one has responsibility either as a parent or as a person in *loco parentis* for someone below 18 years of age, or is a parent or resident primary carer for someone over 18 years of age with a disability who requires a high degree of support and attention, while the other has a different family status.

(d) *Sexual Orientation:* that they are of a different sexual orientation, be it heterosexual, homosexual or bisexual.

(e) *Religious Belief:* that one has a different religious belief from the other, or that one has a religious belief and the other has not.

(f) *Age:* that they are of different ages. Discrimination is outlawed between all above the maximum age at which a person is statutorily obliged to attend school (currently sixteen).

(g) *Disability:* that one is a person with a disability and the other either has not or is a person with a different disability. Disability is defined to include total or partial absence of bodily or mental facilities, chronic disease, whether manifest or not, and learning or personality disorders.

(h) *Race:* that they are of a different race, colour, nationality, ethnic or national origins.

(i) *Membership of the Traveller Community:* that one is a member of the traveller community and the other is not.

52. Indirect discrimination occurs where a requirement, which may appear on its face not to be discriminatory adversely affects a particular group or class of persons who are protected by these Acts. For example, a requirement that female employees wear uniforms with short skirts, contrary to the religious beliefs of certain groups such as Muslims, could be construed as indirectly discriminatory, even though there might not be any intention by employers to discriminate. However, a case would have to be taken by any such employee to prove this.

53. The legislation seeks to ensure equal payment between persons or a group of persons for 'like work'. For example, if two people are doing 'like work' irrespective of their race, they must receive equal pay. In order to prove 'like work' it must be shown that the work of the person who is claiming equal pay is the same, similar or of equal value of the person that they are comparing themselves to. Employees must be employed by the same employer or an associated employer (which would include different plants within the same group and subsidiary or associated companies controlled directly or indirectly by the same body corporate). It is worth noting, however, that it is not unlawful for an employer to provide a different rate of pay for work of a particular description performed by an employee with a disability if, as a result of that disability, the employee is restricted in their capacity to do the same amount of work (or to work similar hours) as a person employed to perform work of that description, but who is without that disability.

54. Harassment in the workplace or in the course of employment on grounds of gender, marital status, family status, sexual orientation, religious belief, age, disability, race or membership of the traveller community, is also outlawed. Harassment, including sexual harassment, is defined as any act or conduct which is unwelcome and offensive, humiliating or intimidating, including acts of physical intimacy, spoken words, gestures, the production, display or circulation of written material, pictures, or requests for sexual favours. An obligation is placed on employers to take all reasonable steps to ensure a harassment free environment and to prevent a person being treated differently because of rejection or acceptance of harassment which takes place in the workplace, in the course of employment or outside the workplace. Employers are liable for acts of harassment by employees, clients, customers or other business contacts done in the course of employment whether or not they were done with their knowledge or approval, unless they can display that they took reasonable steps to prevent such harassment.

55. Certain exemptions from the scope of legislation are permitted. An employer may discriminate on the grounds of gender and grant special beneficial treatment to women connected with pregnancy, maternity or adoption. Discrimination is also permitted where gender amounts to an occupational qualification, for example, an artist's model, an actor or where laws or customs preclude women.

Likewise, where the employment consists of the performances of services of a personal nature, for example the care of an elderly or incapacitated person in that person's home. Finally, limited exemptions for discrimination on the grounds of gender exist for the Garda Síochána and prison service, in the interests of privacy and decency, in violent situations such as riots, as regard height requirements and to allow for the maintenance of an appropriate gender balance for the purpose of both services.

56. Exclusions are also permitted where a religious, educational or remedial institution that is under the direction or control of a body established for religious purposes, or whose objective include the provision of services in an environment which promotes certain religious values, gives more favourable treatment, on the grounds of religious belief, to an employee or a prospective employee where it is reasonable to do so in order to maintain the religious ethos of the institution or prevent the undermining of it.

57. The Employment Equality Acts 1998–2007 provided for the establishment of the Equality Authority and its functions are to:

(a) Work towards the elimination of discrimination in employment, in the provision of goods and services, education, property and other opportunities to which the public generally have access.
(b) Promote equality of opportunity in matters to which the legislation applies.
(c) Provide information to employers, service providers, individuals, trade unions and the legal profession on the Employment Equality Acts 1998–2007, the Equal Status Acts 2000–2004, the Maternity Protection Acts 1994–2004, the Adoptive Leave Acts 1995–2005, the Parental Leave Acts 1998–2006 and the Pensions Acts 1990–2007.
(d) Monitor and review the operations of the aforementioned employment equality legislation.

58. A new statutory office, the Equality Tribunal, has been created which investigates or mediates complaints of unlawful discrimination under the equality legislation. All cases, other than those involving dismissal and gender discrimination, must be referred in the first instance to the Equality Tribunal. Each case will be investigated by the Equality Tribunal (except those referred to and resolved at mediation) and a decision issued which is binding and enforceable through the Circuit Court. The Equality Tribunal may, in equal pay cases, order equal pay and arrears in respect of a period not exceeding three years preceding the reference of the case, and in other cases order equal treatment and compensation of up to a maximum of two years pay (or €12,697 where the person was not an employee). In addition, the Equality Tribunal may order any person to take a specified course of action to avoid future discrimination. All decisions may be appealed to the Labour Court within forty-two days of issue, which in turn will issue legally binding determinations. These may be appealed to the High Court on points of law, whilst the Labour Court may refer questions as to the interpretation of Community Law to the European Court of Justice.

59. Dismissal cases, except those on the grounds of gender, may be referred in the first instance to the Labour Court for a determination. However, the Labour Court can refer them initially to the Equality Tribunal if it wishes. In such cases, the Labour Court may order reinstatement or re-engagement with or without financial compensation. Alternatively, complainants on the grounds of gender can apply directly to the Circuit Court for redress, which may in turn require the Equality Tribunal to have a report prepared by an equality officer for the court. The Circuit Court is not limited to the normal ceiling on awards and may order compensation as appropriate in each case. This can be appealed to the High Court in accordance with the rules of the court.

Equal Status Acts 2000–04

60. The Equal Status Acts 2000-04 complement the Employment Equality Acts 1998–2007 by providing protection against discrimination in non-employment areas such as the provision of goods, facilities and services, education, accommodation and membership of private registered clubs. All services which are generally available to the public are covered by this legislation, including access to public places, banking and insurance services, entertainment, facilities for refreshments and transport facilities.

61. Direct and indirect discrimination, sexual harassment, harassment and victimisation are prohibited on the same nine grounds as in the Employment Equality Acts 1998–2007, namely, gender, marital status, family status, sexual orientation, religion, age, disability, race or membership of the traveller community.

62. The Equal Status Acts 2000–04 address, in particular, discrimination relating to disability. Those selling goods or providing services, providers of accommodation, educational institutions and private clubs must do all that is reasonably possible to accommodate the needs of a person with a disability. This includes providing special treatment or facilities in circumstances where, without these, it would be impossible or unduly difficult to avail of the services. However, they are not obliged to make such arrangements where the cost involved is more than a nominal cost, the definition of which depends on the circumstances of each case. These include the size and resources of the service provider, as well as any State grants or aids for assistance in providing special treatment or facilities. The Disability Act 2005 provides a statute-based right for people with disabilities to an assessment of disability-related health, personal social service and education needs, and also place obligations on public bodies to make their services and information accessible to people with disabilities.

63. There are several significant exemptions in the Acts, the broadest being that anything mandated by an Act of the Oireachtas or EU law is allowed. There are also exemptions where a service provider can refuse access if a reasonable individual, having knowledge and experience of the provider, would form the belief that the provision of the service to the customer would produce a substantial risk of criminal or disorderly conduct or behaviour, or damage to property, in or around the area where the service is provided. Finally, there are specific exemptions that apply to each of the nine grounds mentioned above, but these should be read restrictively and should not be allowed to unduly restrict the general prohibition of discrimination.

64. Anyone wishing to make a claim of discrimination must notify the person(s) against whom the claim is being made, in writing, within two months of the date of the most recent occurrence of the discrimination. If there is no reply or if the reply is unsatisfactory, the complaint should be referred to the Equality Tribunal within six months of the discrimination. The complaint can be addressed through investigation and decision or through mediation. An investigation is a process carried out by an Equality Officer who first considers submissions from both parties, before arranging a joint hearing of the case to reach a decision. Mediation is an alternative approach to resolving conflicts, arriving at a resolution through agreement rather than through investigation and decision. If there is a finding in favour of the person making the complaint, compensation of up to €6,350 can be ordered. The Equality Officer can also order specified courses of action to be taken. All decisions may be appealed to the Circuit Court not later than 42 days from the date of the decision. There is no further right of appeal except to the High Court on a point of law.

Protection of Young Persons (Employment) Act 1996
65. The Act extends the scope of the legislative protection given to young workers under the age of eighteen. It contains provisions as to:

(a) the minimum age for entry into employment;
(b) limits to the working hours of young people;
(c) rest intervals; and
(d) prohibition of night work.

66. An employer may not employ anyone under eighteen years of age, without first requiring the production of a birth certificate. Furthermore, an employer must obtain written permission from the parent or guardian before employing a person under sixteen years.

67. The employment of children under fifteen is generally prohibited. However, children over fourteen may be permitted to do light, non-industrial work, during school holidays, provided that it does not interfere with their schooling and is not harmful to health or normal development.

68. The limitation on hours of work of young persons is a maximum of eight hours in any day and forty hours in any week.

69. Young persons aged under sixteen must be allowed at least a twenty-one day break from work in the summer, and a half-hour rest break after four hours' work.

70. They are entitled to fourteen consecutive hours off each day, and two days off in every week (to be consecutive as far as is practicable).

71. Young persons aged between sixteen and eighteen must be allowed a thirty-minute break after working more than four-and-a-half hours.

72. They are entitled to twelve consecutive hours off each day, and two days off in every week (to be consecutive as far as is practicable).

73. Employers are not allowed to require employees under sixteen to work before 8 am or after 8 pm. In general, young persons aged between sixteen and eighteen are not allowed to work before 6 am and after 10 pm.

74. The Act also requires employers to keep a record of the following particulars of each employee under age eighteen:

(a) full name;
(b) date of birth;
(c) time of commencement of work each day;
(d) time of termination of work each day;
(e) rate of wages or salary paid for normal working hours per day, week, month or year, as the case may be;
(f) total wages or salary paid.

Maternity Protection Acts 1994–2004

75. The Acts provide the statutory minimum entitlements for all pregnant employees, including casual workers, apprentices, employees on probation and employment agency workers, regardless of the length of time employed by the organisation or the number of hours worked per week.

76. Expectant employees are entitled to take twenty-six weeks' maternity leave, taking at least two weeks before the end of the week of the expected birth and four weeks afterwards. They are also entitled to attend a complete set of ante-natal classes without loss of pay, whilst the father has the right once only to paid time off to attend the last two ante-natal classes of a series.

77. Employees are entitled to take time off from work without loss of pay for the purposes of ante-natal and post-natal care. Written notice about taking the time off must be given to the employer at least two weeks beforehand on each occasion, and except in the case of the first appointment, the appointment card (or other appropriate document) must be produced by the employee if requested to do so.

78. To exercise her right to take maternity leave, an employee must:

(a) notify her employer in writing, at least four weeks before she intends to go on maternity leave, of her intention to take the leave; and

(b) give her employer, or produce for her employer's inspection, a medical certificate, confirming her pregnancy and indicating the expected week of her confinement.

79. A claim may be made for pay-related maternity benefit during maternity leave by employees who satisfy the contribution conditions. It is payable for a basic period of twenty-six weeks, with a possibility of extension of this period in certain cases of late birth. The amount payable is 70 per cent based on a weekly average of gross yearly earnings in the relevant income tax year. It is tax-free and, in addition, the employee may benefit from a tax refund or tax credit. There is a minimum payment.

80. An employee may take up to sixteen consecutive weeks' additional maternity leave immediately after her maternity leave, even where that has been extended for a late birth. The employer is not obliged to pay an employee during additional maternity leave. Neither is maternity benefit payable. An employee who chooses to take additional maternity leave must ensure that her employer is notified in writing not later than four weeks before the end of her maternity leave.

81. The Act does not oblige an employee who has taken maternity leave to return to work afterwards. But if she does wish to return, she must give prior notice to her employer in writing of her intention to return to work, not later than four weeks before the date on which she expects to return.

82. Where the employer cannot comply with this right of the employee, suitable alternative employment must be offered to the employee. The Employment Appeals Tribunal will determine any disputes arising from this arrangement.

83. Pregnant employees, employees who have recently given birth and employees who are breastfeeding may be granted health and safety leave (in addition to maternity leave), in accordance with regulations made under the Safety, Health and Welfare at Work Act 2005, where a risk to these employees is identified in the workplace, and it is not feasible for the employer to remove the risk or move the employees to suitable other work.

84. An employee on maternity leave is entitled to her full annual leave entitlement and to leave in lieu of public holidays occurring during such absences, or to one of the alternatives prescribed under the Organisation of Working Time Act 1997. An employee on health and safety leave is likewise entitled to retain her entitlement to annual holidays, but does not have such an entitlement to time off in lieu of public holidays occurring during her absence.

Adoptive Leave Acts 1995–2005

85. These Acts entitle an adopting mother or a sole male adopter who is in employment to a minimum of twenty-four consecutive weeks of adoptive leave from work commencing on the day of placement of the child, as well as up to sixteen weeks of additional adoptive leave following immediately on the original period. In the case of a foreign adoption, however, some or all of the additional adoptive leave may be taken at the request of the employee immediately before the day of placement and subject to compliance notification and evidence requirements.

86. An employed adopting mother is defined by the Act as any female employee in whose care a child (of whom she is not the natural mother) has been placed or is about to be placed with a view to the making of an adoption order, or to the effecting of a foreign adoption or following any such adoption. Likewise, a sole male adopter has been defined as a male employee in whose sole care a child has been placed or is about to be placed with a view to the making of an adoption order, or to the effecting of a foreign adoption or following any such adoption. Adopting parents are entitled to paid time off work to attend preparation classes and pre-adoption meetings with social workers or health service executives during the pre-adoption process.

87. Employees must give advance notice in writing to the employer at least four weeks prior to the expected placement of the child, informing the employer in writing of the specific day of placement as soon as is reasonably practicable. Likewise, employees must give advance notice in writing to the employer at least four weeks prior to taking additional adoptive leave. During an absence from work on additional adoptive leave, the period of employment before the absence will be regarded as continuous with the period of employment after the absence.

88. Following a period of adoptive leave or additional adoptive leave, the employee has a right to return to work, provided that the employer has been informed in writing by the employee at least four weeks before the scheduled date of return. Redress is available under the Unfair Dismissals Acts 1977–2007, in the event of a dismissal arising due to the exercise or contemplated exercise of the right to adoptive leave or additional adoptive leave.

Parental Leave Acts 1998–2006

89. These Acts entitle parents to 14 weeks' unpaid parental leave for each child born or adopted. The leave must be taken before the child reaches eight years of age, except in certain circumstances in the case of adopted children. Parental leave may be taken either as a continuous block of 14 weeks or, with the agreement of the employer, in separate time blocks or by reduced working hours. Each parent is entitled to a separate period of leave which is non-transferable between parents (unless both work for the same employer and negotiate such an arrangement).

90. Notification of an intention to take parental leave must be provided in writing not later than six weeks prior to the proposed date of commencement. This may, however, be waived at the discretion of an employer. A confirmation document must be prepared and signed jointly by the employee and employer at least four weeks prior to the proposed date on which leave will commence, and this document can be altered or revoked only with the agreement of both parties.

91. Employees must have at least one year's continuous service with the employer prior to entitlement to take parental leave; although limited exceptions are included in the legislation on this matter. Likewise, an employee is restricted to a maximum of fourteen weeks' parental leave in any twelve-month period, unless the employer agrees otherwise, where they qualify for parental leave in respect of more than one child. This restriction does not apply in the case of children of a multiple birth.

92. Employees are entitled to *force majeure* leave with pay from the employer due to urgent family business owing to the injury or illness of a child or adoptive child of the employee, the spouse of the employee or a person with whom the employee is living as husband or wife, a person to whom the employee is in *loco parentis*, a brother or sister of the employee or a parent or grandparent of the employee. An employee may not be absent on *force majeure* leave for more than three days in any consecutive months or five days in any thirty-six consecutive months, and it cannot be treated as part of any other leave to which the employee is entitled.

93. In the event of any dispute or difference between an employer and an employee in relation to *force majeure* leave, either party may refer the issue to a rights commissioner, the decision of which may be appealed to the Employment Appeals Tribunal.

Carer's Leave Act 2001

94. The Carer's Leave Act 2001 enables employees working under a contract of employment or apprenticeship, employed through an employment agency or holding office under, or in the service of, the State to avail of unpaid leave from their employment to enable them to personally provide full-time care and attention for a person who is in need of such care.

95. There is an entitlement to leave subject to a maximum of sixty-five weeks in respect of any one care recipient, whilst the minimum statutory entitlement is thirteen weeks. They must have completed at least twelve months continuous service with the employer from whose employment the leave is taken before the commencement of the leave, and they must intend to take leave for the purpose of personally providing full-time care and attention to a person who is in need of such and must do so for the duration of the leave.

96. Employees are regarded as still working in their employment during an absence on carer's leave, and their rights and obligations relating to the employment cannot be affected by taking leave. However, there are no rights to remuneration or superannuation benefits and any obligation to pay superannuation contributions in, or in respect of, the employment. Furthermore, the right to annual leave or public holidays is restricted to the period comprising the first thirteen weeks only of the carer's leave entitlement.

97. Written notice of an intention to take carer's leave must be given to an employer not later than six weeks before the employee proposes to commences the leave, and must contain details of the date of commencement and the duration of the leave, a statement that an application for a decision that the person to be cared for is a relevant person for the purposes of the Carer's Leave Act 2001 has been made to the Department of Social, Community and Family Affairs, and the employee's signature and date. However, where an employee who is entitled to carer's leave has taken leave purporting to be carer's leave but has not complied with the notice requirements, the employer may apply discretion to treat it as carers' leave for the purpose of the Carer's Leave Act 2001. If the employer refuses to do so, a written statement specifying the grounds for such refusal must be provided to the employee.

98. Following notification of an intention to take carer's leave, an employee must give to the employer a copy of the decision from the deciding officer of the Department of Social, Community and Family Affairs that the person has been medically certified as requiring full-time care and attention. An employer and employee may at this stage prepare, sign and date a confirmation document detailing the date on which the leave period will commence and the duration of the period of leave. It cannot be subsequently altered unless both parties agree.

99. An employer must make a record of the carer's leave taken by employees, specifying the period of employment of each employee and the dates and times of the leave taken, and such records must be kept for eight years. Failure to do so is an offence liable to a fine of up to €3,000.

100. At the end of a period of carer's leave, employees are entitled to return to work to the employer with whom they worked immediately before the absence, and under the same contract and terms and conditions of employment. They must notify their employer of the intention to return to work not less than four weeks before the date on which the employee is due to return to work.

101. An employee has a right of complaint to a Rights Commissioner which must be made in writing within six months. Either party may appeal a recommendation of the Rights Commissioner to the Employment Appeals Tribunal, and may make a subsequent appeal to the High Court on a point of law.

Protection of Employees (Part-Time Work) Act 2001

102. These Acts repeal the Worker Protection (Regular Part-Time Employees) Act 1991, which originally brought regular part-time employees within the scope of existing employment legislation and provided that part-time employees could not be treated in a less favourable manner than comparable full-time employees in relation to conditions of employment. These were previously excluded by virtue of provisions relating to hours worked or PRSI status.

103. The 2001 Act repeals the requirement that a part-time worker should be in the continuous service of the employer for not less than 13 weeks and should be normally expected to work not less than 8 hours per week for that employer. However, part-time employees will still be required to have 12 months continuous service under the Unfair Dismissals Acts and 2 years continuous service under the Redundancy Payments Acts to be entitled to protection under these statutes.

Protection of Employees (Fixed-Term Work) Act 2003

104. A fixed-term employee is a person who has entered into a contract of employment with an employer where the end of the contract is determined by an objective condition such as arriving at a specific date, completing a specific task or the occurrence of a specific event. The Act provides that an employer must inform a fixed-term employee in writing, as soon as practicable after employment, of the objective condition determining the contract.

105. This legislation also protects fixed-term employees by ensuring that they cannot be treated less favourably than comparable permanent workers and that employers cannot continually renew fixed-term contracts.

106. Where an employer proposes to renew a fixed-term contract, the employee must be informed in writing of the objective grounds justifying the renewal and explaining the failure to offer a permanent contract. This must happen not later than the date of renewal. Under the Act, employees can only work one or more fixed-term contracts for a continuous period of four years. After this, the employee is assumed to have a permanent contract.

National Minimum Wage Act 2000

107. All experienced adult employees, except apprentices and close relatives of the employer, are entitled from July 2007 to a national minimum rate of pay of €8.65. Employers can pay less than this to inexperienced workers. For new workers over eighteen in the first year of a job, the minimum rate is €6.92 per hour. In the second year of employment, it increases to €7.79 per hour. For employees under the age of eighteen, the minimum rate of pay is €6.06 per hour.

108. Employees are entitled, on request, to a written statement outlining their reckonable pay, working hours, average hourly rate of pay and statutory minimum hourly rate of pay entitlement under the Act. Employers are required to keep all records necessary to prove that this Act is being complied with in relation to employees for at least three years from the date any record is made.

109. A dispute may be referred to a Rights Commissioner where the employer fails to supply the written statement of the average hourly rate of pay, and the decision of a Rights Commissioner can in turn be appealed to the Labour Court. Dismissal of employees for exercising or proposing to exercise their rights under the legislation is an unfair dismissal within the meaning of the Unfair Dismissals Acts 1977–2007.

Employment Permits Acts 2003–06

110. The Acts provide for the granting of employment permits to foreign nationals from outside the European Economic Area (not including Romania and Bulgaria) and Switzerland. The foreign national must be directly employed by the organisation offering the job, which itself must be registered with the Companies Registration Office and the Revenue Commissioners and trading in Ireland.

111. The employer is required to pay the fee for the applicant. The permit itself is issued to the employee, with a copy being sent to the employer. Employees are generally expected to stay with the employer for one year on the first permit.

112. The Acts contain certain protections which include inspections by authorised officers, a requirement on employers to retain certain books and records, a prohibition on deduction of any expenses involved in the recruitment of foreign nationals or the retention of any personal documents, and a surrender of the permit when there is a cessation or termination of employment.

Employees (Provision of Information and Consultation) Act 2006

113. This Act, transposing EU Council Directive 2002/14/EC, provides for the establishment of systems to inform and consult with employees, in advance of certain proposed organisational and structural changes which directly affect them, in workplaces with at least fifty employees.

114. Employers have the option of putting in place 'pre-existing agreements' which can be tailored to suit the circumstances and culture of their own organisation. Alternatively, once ten per cent of employees (subject to a minimum of fifteen and a maximum of a hundred) request an employer to set up an information and consultation process, negotiations must be entered into so as to reach such an agreement. Finally, an information and consultation forum comprising between three and thirty elected employee representatives may be assigned to meet with the employer twice a year and in advance of any significant organisational developments.

115. Employers are obliged to provide information and consultation on issues such as probable development of the organisation's activities and economic situation, the structure and probable development of employment within the organisation and any anticipatory measures envisaged, and any decisions likely to lead to substantial changes in work organisation or contractual relations. Information must be given at such time, in such fashion and with such content as are appropriate to enable, in particular, employee representatives to conduct an adequate study and, where necessary, prepare for consultation.

Termination of the contract

116. Under common law, a contract of employment may be terminated by:

(a) agreement with notice;
(b) death of the employer or employee;
(c) frustration;
(d) insolvency; or
(e) breach.

Termination by agreement with notice

117. The ending of a contract of employment is most often achieved without any breach of its terms. A contract can be terminated at common law by either party giving the notice required by the terms of the contract, or by giving reasonable notice where none is specified in the contract. What is regarded as reasonable notice will depend on a number of factors, such as the nature of the work, the method of payment and the custom of the trade. Alternatively, an employer may pay wages in lieu of notice, subject to the protection given to employees under the Unfair Dismissals Acts 1977–2007.

Case: McDonnell v. Minister for Education (1940)

The plaintiff, a lecturer, was employed by the defendant. She was given three months' notice of termination of her contract of employment upon her marriage. She took an action against the defendant for wrongful dismissal.

Held: As no notice was specified in the contract of employment, six months was a reasonable period in the circumstances.

118. If an employee is an office holder, i.e. a person occupying a relatively permanent position created by statute, charter, articles of association, or statutory regulation, termination by notice is not sufficient. Such an employee is entitled to be notified of the grounds of their dismissal and to be given an opportunity of defending themselves.

Termination by death of the employer or employee

119. Death of either the employer or the employee will end the contract, unless there is an express or implied term to the contrary. This will not apply if the person is employed by a company, which may have perpetual existence. Any liabilities arising under the contract of employment are not extinguished upon the death of either party. For example, any outstanding remuneration must be paid to the estate of the employee.

Termination by frustration

120. If either party is incapable of performing their part of the contract due to circumstances beyond their control, it will be terminated by frustration. Illness may be a frustrating event if it renders future performance impossible or fundamentally different from that envisaged by the parties when they entered into the contract. A period of imprisonment may also frustrate a contract of employment.

Termination by insolvency

121. Insolvency or bankruptcy of either party will not automatically terminate the contract of employment, unless it is an essential element of the relationship. In practice, however, an employer who becomes insolvent will not be in a position to pay remuneration to their employees. An employee may submit a claim in bankruptcy for remuneration outstanding, and, in the absence of proper notice, a claim for wrongful dismissal. They may also lodge a claim for redundancy payments.

122. An order for compulsory winding-up (liquidation) of a company terminates the contracts of employment of all the employees. However, a voluntary winding-up will not automatically terminate employees' contracts if the liquidator chooses to carry on the business – unless it is obvious that the company will be unable to fulfil its obligation under the contracts.

Termination by breach

123. A contract of employment may be ended by breach if the employee resigns without sufficient reason and without notice, or goes on strike or fails to perform the contract and to observe its conditions.

124. It may also be ended by breach if the employer dismisses the employee without notice when the employer has not sufficient justification to do so, or if the employer repudiates some essential term of the contract, e.g. a complete change of duties.

Case: Phelan v. Bic (Ireland) Ltd, Biro Bic Ltd, Societe Bic SA and Robert McDonald (1997)

At a meeting of the Board of Directors of the first named defendant, a decision was taken to terminate the contract of employment of the plaintiff, who had held the position of managing director since 1972. The plaintiff refused an offer of two month's salary in lieu of notice, insisting that his contract provided for a reasonable period of notice in the event of its termination. He sought an interlocutory injunction restraining the defendants from removing him from his office, publishing any statement to the effect that he was no longer managing director of the company and implementing the termination of his employment in this manner.

Held: There was no power in the Articles of Association to terminate the position of managing director summarily. Likewise, a serious issue arose as to breach of contract on the part of the defendants. A person such as the plaintiff in the position of managing director, earning a substantial salary, might be entitled to at least twelve months' notice. Finally, the provisions of the Redundancy Payments Act 1967 had been violated by the absence of any formal redundancy notice or offer of a lump sum to the plaintiff. Therefore, the plaintiff was prima facie entitled to exemplary damages or to an order reinstating him to his original position, and initial relief in the form of an interlocutory injunction was granted.

Case: Philpott v. Ogilvy and Mather Ltd (2000)

The plaintiff, who had commenced employment as a creative director with the defendant in March 1999, claimed he had been summarily dismissed on 4 February 2000, without warning or notice. He sought an interlocutory injunction restraining the defendant from giving effect to the purported dismissal, and a mandatory injunction requiring the defendant to pay his salary as it fell due.

Held: The relief at common law for wrongful dismissal was damages. The Court was unable to provide any other injunctive relief.

125. These common law rules have been supplemented by statute.

Minimum Notice and Terms of Employment Acts 1973–2005
126. The Acts establish minimum periods of notice which have to be given by employers and employees prior to the termination of a contract of employment. Employees who have at least thirteen weeks' continuous service with the same employer are covered by this legislation, except:
(a) the immediate family of the employer working in a private house or farm;
(b) members of the Defence Forces and Garda Síochána; and

(c) persons employed under the Merchant Shipping Acts.

127. The minimum period of notice due to an employee varies according to length of service as follows:

Length of Service	Minimum Notice
Thirteen weeks to two years	One week
Two years to five years	Two weeks
Five years to ten years	Four weeks
Ten years to fifteen years	Six weeks
More than fifteen years	Eight weeks

128. An employee with in excess of thirteen weeks' service with their employer, and wishing to terminate their contract of employment, must give at least one week's notice of termination. The required period may be greater than this if so provided for in the contract of employment.

129. The Acts allow either employee or employer to voluntarily waive their rights to notice. Employees can accept payment in lieu of notice, in which case the date of termination of the contract of employment is that upon which the employee physically leaves the employment. For statutory redundancy purposes, however, the date of termination of employment is deemed to be that on which notice, if given, would have expired.

Unfair Dismissals Acts 1977–2007

130. The Acts protect employees from being unfairly dismissed from their jobs by laying down criteria by which dismissals are to be judged unfair, and by providing an adjudication system and redress for an employee whose dismissal has been found to be unjustified.

131. Many workers are excluded from the protection of the Acts. The most important of these are:

(a) employees with less than one year's continuous service, but this does not apply when the dismissal results from pregnancy or trade union activities – dismissal for such reasons is indefensible;
(b) employees who have reached normal retiring age;
(c) close relatives of the employer, employed and living at the employer's residence or farm;
(d) members of the Defence Forces or Gardaí;
(e) FÁS trainees or apprentices;
(f) State employees (except specified industrial grades);
(g) officers of a local authority, health board, vocational education committee or county committee of agriculture;

(h) persons working under fixed-term contracts (in some cases);
(i) persons who, under their contract, ordinarily work outside the State;
(j) persons undergoing promotion or training for a year or less, and this is specified in a written contract of employment;
(k) persons undertaking training for the purpose of obtaining qualifications or registration as a nurse, pharmacist, health inspector, etc.; or
(l) persons working under illegal contracts of employment.

132. An employee is deemed to have been dismissed if:

(a) the employer terminates the contract of employment, with or without notice ('actual dismissal');
(b) the employee, because of the conduct of the employer, terminates the contract of employment, with or without notice ('constructive dismissal'); or
(c) the contract is for a fixed term and is not renewed.

Case: Kiernan v. Iarnród Éireann (1996)

The plaintiff claimed that he had received no notification from the defendant upon taking up employment as a boy porter that he would have to retire on reaching twenty years of age. The defendant argued that employment had been on a fixed term contract basis, that this would have been put to the plaintiff when he was being interviewed, and that the plaintiff had not been dismissed, but had retired on reaching this age in accordance with his conditions of service.

Held: The precise age of retirement should have been given to the plaintiff in writing. Failure to notify him accordingly rendered the dismissal unfair, and compensation was awarded.

133. Any dismissal is presumed to be unfair unless and until the employer proves to the contrary. To justify a dismissal, an employer must show that it resulted from one or more of the following causes, or that there were other 'substantial grounds' for the dismissal:

(a) lack of skill, or physical or mental ability, or adequate health, or such formal professional or technical qualifications as are appropriate for the work the employee was employed to do;
(b) conduct of the employee of such a serious or continuing nature as to amount to serious misconduct. This will not include isolated acts or behaviour which has not warranted a warning by the employer;
(c) redundancy, in accordance with fair or agreed procedures;
(d) the fact that continuation of employment would contravene another statutory restriction. For example, to continue to employ an under-age employee would be a contravention of the law.

Case: P v. S and Cornwall County Council (1996)

The plaintiff, a senior manager in an educational establishment, was given notice of the termination of her employment when she informed her employers that she was undergoing gender reassignment and wished to come back to work as a woman. Her period of employment terminated without her returning to work, and she brought an action before an industrial tribunal claiming that she had suffered discrimination on the grounds of sex and that she ought not to have been dismissed. The defendants claimed that, on the contrary, she had been dismissed by reason of redundancy.

Held: The industrial tribunal found that whilst there was a case for redundancy, the true reason for dismissal was the objection to P's intention to undergo gender reassignment. However, since statute law provided no protection for transsexuals, all the employers needed to show was that they would have treated a transsexual of either (natally recorded) sex in the same manner. In the subsequent ground-breaking appeal, the European Court of Justice ruled that European Council Directive 76/207/EEC on the principle of equal treatment for men and women should be held to cover transsexuals, and that the plaintiff ought not to have been dismissed.

134. An employer who has dismissed an employee must, if asked, furnish in writing within fourteen days the reason for the dismissal. Dismissals will be always automatically unfair, and can never be justified where it is shown that they have resulted wholly or mainly from any of the following:

(a) trade union membership or activities, either outside working hours or during working hours at times permitted by the employer;
(b) religious or political opinions;
(c) race or colour or sexual orientation;
(d) participation in legal proceedings against the employer;
(e) unfair selection for redundancy, where there are no grounds for a redundancy, or where an employee is selected for redundancy contrary to a fair or agreed procedure;
(f) pregnancy, or the exercise by an employee of her rights under the Maternity Protection Acts 1994–2004;
(g) exercise or contemplated exercise by an employee of the right to adoptive leave or additional adoptive leave under the Adoptive Leave Acts 1995–2005;
(h) age;
(i) membership of the travelling community.

135. Claims of unfair dismissal must be made within six months of the date of dismissal. The time-limit can be extended to twelve months in cases where exceptional circumstances have prevented the lodgment of the claim within the specified time-limit.

136. An employee can initiate the claim before a Rights Commissioner, who must send the ex-employer a copy of the application. The Rights Commissioner hears the evidence in private and issues a recommendation. If the action is settled, no further claim on the same issue is allowed. If the recommendation is not acceptable, either party may appeal to the Employment Appeals Tribunal within six weeks.

137. Alternatively, the case may be referred to the Employment Appeals Tribunal in the first place, if the employer objects to it being heard by a Rights Commissioner or if the employee so wishes. The Tribunal is responsible for sending a copy of the employee's claim to the ex-employer.

138. The Employment Appeals Tribunal will issue a determination on a case coming before it either by way of appeal or by original claim. This may in turn be appealed to the Circuit Court, and from there to the High Court and Supreme Court, if necessary.

139. If an employer does not comply with the terms specified in a determination within six weeks, the Minister for Enterprise and Employment may take the case to the Circuit Court on behalf of the employee to enforce the redress.

140. Apart from showing that the dismissal was for a fair reason, employers are also obliged to establish that they acted reasonably in deciding to dismiss. Employers must:

(a) conduct an adequate investigation of the circumstances before deciding to dismiss, so that the dismissal is not based on incorrect or incomplete information;
(b) give the employee a chance to 'state their case' before being dismissed;
(c) give the employee at least one warning before being dismissed, which allows sufficient time to improve, a reasonable work situation within which to do so and a fair process for monitoring progress;
(d) relate the penalty proportionally to the offence; and
(e) follow agreed disciplinary procedures.

141. Where an employee has been held to have been unfairly dismissed, the following remedies are available to the Rights Commissioner, the Employment Appeals Tribunal or the Circuit Court, depending on the merits of the case:

(a) the reinstatement of the employee in the same position and on the same terms as before dismissal. The employee will be entitled to all arrears of salary and there will be no break in service;
(b) the re-engagement of the employee in the same position, or in a reasonably

suitable alternative one, on such terms and conditions as the adjudicating body considers reasonable; or

(c) financial compensation, up to a maximum of 104 weeks' pay, in respect of such loss suffered by the employee as a result of the dismissal. The exact amount depends, among other things, on where the responsibility for the dismissal lies, the measures taken to reduce the financial loss or the extent to which negotiated procedures were followed.

142. An employee found to have been unfairly dismissed, but who has not suffered any financial loss, may be awarded compensation of not more than four weeks' pay.

Redundancy Payments Acts 1967–2007

143. The Acts impose a statutory obligation on employers to pay compensation to employees dismissed for reasons of redundancy. They provide for lump-sum payments to be made to redundant workers based on their years of continuous service and gross weekly wages. Redundancy arises where the employer's requirement for employees has ceased or diminished. Examples of when redundancy can occur include:

(a) the employer has ceased to carry on the business;
(b) the requirements of that business have ceased;
(c) the employer has decided to carry on the business with fewer employees;
(d) the employer has decided that the work should be done differently; or
(e) the employer has decided that the work should be done by a person who is capable of doing other work for which the employee is not qualified.

144. A Social Insurance Fund is operated by the State, financed by contributions paid by employees and employers. The fund is used:

(a) to give rebates on lump-sum payments made by the employer;
(b) to pay a lump sum directly to an employee where the employer refuses; or
(c) to pay outstanding sums due to employees in the event of an employer being unable to pay because of insolvency.

An employer is entitled to a rebate of sixty per cent of statutory redundancy payments, provided that the requisite two weeks' written notice of redundancy has been given to each employee on the prescribed form.

145. To be entitled to redundancy payment, an employee must be:

(a) over sixteen years of age;
(b) in employment that is insurable under the Social Welfare Acts; and
(c) employed continuously by the same employer for at least two years by the

date the employment was terminated due to redundancy. The following events do not break continuity:

(i)   change in job with the same employer;
(ii)   change in ownership of the business;
(iii)   engagement by an associated employer;
(iv)   absence up to eighteen months due to sickness or injury;
(v)   absence of up to thirteen weeks taken for purposes of pregnancy, a lay-off or holidays;
(vi)   a lockout or participation in a strike; or
(vii)   any other causes authorised by the employer which do not last longer than twenty-six weeks.

146. Dismissal must be deemed to have been by reason of redundancy. There is no dismissal, and therefore no redundancy payment, where an employee leaves voluntarily or where the contract is frustrated. The dismissal is presumed to have been by reason of redundancy unless the employer can prove to the contrary. However, case-law has shown that an employee will not have a justifiable claim for redundancy payment if:

(a) the contract of employment is renewed; or
(b) the employee unreasonably refuses a suitable offer of alternative employment.

147. The amount of the payment is related to the employee's length of continuous employment and wage. The calculation of redundancy pay is carried out as follows:

(a) one week's pay; plus
(b) two weeks' pay, irrespective of age, for every continuous year of employment, subject to a ceiling of €600 per week.

148. An employee may, if possible, negotiate a higher redundancy payment but, where applicable, must get the statutory minimum.

Protection of Employment (Exceptional Collective Redundancies and Related Matters) Act 2007
149. This Act seeks to prevent large-scale compulsory replacement of workers in Ireland by lower-paid alternatives. Such redundancies may commonly arise in cases of outsourcing, although the Act does not apply to redundancies which are voluntary. An exceptional collective redundancy is a dismissal which is collective and effected on a compulsory basis, and which takes place in circumstances where the dismissed employees have been replaced by others who are employed to perform essentially the same functions on terms and conditions materially inferior to those of the dismissed employees.

150. The Act provides for the establishment of a Redundancy Panel to whom certain proposed collective redundancies can be referred to for consideration. A referral can be made by either the employer or employee representative, and the Redundancy Panel may give notice to the Minister that they require the assistance of the Labour Court if they are satisfied that the proposed redundancies are of an exceptional nature and that other avenues of dispute resolution have been exhausted.

151. Where the Labour Court has determined the dismissal to be 'exceptional' and the employer proceeds to dismiss the employees regardless, the employer is open to a claim under the Unfair Dismissals Acts 1977-2007. Maximum compensation of 260 weeks is payable to employees with more than twenty years' continuous service, while compensation of 208 weeks is payable to those with less than twenty years' continuous service. Moreover, the employer may not be entitled to avail of the rebate under the Redundancy Payments Acts 1967–2007.

IMPORTANT CASES

Numbers in brackets refer to paragraphs of this chapter

IMPORTANT STATUTES

Numbers in brackets refer to paragraphs of this chapter

PROGRESS TEST

Numbers in brackets refer to paragraphs of this chapter

1. When may formality be required in a contract of employment? (3)
2. Identify the common law duties of an employee to the employer. (8)
3. List some of the terms of employment which an employer is required to supply in writing to a new employee. (15)
4. What are the obligations imposed on employers under the Safety, Health and Welfare at Work Act 2005? (46–7)
5. Describe those circumstances whereby a man and a woman are to be regarded as being employed on like work. (53)
6. What are the functions of the Equality Authority and the Equality Tribunal? (57, 58, 64)
7. Identify those details which an employer is required to keep a record of, relating to the employment of each employee under age eighteen. (74)
8. How may an employee exercise her right to take maternity leave? (78)
9. Describe five methods by which a contract of employment may be terminated. (116–125)
10. What workers are excluded from the protection of the Unfair Dismissals Acts 1977–2007? (131)
11. How may an employer justify a dismissal on 'substantial grounds'? (133)
12. What redress is available to an employee who has been held to have been unfairly dismissed? (141)
13. What are the prerequisites for an employee to be entitled to redundancy payment? (145)

INTERNET RESOURCES

Department of Enterprise, Trade and Employment
  www.entemp.ie
Employment Appeals Tribunal
  www.eatribunal.ie
Equality Authority
  www.equality.ie
Equality Tribunal
  www.equalitytribunal.ie
Health and Safety Authority
  www.hsa.ie
Labour Court
  www.labourcourt.ie
National Employment Rights Authority (NERA)
  www.employmentrights.ie
Rights Commissioner (Labour Relations Commission)
  www.lrc.ie

Part 6: Employment Law

EXAMINATION QUESTIONS

1. Given the nature of the employment market in the Irish economy it is important to be able to distinguish between the types of employment relationships. Distinguish between a contract of service and a contract for services. Why is this distinction important?

   ICPA (Summer 2007)

2. John and Mary maintain the gardens of a large country hotel. They use their own equipment and set their own hours. Explain the test to be applied to determine whether or not they are employed under a contract of service or a contract for services and whether or not the Unfair Dismissals legislation applies to them.

   IATI (Autumn 2007)

3. Distinguish between a contract of service and a contract for services, and explain the importance in this distinction.

   ICPA (Autumn 2006)

4. Michael agreed to build a new garage for Peter on his property at an agreed price of €50,000. Michael hired Ted to construct the garage for €20,000. Ted was obliged to use materials supplied by Michael and to follow his specifications. Michael monitored the progress of the construction but did not tell Ted what to do or how to do it. Michael also engaged other workers to carry out similar construction work in accordance with his specifications at other locations. Ted was a skilled and experienced builder and had done similar work before for Michael. Ted was recently injured while on the job. He needs to know whether he is an employee of Michael or an independent contractor. Advise Ted.

   ICPA (Summer 2006)

5. Healthfoods Ltd manufactures its own products, which it used to sell through its own retail shop. Ida, who is 42 years old, was employed by Healthfoods Ltd for six years as the manager of the shop. Healthfoods Ltd decided to close its shop and concentrate solely on manufacturing. As a result, the company told Ida that her services would no longer be required after she had served her period of notice. The company also told Ida that she was not entitled to receive any recompense for her loss of employment.

   Required: Advise Ida as to the likelihood of her successfully claiming for unfair dismissal or redundancy.

   ACCA (June 2007)

6. (a) Under the Unfair Dismissal legislation, which categories of persons may bring an action for unfair dismissal and which categories may not.
   (b) In what circumstances will a dismissal be deemed to be unfair?

IATI (Summer 2007)

7. Fritz ran a publishing business which specialised in producing legal textbooks. Gus and Hilda worked for Fritz as proofreaders and editors for a period of three years. They were both described as self-employed and both paid tax as self-employed persons. Fritz provided all of their computer equipment. Gus was required to work solely on the projects Fritz provided, and he had to attend at his premises every day from 9 a.m. till 5 p.m. Hilda, on the other hand, usually worked at home and was allowed to work on other projects. Hilda could even arrange for her work for Fritz to be done by someone else if she was too busy to do it personally. Also, Gus received payment when he could not work because of illness, but Hilda received no such payment.

Last month, Fritz decided to move out of the law textbook market and, instead, to specialise in scientific textbooks. As a result, he told Gus and Hilda that there would be no more work for them.

Advise Gus and Hilda:

(a) why it is important to distinguish between contracts of service and contracts for services;
(b) how the courts decide whether someone is self-employed or is an employee;
(c) whether each of them will be considered to be self-employed or an employee; and
(d) what claim, if any, they can make against Fritz.

ACCA (June 2006)

8. Vanessa was employed for the past four years as a structural engineer with ABC Engineering Company. Her work has been excellent and last year she was promoted to head the bridge design team. However, on recently learning that Vanessa was pregnant, her boss, Ms Anderson, dismissed her. Under the Unfair Dismissals legislation, advise Vanessa of her rights and what her entitlements are.

IATI (Summer 2005)

9. In relation to employment law, explain:
   (a) the grounds upon which dismissal may be fair;
   (b) the meaning and effect of constructive dismissal.

ACCA (December 2006)

10. David has worked for a local computer software company 'Webnet' for the past 18 months. The company has recently dismissed him after he was seen talking to an employee of a rival company. 'Webnet' has accused David of discussing the company's new software with their rival. Advise David as to the common law duties he owes to 'Webnet' and the three remedies available to an employee who has been unfairly dismissed, if this turns out to be the case.

IATI (Autumn 2006)

11. Impact College Ltd provides private tuition. The college is managed by Jack, who also has responsibility for personnel matters. The college has lost a considerable number of its clients in recent years and the decision has been taken to reduce the staff numbers by ten. Fred, Gale and Hilda are amongst the 60 lecturers currently employed by Impact College Ltd. They have all worked for Impact College for the past six years. Fred has been the staff trade union representative for the past three years and has had several confrontations with Jack as to the working conditions of the college's employees. Gale has been off work twice in the past four years on maternity leave, to Jack's stated annoyance, and is pregnant once again. Last year, Hilda reported the college for breaching health and safety requirements and the college was fined a substantial sum of money. It has transpired that Fred, Gale and Hilda are among the ten members of staff to be selected for dismissal by the college, and they suspect that Jack has pursued a personal vendetta against them.

Advise Fred, Gale and Hilda, and the other seven members of staff to be dismissed, as to what action they can take against their employer.

ACCA (December 2005)

Part 7

LAW OF PERSONS

chapter 31

PARTNERSHIPS

Topics covered

- Definition
- Formation
- Relationship with third parties
- Relationship with each other
- Dissolution
- Limited Partnerships Act 1907

Summary

Partnerships are most commonly used nowadays as a form of association by professional people, such as accountants and solicitors, since they must maintain individual professional accountability to their clients. This chapter examines how the relationship between such people and their clients is regulated.

• Definition

1. In s. 1 of the Partnership Act 1890, a partnership is defined as a 'relation which subsists between persons carrying on a business in common with a view to profit'.

2. A 'business' includes 'every trade, occupation or profession'. (s. 45)

3. It should be noted that it is not possible for complete strangers to carry on business in common, since there will be an absence of mutual obligation between the parties. Furthermore, if a business is carried on with the intention of making a profit, it is not necessary that a profit be made in order for a partnership to exist.

• Formation

4. No formalities are required for the formation of a partnership. The relationship may come into existence when the parties make an express contract, as where they execute formal 'articles of partnership', or when they make an implied contract, as where their conduct indicates an implied partnership agreement between the parties.

5. However, while a contract of partnership may be created orally or by implication, such informality is rare. Generally, the partners have a written agreement or deed drawn up, called the 'articles of partnership', which contains all the provisions of the partnership contract. A partnership agreement will usually provide for the following matters:

(a) the place and nature of the business;

(b) the name of the firm;

(c) the date of commencement and duration of the partnership;

(d) the capital of the firm and the proportion being contributed by each partner;

(e) the salary, if any, to be paid to each partner;

(f) the ratio in which profits and losses are to be divided;

(g) the method for keeping regular accounts and preparing an annual profit and loss account and balance sheet;

(h) the amount of drawings which each partner may take from the business;

(i) the death, retirement or bankruptcy of a partner;

(j) the dissolution of the partnership;

(k) the admission and expulsion of partners;

(l) the calculation of goodwill in the event of the death or retirement of a partner;

(m) the powers and duties of partners;

(n) the procedure to be used in solving disputes.

Case: Macken v. the Revenue Commissioners (1962)

A painting contractor, his son and daughter agreed, in or around September 1953, that they should form a partnership effective from 1 January 1954. A partnership deed to this effect was signed on 30 April 1954. The defendants took an action so as to have the court declare that a partnership existed from 1 January 1954.

Held: No partnership existed until the deed was executed. All that had existed was an intention to form a future relationship effective from 1 January 1954.

6. A partnership requires a minimum of two members. The maximum membership is restricted by statute. The upper limit of partners in a limited partnership (i.e. one where *some* of the partners have limited liability) was fixed to twenty for an ordinary business and ten for a banking partnership by the Limited Partnerships Act 1907. This restriction was extended to general partnerships (i.e. where *each* partner is liable for the debts of the partnership) by the Companies Act 1963, but was amended by the Companies (Amendment) Act 1983 to exclude persons practising as accountants or solicitors.

7. Persons acting in partnership are collectively known as the 'firm', and the name under which trading takes place is called the 'firm name'. Where a partnership is carried on under a name which does not consist of the true surnames of all the partners, the partnership name must be registered under the Registration of Business Names Act 1963, and the true names of each of the partners have to be disclosed on every business letter, trade circular, trade catalogue or showcard issued by the firm.

• Relationship with third parties

8. Every partner is an agent of the firm and the other partners for the purpose of the business of the partnership; and the acts of every partner who does any act for carrying on in the usual way business of the kind carried on by the firm of which this person is a member bind the firm and the partners, unless the partner so acting has in fact not authority to act for the firm in the particular matter, and the third party with whom this partner was dealing either knows that this person does not have authority, or does not believe this person to be a partner. (s. 5, Partnership Act 1890)

9. Acts carried out by a partner within the scope of apparent authority, even when no actual authority has been obtained, will bind the firm and the partners.

Case: Mercantile Credit Co. of Ireland Ltd v. Garrod (1962)

A partnership existed for the purpose of the letting of garages and the provision of a motor repair service. The deed of partnership expressly excluded the buying and selling of cars, but the defendant, a co-partner, sold a car to the plaintiffs. The plaintiffs sued the firm.

Held: The transaction was valid and binding on the firm, since the co-partner had acted in a manner which could be considered as commonly practised in a garage.

10. Partners have been held to have apparent authority to:

(a) purchase on account goods necessary for the business;
(b) sell the firm's goods or personal chattels;
(c) engage and discharge employees;
(d) accept payment of debts owing to the firm;
(e) sign cheques;
(f) borrow money and pledge security; and
(g) employ a solicitor to represent the firm in legal proceedings.

11. However, a partner will not have apparent authority to:

(a) execute a deed;
(b) guarantee a loan;
(c) accept property other than money in payment of a debt; or
(d) submit a dispute to arbitration.

12. An act, or instrument, relating to the business of the firm and done, or executed, in the firm name, or in any other manner showing an intention to bind the firm, by any person so authorised, whether a partner or not, is binding on the firm and on all the partners. (s. 6)

13. Where a partner pledges the credit of the firm for a purpose apparently unconnected with the ordinary business of the firm, the firm is not bound by such a pledge unless it has been specifically authorised by the other partners. The partner will be personally liable. (s. 7)

14. The firm is not bound by the act of a partner whose power to bind the firm has been restricted, and who contracts in excess of powers with a third party who has notice of this restricted authority. (s. 8)

Personal liability of partners
15. Each partner is jointly liable for the whole of the firm's debts and obligations incurred while a partner. (s. 9)

16. Therefore, if a creditor obtains a judgment against the firm, the judgment operates against each of the partners to the full extent of their wealth. However, if instead of proceeding against the firm the creditor proceeds against only some of the partners and obtains a judgment, the other partners are discharged from liability.

17. Where a partner is responsible for any wrongful act or omission done in the ordinary course of the firm's business or with the authority of the other partners, the firm is liable for any loss, damage or injury caused to a third party. (s. 10)

Case: Hamlyn v. Houston & Co. (1903)

A partner of the defendant firm bribed the plaintiff's clerk in order to obtain information.

Held: The partnership was liable in tort, since it was the business of the partnership to obtain such information by legitimate means.

Misapplication of funds
18. Where a partner receives money or property while acting within the scope of actual or apparent authority, the firm is liable in the event of its misapplication. (s. 11)

Case: Cleather v. Twisden (1884)

The plaintiffs, trustees of a will, deposited bonds with a partner of the defendant firm of solicitors. The partner converted the bonds and disappeared with the proceeds. The plaintiffs took an action against the remaining partner to recover the misappropriated amount.

Held: The defendant was not liable for the loss, since it was not within the ordinary scope of the business of solicitors to retain bonds for their clients.

19. People who represent themselves by words spoken or written, or by conduct, or who knowingly allow themselves to be represented as partners in a particular firm, are liable to any third parties who have, on the faith of such representations, given credit to the firm. (s. 14)

20. However, the estate of a deceased partner will not be liable for partnership debts incurred after the date of death where the partner's name continues to be used, unless the deceased partner's personal representatives allow the deceased to be represented as still alive.

• Relationship with each other

21. The relations of partners to one another are generally provided for by the articles of partnership but, in the absence of such, the provisions of the Partnership Act 1890 are used as the basis for solving any difficulties which subsequently arise.

22. The mutual rights and duties of partners may be varied with the consent of all the parties. This consent may be either express or implied from the conduct of the partners. (s. 19)

Partnership property

23. Partnership property consists of all property, and rights and interests in property, originally brought into the partnership or subsequently acquired, for the purpose and in the course of the partnership. Partnership property must be held and applied exclusively for the purpose of the partnership and in accordance with the partnership agreement. (s. 21)

24. A creditor can only issue an execution order against the partnership property if a judgment is obtained against the firm. A charging order, however, may be obtained against any partner's interest in the partnership property, and the court may appoint a receiver to collect all profits attributable to the partner's share of the business and to apply them to the money due. The other parties may at any time pay the creditors and redeem the interest charged, or purchase the partner's share in the business if it is offered for sale. (s. 23)

Rights and duties

25. In the absence of an agreement as to the rights and duties of the partners, or if the agreement made by them does not cover a particular difficulty that subsequently arises, the general rules governing these matters are contained in ss. 24, 25, 28, 29 and 30 of the Partnership Act 1890.

26. All the partners are entitled to share equally in the capital and profits of the business, and must contribute equally towards the losses, whether of capital or otherwise, sustained by the firm. (s. 24(1))

27. The firm must indemnify every partner in respect of payments made and personal liabilities incurred in the ordinary and proper conduct of the partnership business, or in relation to anything necessarily done for the preservation of partnership business or property. (s. 24(2))

28. Any partner who makes a payment or advance of capital beyond the agreed amount to be subscribed is entitled to interest at the rate of five per cent per annum from the date of the payment or advance. (s. 24(3))

29. No partner is entitled to receive interest on the capital subscribed before the profits have been ascertained. (s. 24(4))

Management

30. Every partner has the right to take part in the management of the business. (s. 24(5))

31. Partners are not entitled to remuneration for acting in the business. (s. 24(6))

32. No new partners may be introduced without the unanimous consent of all the existing partners. (s. 24(7))

33. Any differences arising in relation to ordinary matters connected with the partnership business may be decided by a majority of the partners, but unanimous consent is required in relation to a change in the nature of the partnership business. (s. 24(8))

34. Every partner has the right to have access to and inspect and copy the partnership books, which are to be kept at the principal place of business of the partnership. (s. 24(9))

35. A partner cannot be expelled from the partnership by a majority decision of the other parties unless there is an express power of expulsion conferred by the partnership agreement and this has been exercised in good faith and for a proper purpose. (s. 25)

36. Partners are bound to give true accounts and full information of all things relating to the partnership to any other partner or to their legal representative. (s. 28)

37. Every partner must account to the firm for any personal benefit obtained without the consent of the other partners from any transaction concerning the partnership or from the use of the firm's property, name or business connection. This duty extends to transactions undertaken after a partnership has been dissolved and before the affairs of the partnership have been completely wound up.

Case: Bentley v. Craven (1853)

Both parties were co-partners, carrying on business as sugar refiners. The defendant, the firm's buyer, purchased sugar very cheaply and sold it to the firm at market price, retaining the profit he had made on the transaction.

Held: The defendant was obliged to pay over the full profit to the firm.

38. A partner who carries on a business of the same nature as, and competing with, the partnership business without the consent of the other partners must account for and hand over all profits made in that business to the partnership. (s. 30)

• Dissolution

39. Subject to any clause or clauses in the articles of partnership, the Partnership Act 1890 provides a number of ways by which a partnership may be dissolved and terminated.

40. A partnership is dissolved by:

(a) passage of time, if the partnership was entered into for a fixed term;
(b) termination of the venture or undertaking, if the partnership was entered into for a single venture or undertaking;
(c) any partner giving notice to the other partners of an intention to dissolve the partnership, if it was a partnership-at-will (i.e. for an undefined time);
(d) the death or bankruptcy of any partner;
(e) subsequent illegality, being the happening of any event which makes it unlawful for the business of the partnership to be carried on, or for the members of the firm to carry on in partnership; or
(f) order of the court. (ss. 32–5)

41. The court may issue a decree for the dissolution of the partnership in any of the following circumstances:

(a) if a partner has been shown to the satisfaction of the court to have become a lunatic or permanently insane;
(b) if a partner has become otherwise permanently incapable of carrying out duties in accordance with the partnership agreement;
(c) if a partner has been found guilty of any conduct which is seriously damaging to the carrying on of the business of the firm;
(d) if a partner wilfully and persistently breaks the partnership agreement;
(e) if the business of the partnership can only be carried on at a loss;
(f) if, in the opinion of the court, circumstances render it just and equitable that there should be a dissolution. (s. 35)

42. Any partner may notify the public of dissolution of the partnership and may require the other partners of the firm to concur for that purpose. (s. 37)

43. After the dissolution of a partnership, the authority of each partner to bind the firm continues, so far as may be necessary, to complete transactions begun but unfinished at the time of the dissolution, and to wind up the affairs of the partnership, but not otherwise. However, the other partners are in no way bound by the acts of a partner who has become bankrupt unless they hold this partner out as having authority for particular transactions. (s. 38)

44. Every partner is entitled, on the dissolution of a partnership, to have the partnership property applied in payment of the debts and liabilities of the firm. Any surplus after such payment may then be applied in payment of what may be due to the partners themselves. Any partner may, on dissolution of the partnership, apply to the court to wind up the affairs of the partnership. (s. 39)

45. Where one partner has paid a premium to another on entering into a partnership for a fixed term, and the partnership is dissolved before the expiration of that term otherwise than by the death of a partner, an application may be made to the court for the repayment of all, or part, of that premium. The court will not order repayment, however, where the dissolution is wholly or chiefly due to the misconduct of that partner who paid the premium, or where the partnership has been dissolved by an agreement containing no provision in relation to a return of any part of the premium. (s. 40)

46. Where a partnership contract is rescinded due to fraud or misrepresentation of one of the partners, the partner who rescinded it is, without prejudice to any other right, entitled to:

(a) a lien on, or right of retention of, the surplus of the partnership assets after satisfying the liabilities, for any sum of money paid by the partner for the purchase of a share in the partnership and for any capital contributed;
(b) stand in the place of creditors of the partnership for payments made towards partnership liabilities; and
(c) be indemnified by the guilty partner against all the debts and liabilities of the firm. (s. 41)

47. Where the surviving or continuing partners of the partnership carry on the business of the firm with its capital or assets without any final settlement of accounts with the outgoing partner, then in the absence of agreement to the contrary, the outgoing partner or nominated representatives are entitled to such share of the profits made since the dissolution as the court may find to be attributable to the use of the partner's share of the partnership assets. (s. 42)

48. The amount due from surviving or continuing partners to an outgoing partner or nominated representatives is, subject to any agreement between the partners, a debt accruing at the date of the dissolution or death. (s. 43)

49. After a dissolution of partnership, the partnership property must be converted into money and applied, subject to any agreement, as follows:

(a) Losses are to be paid:

 (i) firstly out of profits, if any;
 (ii) next, out of capital; and
 (iii) finally, if necessary, by the partners individually in the ratio to which they were entitled to share profits.

(b) The assets of the firm, including sums, if any, contributed by the partners to make up losses, are to be applied to pay:

 (i) the debts and liabilities of the firm to non-partners;
 (ii) each partner rateably the amount due from the firm for advances, as distinct from capital;
 (iii) each partner rateably the amount due from the firm for capital contributions; and
 (iv) the ultimate residue, if any, to the partners in the ratio to which they shared profits and losses.

• Limited Partnerships Act 1907

50. A limited partnership consists of one or more general partners with full liability for the firm's debts and obligations, and one or more limited partners whose liability is limited to their initial capital contributions, which must be left in the firm during its existence. (s. 4)

51. A limited partnership must be registered with the Registrar of Companies, and the register is open to scrutiny by the public. (s. 5)

52. The statement of registration, signed by all the partners, must contain the partnership name, the nature of business, the place of business, the full name of each of the partners, a statement that the partnership is limited, the name of each limited partner, the amount contributed by each partner, the term of the partnership and its date of commencement. (s. 8)

53. A limited partner cannot become involved in the management of the firm. However, if this happens, the limited partner becomes fully liable for the debts and liabilities of the firm incurred at that time. (s. 6)

54. The death, lunacy or bankruptcy of a limited partner does not cause a dissolution of the partnership.

55. The limited partnership became virtually redundant with the passing of the

Companies Act 1963, which made it possible to form a private company consisting of only two members, and which also had benefits of a limited liability.

IMPORTANT CASES

Numbers in brackets refer to paragraphs of this chapter

Macken v. the Revenue Commissioners (1962) .... (5)
Mercantile Credit Co. of Ireland Ltd v. Garrod (1962) .... (9)
Hamlyn v. Houston & Co. (1903) .... (17)
Cleather v. Twisden (1884) .... (18)
Bentley v. Craven (1853) .... (37)

IMPORTANT STATUTES

Partnership Act 1890
Limited Partnerships Act 1907
Registration of Business Names Act 1963

PROGRESS TEST

Numbers in brackets refer to paragraphs of this chapter

1. Define a partnership. (1)
2. What formalities are required for the formation of a partnership? (4–5)
3. May a firm be bound by the acts of a partner without the co-partners providing the authority to do so? (8–9)
4. To what extent is a partner liable for the debts and obligations of the firm? (15–20)
5. What is partnership property, and in what circumstances may a creditor issue an execution order against the same? (23–4)
6. Describe the rules governing the rights and duties of the partners, contained in the Partnership Act 1890, in the absence of an agreement as to these matters. (26–38)
7. How may a partnership be dissolved? (40)
8. Under what circumstances may a court issue a decree for the dissolution of a partnership? (41)
9. What rights has a partner who rescinds a partnership contract due to fraud or misrepresentation? (46)
10. How, subject to any agreement, must partnership property be applied after a dissolution of partnership? (49)
11. Define a limited partnership, and describe the registration requirements of the same. (50–52)

chapter 32

COMPANIES

Topics covered

- Origins of company law
- Director of Corporate Enforcement
- Formation of a company
- Share capital
- Management and administration

- Liquidations, receiverships and examinerships
- Comparisons between partnerships and companies

Summary

A company is a separate legal entity which provides stability, limited liability and, above all, continuity of existence to its members. This chapter examines the rights and powers of such entities, as regulated by statute.

• Origins of company law

1. Up to 1963, there were a number of Companies Acts on the statute book. The Companies Act 1963 repealed and consolidated the Companies (Consolidation) Act 1908, the Companies Act 1913, the Companies (Particulars as to Directors) Act 1917 and the Companies Act 1959. The Companies Act 1963, containing 399 sections and thirteen schedules, is the largest Act to have been passed in the Dáil.

2. The Companies (Amendment) Act 1983 enacted into Irish law the provisions of the EC Second Directive on Company Law. It had the effect of regulating the maintenance and alteration of capital, the formation of public companies and the reregistration procedure for companies.

3. The Companies (Amendment) Act 1986 complied with Ireland's obligations under the EC Fourth Directive on Company Law. It provides that companies are required to file financial statements in a specified format with their annual returns in the Companies Registration Office. The detail required is dependent on whether the company is defined as 'large', 'medium' or 'small', for the purpose of the Companies (Amendment) Act 1986.

4. The Companies Act 1990 is by far the most thorough reform of company law since 1963. Its provisions are designed to curb abuse of limited liability, deal with the problem of insider dealing, give creditors greater redress in cases of malpractice by directors, and improve the management of companies.

5. The Companies (Amendment) Act 1990 provides for the introduction of an examiner, under the protection of the court, to give companies experiencing difficulties every opportunity to reorganise themselves so that they can survive.

6. The Companies (Amendment) Act 1999 amends and extends Part IV (relating to disclosure of interest in shares) and Part V (relating to insider dealing) of the Companies Act 1990, so as to facilitate price stabilising on the Irish Stock Exchange in connection with new issues of securities and large offers of existing securities.

7. The Companies (Amendment) (No. 2) Act 1999 exempts certain companies from the requirement to have accounts audited, requires Irish companies to conduct an activity within the State, demands that one director of an Irish incorporated company be resident in the State, limits to 25 the number of directorships any individual can have, provides the Registrar of Companies with increased powers to strike off companies, and amends aspects of legislation relating to court protection procedure.

8. The Company Law Enforcement Act 2001 improves compliance with and enforcement of company legislation. It established the independent office of the Director of Corporate Enforcement, and transferred to the Director the powers of the Minister for Enterprise, Trade and Employment in the areas of investigations and company law prosecutions. It also conferred the Director with powers relating to insolvent companies, whether in liquidation or not, the restriction and disqualification of company directors and other persons, and the supervision of liquidators and receivers.

9. The Companies (Auditing and Accounting) Act 2003 addresses the regulation and professional rules governing the auditing profession. It provides for the establishment on a statutory basis of an independent regulatory body, the Irish Auditing and Accounting Supervisory Authority (IAASA), the principal function of which is to supervise how the prescribed accountancy bodies regulate and monitor their members. The IAASA has the power, among other things, to intervene in the disciplinary process of the accountancy bodies where it deems it necessary, to carry out independent investigations in public interest cases, and to apply to the courts to compel directors of a company to amend accounts that are not in line with accounting standards.

10. The Investment Funds, Companies and Miscellaneous Provisions Act 2005 provides greater flexibility to the funds industry whilst keeping appropriate controls in place. It also increases the amount of shares that a member may hold and other financial limits for industrial and provident societies (cooperatives), as well as raising the levels of fines which can be imposed on parties found guilty of breaches of specific consumer legislation. The main provisions of the Investment

Funds, Companies and Miscellaneous Provisions Act 2006 include an increase of audit exemption thresholds, a new definition of private companies, a transposing into Irish law of the EU Transparency Directive and an amendment to the Consumer Information Act 1978 for the appointment of a person to perform the functions of the Director of Consumer Affairs for a period of more than 6 months.

11. In May 2007, the chair of the Company Law Review Group presented a report on the Companies Consolidation and Reform Bill with a view to replacing thirteen Companies Acts and numerous statutory instruments with a single piece of legislation. This Bill is expected to simplify many of the existing procedures for setting up and running a company, whilst ensuring that creditors and shareholders remain strongly protected. Some likely changes include a single-document constitution in place of the current memorandum and articles of association, the introduction of single-director private companies, a variation in the criteria for classifying small- and medium-sized companies, and an extension in the powers of the Director of Corporate Enforcement to petition the court to wind up a company.

Director of Corporate Enforcement
12. The Company Law Enforcement Act 2001 provided for the establishment of an independent officer, the Director of Corporate Enforcement, who has statutory responsibility for enforcing and ensuring compliance with company law.

13. The functions of the Director are specified in s. 12(1), Company Law Enforcement Act 2001 as being:

(a) to enforce the Companies Acts, including the prosecution of offences by way of summary proceedings;
(b) to encourage compliance with the Companies Acts;
(c) to investigate instances of suspected offences under the Companies Acts;
(d) at his or her discretion, to refer cases to the Director of Public Prosecutions where the Director of Corporate Enforcement has reasonable grounds for believing that an indictable offence under the Companies Acts has been committed;
(e) to exercise, insofar as the Director feels it necessary or appropriate, a supervisory role over the activity of liquidators and receivers in the discharge of their functions under the Companies Acts;
(f) for the purpose of ensuring the effective application and enforcement of obligations, standards and procedures to which companies and their officers are subject, to perform such other functions in respect of any matters to which the Companies Acts relate as the Minister considers appropriate and may by order confer on the Director; and

(g) to perform such functions for a purpose referred to in paragraph (f) as may be assigned to him or her by or under the Companies Acts or any other act.

14. A number of the Minister's functions are transferred to the Director under s. 1, including the power of the Minister to direct the calling of an AGM and the power to apply to the court for the production and inspection of books when the Minister believes an offence (in connection with the management of a company's affairs) has been committed.

15. The Director of Corporate Enforcement is required under s. 16 to make an annual report about the performance of the Director's functions and other activities of the Director to the Minister no later than 31 March in the following year. The Minister must lay that report before each house of the Oireachtas within two months of receiving that report.

16. The Strategy Statement for 2003–5 produced by the Director of Corporate Enforcement clearly defined and set out the long-term objectives of the office by identifying five key goals, namely:

(a) encouraging improved compliance with the Companies Acts;
(b) uncovering suspected breaches of Company Law;
(c) prosecuting detected breaches of the Companies Acts;
(d) sanctioning improper conduct with respect to insolvent companies; and
(e) providing quality services to internal and external customers.

• Formation of a company

17. The normal method of incorporation is by registration in accordance with the provisions of the Companies Acts 1963–2006. A company may be registered as a private or public limited company.

18. A private company is a company with share capital and which:

(a) restricts the rights to transfer its shares;
(b) must have at least two members and not more than ninety-nine, excluding employees and past employees;
(c) prohibits any invitation to the public to subscribe for any shares or debentures in the company. (The 2006 Act provides that certain offers of shares or debentures do not constitute offers to the public for the purposes of this definition.)

19. A public company is any registered company which is not private. It can have from seven members upwards.

20. For the purposes of the registration of a *private* company, the following documents must be prepared and sent to the Registrar of Companies:

(a) memorandum of association (s. 17, Companies Act 1963);

(b) articles of association (s. 17, Companies Act 1963);

(c) a statutory declaration by a solicitor or a person named in the articles of association as a director or secretary that all the requirements for registration have been complied with s. 5(4) Companies (Amendment) Act 1983;

(d) a letter of confirmation from the Minister for Enterprise, Trade and Employment as to the availability of a proposed name for the company (s. 21, Companies Act 1963);

(e) a statement of capital duty, in accordance with the Finance Act 1973;

(f) a statement of (i) the particulars of the first directors' names, addresses, nationalities and occupations; (ii) the details of the first secretary or secretaries; (iii) the situation of the registered office of the company (s. 3, Companies (Amendment) Act 1983); and

(g) a bank draft for the registration fee (s. 369, Companies Act 1963).

21. For the purpose of the registration of a *public limited* company, it is necessary to deliver to the Registrar of Companies, in addition to the above, a statutory declaration stating:

(a) the nominal value of the company's allotted share capital is not less than €38,092;

(b) the amount paid up, at the time of the application, on the allotted share capital of the company (s. 6, Companies (Amendment) Act 1983);

(c) the amount, or estimated amount, of the preliminary expenses of the company and the persons to whom these expenses have been paid or are payable; and

(d) any amount or benefit paid or given or intended to be paid or given to any promoter of the company and the consideration for the payment or benefit.

22. When all of the documents and fees have been received, examined and approved of by the Registrar of Companies, the company is registered and receives a certificate of incorporation, which is conclusive proof of the existence of the company.

23. A company may be registered with either limited or unlimited liability.

24. A company may be *limited by guarantee,* whereby the members' liability is limited to the amount which each member has guaranteed in writing to contribute to the company in the event of the assets of the company being insufficient to discharge all the debts of the company when it is being wound up. If a company is limited by guarantee, it is prevented by s. 7, Companies (Amendment) Act 1983 from being a public limited company. This type of company, therefore, is best suited for non-profit-making and charitable organisations.

25. A company may be *limited by shares*, whereby the members' liability is limited to the nominal value of the shares held by them in the company. If the shares are not fully paid up, the individual member's liability to unpaid creditors is limited to the amount unpaid or outstanding on the shares in the event of the company going into liquidation.

26. Finally, a company may have *unlimited liability*, whereby the members are liable for all the debts of the company, even if this results in the debts having to be paid from their own private assets.

27. The most important consequence of registration is that a company is recognised by law as having an existence and reality which is separate from its members. Some of the consequences of this separate legal entity are that a company can make contracts, can sue and be sued, and can own property.

Case: Salomon v. Salomon & Co. (1897)

The plaintiff, with his wife and five children, formed a limited company, and sold his business to the company as a going concern. The price was paid by the issue of 20,000 fully paid £1 shares, and debentures to the value of £10,000 secured on the company's assets. The company ran into financial difficulties and, on liquidation, the assets only realised about £6,000, whereas it owed £7,000 to unsecured creditors and £10,000 to the plaintiff as holder of the secured debentures. The liquidator, on behalf of the unsecured creditors, claimed that Salomon, the virtual owner of the company, should not be paid on his secured debentures until the other creditors were paid first.

Held: The company was completely separate from the plaintiff, who was entitled to have his loan repaid to him. Since the shares were fully paid up, the debts of the company were its own affair and not those of the plaintiff, who was merely the company's agent.

28. It is only on rare occasions that the law will ignore the separate legal personality of the company, and will 'lift the veil of incorporation' to hold the members personally liable for the actions of the company. Some such situations, as when membership falls below the legal minimum, are outlined in the Companies Act 1963. In other cases, the law will look at the realities if the company is being used to evade legal obligations or is acting solely as the agent of another company.

Case: Gilford Motor Co. v. Horne (1933)

The defendant entered into a contract of employment which provided that he would not solicit his employer's customers upon the termination of his employment. The defendant set up a company with his wife and son as directors and shareholders after the termination of his employment, which subsequently issued circulars to his former employer's clients. The plaintiffs sought an injunction to restrain the defendant and the company from soliciting their customers.

Held: The court would lift the veil of incorporation to see that the company was but a device by which the defendant sought to avoid his contractual obligations. The court granted the injunction, thereby preventing both the defendant and the company from distributing the circulars to the plaintiffs' customers.

Memorandum of association

29. A memorandum of association must be delivered to the Registrar of Companies before incorporation can take place. The document contains the rules and regulations that govern the company's dealings with the outside world. Section 6, Companies Act 1963 requires the memorandum to contain the following clauses:

(a) name clause;
(b) objects clause;
(c) limited liability clause;
(d) share capital clause;
(e) association clause.

(a) Name clause

The memorandum of association must contain the company's name, which in the case of a company limited by shares or by guarantee must be followed by the word 'Limited' or 'Teoranta' (or the abbreviation 'Ltd' or 'Teo' respectively). Furthermore, in accordance with s. 4, Companies (Amendment) Act 1983, in the case of a public limited company the name must be followed by the words 'public limited company' or 'cuideachta phoiblí theoranta' (or the abbreviation 'plc' or 'cpt' respectively). A company is restricted in the name it chooses. The Minister for Enterprise, Trade and Employment may consider a name to be undesirable and refuse its registration if:

(i)   it is the name of an existing company;
(ii)   it suggests or implies a connection with any government department, local authority or state agency;
(iii) it is regarded as being misleading;
(iv)   it includes a registered trade mark, without production of the consent of its owner.

Case: Irish Permanent Building Society v. Cauldwell and Irish Life Building Society (1981)

The plaintiffs requested that the defendants be refused the right to register with the name specified, on the grounds that it would lead unsuspecting people to believe that the resources of the Irish Life Assurance Company Limited were behind the company should they get into difficulty.

Held: Although the defendant building society was founded by employees of the Irish Life Assurance Company Limited and its directors were nominees of the assurance company, it was a separate legal entity and should be allowed to register on that basis.

(b) Objects clause

The memorandum of association must specify the objects or aims of the company, which limit the company's contractual capacity. A company may adopt any object it wishes provided such objects are legal, and it is usual for promoters to include a wide variety of objects. Where a company enters into a contract which is beyond the powers granted to it by virtue of the objects clause, the contract is said to be *ultra vires* (beyond its powers), and null and void. However, although the contract is *ultra vires*, the third party may be able to enforce it against the company by virtue of s. 8, Companies Act 1963 which provides that the company cannot defeat the third party's claim unless it can be shown that the third party was actually aware at the time of entering the contract that the act or thing was not within the powers of the company. This provision has since been joined by Regulation 6, European Communities (Company) Regulations 1973, which provides that if a third party contracts with a limited company in good faith, there is an entitlement to enforce an *ultra vires* contract against the company. Under no circumstances, however, may a company ratify an act of its own, or its directors, which is *ultra vires*.

Case: Northern Bank Finance Corporation Ltd v. Quinn and Achates Investment Co. (1979)

The plaintiffs had agreed to lend money to a third party on condition that the defendants mortgaged some of their property as security to the plaintiffs. The defendants submitted their memorandum and articles of association to the plaintiffs, which were examined and cleared by the latter's solicitor. The solicitor failed to observe that the company was precluded in its objects clause from guaranteeing loans to any third party, and the loan was granted. When the third party defaulted on the loan and the plaintiffs sought to enforce the guarantee, the defendants argued that this had been an *ultra vires* contract of which the plaintiffs were aware, and hence the transaction was null and void.

Held: Even though the plaintiffs' solicitor did not appreciate the significance of the objects clause in the memorandum of association, the plaintiffs were deemed to have been aware that the defendants were acting *ultra vires*, and therefore were unable to enforce the guarantee. Neither could they rely on the provisions of Regulation 6, European Communities (Companies) Regulations 1973, because the defendants were an unlimited company.

(c) Limited liability clause

The memorandum of association must state that the liability of the member is limited, if the company is to be limited by shares or by guarantee. No member will be required to pay a sum greater than the amount unpaid, if any, on the shares in the event of a winding-up of the company. Limited liability may be lost, however, where the membership of a private company or a public company falls below two or seven respectively, and the company continues to operate for more than six months after this event. In such a case, each member who is aware that the company is operating below the required membership becomes liable for debts incurred throughout this period. Likewise, limited liability may also be withdrawn where it can be proven that members, and others, knowingly operated the business with the intention of defrauding the company's creditors, or for any other fraudulent purpose.

(d) Share capital clause

The memorandum of association must state the amount of the proposed share capital and its divisions into different classes of a fixed amount. No subscriber of the memorandum may take less than one share. The minimum authorised share capital of a public limited company, in accordance with s. 5, Companies (Amendment) Act 1983, is €38,092.

(e) Association clause

The memorandum of association must contain the witnessed signatures of the subscribers, whereby they agree to be bound to the provisions of the memorandum, and the number of shares which each subscriber wishes to take in the company.

30. A company may alter its memorandum of association. The name clause can be changed by special resolution in a general meeting and with the approval of the Minister. Likewise, the objects clause and share capital clause can be amended by special resolution.

Articles of association

31. The articles of association of a company contain the rules and regulations governing the internal management of the company and the rights of the shareholders.

32. In this respect, the articles of association are also of importance to outsiders dealing with the company. The power to bind the company depends on the authority conferred upon the directors, and any director acting beyond this authority does not bind the company, but is personally liable to the outsider.

33. A company may draft special articles for its own use or it may adopt all or any of the model sets of articles contained in Table A of the Companies Act 1963.

34. Part I of Table A contains a model set of articles of association for a public company limited by shares, and Part II contains a model set of articles of association for a private company limited by shares.

35. The following are some of the more usual matters dealt with in articles of association:

(a) division of share capital, shareholders' rights, transfer and forfeiture of shares, alterations of capital;

(b) appointment, rotation and removal of directors, powers and duties of directors, appointment and removal of the secretary and the use of the company seal;

(c) declaration of dividends, transfers to reserves, preparation of accounts and holding of audits;

(d) winding-up of a company.

36. Unless a particular article in Table A is specifically excluded, it applies to a company. It is therefore advisable to identify by number those articles in Table A which the company wishes to exclude.

37. The articles of association must be printed, divided into paragraphs, numbered consecutively, bear a stamp as if they were contained in a deed and be signed by each subscriber of the memorandum in the presence of at least one witness, who must attest the signature.

38. Once registered with the Registrar of Companies, the memorandum and articles of association are binding on each member of the company just as if they had been respectively signed and sealed by each member, and create a contract which can be enforced by the company against the members, by the members as against each other, and by the members as against the company.

Case: Securities Trust Ltd v. Hugh Moore & Alexander Ltd (1964)

A shareholder in the defendant company requested and obtained a copy of its memorandum and articles of association. The shareholder was also chair and managing director of the plaintiff company, which subsequently purchased shares in the defendant company registered in its own name. There had been a serious printer's error in the articles of association and, when a resolution to wind up the company had been passed, the plaintiff company suffered loss. They took an action for damages for negligent misrepresentation by the defendant company.

Held: The copy of the articles of association were not supplied to the shareholder as agent for the plaintiff company. Therefore, the defendant company owed no duty of care to the plaintiff company to ensure that the copy supplied was a correct copy.

39. The articles of association may be amended, subject only to the provisions of the memorandum and the Companies Acts 1963–2006, by the passing of a special resolution by the members in a general meeting.

• Share capital

40. Share capital is a term used in a variety of senses, which include:

(a) *Authorised* (or nominal) share capital is the total amount fixed in the memorandum of association which the company is authorised to issue.

(b) *Issued* share capital is that portion of the authorised share capital which has been issued to members.

(c) *Paid-up* share capital is the total sum of money paid up on shares which have been issued.

(d) *Called-up* share capital is that portion of the issued share capital which has been called up and which members have been required to pay.

(e) *Uncalled-up* share capital is that portion of the issued share capital which has not been called up and for which the members are still liable.

(f) *Reserved* share capital is that portion of a company's uncalled-up share capital which a company has determined by special resolution will not be called up unless in the circumstances of the company being wound up.

41. A share is the interest of a shareholder in a company. A company may in its memorandum of association, but more usually in its articles of association, confer different rights on different classes of shares. It is usual for the capital of a company to consist of two classes of shares, namely: (a) ordinary shares; (b) preference shares.

(a) *Ordinary shares* give holders full members' rights. These include voting rights at a general meeting, the right to receive a dividend declared by the board of directors, and the right to participate in the distribution of capital in the event of the winding-up of the company when all debts have been paid. However, although holders of ordinary shares may receive substantial dividends if profits are high, they do not receive a guaranteed return on their dividends and may, as a result, not receive dividends if profits are low.

(b) *Preference shares* normally carry no voting rights, but are entitled to a fixed percentage dividend each year with priority over that payable on the ordinary shares, and enjoy the same priority over ordinary shares in the distribution of capital in the event of the winding-up of the company. Preference shares may be cumulative, whereby the holder is entitled to arrears of dividends together with current dividends, or non-cumulative. Preference shares are usually redeemable, whereby the company may buy them back from the holders at some future time, though they may also be non-redeemable.

42. A company may also create *debentures*, which are written acknowledgments of loans given to the company by third parties. Strictly, debentures do not form part of a company's true capital; they may, however, be described as 'borrowed' or 'loan' capital and are included in this section for that reason. The position of a debenture holder is completely different to that of a member of the company. Debenture holders do not have any voting rights; they receive a fixed interest payment before any shareholders receive a dividend and, in the event of a winding-up of a company, they are entitled to a repayment of their loans before any of the members receive a refund of their share capital.

Allotment of shares

43. Subscribers to the memorandum of association are a company's initial shareholders. Other shareholders of a company include those parties who have agreed to become members and whose names have been entered in a company's register of members. This is done by a party agreeing to take an allotment of shares from a company or by receiving a transfer of shares from an existing member. Share purchase or subscription is covered by contract law. An offer is made by a prospective shareholder and acceptance arises when allotment is made by the company.

44. Under the Companies (Amendment) Act 1983, the directors of a company may not allot shares unless they are expressly authorised to do so in the articles of association or by a resolution at a general meeting. The authority to allot may be specific or general, and it must state the maximum number of shares which may be allotted. It must also state the date on which the authority expires. Authority to allot expressly included in the articles of association expires after five years.

45. The Companies (Amendment) Act 1983 also provides that where a company issues ordinary shares wholly for cash, it must first offer them to existing ordinary shareholders in proportion to the nominal value of their holdings. The holders of registered shares must receive notice of this pre-emption offer in writing, and the offer must remain open for at least twenty-one days. No allotment may be made until the offer has expired, or every offer made has been accepted or refused. Private companies will not be bound by this pre-emption right if their memorandum or articles of association specifically exclude it.

Consideration for shares

46. In general, shares in any company must be paid for in full and by cash.

47. Part payment is permitted in certain circumstances, however, where the company does not require the full amount immediately. An example of this is where a company can allot shares upon payment of part of the nominal amount of the share and a promise of payment of the outstanding sum upon request. A public company may not allot shares unless 25 per cent of their nominal value and the whole of any premium is paid up.

48. A public company is prohibited by the Companies (Amendment) Act 1983 from allotting shares (whether as fully or partly paid) for a non-cash consideration, unless:

(a) the company receives such consideration within five years from the date of allotment;
(b) the non-cash consideration has been independently valued by someone qualified to be an auditor of the company; and
(c) a report on the valuation has been made to the company and filed with the Registrar of Companies.

49. A private company may allot shares (whether as fully or partly paid) for a non-cash consideration by filing with the Registrar of Companies, within one month from the date of allotment, either:

(a) a copy of the written contract; or
(b) written particulars of the allotment and a return stating the number and nominal amount of shares so allotted, the extent to which they are to be treated as paid up, and the consideration for which they were allotted.

50. Generally, the allotment of shares *at a discount*, that is, at a price lower than their nominal value, is prohibited. Provision is made in the Companies (Amendment) Act 1983 that where shares are allotted at a discount, the allottee is liable to pay the amount of the discount to the company together with interest. However, commission not exceeding 10 per cent of the nominal value of the shares may be paid to a third party in consideration for an agreement to take a company's shares.

51. Where shares are issued *at a premium*, that is, at a price exceeding their nominal value, an amount equal to the aggregate amount of the premium must be transferred to a share premium account. This account can be used for four purposes only, namely:

(a) writing off of preliminary expenses;
(b) writing off the expenses, commission or discount relating to any issue of shares or debentures;
(c) providing the premium payable on the redemption of shares or debentures; and
(d) issuing fully paid bonus shares to existing members.

52. A *bonus* (capitalisation) issue is when a company applies its reserves to paying up unissued shares which are then allotted to existing members. A *rights* issue, on the other hand, is an allotment (or an offer of allotment) of additional shares to existing members. Rights not taken up can be sold on.

Transfer of shares

53. A share certificate is a document bearing the common seal of the company and which, when issued to a member, provides prima facie evidence of a holder's ownership of shares in a company. It states that the party mentioned therein is the registered holder of shares in the company, the extent to which such shares are paid up and the distinguishing numbers, if any, of the shares. The true evidence of title to a share certificate is the entry of the holder's name on the register of members.

Case: Kinsella and Others v. Alliance & Dublin Consumers Gas Co. (1982)

The plaintiff shareholders, having called an extraordinary general meeting to remove the directors of the defendant company, transferred a number of shares to nominees in order to increase their voting strength. Owing to the volume of transfers, the secretary of the defendant company was physically unable to enter in its register of members all of the nominees in time for the extraordinary general meeting. Consequently, the votes of unregistered nominees were disallowed at the extraordinary general meeting, and the plaintiffs issued proceedings challenging the validity of the extraordinary general meeting.

Held: All reasonable efforts to register transfers had been made, and the meeting had been properly held on the basis of the register of members as it then existed.

54. Every company must keep a register of members and must enter in it the following details:
(a) name and address of each member;
(b) number of shares (with its distinguishing numbers) held by each member;
(c) amount paid up on shares; and
(d) date of becoming and ceasing to be a member.

55. Any member of a company or a member of the public may inspect the register of members during business hours. The register must be located at the company's registered office and, in the case of public companies, it must be accompanied by an index of the names of members which can readily enable the account of any member to be found.

56. Every company must make an annual return of the register of members to the Registrar of Companies, which includes:

(a) the address of the registered office;
(b) the type of company and its business;
(c) the number of issued shares; and
(d) the names, addresses and other details of the directors and the secretary.

57. The memorandum or articles of association of a company usually provide that a member may freely transfer their interest to another person. Where a member of a company wishes to transfer shares to a third party, they execute a document of transfer and forward it and the related share certificate to the transferee. The third party executes the document in turn and forwards it and the share certificate to the company. A new share certificate in the transferee's name is issued in due course, and the name of the transferee replaces that of the transferor in the register of members.

58. A private company may, by its articles of association, refuse to register any transfer of shares provided that this power is exercised by the directors in good faith and for the company's benefit. The directors do not have to give any reason for such a refusal unless the articles of association say otherwise. Likewise, a private company may require that a member intending to transfer shares must first offer them to the other members of the company at a price based on a formula included in the articles of association.

Capital maintenance

59. The Companies Acts 1963–2006 contain various provisions which are designed to ensure that a company maintains its capital, that is, by compelling the directors to warn the shareholders when a serious situation affecting the capital has developed, and by preventing a company from acquiring an interest in its own shares directly or indirectly, except under strict conditions.

60. A company may purchase its own shares, subject to authorisation in its articles of association and the observation of a complex procedure as outlined in the Companies Act 1990, the main purpose of which is to ensure that the company does not make itself insolvent.

61. Companies are generally prohibited from giving financial assistance to third parties to purchase shares in that company. Such assistance is permitted, however, where a special resolution has been passed within the previous twelve months and each member is issued with a copy of a statutory declaration made by the directors stating the name of the parties to be assisted, the purpose of the assistance and the form of the assistance. Members holding at least 10 per cent of the issued share capital have a right to apply to the High Court to have the special resolution cancelled. However, where a company lends money in the ordinary course of business, such as in the case of a bank, it may lend money to customers to buy shares in that company without needing to pass any such special resolution.

62. A company so authorised by its articles of association may, by resolution at a general meeting, alter the memorandum of association to increase its authorised share capital by the issue of new shares of such amount as it considers appropriate.

Notification of such an alternation of share capital must be given to the Registrar of Companies within fifteen days. It may also convert any of its paid-up shares into stock, reconvert stock into shares or consolidate its shares into one of larger amounts by adhering to the same requirements as above, provided that notification of such an alteration is given to the Registrar of Companies within one month.

63. A company may reduce its share capital, if so authorised by its articles of association or by special resolution, subject to confirmation by the High Court. Before confirming the reduction, the court must be satisfied that the company has provided for the debts of existing creditors or that consent has been received from them for the reduction of share capital. The court must also satisfy itself that the reduction of capital is not unfair or oppressive to the minority shareholders of the company. The burden of proof, to this extent, rests on the company itself.

Case: Re John Power & Son Ltd (1934)

The directors put proposals to the ordinary and preference shareholders at separate meetings to reduce the share capital of the company, by reducing the nominal value of the ordinary shares and converting the preference shares into debenture stock. The scheme was unanimously approved by the ordinary shareholders and by the preference shareholders in the ratio of 6 : 1. Upon application to the court for sanction of the proposals, the dissenting preference shareholders argued that the circular convening the meeting was misleading and that the scheme was unfair and inequitable.

Held: The circular did not mislead by any positive statement or by inference, and the scheme itself was both fair and equitable.

Dividends

64. A dividend is that part of a company's profits which is distributed to its shareholders in proportion to their respective shareholdings. In most cases, the power to declare a dividend and other provisions relating to declaration and payment of dividends are set out in a company's articles of association, subject to the overriding rules of the Companies Acts 1963–2006.

65. All companies are forbidden from making any distribution except out of profits legally available for the purpose. Distributable profits may be defined as accumulated realised profits less accumulated realised losses. Provided that this leaves a positive balance, this is the fund available for distribution.

66. A public company may, in addition, only make a distribution if at the time the amount of its net assets is at least equal to the aggregate of its paid-up share capital and undistributable reserves.

67. The right to make, and the amount of, any distribution, whether an interim or final dividend, is dependent upon the company being able to produce accounts which demonstrate the justification for such a distribution.

• Management and administration

68. Membership of a company allows a party to invest money and benefit from its rewards without necessarily taking on responsibilities of management. A company, being an artificial person, can only be represented by and act through agents. The management of a company's business, therefore, is performed by a body of persons elected by the shareholders known as the board of directors.

Directors

69. The Companies Acts 1963–2006 provide that every company must have at least two directors, who collectively manage the company in accordance with the provisions of the company's articles of association. The method of appointing directors, along with their rotation and co-option, is controlled by the articles of association, allowing a company a wide discretion in the matter.

70. It is required under s. 43(1) Companies (Amendment) (No. 2) Act 1999 that at least one director of a company shall be resident in the State. This requirement will not apply if the company holds a bond to the value of €25,395 to satisfy any failure of the company to pay fines or penalties under the Companies Acts and certain Taxes Acts, or the Registrar of Companies has issued a certificate that the proposed company has a real and continuous link with one or more economic activities that are being carried on in the State. (s. 44)

71. The Companies (Amendment) (No. 2) Act 1999 also provides that the number of directorships of Irish incorporated companies that any individual can have is limited to twenty-five. However, directorships of public companies are excluded, holding companies and their subsidiaries are counted as one company, and companies holding a banking licence are exempt from calculation in this regard.

72. The first directors are usually named in the articles of association, but not uncommonly the articles, instead of naming them, contain a power for the subscribers, or the majority of them by writing, to appoint them. Subsequent directors are appointed by an ordinary resolution of the shareholders in general meeting or by a resolution of the board where the articles give the directors powers to appoint a person as a director either to fill a casual vacancy or as an additional director.

73. The appointment of directors to a public company must be voted on individually, unless the members present agree by resolution without dissent to a single resolution appointing two or more directors. It is normal for directors to retire by rotation, a specified proportion retiring at each annual general meeting. A director, retiring by rotation, may be re-elected by the members at an annual general meeting.

74. The articles of association may provide regulations for the removal of a director from office, but any such provisions are overridden by statute, allowing removal by ordinary resolution with special notice. The director may require a memorandum to be circulated to the members of the company and has a right to speak to the meeting on the resolution.

75. Certain persons are disqualified from acting as directors. For example, directors of insolvent companies are restricted by s. 150, Companies Act 1990 from becoming directors of other companies for five years. This restriction may be appealed to the High Court where the director has acted honestly and responsibly in the conduct of the insolvent company's business. Furthermore, under s. 41, Company Law Enforcement Act 2001, disqualification does not apply if the other company is a public limited company with an allotted share capital of €317,435 or a private company with an allotted share capital of €63,487, provided that the allotted share capital is fully paid up in cash. However, the grounds for disqualification have been extended under s. 42, Company Law Enforcement Act 2001, where a person has been guilty of two or more 'proper books of accounts' offences, or a person was a director of a company struck off the Registrar of Companies, or a person stands disqualified from acting as director or company secretary in another jurisdiction under circumstances which, had they occurred in Ireland, would have led to a disqualification order. Finally, in addition to statutory disqualifications, a company's articles commonly specify certain circumstances in which a director is to vacate office by reason of disqualification. Examples include if the director becomes mentally ill, or if the director fails to attend meetings for a specified length of time.

Case: Dunleckney Ltd, Re. (1999)

Dunleckney Ltd was struck off the register of companies on 6 November 1990 for failure to file annual returns. The company was restored on 21 October 1991 on the petition of the revenue commissioners, and a compulsory liquidation of the company was ordered on the same day. The two directors of the company were ordered, under s. 150, Companies Act 1990, which came into operation on 1 August 1991, to file a statement of affairs within three weeks to determine whether the directors had acted honestly and responsibly in relation to the affairs of the company. The surviving director (the other having died) argued the provisions of the Companies Act 1990 were not retrospective.

Held: The Court could look at the director's conduct after the commencement of the winding up to determine whether it would be just and equitable that the director be made subject to the restrictions under the section. The failure to fulfil the statutory obligation by filing a statement of affairs and the failure to explain why was sufficient reason to make a declaration under s. 150, Companies Act 1990.

Case: Squash (Ireland) Ltd, Re. (2001)

The two directors had been such for some eighteen years. By the 1990s the company got into financial difficulties, and the directors organised loans for the company and one of the directors did not draw a salary for a period of up to one year. The company sought to sell a premises it held from the Department of Education to clear its debts, but because the entitlement to a statutory tenancy did not apply to State property, it was realised that this sale would not generate adequate funds. After receiving counsel's advice, the company was placed into liquidation, but not before reminders in relation to subscription renewals had been sent out to members. The directors appealed a decision by the High Court that they be restricted under s. 150, Companies Act 1990 on the basis that they had acted irresponsibly.

Held: There was no suggestion that the Companies Acts had not been complied with. The directors' plan, whilst perhaps overly optimistic, was not incompetent or irresponsible. Furthermore, the directors were neither responsible for the company's insolvency nor the net deficiency in assets. Finally, whilst the directors might have notified their members earlier, it was understandable that they did not stop the automatic subscription renewal notices until they had received counsel's opinion on the sale of the premises to clear the company's debts. Therefore, although the directors were open to criticism, they were not to be characterised as irresponsible. The High Court order restricting the two directors was reversed.

76. The restriction and disqualification of company directors is one of the key powers of the Director of Corporate Enforcement. Liquidators are obliged under s. 56, Company Law Enforcement Act 2001, to provide a report to the Director of Corporate Enforcement on the conduct of each of the directors of an insolvent company no later than six months after the date of the appointment as liquidator. Such reports cover the circumstances in which the insolvency occurred, whether proper books of account were kept by the directors of the company, and the extent, if any, to which the directors of the company are considered to have contributed to the insolvency. Furthermore, the liquidator must apply to the court for a restriction order in respect of each of the directors of the company under s. 150, Companies Act 1990 no later than five months after the date of making the required report, unless advised to the contrary by the Director of Corporate Enforcement.

77. The powers of directors are defined by the articles of association, which generally provide that the directors may exercise all such powers as are not, by statute or the articles, required to be exercised by the company in general meeting. If the company's articles vest the powers of management in the directors, a general meeting of the company cannot interfere with a decision of the directors unless they are acting contrary to the Companies Acts 1963–2006 or the company's articles of association.

78. The individual director has limited powers to act independently on behalf of the company, and such powers are really derived from collective decisions taken by the board of directors as a body. The articles of association will usually provide that the board of directors has the power to recommend a dividend payment, to borrow money on behalf of the company, to allot shares, and to appoint one or more of their number to the post of managing director for such period and on such terms as they see fit.

79. Directors are, in the eyes of the law, agents of the company for which they act, and the general principles of the law of agency regulate in many respects the relationship of the company as principal, and the directors as agents.

80. The managing director's rights and duties depend on contractual terms and conditions. Generally, however, the managing director is given the responsibility of ensuring that the objectives and policies formulated by the board of directors are implemented. The managing director has apparent authority to make business contracts on behalf of the company, while actual authority is that which is provided by the board of directors. The powers of a managing director may be revoked, or the appointment terminated, by the board of directors if it so sees fit.

Case: Battle v. Irish Art Promotion Centre Ltd (1968)

The managing director, who was also the major shareholder, of the defendant company applied to the court for leave to conduct the company's defence on its behalf, saying that the company had not sufficient assets to engage a solicitor and counsel.

Held: A registered company cannot be represented in court proceedings by its managing director or other officer or servant.

81. While the authority of the directors to bind the company as agents normally depends on their acting collectively as a board, their duties of good faith are owed by each individual director. The directors, as agents of the company, are required to exercise only such skill as they possess and such care and diligence as would be displayed by a reasonable person in similar circumstances. While not required to give continuous attention to the company's affairs or to attend every board meeting, directors have a common law duty of reasonable competence based on their knowledge and experience.

Case: Healy v. Healy Homes Ltd (1973)

The plaintiff, a director of the defendant company, sought an inspection of the register of members, the minutes book and the books of account of the company.

He specified that he wished to have an accountant with him while he was doing this. The defendants refused to allow anyone except the plaintiff to see the books of account.

Held: In exercising his statutory right to inspect the books of account at all reasonable times, a director of a company may be accompanied by an accountant and may make copies of such documents. An accountant, if so authorised by the director in writing, may inspect alone the books of account. However, he may be required to provide a written undertaking to use such information acquired by him only for the purpose of advising the director.

82. Directors also owe a number of strictly applied fiduciary duties to the company. They must:

(a) exercise their powers in what they honestly believe to be the best interests of the company, and for the purpose for which the powers are given;
(b) retain their freedom of action and not limit their discretion by agreeing to vote as some other party may direct;
(c) avoid conflicts of duty and personal interest; and
(d) avoid personal gain from the position of director without the consent of the company.

Case: Mehigan v. Duignan (1997)

The court ordered that Mantruck Services Ltd be wound up and appointed the applicant as official liquidator. Following his appointment, he examined the books and records of the company and reported that he believed there were 'significant and extensive' omissions. As a result, he said that he could not determine the financial position of the company. There was no proper record of the assets and liabilities, no proper record of invoices and no proper record of money received or expended. An application was made to make the respondent director, Mr. Duignan, personally liable for the debts of the company due to his failure to ensure that his company complied with reporting requirements, such contravention contributing to the company's inability to pay its debts and the substantial impediment of the orderly winding up of the company.

Held: The respondent had knowingly and wilfully permitted the contravention of s. 202 of the Companies Act 1990 and was personally liable to the company for the professional fees involved in overcoming the deficiencies in the books and records of the company. A five year restriction was imposed on him preventing him from being appointed as a director or secretary or taking part in the promotion or formation of any company with an allotted share capital of less than certain limits as set out in s. 150 of the Companies Act 1990.

Secretary

83. Every company must have a secretary, who may also be a director of the company. The Companies Acts 1963–2006 impose a duty on directors to satisfy themselves that the person appointed as secretary can adequately fulfil the position.

84. The secretary is responsible for seeing that the legal obligations of the company are complied with, such as ensuring that proper books and accounts are maintained and that the various statutory returns are made to the Registrar of Companies. The secretary also has the responsibility for taking and keeping the minutes of both board and company meetings, for the maintenance of the share register, for corresponding with shareholders as regards calls, transfers, forfeiture and otherwise, and for ensuring that interest and dividend payments are correctly made.

85. The secretary can also, to some extent, be an agent of the company, with power to bind it if acting:
(a) within the scope of their duties as secretary;
(b) with the express authority of the directors, in respect of any act which the directors themselves have power to delegate; or
(c) with the express authority of the company in general meeting.

Auditors
86. Every company must appoint an auditor, or auditors, at each annual general meeting, to hold office until the conclusion of the next annual general meeting of the company.

87. By virtue of the Investment Funds, Companies and Miscellaneous Provisions Act 2006, private companies whose turnover does not exceed €7.3 million and whose balance sheet amounts do not exceed €3.65 million are entitled to avail of an exemption from the statutory audit requirement. The obligation to annex accounts to the annual return for filing with the Registrar of Companies remains.

88. The auditors have a duty to:

(a) conduct an examination of the financial books and accounts of a company, and a scrutiny of the balance sheet and profit and loss account made up from these financial books and accounts;
(b) report to the members in general meeting whether in their opinion the accounts of the company have been prepared in accordance with the Companies Acts 1963–2006, and whether they give a true and fair view of the company's affairs. If they do not, the auditors must state why and, if possible, quantify the difference;
(c) report on particulars of assets and liabilities, profits and dividends included in any prospectus issued by the company;
(d) report to the Director of Corporate Enforcement if, in the course of the audit, they form an opinion that there are reasonable grounds for believing that a

company or any of its officers or agents has committed an indictable offence (where the accused is entitled as a right to trial by jury) under the Companies Acts (Company Law Enforcement Act 2001).

89. The auditors are entitled to:

(a) have free access to the books and accounts of the company at all times;
(b) require from officers of the company any information and explanations as they think necessary in the performance of their duties;
(c) receive the same notices as members are entitled to of all general meetings of the company; and
(d) attend and be heard at general meetings of the company on any business with which they are concerned.

90. The auditors must exercise reasonable care and skill in carrying out their investigations, and are liable to the company for any loss resulting from negligence or fraud in the performance of their duties.

Shareholders

91. The ultimate control of a company rests with its members in general meeting. A member is any person holding shares in a company. In general, all shareholders have a right to vote, though this is subject to the principles of the articles of association. A shareholder who is entitled to vote may exercise this right in any way they choose, even if such a vote is entirely adverse to the interests of the company as a whole. Likewise, shareholders are permitted to enter into agreements restricting, or determining, the way in which they exercise their voting rights.

92. Generally, shareholders exercise their voting rights at a meeting of the company. Meetings may be attended by members of a company with the right to vote. These members may alternatively appoint another party, known as a 'proxy', whether a member of the company or not, to attend and vote. There are two types of general meetings of members of a company:

(a) annual general meetings; and
(b) extraordinary general meetings.

93. The Companies Acts 1963–2006 provide that a company must convene the first general meeting within eighteen months of its incorporation. It must hold an annual general meeting in each calendar year thereafter, with an interval of not more than fifteen months between each. The articles of association usually determine the business of the annual general meeting, which normally convenes to declare a dividend, consider the accounts and balance sheet and the directors' and auditors' reports, elect directors and appoint auditors until the conclusion of the next annual general meeting of the company.

94. Other general meetings, known as extraordinary general meetings, may be convened by the directors whenever they think fit or on the requisition of members if they constitute one-tenth of the paid-up share capital carrying voting rights. An extraordinary general meeting may also be called by the High Court on a director's or member's application.

95. In order to make valid and binding decisions, a meeting must be properly convened. The length of notice of meetings and how and to whom notice shall be given depend primarily on the articles of association of the company, but the Companies Acts 1963–2006 lay down certain minimum requirements, namely, twenty-one days for an annual general meeting and not less than fourteen days for extraordinary general meetings. In most circumstances, a prescribed number of members may waive this period should they so wish. The notice must be sent to every person whose shares give them a right to attend and vote, and must include any information reasonably necessary to allow shareholders to know in advance what is to be done and to decide whether they will attend the meeting or not.

96. Decisions of the company are made by resolutions of its members, passed at meetings of the members. An ordinary resolution is used for all matters not requiring a special resolution under the Companies Acts 1963–2006 or the company's articles of association. It requires fourteen days' notice and a simple majority of votes cast in order to be passed.

97. Special resolutions are required before the company can make important constitutional changes, such as altering the articles or objects of the company, changing its name, reducing its capital or purchasing its own shares. A special resolution requires twenty-one days' notice and it must be passed by a three-quarters majority. The notice must specify that it is to be a special resolution.

Minority protection

98. From what has been said above, it is clear that the general rule is that of majority rule. Control is exercised by a company's shareholders in general meeting by a simple majority unless the act is one which by statute or the articles of association requires a larger majority. Shareholders in general meeting, whether or not directors, are entitled to vote in whatever way they choose, even if the result will be to assure the passing of a resolution in their own interests.

99. The separate personality which a company acquires on its incorporation means that if a complaint is made that the directors have breached their duties, the company is the proper plaintiff in an action against them. Thus, in general, decisions made or ratified by the majority cannot be disputed by the minority.

Case: Foss v. Harbottle (1843)

Two shareholders of The Victoria Park Company brought an action on behalf of themselves and all other shareholders except the defendants, who were the directors, claiming that the directors had fraudulently misapplied funds of the company.

Held: Only the company itself could sue for redress where a wrong had been done to the company which could validly be ratified or forgiven by a majority of the members in general meeting.

100. Majority rule, however, is not absolute, and *Foss* v. *Harbottle* does not apply to prevent actions by an individual member to restrain an act which:

(a) is illegal or *ultra vires* the company;
(b) has been sanctioned by a simple majority when a special resolution is required;
(c) infringes the personal rights of an individual member; or
(d) constitutes a fraud by the majority on the minority.

101. In addition, there is a series of statutory remedies which may be available not only when some wrongful act has occurred but also when there has been a course of oppression or unfair prejudicial treatment of the minority shareholders.

102. Under s. 213 of the Companies Act 1963, application can be made to the High Court by minority shareholders on the grounds that the company's affairs are being, have been or will be conducted in a manner unfairly prejudicial to them. Where such oppression has been proved, the High Court may order that the company be wound up on the grounds that it is just and equitable to do so.

Case: Re Murph's Restaurants Ltd (1979)

There were three equal shareholders and directors in the company. The affairs of the company had been conducted on a very informal basis, with no annual meetings, no annual accounts and no payment of directors' fees or dividends. All profits of the company had been distributed as directors' remuneration. When one of the directors was informed that he was being relieved of his responsibilities as a working director and was being offered three months' salary in lieu of notice, he applied to have the company wound up under s. 213 of the Companies Act 1963.

Held: The action of the other two equal shareholders and directors was wholly unjustified, irregular and oppressive. The court ordered the winding-up of the company on just and equitable grounds.

103. However, very often it is not in the interests of the minority shareholders to have the company wound up, since such a liquidation may result in the sale of assets at a break-up value without regard to the company's intangible assets, goodwill and know-how. In an attempt to meet such cases, s. 205 of the Companies Act 1963 gives an alternative remedy, namely that the High Court may order the other members of the company to purchase the shares of the oppressed shareholders.

Case: Re Greenore Trading Co. Ltd (1980)

The company had three equal shareholders and directors. One of the directors, when resigning, sold his shares to a fellow director, part of the consideration for which was a cheque drawn on the company. The third director, upon learning of this, applied for relief under s. 205 of the Companies Act 1963 on the ground that the company's affairs were being conducted in an oppressive manner.

Held: The petitioner's shares were to be purchased by the majority shareholder at a fair price set by the court.

Charges

104. Upon incorporation, an express or implied power of a registered company to borrow brings with it the implied power to charge the company's property as security for the repayment of the loan. A charge over the assets of a company, therefore, gives a creditor a prior claim over other creditors to payment of the debt out of these assets.

105. Charges may be either fixed or floating. A fixed (or specific) charge is secured against a specific asset or group of assets on creation, and the company is prevented from realising and disposing of that property without the consent of the holders of the charge. Fixed charges rank according to the order of creation, and are usually given by a company over its fixed assets, such as land or premises. A floating charge, on the other hand, is one that is generally secured over all the assets until such time as it crystallises, or becomes fixed, such as when a receiver is appointed to the company or when it ceases to carry on its business and begins the winding-up process. Assets disposed of by a company in the ordinary course of business cease to be subject to the floating charge, whilst all new assets acquired by a company become subject to it.

Case: Re Keenan Bros Ltd (1985)

The company created two charges over its present and future book debts, both of which required the company to pay all moneys it received 'in respect of the bank and other debts' into designated bank accounts, withdrawals from which could only be made with the consent of the relevant bank. On the liquidation of the company, the question arose whether the charges were fixed or floating.

Held: The charges created were fixed charges, since the banks had deprived the company of its freedom to deal with the book debts in the ordinary course of business such as it would have been entitled to under a floating charge.

106. The Companies Act 1963 provides that every charge must be registered with the Registrar of Companies within twenty-one days of its creation. Failure to do so will render the charge void against the liquidator and any person who acquires an interest in property subject to the charge. The loan remains valid but unsecured. If default is shown to be accidental or inadvertent, the time for registration may be extended by the High Court.

• Liquidations, receiverships and examinerships

107. A company will continue to exist despite the fact that there may be a change in its membership. A company does not terminate because its shares are transferred, its directors retire or a member dies. It has the possibility of 'perpetual succession', and will only cease to exist where it is 'wound up' or dissolved.

Liquidations

108. A liquidation is the legal winding-up of a company and the administration of its property for the benefit of its creditors and members when:

(a) it has completed the business for which it was created;
(b) the members of the company decide to withdraw from business; or
(c) the company is unable to meet its obligations.

109. A *compulsory* liquidation may be ordered by the court upon petition by the company, any creditor, the Minister for Enterprise, Trade and Employment or, in certain circumstances, by a past or present member of the company where:

(a) the company has passed a special resolution to be wound up by the court;
(b) the company does not begin business within a year from its incorporation or suspends its business at any other time for a whole year;
(c) the number of the company's members is reduced below two for a private company or below seven in the case of a public company;
(d) the company is unable to pay its debts;
(e) the court is of the opinion that it is just and equitable that the company should be wound up; or
(f) the court is satisfied that the company's affairs are being conducted, or the powers of the directors are being exercised, in a manner oppressive to any member of the company.

Case: Irish Tourist Promotions Ltd (1974)

One of the directors brought proceedings to have the company wound up by the court on the grounds that it was insolvent and that the petitioner and another director were on such bad terms that a complete deadlock in the company's management existed. The majority of the creditors, however, did not wish the company to be wound up.

Held: Due to the deadlock between the sole shareholders/directors, there was no prospect that the company would ever trade profitably. In these circumstances, the court ordered that the petition should be granted.

110. In a compulsory liquidation, it is the High Court which appoints the liquidator to the company.

111. A *voluntary* liquidation may be initiated by the members of a company or its creditors. This is the method most commonly adopted, since it enables the company concerned and its creditors to settle their affairs without many of the formalities described in a compulsory liquidation. A company may be wound up voluntarily if:

(a) the period laid down by the articles of association for the duration of the company expires or an event takes place on the occurrence of which the articles of association state that the company is to be dissolved;
(b) the company resolves by special resolution that the company be wound up voluntarily; or
(c) the company, in general meeting, resolves by ordinary resolution that the company, by reason of its liabilities, cannot continue in business. (s. 251, Companies Act 1963)

Case: Re Galway and Salthill Tramways Co. (1918)

The directors of the company had presented a petition in the name of the company seeking to have it wound up on the grounds of inability to pay its debts. Some of the shareholders opposed the winding-up petition.

Held: The court refused to make the order for the winding up of the company, asserting that such a proposal could only be filed with the express authority of the shareholders obtained at a general meeting of the company.

112. A *members' voluntary winding-up* is achieved by the directors making a statutory declaration to the effect that, having made a full enquiry into the company's affairs, they are of the opinion that the company will be able to pay its debts in full within a period not exceeding twelve months from the commencement of the winding-up.

113. In a members' voluntary liquidation, it is the members of the company who appoint the liquidator to the company.

114. A *creditors' voluntary winding-up* may be made in the absence of a statutory declaration of solvency. The company must organise a creditors' meeting to be held not later than one day after the company meeting at which the voluntary winding-up is to be proposed. The directors must present a full statement of the company's affairs, together with a list of their claims, to this creditors' meeting.

115. A liquidator may be appointed at both the company and creditors' meetings, but s. 47 Company Law Enforcement Act 2001 provides that a resolution at a creditors' meeting for the appointment of a creditors' nominee ignores those who abstain, and can be passed only by a majority in value of the creditors voting on the resolution. In the event of no liquidator being nominated by the creditors, the members' choice prevails. An appeal for an alternative nomination can be made to the Court by any director, member or creditor of the company within 14 days of the creditors' meeting. The creditors may also appoint a committee of inspection to supervise the liquidator, to which the members of the company may appoint representatives.

116. The liquidator takes control of the company and, in accordance with the Companies Acts 1963–2006:

(a) collects and realises its assets;
(b) pays the liquidation expenses and the other debts and liabilities; and
(c) distributes the surplus, if any, amongst the members of the company according to their rights.

When this is done, the company is dissolved.

117. The Director of Corporate Enforcement has been empowered by s. 56, Company Law Enforcement Act 2001 to receive from a liquidator a report on each of the directors of an insolvent company no later than six months after the date of appointment of the liquidator. Such a report includes information on how the insolvency occurred and the extent to which the actions of each of the company directors contributed to the insolvency. This will assist the Director to determine whether or not to relieve the liquidator of the obligation to make an application to the High Court for the restriction of each of the directors of the company under s. 150 of the Companies Act 1990. Relief will only be granted when the liquidator makes a clear and unambiguous statement, with accompanying evidence, to the effect that the directors have behaved honestly and responsibly. Otherwise, a s. 150 application must be made not earlier than three months and not later than five months from the date that the report has been submitted.

118. Under s. 57, Company Law Enforcement Act 2001, the liquidator is also required upon request of the Director of Corporate Enforcement to produce for examination books of account, and to answer questions with regard to the contents of the books and the conduct of the liquidation.

Receiverships

119. A receivership is an alternative to liquidation. A receiver may be appointed by the court or under the terms of a deed of debenture if the company appears to be unable to pay its debts.

120. The basic function of the receiver is to collect and realise the assets which provide the security for the loan and to pay the debenture holder the amount due to them. Companies put into receivership do not necessarily finish up in liquidation, since the business continues after the cessation of the receiver's powers but, in practice, creditors are frequently induced into petitioning for a wind-up of the company upon the appointment of a receiver.

Case: Irish Oil & Cake Mills Ltd v. Donnelly (1983)

The defendant was appointed receiver and manager of the plaintiff company by the Northern Bank, under the terms of two floating charges. The directors of the company subsequently failed to provide a statutory statement of affairs verified by affidavit. After four months, the company wrote to the receiver requesting detailed accounts and information of the receivership. When this was refused, the company sought a mandatory injunction directing the defendant receiver to supply the requested material.

Held: A receiver/manager has a duty to account to the company whose affairs he is managing, but the failure of the directors to comply with their statutory duties relieved the receiver from disclosing the information they were seeking.

121. A receiver upon ceasing to act is required under s. 52, Company Law Enforcement Act 2001 to forward a statement of opinion to the Registrar of Companies as to whether or not the company is solvent. A copy of this statement shall in turn be forwarded to the Director of Corporate Enforcement, who is entitled under s. 53 to secure the production of a receiver's books for examination, as well as to have questions answered concerning the content of the books and the conduct of the receivership.

Examinerships

122. An examiner may be appointed by the High Court, under the provisions of the Companies (Amendment) Act 1990, when it appears that a company is unable to pay its debts and no order for winding-up has been made, and the court considers that such action would be likely to facilitate the company's survival as a going concern. Under the Companies (Amendment) (No. 2) Act 1999, the High Court will not appoint an examiner unless there is a 'reasonable prospect' of survival. A report of an independent accountant, indicating the extent of the funding required for trading during the examinership period and the source of that funding, must now accompany a petition for the appointment of an examiner.

123. A petition to the High Court to appoint an examiner may be made by a company, a creditor, directors, or members constituting at least one-tenth of the paid-up share capital carrying voting rights. The usual period of the appointment is three months, but the court may extend that period for a further thirty days.

124. During this period, the company is under the protection of the High Court, which effectively means that:

(a) a receiver may not be appointed;
(b) resolutions for the winding-up of the company may not be passed;
(c) legal proceedings may not be put into effect against the company's assets without the consent of the examiner;
(d) fixed or floating charges against the company's property may not be realised without the consent of the examiner; and
(e) goods in the company's possession under hire-purchase agreements may not be repossessed without the consent of the examiner.

125. The examiner must prepare a report to be presented to the High Court within twenty-one days or such longer period as the court permits, showing full details of the assets, liabilities and debts of the company. It must contain proposals with regard to the possible future of the company and propose schemes of arrangement to facilitate the survival of the company and the whole or any part of its undertaking as a going concern.

126. Such proposals require court approval before they can be implemented. If, however, the court rejects the examiner's proposals or the examiner considers that the company does not have a viable future, the court will order the winding-up of the company.

• Comparisons between partnerships and companies

127. A partnership is formed by the express or implied agreement of the partners, with no formal written requirements. Its existence is a question of fact, to be decided by the court based on the intentions and conduct of the parties. A company is formed by registration under the provisions of the Companies Acts 1963–2006.

128. A partnership has no legal personality distinct from its members. Although a partnership may sue and be sued in the firm's name, it is also possible for each of the partners to be sued in their individual capacity. A company has a legal personality distinct from its members and officers, and it may make contracts, own property and sue and be sued in its own name.

129. A partnership must have at least two partners but, with the exception of solicitors, accountants and bankers, cannot have more than twenty partners. A private limited company must have at least two members and not more than fifty, while a public limited company must have at least seven members and has no upper limit.

130. Partners have, in general, unlimited liability with respect to debts incurred while being a member of the partnership. Under the Limited Partnerships Act 1907, a limited partnership may be formed whereby it is possible for one or more of the partners to limit their liability. The members of a company may have limited liability by shares or by guarantee.

131. Partners are entitled to take part in the management of the partnership, unless they are limited partners or the partnership agreement provides otherwise. Members of a company are not entitled to take part in the management of the company unless they become directors.

132. Partners, with the exception of limited partners, have the implied authority to bind the partnership with their acts. Members of a company cannot bind a company by their acts if they are *ultra vires*, i.e. outside the objects contained within the memorandum of association of the company.

133. Partners cannot transfer their share of the business without the consent of all the partners. Members of a public limited company may transfer their shares freely, while members of a private limited company must generally receive the consent of the directors of the company to transfer their shares.

134. The assets of a partnership belong to the partners involved, but are the partnership's property to be used for the business of the partnership. The assets of a company are vested in the company as a separate legal entity and are not the assets of the members.

135. Except in the case of limited partners, the creditors of a partnership can sue the partnership in the firm's name with the partners jointly and severally liable. The creditors of a company can sue the company as a separate legal entity but not the members.

136. Partnerships are dissolved by the death, bankruptcy or retirement of any partner. They may be dissolved with or without court action. Companies are not dissolved by the death, bankruptcy or retirement of any of their members or officers. Companies are dissolved, on application to the court, by a liquidator appointed by either the court, the creditors or the members of the company.

IMPORTANT CASES

Numbers in brackets refer to paragraphs of this chapter

Salomon v. Salomon & Co. (1897) .... (27)
Gilford Motor Co. v. Horne (1933) .... (28)

IMPORTANT STATUTES

Companies Act 1963
Companies (Amendment) Act 1983
Companies (Amendment) Act 1986
Companies Act 1990
Companies (Amendment) Act 1990
Companies (Amendment) Act 1999
Companies (Amendment) (No. 2) Act 1999
Company Law Enforcement Act 2001
Companies (Auditing and Accounting) Act 2003
Investment Funds, Companies and Miscellaneous Provisions Act 2005
Investment Funds, Companies and Miscellaneous Provisions Act 2006

PROGRESS TEST

Numbers in brackets refer to paragraphs of this chapter

1. What is the function of the Director of Corporate Enforcement? (13)
2. Define a private company. (18)
3. What documents must be submitted for the purposes of the registration of a company? (20–21)

4. Describe how a company may (a) be limited by guarantee, (b) be limited by shares, and (c) have unlimited liability. (24–6)
5. Explain what is meant by 'lifting the veil of incorporation'. (28)
6. List the clauses which must be contained in a memorandum of association. (29)
7. State some of the more usual matters dealt with in articles of association. (35)
8. Differentiate between (a) ordinary shares, (b) preference shares, and (c) debentures. (41–2)
9. Define a share certificate. (53)
10. What are the statutory requirements associated with a registrar of members? (54–6)
11. How may a member of a company transfer a share to a third party? (57)
12. Explain how a company may (a) increase and (b) decrease its share capital. (62–3)
13. Discuss the restriction and disqualification of company directors. (75–6)
14. Identify some of the powers vested in the directors of a company. (77–9)
15. What are the primary duties of the directors of a company? (81–2)
16. Explain the function of a company secretary. (84)
17. What criteria must a company meet to avail of an exemption from the statutory audit requirement? (87)
18. What are the principal duties of the auditors to the members of a company? (88)
19. Differentiate between (a) annual, and (b) extraordinary general meetings. (92–5)
20. Under what circumstances may a compulsory liquidation be ordered? (109)
21. Explain the difference between a members' voluntary wind-up and a creditors' voluntary wind-up. (112–15)
22. What is the function of a receiver? (120)
23. Under what conditions may an examiner be appointed to a company, and what responsibilities does the examiner have in such circumstances? (122–5)
24. List five major differences between a partnership and a company. (127–36)

INTERNET RESOURCES

Companies Registration Office
   www.cro.ie
Company Law Review Group
   www.clrg.org
Department of Enterprise, Trade and Employment
   www.entemp.ie
Director of Corporate Enforcement
   www.odce.ie
Irish Auditing and Accounting Supervisory Authority
   www.iaasa.ie

Part 7: Law of Persons

EXAMINATION QUESTIONS

1. Distinguish between a limited partnership and an unlimited partnership.
   IATI (Summer 2007)

2. Mary, Lorna and Lucy are planning to form a partnership. They seek your advice on the following:
   (a) Is it necessary to obtain agreement between the partners on the employment of staff to conduct the business of the firm?
   (b) Whether each partner has implied authority to borrow money on the credit of the firm?
   (c) Must all partners take equal liability of the debts of the partnership?
   (d) What is the maximum number of people that can be partners in a firm?
   (e) When a partner retires from the firm, do they still remain liable for the debts of the partnership?
   (f) What provisions are usually included in a partnership agreement?
   IATI (Summer 2007)

3. Explain the duties that the members of a partnership owe to one another.
   ACCA (June 2006)

4. Tom, Richard and Patrick are equal partners in a partnership which was established for the purposes of selling overseas property. Business is booming. However, Tom and Richard have recently discovered that Patrick has set up a firm which is competing directly against their partnership. In addition, it appears that Patrick may have used deposits paid by their clients to fund his own company. Tom and Richard seek your advice on the following:
   (a) Does the partnership have any remedy against Patrick for competing against the partnership?
   (b) Is it possible to expel Patrick as a partner?
   (c) Can Tom and Richard be liable for Patrick's misapplication of clients' money?
   IATI (Autumn 2006)

5. In relation to partnership law explain the grounds upon which a partnership can be dissolved.
   ACCA (June 2007)

6. Karl and Kenny are partners in a firm of solicitors. Michael, a client of the firm, handed Kenny €50,000 to invest on his behalf. Kenny absconded with

the money. Karl, who was unaware that Kenny had been given any money, has been threatened with legal action by Michael for the return of the money. Advise Karl as to his potential liability.

IATI (Autumn 2007)

7. In relation to partnership law:

    (a) explain the difference between an ordinary partnership and a limited partnership;
    (b) explain the advantages of a private limited company compared to a partnership.

ACCA (December 2006)

8. Discuss the grounds upon which a partnership can be dissolved.

IATI (Autumn 2007)

9. Susan owns a premises in a prime retail location in the centre of town. Mary has recently returned to Ireland having spent years working for a world-famous lady's fashion label. Both had been old college classmates and decided that they would open a lady's boutique. They agreed that they would trade from Susan's premises and would split profits and losses equally. Unfortunately, two years on their business venture has not reached its potential and is accruing considerable losses. Susan believes it is inevitable that their partnership will not last and seeks your advice on the following:

    (a) Has Mary gained any legal or beneficial interest in Susan's premises because of their partnership?
    (b) Mary personally financed the purchase of many items when refurbishing the premises. These items were solely purchased for the business. Are these items partnership property?
    (c) How, and by whom, are the partnership debts to be paid?

IATI (Summer 2006)

10. Distinguish between a partnership and a limited company.

IATI (Autumn 2006)

11. What are the primary characteristics of a limited company?

IATI (Autumn 2007)

12. Explain the principle that a registered company is a separate and distinct legal person from those who own and control such a company.

MII (August 2005)

13. Outline the circumstances in which the veil of incorporation of a company will be pierced.

IATI (Summer 2007)

14. List and explain the different types of companies which can be incorporated.

IATI (Summer 2006)

15. Outline the statutory requirements for registration of a private company limited by shares.

IATI (Autumn 2006)

16. Explain the meaning and consequence of the following terms when found at the end of names of business organizations:
    (a) & Co.
    (b) Ltd
    (c) plc

ACCA (June 2006)

17. Michael has been running a very successful business for a number of years. Up to now, he has been trading as a sole trader. He has decided to set up a limited liability company. However, he does not understand what the Memorandum of Association and Articles of Association are. He is also concerned about whether he can change the Memorandum of Association and Articles of Association. Advise Michael.

IATI (Autumn 2007)

18. In relation to company law, explain briefly:
    (a) the clauses that are required to be contained in a company's memorandum of association;
    (b) the legal limitations on the names that may be adopted by companies.

ACCA (June 2007)

19. Write a note on four of the following:
    (a) Articles of Association;
    (b) Memorandum of Association;
    (c) Certificate of Incorporation;
    (d) Redemption of shares;
    (e) Forfeiture of shares.

IATI (Summer 2006)

20. In relation to company law, explain the procedure that must be followed in order for a company to reduce its issued capital.

ACCA (December 2006)

21. Define four of the following:
    (i)   preference share;
    (ii) ordinary share;
    (iii) declaration of a dividend;
    (iv) redeemable preference share;
    (v)   debenture.

IATI (Autumn 2006)

22. In relation to private companies, explain the meaning of and the procedure involved in:
    (a) passing a written resolution;
    (b) paying a dividend.

ACCA (December 2005)

23. You are a legal advisor to Mr Smith, a shareholder in Fusion Ltd. Write a letter to Mr Smith explaining what an Annual General Meeting is and whether he should attend the AGM of Fusion Ltd.

IATI (Autumn 2006)

24. Alex has recently been appointed to a Board of Directors. The Board of Directors are scheduled to meet next month. One of the motions tabled is whether a dividend should be declared. Alex has little experience and seeks your advice on the power of the Board to declare a dividend.

IATI (Summer 2007)

25. In relation to company law, explain the powers of the following to bind their company:
    (a) the Board of Directors;
    (b) the managing director;
    (c) individual directors.

ACCA (December 2006)

26. Discuss a director's duty to avoid conflicts between the interests of the company and his/her own personal or business interests.

IATI (Summer 2007)

27. Peter has been invited to join the Board of Directors of a limited liability company. He has little or no experience in the business world. Therefore, he has sought your advice on what duty of skill and care he would owe the company.

IATI (Summer 2006)

28. Three years ago Norm, a wealthy retired accountant, agreed to become a director of his son Owen's company, Push Ltd, which had been established

three years previously. Owen told Norm that he only wanted his name among the directors in order to give Push Ltd increased credibility. Norm never actually took part in the management of the company and never attended any company meetings. Norm has now learned that Push Ltd is insolvent and owes considerable debts. Owen has confessed to Norm that he had deliberately hidden the fact that Push Ltd has been insolvent and carried on trading for the past two years, in which time Push Ltd's debts have increased from €50,000 to €300,000.

Required: Advise Norm in regard to the following:

(a) the common law duty of care owed by directors to their companies;
(b) any potential liability on behalf of himself or Owen for fraudulent trading under s. 297 of the Companies Act 1963;
(c) any potential liability of himself or Owen for reckless trading under s. 297A of the Companies Act 1963.

ACCA (June 2007)

29. Outline the primary duties of an auditor.

IATI (Autumn 2007)

30. Richard is interested in purchasing shares in a company. He seeks your advice on what rights he will acquire when he purchases the shares.

IATI (Autumn 2007)

31. Write a note on each of the following:
(a) the Register of Members;
(b) the Register of Directors and Secretaries.

IATI (Autumn 2006)

32. In relation to company law, explain the difference between and the procedures involved in:
(a) a members' voluntary winding-up;
(b) a creditors' voluntary winding-up.

ACCA (June 2007)

33. How is a Receiver appointed and what are the duties of a Receiver?

IATI (Summer 2007)

34. Explain what an Examiner is and how one is appointed.

IATI (Summer 2006)

SCHEDULES

Sections, 2, 13,
16, 395.

FIRST SCHEDULE.

TABLE A, TÁBLA A, AND TABLES B, C, D AND E.

TABLE A.

PART I.

REGULATIONS FOR MANAGEMENT OF A COMPANY LIMITED BY
SHARES NOT BEING A PRIVATE COMPANY.

Interpretation.

1. In these regulations:

"the Act" means the Companies Act, 1963 (No. 33 of 1963);

"the directors" means the directors for the time being of the company or the directors present at a meeting of the board of director and includes any person occupying the position of director by whatever name called;

"the register" means the register of members to be kept as required by section 116 of the Act;

"secretary" means any person appointed to perform the duties of the secretary of the company;

"the office" means the registered office for the time being of the company;

"the seal" means the common seal of the company.

Expressions referring to writing shall, unless the contrary intention appears, be construed as including references to printing, lithography, photography, and any other modes of representing or reproducing words in a visible form.

Unless the contrary intention appears, words or expressions contained in these regulations shall bear the same meaning as in the Act or in any statutory modification thereof in force at the date at which these regulations become binding on the company.

Share Capital and Variation of Rights.

2. Without prejudice to any special rights previously conferred on the holders of any existing shares or class of shares, any share in the company may be issued with such preferred, deferred or other special rights or such restrictions, whether in regard to dividend, voting, return of capital or otherwise, as the company may from time to time by ordinary resolution determine.

3. If at any time the share capital is divided into different classes of shares, the rights attached to any class may, whether or not the company is being wound up, be varied or abrogated with the consent in writing of the holders of three-fourths of the issued shares of that class, or with the sanction of a special resolution passed at a separate general meeting of the holders of the shares of the class.

4. The rights conferred upon the holders of the shares of any class issued with preferred or other right shall not, unless otherwise expressly provided by the terms of issue of the shares of that class, be deemed to be varied by the creation or issue of further shares ranking *pari passu* therewith.

5. Subject to the provisions of these regulations relating to new shares, the shares shall be at the disposal of the directors, and they may (subject to the provisions of the Companies Acts, 1963 to 1983) allot, grant options over or otherwise dispose of them to such persons, on such terms and conditions and at such times as they may consider to be in the best interests of the company and its shareholders, but so that no share shall be issued at a discount and so that in the case of shares offered to the public for subscription by a public limited company, the amount payable on application on each share shall not be less than one-quarter of the nominal amount of the share and the whole of any premium thereon.

6. The company may exercise the powers of paying commissions conferred by section 59 of the Act, provided that the rate per cent and the amount of the commission paid or agreed to be paid shall be disclosed in the manner required by that section, and the rate of the commission shall not exceed the rate of 10 per cent. of the price at which the shares in respect whereof the same is paid are issued or an amount equal to 10 per cent. of such price (as the case may be). Such commission may be satisfied by the payment of cash or the allotment of fully or

partly paid shares or partly in one way and partly in the other. The company may also, on any issue of shares, pay such brokerage as may be lawful.

7. Except as required by law, no person shall be recognised by the company as holding any share upon any trust, and the company shall not be bound by or be compelled in any way to recognise (even when having notice thereof) any equitable, contingent, future or partial interest in any share or any interest in any fractional part of a share or (except only as by these regulations or by law otherwise provided) any other rights in respect of any share except an absolute right to the entirety thereof in the registered holder: this shall not preclude the company from requiring the members or a transferee of shares to furnish the company with information as to the beneficial ownership of any share when such information is reasonably required by the company.

8. Every person whose name is entered as a member in the register shall be entitled without payment to receive within 2 months after allotment or lodgement of a transfer (or within such other period as the conditions of issue shall provide) one certificate for all his shares or several certificates each for one or more of his shares upon payment of 12½ new pence for every certificate after the first or such less sum as the directors shall from time to time determine, so, however, that in respect of a share or shares held jointly by several persons the company shall not be bound to issue more than one certificate, and delivery of a certificate for a share to one of several joint holders shall be sufficient delivery to all such holders. Every certificate shall be under the seal or under the official seal kept by the company by virtue of section 3 of the Companies (Amendment) Act, 1977, and shall specify the shares to which it relates and the amount paid up thereon.

9. If a share certificate be defaced, lost or destroyed, it may be renewed on payment of 2s. 6d. or such less sum and on such terms (if any) as to evidence and indemnity and the payment of out-of-pocket expenses of the company of investigating evidence as the directors think fit.

10. The company shall not give, whether directly or indirectly, and whether by means of a loan, guarantee, the provision of security or otherwise, any financial assistance for the purpose of or in connection with a purchase or subscription made or to be

made by any person of or for any shares in the company or in its
holding company, but this regulation shall not prohibit any
transaction permitted by section 60 of the Act.

Lien.

11. The company shall have a first and paramount lien on
every share (not being a fully paid share) for all moneys (whether
immediately payable or not) called or payable at a fixed time in
respect of that share; but the directors may at any time declare
any share to be wholly or in part exempt from the provisions of
this regulation. The company's lien on a share shall extend to all
dividends payable thereon.

12. The company may sell, in such manner as the directors
think fit, any shares on which the company has a lien, but no sale
shall be made unless a sum in respect of which the lien exists is
immediately payable, nor until the expiration of 14 days after a
notice in writing, stating and demanding payment of such part of
the amount in respect of which the lien exists as is immediately
payable, has been given to the registered holder for the time
being of the share, or the person entitled thereto by reason of his
death or bankruptcy.

13. To give effect to any such sale, the directors may authorise
some person to transfer the shares sold to the purchaser thereof.
The purchaser shall be registered as the holder of the shares
comprised in any such transfer, and he shall not be bound to see
to the application of the purchase money, nor shall his title to the
shares be affected by any irregularity or invalidity in the
proceedings in reference to the sale.

14. The proceeds of the sale shall be received by the company
and applied in payment of such part of the amount in respect of
which the lien exists as is immediately payable, and the residue,
if any, shall (subject to a like lien for sums not immediately
payable as existed upon the shares before the sale) be paid to the
person entitled to the shares at the date of the sale.

Calls on Shares.

15. The directors may from time to time make calls upon the
members in respect of any moneys unpaid on their shares
(whether on account of the nominal value of the shares or by way
of premium) and not by the conditions of allotment thereof made

payable at fixed times, provided that no call shall exceed one-fourth of the nominal value of the share or be payable at less than one month from the date fixed for the payment of the last preceding call, and each member shall (subject to receiving at least 14 days' notice specifying the time or times and place of payment) pay to the company at the time or times and place so specified the amount called on his shares. A call may be revoked or postponed as the directors may determine.

16. A call shall be deemed to have been made at the time when the resolution of the directors authorising the call was passed and may be required to be paid by instalments.

17. The joint holders of a share shall be jointly and severally liable to pay all calls in respect thereof.

18. If a sum called in respect of a share is not paid before or on the day appointed for payment thereof, the person from whom the sum is due shall pay interest on the sum from the day appointed for payment thereof to the time of actual payment at such rate, not exceeding 5 per cent. per annum, as the directors may determine, but the directors shall be at liberty to waive payment of such interest wholly or in part.

19. Any sum which by the terms of issue of a share becomes payable on allotment or at any fixed date, whether on account of the nominal value of the share or by way of premium, shall, for the purpose of these regulations, be deemed to be a call duly made and payable on the date on which, by the terms of issue, the same becomes payable, and in case of non-payment all the relevant provisions of these regulations as to payment of interest and expenses, forfeiture or otherwise, shall apply as if such sum had become payable by virtue of a call duly made and notified.

20. The directors may, on the issue of shares, differentiate between the holders as to the amount of calls to be paid and the times of payment.

21. The directors may, if they think fit, receive from any member willing to advance the same, all or any part of the moneys uncalled and unpaid upon any shares held by him, and upon all or any of the moneys so advanced may (until the same would, but for such advance, become payable) pay interest at such rate not exceeding (unless the company in general meeting otherwise directs) 5 per cent. per annum, as may be agreed upon

between the directors and the member paying such sum in advance.

Transfer of Shares.

22. The instrument of transfer of any share shall be executed by or on behalf of the transferor and transferee, and the transferor shall be deemed to remain the holder of the share until the name of the transferee is entered in the register in respect thereof.

23. Subject to such of the restrictions of these regulations as may be applicable, any member may transfer all or any of his shares by instrument in writing in any usual or common form or any other form which the directors may approve.

24. The directors may decline to register the transfer of a share (not being a fully paid share) to a person of whom they do not approve, and they may also decline to register the transfer of a share on which the company has a lien. The directors may also decline to register any transfer of a share which, in their opinion, may imperil or prejudicially affect the status of the company in the State or which may imperil any tax concession or rebate to which the members of the company are entitled or which may involve the company in the payment of any additional stamp or other duties on any conveyance of any property made or to be made to the company.

25. The directors may also decline to recognise any instrument of transfer unless —

> *(a)* a fee of 2s. 6d. or such lesser sum as the directors may from time to time require, is paid to the company in respect thereof; and

> *(b)* the instrument of transfer is accompanied by the certificate of the shares to which it relates, and such other evidence as the directors may reasonably require to show the right of the transferor to make the transfer; and

> *(c)* the instrument of transfer is in respect of one class of share only.

26. If the directors refuse to register a transfer they shall, within 2 months after the date on which the transfer was lodged

with the company, send to the transferee notice of the refusal.

27. The registration of transfer may be suspended at such times and for such periods, not exceeding in the whole 30 days in each year, as the directors may from time to time determine.

28. The company shall be entitled to charge a fee not exceeding 2s 6d. on the registration of every probate, letters of administration, certificate of death or marriage, power of attorney, notice as to stock or other instrument.

Transmission of Shares.

29. In the case of the death of a member, the survivor or survivors where the deceased was a joint holder, and the personal representatives of the deceased where he was a sole holder, shall be the only persons recognised by the company as having any title to his interest in the shares; but nothing herein contained shall release the estate of a deceased joint holder from any liability in respect of any share which had been jointly held by him with other persons.

30. Any person becoming entitled to a share in consequence of the death or bankruptcy of a member may, upon such evidence being produced as may from time to time properly be required by the directors and subject as hereinafter provided, elect either to be registered himself as holder of the share or to have some person nominated by him registered as the transferee thereof, but the directors shall, in either case, have the same right to decline or suspend registration as they would have had in the case of a transfer of the share by that member before his death or bankruptcy, as the case may be.

31. If the person so becoming entitled elects to be registered himself, he shall deliver or send to the company a notice in writing signed by him stating that he so elects. If he elects to have another person registered, he shall testify his election by executing to that person a transfer of the share. All the limitations, restrictions and provisions of these regulations relating to the right to transfer and the registration of transfers of shares shall be applicable to any such notice or transfer as aforesaid as if the death or bankruptcy of the member had not occurred and the notice or transfer were a transfer signed by that member.

32. A person becoming entitled to a share by reason of the death or bankruptcy of the holder shall be entitled to the same dividends and other advantages to which he would be entitled if he were the registered holder of the share, except that he shall not, before being registered as a member in respect of the share, be entitled in respect of it to exercise any right conferred by membership in relation to meetings of the company, so, however, that the directors may at any time give notice requiring any such person to elect either to be registered himself or to transfer the share, and if the notice is not complied with within 90 days, the directors may thereupon withhold payment of all dividends, bonuses or other moneys payable in respect of the share until the requirements of the notice have been complied with.

Forfeiture of Shares.

33. If a member fails to pay any call or instalment of a call on the day appointed for payment thereof, the directors may, at any time thereafter during such time as any part of the call or instalment remains unpaid, serve a notice on him requiring payment of so much of the call or instalment as is unpaid together with any interest which may have accrued.

34. The notice shall name a further day (not earlier than the expiration of 14 days from the date of service of the notice) on or before which the payment required by the notice is to be made, and shall state that in the event of non-payment at or before the time appointed the shares in respect of which the call was made will be liable to be forfeited.

35. If the requirements of any such notice as aforesaid are not complied with, any share in respect of which the notice has been given may at any time thereafter, before the payment required by the notice has been made, be forfeited by a resolution of the directors to that effect.

36. A forfeited share may be sold or otherwise disposed of on such terms and in such manner as the directors think fit, and at any time before a sale or disposition the forfeiture may be cancelled on such terms as the directors think fit.

37. A person whose shares have been forfeited shall cease to be a member in respect of the forfeited shares, but shall, notwithstanding, remain liable to pay to the company all moneys which, at the date of forfeiture, were payable by him to the

company in respect of the shares, but his liability shall cease if and when the company shall have received payment in full of all such moneys in respect of the shares.

38. A statutory declaration that the declarant is a director or the secretary of the company, and that a share in the company has been duly forfeited on a date stated in the declaration, shall be conclusive evidence of the facts therein stated as against all persons claiming to be entitled to the share. The company may receive the consideration, if any, given for the share on any sale or disposition thereof and may execute a transfer of the share in favour of the person to whom the share is sold or disposed of and he shall thereupon be registered as the holder of the share, and shall not be bound to see to the application of the purchase money, if any, nor shall his title to the share be affected by any irregularity or invalidity in the proceedings in reference to the forfeiture, sale or disposal of the share.

39. The provisions of these regulations as to forfeiture shall apply in the case of nonpayment of any sum which, by the terms of issue of a share, becomes payable at a fixed time, whether on account of the nominal value of the share or by way of premium, as if the same had been payable by virtue of a call duly made and notified.

Conversion of Shares into Stock.

40. The company may by ordinary resolution convert any paid up shares into stock, and reconvert any stock into paid up shares of any denomination.

41. The holders of stock may transfer the same, or any part thereof, in the same manner, and subject to the same regulations, as and subject to which the shares from which the stock arose might previously to conversion have been transferred, or as near thereto as circumstances admit; and the directors may from time to time fix the minimum amount of stock transferable but so that such minimum shall not exceed the nominal amount of each share from which the stock arose.

42. The holders of stock shall, according to the amount of stock held by them, have the same rights, privileges and advantages in relation to dividends, voting at meetings of the company and other matters as if they held the shares from which the stock arose, but no such right, privilege or advantage (except

participation in the dividends and profits of the company and in the assets on winding up) shall be conferred by an amount of stock which would not, if existing in shares, have conferred that right, privilege or advantage.

43. Such of the regulations of the company as are applicable to paid up shares shall apply to stock, and the words "share" and "shareholder" therein shall include "stock" and "stockholder".

Alteration of Capital.

44. The company may from time to time by ordinary resolution increase the share capital by such sum, to be divided into shares of such amount, as the resolution shall prescribe.

45. The company may by ordinary resolution —

   (a) consolidate and divide all or any of its share capital into shares of larger amount than its existing shares;

   (b) subdivide its existing shares, or any of them, into shares of smaller amount than is fixed by the memorandum of association subject, nevertheless, to section 68 (1) *(d)* of the Act;

   (c) cancel any shares which, at the date of the passing of the resolution, have not been taken or agreed to be taken by any person.

46. The company may by special resolution reduce its share capital, any capital redemption reserve fund or any share premium account in any manner and with and subject to any incident authorised, and consent required, by law.

General Meetings.

47. All general meetings of the company shall be held in the State.

48. (1) Subject to paragraph (2) of this regulation, the company shall in each year hold a general meeting as its annual general meeting in addition to any other meeting in that year, and shall specify the meeting as such in the notice calling it; and not more than 15 months shall elapse between the date of one annual general meeting of the company and that of the next.

(2) So long as the company holds its first annual general meeting within 18 months of its incorporation, it need not hold it in the year of its incorporation or in the year following. Subject to regulation 47, the annual general meeting shall be held at such time and place as the directors shall appoint.

49. All general meetings other than annual general meetings shall be called extraordinary general meetings.

50. The directors may, whenever they think fit, convene an extraordinary general meeting, and extraordinary general meetings shall also be convened on such requisition, or in default, may be convened by such requisitionists, as provided by section 132 of the Act. If at any time there are not within the State sufficient directors capable of acting to form a quorum, any director or any 2 members of the company may convene an extraordinary general meeting in the same manner as nearly as possible as that in which meetings may be convened by the directors.

Notice of General Meetings.

51. Subject to sections 133 and 141 of the Act, an annual general meeting and a meeting called for the passing of a special resolution shall be called by 21 days' notice in writing at the least, and a meeting of the company (other than an annual general meeting or a meeting for the passing of a special resolution) shall be called by 14 days' notice in writing at the least. The notice shall be exclusive of the day on which it is served or deemed to be served and of the day for which it is given, and shall specify the place, the day and the hour of the meeting, and in the case of special business, the general nature of that business, and shall be given, in manner hereinafter mentioned, to such persons as are, under the regulations of the company, entitled to receive such notices from the company.

52. The accidental omission to give notice of a meeting to, or the non-receipt of notice of a meeting by, any person entitled to receive notice shall not invalidate the proceedings at the meeting.

Proceedings at General Meetings.

53. All business shall be deemed special that is transacted at an extraordinary general meeting, and also all that is transacted at an annual general meeting, with the exception of declaring a

dividend, the consideration of the accounts, balance sheets and the reports of the directors and auditors, the election of directors in the place of those retiring, the re-appointment of the retiring auditors and the fixing of the remuneration of the auditors.

54. No business shall be transacted at any general meeting unless a quorum of members is present at the time when the meeting proceeds to business; save as herein otherwise provided, three members present in person shall be a quorum.

55. If within half an hour from the time appointed for the meeting a quorum is not present, the meeting, if convened upon the requisition of members, shall be dissolved; in any other case it shall stand adjourned to the same day in the next week, at the same time and place or to such other day and at such other time and place as the directors may determine, and if at the adjourned meeting a quorum is not present within half an hour from the time appointed for the meeting, the members present shall be a quorum.

56. The chairman, if any, of the board of directors shall preside as chairman at every general meeting of the company, or if there is no such chairman, or if he is not present within 15 minutes after the time appointed for the holding of the meeting or is unwilling to act, the directors present shall elect one of their number to be chairman of the meeting.

57. If at any meeting no director is willing to act as chairman or if no director is present within 15 minutes after the time appointed for holding the meeting, the members present shall choose one of their number to be chairman of the meeting.

58. The chairman may, with the consent of any meeting at which a quorum is present, and shall if so directed by the meeting, adjourn the meeting from time to time and from place to place, but no business shall be transacted at any adjourned meeting other than the business left unfinished at the meeting from which the adjournment took place. When a meeting is adjourned for 30 days or more, notice of the adjourned meeting shall be given as in the case of an original meeting. Save as aforesaid it shall not be necessary to give any notice of an adjournment or of the business to be transacted at an adjourned meeting.

59. At any general meeting a resolution put to the vote of the

meeting shall be decided on a show of hands unless a poll is (before or on the declaration of the result of the show of hands) demanded —

(*a*) by the chairman; or

(*b*) by at least three members present in person or by proxy; or

(*c*) by any member or members present in person or by proxy and representing not less than one-tenth of the total voting rights of all the members having the right to vote at the meeting; or

(*d*) by a member or members holding shares in the company conferring the right to vote at the meeting being shares on which an aggregate sum has been paid up equal to not less than one-tenth of the total sum paid up on all the shares conferring that right.

Unless a poll is so demanded, a declaration by the chairman that a resolution has, on a show of hands, been carried or carried unanimously, or by a particular majority, or lost, and an entry to that effect in the book containing the minutes of the proceedings of the company shall be conclusive evidence of the fact without proof of the number or proportion of the votes recorded in favour of or against such resolution.

The demand for a poll may be withdrawn.

60. Except as provided in regulation 62, if a poll is duly demanded it shall be taken in such manner as the chairman directs, and the result of the poll shall be deemed to be the resolution of the meeting at which the poll was demanded.

61. Where there is an equality of votes, whether on a show of hands or on a poll, the chairman of the meeting at which the show of hands takes place or at which the poll is demanded, shall be entitled to a second or casting vote.

62. A poll demanded on the election of a chairman or on a question of adjournment shall be taken forthwith. A poll demanded on any other question shall be taken at such time as the chairman of the meeting directs, and any business other than that on which a poll is demanded may be proceeded with pending the

taking of the poll.

Votes of Members.

63. Subject to any rights or restrictions for the time being attached to any class or classes of shares, on a show of hands every member present in person and ever proxy shall have one vote, so, however, that no individual shall have more than one vote, and on a poll every member shall have one vote for each share of which he is the holder.

64. Where there are joint holders, the vote of the senior who tenders a vote, whether in person or by proxy, shall be accepted to the exclusion of the votes of the other joint holders; and for this purpose, seniority shall be determined by the order in which the names stand in the register.

65. A member of unsound mind, or in respect of whom an order has been made by any court having jurisdiction in lunacy, may vote, whether on a show of hands or on a poll, by his committee, receiver, guardian or other person appointed by that court, and any such committee, receiver, guardian or other person may vote by proxy on a how of hands or on a poll.

66. No member shall be entitled to vote at any general meeting unless all calls or other sums immediately payable by him in respect of share in the company have been paid.

67. No objection shall be raised to the qualification of any voter except at the meeting or adjourned meeting at which the vote objected to is given or tendered, and every vote not disallowed at such meeting shall be valid for all purposes. Any such objection made in due time shall be referred to the chairman of the meeting, whose decision shall be final and conclusive.

68. Votes may be given either personally or by proxy.

69. The instrument appointing a proxy shall be in writing under the hand of the appointer or of his attorney duly authorised in writing, or, if the appointer is a body corporate either under seal or under the hand of an officer or attorney duly authorised. A proxy need not be a member of the company.

70. The instrument appointing a proxy and the power of attorney or other authority, if any, under which it is signed, or a

notarially certified copy of that power or authority shall be deposited at the office or at such other place within the State as is specified for that purpose in the notice convening the meeting, not less than 48 hours before the time for holding the meeting or adjourned meeting at which the person named in the instrument proposes to vote, or, in the case of a poll, not less than 48 hours before the time appointed for the taking of the poll, and, in default, the instrument of proxy shall not be treated as valid.

71. An instrument appointing a proxy shall be in the following form or a form as near thereto as circumstances permit—

"
                                                                    Limited.
I/We of ....

in the County of...,being a

member/members of the above-named company hereby appoint ....

....

of ....

or failing him...

of ....

as my/our proxy to vote for me/us on my/our behalf at the (annual or extra-ordinary, as the case may be) general meeting of the company to be held on the .... day of ...., 19 ...... and at any adjournment thereof.

                Signed this ....day of ...., 19............

This form is to be used *in favour of/against, the resolution.

Unless otherwise instructed the proxy will vote as he thinks fit.

*Strike out whichever is not desired."

72. The instrument appointing a proxy shall be deemed to confer authority to demand or join in demanding a poll.

73. A vote given in accordance with the terms of an instrument of proxy shall be valid notwithstanding the previous death or insanity of the principal or revocation of the proxy or of the authority under which the proxy was executed or the transfer of the share in respect of which the proxy is given, if no intimation in writing of such death, insanity, revocation or transfer as aforesaid is received by the company at the office before the commencement of the meeting or adjourned meeting at which the proxy is used.

Bodies Corporate acting by Representatives at Meetings.

74. Any body corporate which is a member of the company may, by resolution of its directors or other governing body, authorise such person as it thinks fit to act as its representative at any meeting of the company or of any class of members of the company, and the person so authorised shall be entitled to exercise the same powers on behalf of the body corporate which he represents as that body corporate could exercise if it were an individual member of the company.

Directors.

75. The number of the directors and the names of the first directors shall be determined in writing by the subscribers of the memorandum of association or a majority of them.

76. The remuneration of the directors shall from time to time be determined by the company in general meeting. Such remuneration shall be deemed to accrue from day to day. The directors may also be paid all travelling, hotel and other expenses properly incurred by them in attending and returning from meetings of the directors or any committee of the directors or general meetings of the company or in connection with the business of the company.

77. The shareholding qualification for directors may be fixed by the company in general meeting and unless and until so fixed no qualification shall be required.

78. A director of the company may be or become a director or other officer of, or otherwise interested in, any company promoted by the company or in which the company may be interested as shareholder or otherwise, and no such director shall be accountable to the company for any remuneration or other benefits received by him as a director or officer of, or from his interest in, such other company unless the company otherwise directs.

Borrowing Powers.

79. The directors may exercise all the powers of the company to borrow money, and to mortgage or charge its undertaking, property and uncalled capital, or any part thereof, and subject to section 20 of the Companies (Amendment) Act, 1983 to issue

debentures, debenture stock and other securities, whether outright or as security for any debt, liability or obligation of the company or of any third party, so, however, that the amount for the time being remaining undischarged of moneys borrowed or secured by the directors, as aforesaid (apart from temporary loans obtained from the company's bankers in the ordinary course of business) shall not at any time, without the previous sanction of the company in general meeting, exceed the nominal amount of the share capital of the company for the time being issued, but nevertheless no lender or other person dealing with the company shall be concerned to see or inquire whether this limit is observed. No debt incurred or security given in excess of such limit shall be invalid or ineffectual except in the case of express notice to the lender or the recipient of the security at the time when the debt was incurred or security given that the limit hereby imposed had been or was thereby exceeded.

Powers and Duties of Directors.

80. The business of the company shall be managed by the directors, who may pay all expenses incurred in promoting and registering the company and may exercise all such powers of the company as are not, by the Companies Act 1963 to 1983 or by these regulations, required to be exercised by the company in general meeting, subject, nevertheless, to any of these regulations, to the provisions of the Act and to such directions, being not inconsistent with the aforesaid regulations or provisions, as may be given by the company in general meeting; but no direction given by the company in general meeting shall invalidate any prior act of the directors which would have been valid if that direction had not been given.

81. The directors may from time to time and at any time by power of attorney appoint any company, firm or person or body of persons, whether nominated directly or indirectly by the directors, to be the attorney or attorneys of the company for such purposes and with such powers, authorities and discretions (not exceeding those vested in or exercisable by the directors under these regulations) and for such period and subject to such conditions as they may think fit, and any such power of attorney may contain such provisions for the protection of persons dealing with any such attorney as the directors may think fit, and may also authorise any such attorney to delegate all or any of the powers, authorities and discretions vested in him.

82. The company may exercise the powers conferred by section 41 of the Act with regard to having an official seal for use abroad, and such powers shall be vested in the directors.

83. A director who is in any way, whether directly or indirectly, interested in a contract or proposed contract with the company shall declare the nature of his interest at a meeting of the directors in accordance with section 194 of the Act.

84. A director shall not vote in respect of any contract or arrangement in which he is so interested, and if he shall so vote, his vote shall not be counted, nor shall he be counted in the quorum present at the meeting but neither of these prohibitions shall apply to —

> (*a*) any arrangement for giving any director any security or indemnity in respect of money lent by him to or obligations undertaken by him for the benefit of the company; or
>
> (*b*) any arrangement for the giving by the company of any security to a third party in respect of a debt or obligation of the company for which the director himself has assumed responsibility in whole or in part under a guarantee or indemnity or by the deposit of a security; or
>
> (*c*) any contract by a director to subscribe for or underwrite shares or debentures of the company; or
>
> (*d*) any contract or arrangement with any other company in which he is interested only as an officer of such other company or as a holder of shares or other securities in such other company;

and these prohibitions may at any time be suspended or relaxed to any extent and either generally or in respect of any particular contract, arrangement or transaction by the company in general meeting.

85. A director may hold any other office or place of profit under the company (other than the office of auditor) in conjunction with his office of director for such period and on such terms as to remuneration and otherwise as the directors may determine, and no director or intending director shall be

disqualified by his office from contracting with the company either with regard to his tenure of any such other office or place of profit or as vendor, purchaser or otherwise, nor shall any such contract or any contract or arrangement entered into by or on behalf of the company in which any director is in any way interested, be liable to be avoided, nor shall any director so contracting or being so interested be liable to account to the company for any profit realised by any such contract or arrangement by reason of such director holding that office or of the fiduciary relation thereby established.

86. A director, notwithstanding his interest, may be counted in the quorum present at any meeting whereat he or any other director is appointed to hold any such office or place of profit under the company or whereat the terms of any such appointment are arranged, and he may vote on any such appointment or arrangement other than his own appointment or the arrangement of the terms thereof.

87. Any director may act by himself or his firm in a professional capacity for the company, and he or his firm shall be entitled to remuneration for professional services as if he were not a director; but nothing herein contained shall authorise a director or his firm to act as auditor to the company.

88. All cheques, promissory notes, drafts, bills of exchange and other negotiable instruments and all receipts for moneys paid to the company shall be signed, drawn, accepted, endorsed or otherwise executed, as the case may be, by such person or persons and in such manner as the directors shall from time to time by resolution determine.

89. The directors shall cause minutes to be made in books provided for the purpose —

   (a) of all appointments of officers made by the directors;

   (b) of the names of the directors present at each meeting of the directors and of any committee of the directors;

   (c) of all resolutions and proceedings at all meetings of the company and of the directors and of committees of directors.

90. The directors on behalf of the company may pay a gratuity

or pension or allowance on retirement to any director who has held any other salaried office or place of profit with the company or to his widow or dependants, and may make contributions to any fund and pay premiums for the purchase or provision of any such gratuity, pension or allowance.

Disqualification of Directors.

91. The office of director shall be vacated if the director —

(*a*) ceases to be a director by virtue of section 180 of the Act; or

(*b*) is adjudged bankrupt in the State or in Northern Ireland or Great Britain or makes any arrangement or composition with his creditors generally; or

(*c*) becomes prohibited from being a director by reason of any order made under section 184 of the Act; or

(*d*) becomes of unsound mind; or

(*e*) resigns his office by notice in writing to the company; or

(*f*) is convicted of an indictable offence unless the directors otherwise determine; or

(*g*) is for more than 6 months absent without permission of the directors from meetings of the directors held during that period.

Rotation of Directors.

92. At the first annual general meeting of the company all the directors shall retire from office, and at the annual general meeting in every subsequent year, one-third of the directors for the time being, or, if their number is not three or a multiple of three, then the number nearest one-third shall retire from office.

93. The directors to retire in every year shall be those who have been longest in office since their last election but as between persons who became directors on the same day, those to retire shall (unless they otherwise agree among themselves) be determined by lot.

94. A retiring director shall be eligible for re-election.

95. The company, at the meeting at which a director retires in manner aforesaid, may fill the vacated office by electing a person thereto, and in default the retiring director shall, if offering himself for re-election, be deemed to have been re-elected, unless at such meeting it is expressly resolved not to fill such vacated office, or unless a resolution for the re-election of such director has been put to the meeting and lost.

96. No person other than a director retiring at the meeting shall, unless recommended by the directors, be eligible for election to the office of director at any general meeting unless not less than 3 nor more than 21 days before the day appointed for the meeting there shall have been left at the office notice in writing signed by a member duly qualified to attend and vote at the meeting for which such notice is given, of his intention to propose such person for election and also notice in writing signed by that person of his willingness to be elected.

97. The company may from time to time by ordinary resolution increase or reduce the number of directors and may also determine in what rotation the increased or reduced number is to go out of office.

98. The directors shall have power at any time and from time to time to appoint any person to be a director, either to fill a casual vacancy or as an addition to the existing directors, but so that the total number of directors shall not at any time exceed the number fixed in accordance with these regulations. Any director so appointed shall hold office only until the next following annual general meeting, and shall then be eligible for re-election but shall not be taken into account in determining the directors who are to retire by rotation at such meeting.

99. The company may, by ordinary resolution, of which extended notice has been given in accordance with section 142 of the Act, remove any director before the expiration of his period of office notwithstanding anything in these regulations or in any agreement between the company and such director. Such removal shall be without prejudice to any claim such director may have for damages for breach of any contract of service between him and the company.

100. The company may, by ordinary resolution, appoint

another person in place of a director removed from office under regulation 99 and without prejudice to the powers of the directors under regulation 98 the company in general meeting may appoint any person to be a director either to fill a casual vacancy or as an additional director. A person appointed in place of a director so removed or to fill such a vacancy shall be subject to retirement at the same time as if he had become a director on the day on which the director in whose place he is appointed was last elected a director.

Proceedings of Directors.

101. The directors may meet together for the despatch of business, adjourn and otherwise regulate their meetings as they think fit. Questions arising at any meeting shall be decided by a majority of votes. Where there is an equality of votes, the chairman shall have a second or casting vote. A director may, and the secretary on the requisition of a director shall, at any time summon a meeting of the directors. If the directors so resolve, it shall not be necessary to give notice of a meeting of director to any director who, being resident in the State, is for the time being absent from the State.

102. The quorum necessary for the transaction of the business of the directors may be fixed by the directors, and unless so fixed shall be two.

103. The continuing directors may act notwithstanding any vacancy in their number but, if and so long as their number is reduced below the number fixed by or pursuant to the regulations of the company as the necessary quorum of directors, the continuing directors or director may act for the purpose of increasing the number of directors to that number or of summoning a general meeting of the company but for no other purpose.

104. The directors may elect a chairman of their meetings and determine the period for which he is to hold office, but if no such chairman is elected, or, if at any meeting the chairman is not present within 5 minutes after the time appointed for holding the same, the directors present may choose one of their number to be chairman of the meeting.

105. The directors may delegate any of their powers to committees consisting of such member or members of the board

as they think fit; any committee so formed shall, in the exercise of the powers so delegated, conform to any regulations that may be imposed on it by the directors.

106. A committee may elect a chairman of its meetings; if no such chairman is elected, or if at any meeting the chairman is not present within 5 minutes after the time appointed for holding the same, the members present may choose one of their number to be chairman of the meeting.

107. A committee may meet and adjourn as it thinks proper. Questions arising at any meeting shall be determined by a majority of votes of the members present, and where there is an equality of votes, the chairman shall have a second or casting vote.

108. All acts done by any meeting of the directors or of a committee of directors or by any person acting as a director shall, notwithstanding that it be afterwards discovered that there was some defect in the appointment of any such director or person acting as aforesaid, or that they or any of them were disqualified, be as valid as if every such person had been duly appointed and was qualified to be a director.

109. A resolution in writing signed by all the directors for the time being entitled to receive notice of a meeting of the directors shall be as valid as if it had been passed at a meeting of the directors duly convened and held.

Managing Director.

110. The directors may from time to time appoint one or more of themselves to the office of managing director for such period and on such terms as to remuneration and otherwise as they think fit, and, subject to the terms of any agreement entered into in any particular case, may revoke such appointment. A director so appointed shall not, whilst holding that office, be subject to retirement by rotation or be taken into account in determining the rotation of retirement of directors but (without prejudice to any claim he may have for damages for breach of any contract of service between him and the company), his appointment shall be automatically determined if he ceases from any cause to be a director.

111. A managing director shall receive such remuneration

whether by way of salary, commission or participation in the profits, or partly in one way and partly in another, as the directors may determine.

112. The directors may entrust to and confer upon a managing director any of the powers exercisable by them upon such terms and conditions and with such restrictions as they may think fit, and either collaterally with or to the exclusion of their own powers, and may from time to time revoke, withdraw, alter or vary all or any of such powers.

Secretary.

113. Subject to section 3 of the Companies (Amendment) Act, 1982, the secretary shall be appointed by the directors for such term, at such remuneration and upon such conditions as they may think fit; and any secretary so appointed may be removed by them.

114. A provision of the Act or these regulations requiring or authorising a thing to be done by or to a director and the secretary shall not be satisfied by its being done by or to the same person acting both as director and as, or in place of, the secretary.

The Seal.

115. The seal shall be used only by the authority of the directors or of a committee of directors authorised by the directors in that behalf, and every instrument to which the seal shall be affixed shall be signed by a director and shall be countersigned by the secretary or by a second director or by some other person appointed by the directors for the purpose.

Dividends and Reserves.

116. The company in general meeting may declare dividends, but no dividend shall exceed the amount recommended by the directors.

117. The directors may from time to time pay to the members such interim dividends as appear to the directors to be justified by the profits of the company.

118. No dividend or interim dividend shall be paid otherwise than in accordance with the provisions of Part IV of the

Companies (Amendment) Act, 1983 which apply to the company.

119. The directors may, before recommending any dividend, set aside out of the profits of the company such sums as they think proper as a reserve or reserves which shall, at the discretion of the directors, be applicable for any purpose to which the profits of the company may be properly applied, and pending such application may, at the like discretion, either be employed in the business of the company or be invested in such investments as the directors may lawfully determine. The directors may also, without placing the same to reserve, carry forward any profits which they may think it prudent not to divide.

120. Subject to the rights of persons, if any, entitled to shares with special rights as to dividend, all dividends shall be declared and paid according to the amounts paid or credited as paid on the shares in respect whereof the dividend is paid, but no amount paid or credited as paid on a share in advance of calls shall be treated for the purposes of this regulation as paid on the share. All dividends shall be apportioned and paid proportionately to the amounts paid or credited as paid on the shares during any portion or portions of the period in respect of which the dividend is paid; but if any share is issued on terms providing that it shall rank for dividend as from a particular date, such share shall rank for dividend accordingly.

121. The directors may deduct from any dividend payable to any member all sums of money (if any) immediately payable by him to the company on account of calls or otherwise in relation to the shares of the company.

122. Any general meeting declaring a dividend or bonus may direct payment of such dividend or bonus wholly or partly by the distribution of specific assets and in particular of paid up shares, debentures or debenture stock of any other company or in any one or more of such ways, and the directors shall give effect to such resolution, and where any difficulty arise in regard to such distribution, the directors may settle the same as they think expedient, and in particular may issue fractional certificates and fix the value for distribution of such specific assets or any part thereof and may determine that cash payments shall be made to any members upon the footing of the value so fixed, in order to adjust the rights of all the parties, and may vest any such specific assets in trustees as may seem expedient to the directors.

123. Any dividend, interest or other money payable in cash in respect of any shares may be paid by cheque or warrant sent through the post directed to the registered address of the holder, or, where there are joint holders, to the registered address of that one of the joint holders who is first named on the register or to such person and to such address as the holder or joint holders may in writing direct. Every such cheque or warrant shall be made payable to the order of the person to whom it is sent. Any one of two or more joint holders may give effectual receipts for any dividends, bonuses or other moneys payable in respect of the shares held by them as joint holder.

124. No dividend shall bear interest against the company.

Accounts.

125. The directors shall cause proper books of account to be kept relating to —

(*a*) all sums of money received and expended by the company and the matters in respect of which the receipt and expenditure takes place; and

(*b*) all sale and purchases of goods by the company; and

(*c*) the assets and liabilities of the company.

Proper books shall not be deemed to be kept if there are not kept such books of account as are necessary to give a true and fair view of the state of the company's affairs and to explain its transactions.

126. The books of account shall be kept at the office or, subject to section 147 of the Act, at such other place as the directors think fit, and shall at all reasonable times be open to the inspection of the directors.

127. The directors shall from time to time determine whether and to what extent and at what times and places and under what conditions or regulations the accounts and books of the company or any of them shall be open to the inspection of members, not being directors, and no member (not being a director) shall have any right of inspecting any account or book or document of the company except as conferred by statute or authorised by the directors or by the company in general meeting.

128. The directors shall from time to time, in accordance with sections 148, 150, 157 and 158 of the Act cause to be prepared and to be laid before the annual general meeting of the company such profit and loss accounts, balance sheets, group accounts and reports as are required by those sections to be prepared and laid before the annual general meeting of the company.

129. A copy of every balance sheet (including every document required by law to be annexed thereto) which is to be laid before the annual general meeting of the company together with a copy of the directors' report and auditors' report shall, not less than 21 days before the date of the annual general meeting be sent to every person entitled under the provisions of the Act to receive them.

Capitalisation of Profits.

130. The company in general meeting may upon the recommendation of the directors resolve that any sum for the time being standing to the credit of any of the company's reserves (including any capital redemption reserve fund or share premium account) or to the credit of profit and loss account be capitalised and applied on behalf of the members who would have been entitled to receive the same if the same had been distributed by way of dividend and in the same proportions either in or towards paying up amounts for the time being unpaid on any shares held by them respectively or in paying up in full unissued shares or debentures of the company of a nominal amount equal to the sum capitalised (such shares or debentures to be allotted and distributed credited as fully paid up to and amongst such holders in the proportions aforesaid) or partly in one way and partly in another, so however, that the only purpose for which sums standing to the credit of the capital redemption reserve fund or the share premium account shall be applied shall be those permitted by sections 62 and 64 of the Act.

130A. The company in general meeting may on the recommendation of the directors resolve that it is desirable to capitalise any part of the amount for the time being standing to the credit of any of the company's reserve accounts or to the credit of the profit and loss account which is not available for distribution by applying such sum in paying up in full unissued shares to be allotted as fully paid bonus shares to those members of the company who would have been entitled to that sum if it were distributed by way of dividend (and in the same proportions), and the directors shall give effect to such resolution.

131. Whenever such a resolution is passed in pursuance of regulation 130 or 130A, the directors shall make all appropriations and applications of the undivided profits resolved to be capitalised thereby and all allotments and issues of fully paid shares or debentures, if any, and generally shall do all acts and things required to give effect thereto with full power to the directors to make such provision as they shall think fit for the case of shares or debentures becoming distributable in fractions (and, in particular, without prejudice to the generality of the foregoing, to sell the shares or debentures represented by such fractions and distribute the net proceeds of such sale amongst the members otherwise entitled to such fractions in due proportions) and also to authorise any person to enter on behalf of all the members concerned into an agreement with the company providing for the allotment to them respectively credited as fully paid up of any further shares or debentures to which they may become entitled on such capitalisation or, as the case may require, for the payment up by the application thereto of their respective proportions of the profits resolved to be capitalised of the amounts remaining unpaid on their existing shares and any agreement made under such authority shall be effective and binding on all such members.

Audit.

132. Auditors shall be appointed and their duties regulated in accordance with sections 160 to 163 of the Act.

Notices.

133. A notice may be given by the company to any member either personally or by sending it by post to him to his registered address. Where a notice is sent by post, service of the notice shall be deemed to be effected by properly addressing, prepaying and posting a letter containing the notice, and to have been effected in the case of the notice of a meeting at the expiration of 24 hours after the letter containing the same is posted, and in any other case at the time at which the letter would be delivered in the ordinary course of post.

134. A notice may be given by the company to the joint holders of a share by giving the notice to the joint holder first named in the register in respect of the share.

135. A notice may be given by the company to the persons entitled to a share in consequence of the death or bankruptcy of a member by sending it through the post in a prepaid letter addressed to them by name or by the title of representatives of the deceased or Official Assignee in bankruptcy or by any like description at the address supplied for the purpose by the persons claiming to be so entitled, or (until such an address has been so supplied) by giving the notice in any manner in which the same might have been given if the death or bankruptcy had not occurred.

136. Notice of every general meeting shall be given in any manner hereinbefore authorised to —

    (a) every member; and

    (b) every person upon whom the ownership of a share devolves by reason of his being a personal representative or the Official Assignee in bankruptcy of a member, where the member but for his death or bankruptcy would be entitled to receive notice of the meeting; and

    (c) the auditor for the time being of the company.

No other person shall be entitled to receive notices of general meetings.

Winding Up.

137. If the company is wound up, the liquidator may, with the sanction of a special resolution of the company and any other sanction required by the Act, divide among the members in specie or kind the whole or any part of the assets of the company (whether they shall consist of property of the same kind or not) and may, for such purpose, set such value as he deems fair upon any property to be divided as aforesaid and may determine how such division shall be carried out as between the members or different classes of members. The liquidator may, with the like sanction, vest the whole or any part of such assets in trustees upon such trusts for the benefit of the contributories as the liquidator, with the like sanction, shall think fit, but so that no member shall be compelled to accept any shares or other

securities whereon there is any liability.

Indemnity

138. Every director, managing director, agent, auditor, secretary and other officer for the time being of the company shall be indemnified out of the assets of the company against any liability incurred by him in defending any proceedings, whether civil or criminal, in relation to his acts while acting in such office, in which judgment is given in his favour or in which he is acquitted or in connection with any application under section 391 of the Act in which relief is granted to him by the court.

PART II.

REGULATIONS FOR THE MANAGEMENT OF A PRIVATE COMPANY LIMITED BY SHARES.

1. The regulations contained in Part I of Table A (with the exception of regulations 8, 24, 51, 54, 84 and 86) shall apply. *As amended by 1977 S5 (4).*

2. The company is a private company and accordingly —

  (a) the right to transfer shares is restricted in the manner hereinafter prescribed;

  (b) the number of members of the company (exclusive of persons who are in the employment of the company and of persons who, having been formerly in the employment of the company, were while in such employment, and have continued after the determination of such employment to be, members of the company) is limited to fifty, so, however, that where two or more persons hold one or more shares in the company jointly, they shall, for the purpose of this regulation, be treated as a single member;

  (c) any invitation to the public to subscribe for any shares or debentures of the company is prohibited;

  (d) the company shall not have power to issue share warrants to bearer.

3. The directors may, in their absolute discretion, and without assigning any reason therefor, decline to register any transfer of any share, whether or not it is a fully paid share.

4. Subject to sections 133 and 141 of the Act, an annual general meeting and a meeting called for the passing of a special resolution shall be called by 21 days' notice in writing at the least and a meeting of the company (other than an annual general meeting or a meeting for the passing of a special resolution) shall be called by 7 days' notice in writing at the least. The notice shall be exclusive of the day on which it is served or deemed to be served and of the day for which it is given and shall specify the day, the place and the hour of the meeting and, in the case of special business, the general nature of that business and shall be given in manner authorised by these regulations to such persons as are under the regulations of the company entitled to receive such notices from the company.

5. No business shall be transacted at any general meeting unless a quorum of members is present at the time when the meeting proceeds to business; save as herein otherwise provided, two members present in person or by proxy shall be a quorum.

6. Subject to section 141 of the Act, a resolution in writing signed by all the members for the time being entitled to attend and vote on such resolution at a general meeting (or being bodies corporate by their duly authorised representatives) shall be as valid and effective for all purposes as if the resolution had been passed at a general meeting of the company duly convened and held, and if described as a special resolution shall be deemed to be a special resolution within the meaning of the Act.

7. A director may vote in respect of any contract, appointment or arrangement in which he is interested, and he shall be counted in the quorum present at the meeting.

8. The directors may exercise the voting powers conferred by the shares of any other company held or owned by the company in such manner in all respects as they think fit and in particular they may exercise the voting powers in favour of any resolution appointing the directors or any of them as directors or officers of such other company or providing for the payment of remuneration or pensions to the directors or officers of such other company. Any director of the company may vote in favour of the exercise of such voting rights, notwithstanding that he may be or may be about to become a director or officer of such other company, and as such or in any other manner is or may be interested in the exercise of such voting rights in manner aforesaid.

9. Any director may from time to time appoint any person who is approved by the majority of the directors to be an alternate or substitute director. The appointee, while he holds office as an alternate director, shall be entitled to notice of meetings of the directors and to attend and vote thereat as a director and shall not be entitled to be remunerated otherwise than out of the remuneration of the director appointing him. Any appointment under this regulation shall be effected by notice in writing given by the appointer to the secretary. Any appointment so made may be revoked at any time by the appointer or by a majority of the other directors or by the company in general meeting. Revocation by an appointer shall be effected by notice in writing given by the appointer to the secretary.

10. Every person whose name is entered as a member in the register shall be entitled without payment to receive within 2 months after allotment or lodgment of a transfer (or within such other period as the conditions of issue shall provide) one certificate for all his shares or several certificates each for one or more of his shares upon payment of 12½ new pence for every certificate after the first or such less sum as the directors shall from time to time determine, so, however, that in respect of a share or shares held jointly by several persons the company shall not be bound to issue more than one certificate, and delivery of a certificate for a share to one of several joint holders shall be sufficient delivery to all such holders. Every certificate shall be under the seal and shall specify the shares to which it relates and the amount paid up thereon.

Inserted by 1977 S5 (5).

Note:—Regulations 3, 4, 5 and 10 of this Part are alternative to regulations 24, 51, 54 and 8 respectively of Part I. Regulations 7 and 8 of this Part are alternative to regulations 84 and 86 of Part I.

As amended by 1977 S5 (6).

Tábla A, Cuid I and Cuid II have not been included here. They are the Irish language version of Table A, Part I and Part II.

INDEX